THE MIND OF MAN

HARPER TORCHBOOKS / The Cloister Library

Tor Andrae	MOHAMMED: *The Man and His Faith* TB/62
Augustine/Przywara	AN AUGUSTINE SYNTHESIS TB/35
Roland H. Bainton	THE TRAVAIL OF RELIGIOUS LIBERTY TB/30
Karl Barth	DOGMATICS IN OUTLINE TB/56
Karl Barth	THE WORD OF GOD AND THE WORD OF MAN TB/13
Nicolas Berdyaev	THE BEGINNING AND THE END TB/14
Nicolas Berdyaev	THE DESTINY OF MAN TB/61
James Henry Breasted	DEVELOPMENT OF RELIGION AND THOUGHT IN ANCIENT EGYPT TB/57
Martin Buber	ECLIPSE OF GOD: *Studies in the Relation Between Religion and Philosophy* TB/12
Martin Buber	MOSES: *The Revelation and the Covenant* TB/27
Jacob Burckhardt	THE CIVILIZATION OF THE RENAISSANCE IN ITALY [Illustrated Edition]: *Vol. I*, TB/40; *Vol. II*, TB/41
Edward Conze	BUDDHISM: *Its Essence and Development* TB/58
F. M. Cornford	FROM RELIGION TO PHILOSOPHY: *A Study in the Origins of Western Speculation* TB/20
G. G. Coulton	MEDIEVAL FAITH AND SYMBOLISM TB/25
G. G. Coulton	THE FATE OF MEDIEVAL ART IN THE RENAISSANCE AND REFORMATION TB/26
H. G. Creel	CONFUCIUS AND THE CHINESE WAY TB/63
Adolf Deissmann	PAUL: *A Study in Social and Religious History* TB/15
C. H. Dodd	THE AUTHORITY OF THE BIBLE TB/43
Johannes Eckhart	MEISTER ECKHART: A Modern Translation TB/8
Mircea Eliade	COSMOS AND HISTORY: *The Myth of the Eternal Return* TB/50
Morton S. Enslin	CHRISTIAN BEGINNINGS TB/5
Morton S. Enslin	THE LITERATURE OF THE CHRISTIAN MOVEMENT TB/6
Austin Farrer, *ed.*	THE CORE OF THE BIBLE TB/7
Ludwig Feuerbach	THE ESSENCE OF CHRISTIANITY TB/11
Harry Emerson Fosdick	A GUIDE TO UNDERSTANDING THE BIBLE TB/2
Sigmund Freud	ON CREATIVITY AND THE UNCONSCIOUS: *Papers on the Psychology of Art, Literature, Love, Religion* TB/45
Maurice Friedman	MARTIN BUBER: *The Life of Dialogue* TB/64
Octavius Brooks Frothingham	TRANSCENDENTALISM IN NEW ENGLAND: *A History* TB/59
Edward Gibbon	THE END OF THE ROMAN EMPIRE IN THE WEST [J. B. Bury Edition; Illustrated] TB/37
Edward Gibbon	THE TRIUMPH OF CHRISTENDOM IN THE ROMAN EMPIRE [J. B. Bury Edition; Illustrated] TB/46
Charles C. Gillispie	GENESIS AND GEOLOGY TB/51
Maurice Goguel	JESUS AND THE ORIGINS OF CHRISTIANITY I: *Prolegomena to the Life of Jesus* TB/65
Maurice Goguel	JESUS AND THE ORIGINS OF CHRISTIANITY II: *The Life of Jesus* TB/66
Edgar J. Goodspeed	A LIFE OF JESUS TB/1
Herbert J. C. Grierson	CROSS-CURRENTS IN 17TH CENTURY ENGLISH LITERATURE: *The World, the Flesh, the Spirit* TB/47
William Haller	THE RISE OF PURITANISM TB/22
Adolf Harnack	WHAT IS CHRISTIANITY? TB/17
Edwin Hatch	THE INFLUENCE OF GREEK IDEAS ON CHRISTIANITY TB/18
Karl Heim	CHRISTIAN FAITH AND NATURAL SCIENCE TB/16
F. H. Heinemann	EXISTENTIALISM AND THE MODERN PREDICAMENT TB/28
Stanley R. Hopper, *ed.*	SPIRITUAL PROBLEMS IN CONTEMPORARY LITERATURE TB/21
Johan Huizinga	ERASMUS AND THE AGE OF REFORMATION TB/19
Aldous Huxley	THE DEVILS OF LOUDUN: *A Study in the Psychology of Power Politics and Mystical Religion in the France of Cardinal Richelieu* TB/60
Søren Kierkegaard	EDIFYING DISCOURSES: A Selection TB/32

(Continued on next page)

Søren Kierkegaard — THE JOURNALS OF KIERKEGAARD TB/52
Søren Kierkegaard — PURITY OF HEART TB/4
Alexandre Koyré — FROM THE CLOSED WORLD TO THE INFINITE UNIVERSE TB/31
Emile Mâle — THE GOTHIC IMAGE: *Religious Art in France of the 13th Century* TB/44
H. Richard Niebuhr — CHRIST AND CULTURE TB/3
H. Richard Niebuhr — THE KINGDOM OF GOD IN AMERICA TB/49
H. J. Rose — RELIGION IN GREECE AND ROME TB/55
Josiah Royce — THE RELIGIOUS ASPECT OF PHILOSOPHY: *A Critique of the Bases of Conduct and of Faith* TB/29
Auguste Sabatier — OUTLINES OF A PHILOSOPHY OF RELIGION BASED ON PSYCHOLOGY AND HISTORY TB/23
George Santayana — INTERPRETATIONS OF POETRY AND RELIGION TB/9
George Santayana — WINDS OF DOCTRINE *and* PLATONISM AND THE SPIRITUAL LIFE TB/24
Friedrich Schleiermacher — ON RELIGION: *Speeches to Its Cultured Despisers* TB/36
Henry Osborn Taylor — THE EMERGENCE OF CHRISTIAN CULTURE IN THE WEST: *The Classical Heritage of the Middle Ages* TB/48
Paul Tillich — DYNAMICS OF FAITH TB/42
Edward Burnett Tylor — THE ORIGINS OF CULTURE TB/33
Edward Burnett Tylor — RELIGION IN PRIMITIVE CULTURE TB/34
Evelyn Underhill — WORSHIP TB/10
Johannes Weiss — EARLIEST CHRISTIANITY: *A History of the Period* A.D. *30–150: Vol. I,* TB/53; *Vol. II,* TB/54
Wilhelm Windelband — A HISTORY OF PHILOSOPHY I: *Greek, Roman, Medieval* TB/38
Wilhelm Windelband — A HISTORY OF PHILOSOPHY II: *Renaissance, Enlightenment, Modern* TB/39

HARPER TORCHBOOKS / The Academy Library

H. J. Blackham — SIX EXISTENTIALIST THINKERS TB/1002
Walter Bromberg — THE MIND OF MAN: *A History of Psychotherapy and Psychoanalysis* TB/1003
G. P. Gooch — ENGLISH DEMOCRATIC IDEAS IN THE SEVENTEENTH CENTURY TB/1006
Francis J. Grund — ARISTOCRACY IN AMERICA TB/1001
Henry James — THE PRINCESS CASAMASSIMA TB/1005
Georges Poulet — STUDIES IN HUMAN TIME TB/1004

HARPER TORCHBOOKS / The Science Library

J. Bronowski — SCIENCE AND HUMAN VALUES TB/505
W. C. Dampier, *ed.* — READINGS IN THE LITERATURE OF SCIENCE TB/512
Arthur Eddington — SPACE, TIME AND GRAVITATION: *An Outline of the General Relativity Theory* TB/510
H. T. Pledge — SCIENCE SINCE 1500: *A Short History of Mathematics, Physics, Chemistry, and Biology* TB/506
George Sarton — ANCIENT SCIENCE AND MODERN CIVILIZATION TB/501
Paul A. Schilpp, *ed.* — ALBERT EINSTEIN: Philosopher-Scientist: *Vol. I,* TB/502; *Vol. II,* TB/503
Friedrich Waismann — INTRODUCTION TO MATHEMATICAL THINKING: *The Formation of Concepts in Modern Mathematics* TB/511
W. H. Watson — ON UNDERSTANDING PHYSICS: *An Analysis of the Philosophy of Physics* TB/507
G. J. Whitrow — THE STRUCTURE AND EVOLUTION OF THE UNIVERSE: *An Introduction to Cosmology* TB/504
A. Wolf — A HISTORY OF SCIENCE, TECHNOLOGY AND PHILOSOPHY IN THE 16TH AND 17TH CENTURIES: *Vol. I,* TB/508; *Vol. II,* TB/509

THE MIND OF MAN

A History of Psychotherapy and Psychoanalysis

WALTER BROMBERG

HARPER TORCHBOOKS / *The Academy Library*

HARPER & BROTHERS • PUBLISHERS • NEW YORK

HARPER TORCHBOOKS / *The Academy Library*

Advisory Editor in the Humanities and Social Sciences: Benjamin Nelson.

THE MIND OF MAN

Printed in the United States of America

This book was originally entitled MAN ABOVE HUMANITY: *A History of Psychotherapy*, published in 1954, and is reprinted by arrangement with J. B. Lippincott Company. It is a revision of THE MIND OF MAN, first published by Harper & Brothers in 1937.

First HARPER TORCHBOOK edition published 1959

Library of Congress catalog card number: 59-10344

THIS BOOK IS DEDICATED TO

MY MOTHER

I sometimes think that never blows so red
The Rose as where some buried Caesar bled.

RUBÁIYÁT, ED. 4, XIX

Preface to the Torchbook Edition

THE labyrinth of man's mind, no less than the extraordinary mechanism of his body, has fascinated man from the earliest days of his self-awareness. His aspirations and wonderments, his creativeness and destructiveness, desires and appetites, have intrigued the philosopher and priest, the physician and scientist. The questions these human characteristics have raised are legion, the answers relatively few. But even that proven knowledge which constitutes the content of mental sciences, gained after much patient labor, is insufficient in the face of the complexities presented by mental aberrations. For the psyche in health and the psyche in illness seem sometimes to be so similar as to be almost identical and sometimes so distant as to be at opposing poles. Moreover, mental illness presents a double problem. Not only the wish for understanding, but the sufferers' urgent requests for help are ever before the mental scientist: this spurs the efforts of mental healers but simultaneously increases their difficulty. Yet man, being what he is, has never ceased to struggle for solution and cure of the enigma of mental illness and emotional distress. Today's striving to understand the underlying riddles and to still the clamor of emotional needs is enormous.

The panorama of psychotherapy has become progressively wider and deeper in the middle decade of the twentieth century. Growth in all branches of psychotherapy has been stimulated by an unexampled public demand for help with emotional problems, with maladjustment in marriage or on the job, with unhappiness and the effects of many types of neuroses. Not only have psychiatrists, clinical investigators, and psychologists continued to develop their methods for mental healing, but educators, clergymen, nurses, public relations experts, industrial management authorities have extended basic concepts, which rightly can be called "psychiatric," into their approach to people. The field of public relations and propaganda, including activities in international affairs, has incorporated psychotherapeutic principles; philosophers, particularly the existentialists and religionists as pastoral psychiatrists, have found therapeutic applications for their thinking. Biochemists and pharmacological chemists have worked unceasingly to find drugs that will increase the effectiveness of tranquilizers. Indeed, it is almost inaccurate nowadays to restrict the tracing of psychotherapy's growth merely to psychiatric and medical workers. Broad movements in this "people-conscious" world of the mid-century, democratization of major political areas of the world, efforts at spreading political equality in backward nations, the psychological implications involved in the "one world" notion, all merge with the psychotherapeutic aim of relieving tension and promoting emotional security. Yet once the ubiquity of the mental health aim is appreciated, a brief discussion of recent advances in psychotherapy will necessarily be limited to several well-defined areas.

The mainstream of thought nourishing scientific psychotherapy remains *psychoanalysis*. Psychoanalytic training has become accepted as indispensable for those psychiatrists who utilize psychological principles in treatment. Nevertheless, in spite of the growth of institutes teaching psychoanalysis in the larger cities of this country and in Europe and the consequent increase in the number of practicing analysts, there has been a tendency to depart from orthodox psychoanalytic technique with patients suffering from neurosis and personality disorders. The cost to each patient and the increase in numbers applying for analytic help have been partial factors. On the other hand, psychotherapeutic clinics have been established throughout the country; one center in New York provided 30,000 hours of psychoanalytically oriented treatment sessions in a given year. While the numbers of distraught individuals applying for psychoanalytic help has increased among private practitioners as well as in clinics, brief psychotherapies along psychoanalytic lines, introduced originally by Franz Alexander and his associates (see page 234) and furthered by many others, are now no novelty.

Another indirect factor which has tended to make psychoanalysis more the guiding philosophy of scientific psychotherapy than its sole tool has been the steady swell of criticism of Freudian theory based on a logical analysis of Freudian premises as well as dissatisfaction with the results from psychoanalytic treatment. The trend to critically evaluate psychoanalysis has proceeded at the same time that the various university centers and institutes have been bringing it closer to clinical psychology. Simultaneously, there has been a tremendous diffusion of Freudian knowledge among psychologists, psychiatric social workers, counselors, and physicians, all of whom use its principles in their contacts with patients.

In the main, the basic principles of Freudian analysis are not contested among the majority of analysts, although stress on the interpretation of "here and now" events in a patient's life, as opposed to the events and situations of the patient's infancy and childhood, has received increased attention. The Jungian analytic psychology, although eclipsed by Freudianism, especially in this country, has never lost stature. This is particularly true since Jung's plea that the integrative power of mankind, which has always been inherent in religion, is being given more attention than psychoanalysis has given it up to now and is heeded among literary groups, especially in England. The modifications by Horney, stressing social factors, have been incorporated in analytic practice. Decreased stress on passivity on the part of the therapist has insensibly influenced psychoanalytic applications in psychotherapy as a consequence of disappointment with prolonged treatment of the transference situation. Directive attitudes on the part of physicians have taken its place, meeting the needs of many patients for quicker aid.

The attitude that *interpersonal relations* in the patient's life have dynamic affects in fashioning his illness (with a minimizing of early trauma and infantile material) has maintained its position in therapeutic thinking. So also the psychobiologic orientation of Adolf Meyer, which has exerted a subtle influence in the practices of American psychotherapists, continues to form the frame of reference for most psychotherapists who do not rigidly adhere to orthodox psychoanalytic schools. This view, congenial to the American temperament, stresses the "common sense" approach involving estimating the patient's mental resources and aiding him in adjusting his life with such ego strengths as can be mustered. There has been a growing recognition of the *eclectic* psychotherapist. These are men trained in the basic sciences of neurology, psychodynamics, and psychobiology who utilize all aspects of neuropsychiatry in their therapy. A recent study of psychiatrists as individuals, their beliefs and aspirations (McIver and Redlich), has pointed out that the eclectics who "show tolerance for all theories and practices . . . are the hope of our profession . . . building a sturdy road toward a unified and scientific psychiatry."

As the issue of the marriage between psychoanalytic psychotherapy and applied psychology, the field of counseling has grown to robust adulthood among colleges and in large industrial enterprises involving many levels of workers where personal interaction is based on minor personality clashes. Here counseling has found a fixed place as part of personal practices. Counseling, which received its impetus from the school of Carl Rogers, is based on a theory of nondirectiveness and serves as psychotherapy for many problems such as marital disharmony, student inadequacies, tension among workers, and child-parent problems. Psychotherapy involved in this counseling has become almost synonymous with "listening as therapy" plus occasional common-sense direction. In this field clinical psychologists, as before, have been active, and to this group have been added increasing numbers of psychiatric social workers and guidance specialists.

Child guidance, originally conceived as the prime tool in the total plan of prevention of mental illness, has developed in two directions: inculcation of mental hygiene principles in education and intensive treatment of the increasing numbers of disturbed children. Today the child-guidance clinic is more apt to form part of a hospital organization or outpatient set-up. Child psychotherapy which involves play technique, featuring puppets, toys, drawing, and finger painting, continues to be utilized in probing the depths of child phobias and behavior changes. The problem of evoking fantasy responses, considering the nonverbality of children, has been partially solved by play techniques applied individually and in groups. Out of the early child play groups (Slavson) have emerged experimental play-therapy groups with adolescents, wherein delinquent, neurotic, and incipient schizophrenic youths are treated. Here the leader warms up the group with play experiences which partake of the currency of adolescent language, thinking, and feeling, and provide an opportunity for the youths to identify with the therapist in sensitive areas of sex, rebellion against authority, social mores, and the like. This work has fanned out to include boys' clubs, street gangs (by probation officers working under a nom-de-plume), state school and reformatory populations. Indeed, group therapy techniques have virtually brought about a revolution in the handling of sociopathic behavior problems—drug addicts, criminal recidivists, potential and fully developed psychopaths—by juvenile detention homes, youth authorities, and penal institutions including state prisons.

Group therapy as a philosophy and technique of handling mental problems can be considered the greatest single development in psychotherapy during the mid-century decade. Of the methods employed, the analytic and psychodramatic methods have the widest vogue. Analytic group therapy, initiated by Slavson, utilizes the transference from the patient to therapist as well as lateral transference from patient to patient. Interpretations are made, emotional weaknesses supported, neurotic problems investigated, the aim being to confront the patient with the psychological essence of his or her problem and eventually to provide insight thereof. The psychodramatic approach, initiated by Moreno, transliterates the patient's problem into a dramatic presentation, thus allowing the patient to re-live in a social dimension (i.e., the social matrix) the nucleus of his neurotic difficulty. Through the mirror image, reversal, and other techniques, the patient is provided the opportunity for the solace for which Robert Burns called:

> Oh wad some power the giftie gie us
> To see oursels as others see us!

Most commonly, group workers adopt a combination of interview, analytic, and psychodramatic methods. These techniques have been found especially helpful in what could be called the "social neurosis" (Schilder), where symptoms of uneasiness, diffidence, social inhibition from whatever cause, and aloofness are prominent. The loss of a sense of isolation consequent upon the patient's entering a community of distraught or neurotic people is found to have done much to reduce the social tension from which neurotic people suffer and to pave the way for further psychological analysis.

Group activity appears in wide use in such autonomous organizations as Alcoholics Anonymous, where the effect of a generalized communal religious experience in conjunction with an open avowal of individual emotional problems has been increasingly successful with an age-old difficulty. Pastoral psychiatry continues its growth wherein the integrative power of faith in revealed religion and religious concepts as an ethical world force is invoked in pastoral counseling. World interest, although fascinated with astronomical and engineering achievements, slowly turns to the uncharted universe of man's nature and the techniques which promise to explore it. Hamlet's lament,

> The time is out of joint; O cursed spite,
> That ever I was born to set it right!

has turned into a victory cry for mental healers.

The chemical treatment of nervous ailments has attained so wide a horizon in the last few years that Joseph Wortis, an early American investigator of insulin therapy, was able to write in 1957 "new drug treatments have practically abolished lobotomy and greatly diminished both the need for electroshock therapy and insulin." Of themselves the vast group of chemical tranquilizers were considered to be direct therapeutic agents which quieted anxiety, reduced obsessional notions and, in disturbed patients, almost obliterated agitation and combativeness. These drugs, used by medical men as well as psychiatrists, have become almost a household remedy, much as bromides were two generations ago. The drugs reserpine, chlorpromazine (Thorazine), Compazine, Equanil, and Miltown, and hundreds of others newly announced almost monthly by pharmaceutical manufacturers, promise an entirely new area of treatment. Borrowed from the term *ataraxia,* a concept prominent in Stoic philosophy, meaning "detachment," these drugs have been called ataractics. As dispensers of detachment they were seized upon as an answer to the anxiety of a nation of worriers. By 1956, thirty million tranquilizer tablets were sold by one drug company alone. By 1958, the nation's pharmacies had dispensed almost two billion tranquilizer pills on prescriptions (U.S. Public Health Service). Public pressure for tranquilizer use became enormous. The threshold of anxiety seemed to have been lowered as psychic pain became less tolerable to the public.

Nevertheless, the main use of tranquilizers was in state hospitals and clinics where psychiatrists eagerly tested their efficiency on serious mental disorders. The properties of tranquilizers were investigated: F. M. Berger analyzed the tranquilizers as falling in two groups: "autonomic suppressants," or tranquilizers in the narrower sense of the word, and "central relaxants." The former comprised the "phenothiazines, reserpine, and the diphenylmethanes," (Thorazine, Sparine, Atarax, etc.). The second group, "central relaxants," "is composed of meprobamate, mephenesin, and related compounds" (Miltown, Equanil, etc.). As new drugs come on the market they are studied carefully by hospital workers. All investigators agree that these drugs modify psychotic behavior, reduce tension, and ameliorate symptoms, mild and severe emotional turmoil and excitement.

Early in the tumultuous history of chemotherapy, reserpine, extracted from the Indian root Rauwolfia, promised the greatest relief for psychotic patients. Later it was supplanted by the phenothiazine derivatives. As comparative studies accumulated it became evident that drugs alone did not remove conflicts or alleviate the basic pathology of neurosis and psychosis. Some physicians even scouted the idea that drugs had any effect at all, implying that the effect was suggestive: the majority, however, agreed that they reduced the duration and intensity of mental illness. Indeed, plans have been made in several of the larger state mental hygiene departments to reduce the number of mental hospital beds as the discharge increased in anticipation of decreased patient-hospital days. Current assessment of the use of ataractic drugs can be stated as follows: the tranquilizer group reduces the intensity of obsessional ideas, of tension and anxiety, of disordered thinking by interfering with the emotional expression and meaning of symptoms to the patient—the underlying psychic constellation that accompanies these symptoms remains unchanged. For this reason psychotherapy has been increasingly combined with chemotherapy, which induces improved receptivity toward psychotherapeutic analysis in the patient.

Electroconvulsive therapy, with its variants, electric stimulation and electronarcosis, is still used in mental states featured by depression but with diminishing frequency. Although a majority of psychiatrists would insist that, for intractible depressions, early schizophrenias, melancholias in middle and old age, electroconvulsive therapy is the treatment of choice, an increasing number are relying on drugs, psychotherapy, and management. State hospitals use electroconvulsive therapy consistently but in shorter series of treatments and on fewer patients. *Insulin coma* therapy has receded rapidly into the background because of uncertain results and the cost involved in administration; but subcoma insulin therapy has reappeared as a prominent type of therapy aimed at milder neuroses and depressions. At a recent international conference on physiological methods in psychiatry, it was maintained that although no agreement among psychiatrists on the therapeutic significance of insulin coma existed they were loath to discontinue its use. At this congress some European commentators held to the opinion that tranquilizers should not replace insulin coma because of the latter's more abiding results.

The other major form of physiological psychotherapy, *lobotomy,* has had a checkered career since its American introduction (see page 269). It has adherents and detractors: in 1958 Walter Freeman, one of psychosurgery's pioneers, stated that "[psychosurgery] is in eclipse, overshadowed by the tranquilizers and euphoriants." Much resistance has developed about psychosurgery because of its drastic nature and, more importantly, the personality changes which follow lobotomy. Still, Freeman and others have reported on thousands of cases in which, in one series, 80 per cent were kept out of a hospital for chronic mental illness and 60 per cent returned to their former activities. The ethical bluntness which follows some lobotomies has been pointed to as an undesirable result. On the other hand, many patients hospitalized for years have become free from complaints, freed of preoccupation with self, and able to return to gainful employment. Lobotomy has proven to be an almost miraculous cure in many cases, particularly for obsessive-compulsive states which do not yield to chemical or psychotherapeutic intervention and chronic anxiety states as well as for regressed and schizophrenic patients. It can be stated that in hospitals with large numbers of chronic patients lobotomy has proven its worth and it is likewise true that it is employed often as a last resort.

Freud's bold thrust into the dark caverns of man's nature has provided a rallying point and given direction to mental healers and psychotherapists of many descriptions. It is not too much to say that modern social life has become therapeutic in its essence. Magazine articles, sermons by clergymen, preachments by teachers in adjustment classes and personal development courses, casual conversation between friends, and the interminable concern with human problems at the bridge table, on the golf course, in the neighborhood bar, at the dinner table and in the family room give evidence of the Age of Self-Awareness.

Whether this concerted effort to help man master his emotions and to diagnose the psychological causes of his unhappiness will result in a tensionless world is a problem for the future to answer. Psychotherapy, if it does not accomplish this gigantic task, has at least implemented Man's eternal search for emotional ease and peace of mind.

WALTER BROMBERG, M.D.

Sacramento, California
March, 1959

Preface

To understand the ramifications of present-day psychiatry, a knowledge of its history is pertinent; to understand the more chaotic field of mental healing, it is *essential* to know its history. This work is an effort to supply this requirement for those who have come upon psychotherapy in the full flower of its modern growth. The present inquiry into the genetic history of psychotherapy started eighteen years ago with a publisher's request that a brief book be written on the "differences between Freud, Jung and Adler." Clear cut as the assignment appeared to be, it soon became evident that analysis of the broad historical-social base of mental healing, transcending study of these schools of analytic psychotherapy, was required to complete the task. An earlier effort in this direction resulted in publication of *The Mind of Man,* which appeared in 1937. The present volume is an extension—a rethinking and a rewriting of that work.

As a history of mental healing the present work necessarily suffers from the lack of completeness manifest in any such recording. The fulfillment of the task of writing a history, complete in every detail, would be gratifying bibliographically but might not be useful operationally. The steps in the evolution of mental healing as an art and a science have been so devious, so unevenly recorded and so uncritically reported, that even the most scrupulous scholar may be satisfied with a "comprehensive" account. Undoubtedly much material was inadvertently omitted, and some was purposely excluded. The author has attempted to steer a clear course between what might have been a "Bartlett's Quotations" of psychiatry and a possibly hazy generalized statement of the field of mental healing. For practical reasons, and because America has taken the lead in psychotherapeutic development in recent years, the accent has been on publications written in English. Omissions from the world literature, notably of the Slavic and the Oriental nations, and to a lesser degree of some Latin countries, may be attributable to reasons stated above.

The author has endeavored to present the currents, the movements, the individual figures in the long evolution of psychotherapy. With this goal in view, mental healers not allied to the medical profession, or loosely affiliated with it, have not been neglected. Because of this wider view of mental healing as the generic endeavor, the author claims sole responsibility for selection and interpretation of the elements comprising this chronicle.

It is a genuine pleasure to acknowledge help which has come from diverse quarters in the preparation of this work. The following individuals have been of invaluable assistance in specific areas with which this book deals: Dr. Winfred Overholser, Superintendent of Saint Elizabeths Hospital, Washington, D. C., critically read the entire manuscript and furnished valuable corrections in many of the sections. Dr. Edward L. Margetts, Honorary Librarian, Department of Psychiatry, McGill University, Montreal, Canada, gave the first five chapters a careful reading and offered important comments on them. Dr. Clarence P. Oberndorf, one of America's pioneer psychoanalysts, evaluated Chapters 8 and 9 and supplied valued suggestions on the history of psychoanalysis. Dr. George S. Stevenson, National and International Consultant of the National Association of Mental Health, examined and criticized Chapter 10, dealing with mental hygiene. Dr. C. J. Ducasse, Professor of Philosophy at Brown University, studied Chapters 2, 3 and 6 and contributed incisive comments on religious healing and the philosophy of faith healing.

Acknowledgment is due Miss Clara Manson, Librarian, Stanford Lane Medical Library, San Francisco, who assisted in the garnering of material, and Mrs. Anne Hoen and her staff, who made material available; Miss Clara Zimmerman and her staff, including Mr. Robert A. Anderson and Mr. Charles K. Atkins, of the California State Library, Sacramento, California, who aided in securing nonmedical material on mental healing; and Dr. Estelle M. Rogers, of the Langley-Porter Clinic, San Francisco, who helped in the translation of several French works. There were many others with whom historical accents and material were discussed. These included Dr. Richard Loewenberg, Bakersfield, California, concerning eighteenth-century psychiatry; Dr. Wladimir Eliasberg, New York, regarding recent psychotherapeutic movements in Germany; Dr. Fabian L. Rouke, Consulting Psychologist, New York, with whom the philosophic implications of religious healing were freely discussed; my wife, Esther B. Bromberg, sociologic implications of psychotherapy; Dr. Ruth L. Green, psychotherapy in state-hospital practice; Mr. Walter Kahoe, of the J. B. Lippincott Company, historical aspects of physiologic methods of psychotherapy.

Acknowledgment is also made to students, hospital assistants and secretaries, the last of whom was Mrs. Dorothy Bruggman, all of whom did yeoman service in the tedious job of checking references, typing, revising and proofreading the manuscript. To all I extend my appreciation and my thanks.

WALTER BROMBERG, M.D.

Sacramento, California

Contents

A section of illustrations follows page 136

THE MIND OF MAN

1

Scope and Meaning of Psychotherapy

Traditionally, history is written in an anterograde manner, from the earliest period for which records are available to the time of writing. This procedure seems natural, even "instinctive," to the investigator and recorder of any area of human interest. Practical advantages of logical consistency and ease of conceptualization, especially in a genetic study of any scientific subject, seem to dictate the wisdom of starting from the beginning. Yet, beyond this lies a psychological factor which it is difficult to repress: it is the compulsive, yet intensely human, wish to consider first things first. But from the standpoint of the emotional stimulus which spurs curiosity, a history of a practical field like psychotherapy should start with the "now." This is a point at which interest in causes and preceding events originates. For that which concerns the practitioner of any discipline, be it medicine, psychiatry, social work or the law, is the "present" with its tensions, distresses, outraged feelings or emergency needs. The immediacy of human needs precludes attention to any but the current period.

In human behavior and thought, however, the "now" does not stand alone. It is compounded of and infiltrated with centuries of "nows," reverberating and re-echoing in obscure ways in our thoughts, inner feelings and reflex or automatic behavior. Just as our physical structures contain palpable reminders of our biologic heritage, so do our psychic functions and institutions carry rational and irrational elements, the possession of those who preceded us. The core of experience which gives an individual his characteristic integrity as a personality relates him to his own ancestors as it does to the entire human race. The exaltations and the defeats of the human spirit are reflected in difficulties now, as in the past, bearing witness to the sameness of human experience.

The history of mental healing, then, may be written starting with the present, winding its serpiginous way back through the fifty centuries to ascertain how others have dealt with these same pressing needs now addressed to the therapist. For one who has endeavored for a quarter of a century to bring mental health to patients through psychological means, an occasional flash illuminates the continuity of his efforts with the strivings of those who wrestled with psychological disorders in the past. A perception arises of an unbroken series of similar inner experiences occurring in similar situations stretching through the years. The inner uniting thread common to all mental healers centers in the challenge of man's imperishable spirit and the vicissitudes to which it is subject. This recognition of historical continuity in the mental healer and psychotherapist, now and in the past, is not a statement of mystical relationship, although it must be conceded that such a notion forms an important part of the mental content of the patient approaching psychotherapy. It is a recognition of the factual (historical) implications within the patient-doctor relationship as it is presented in the "now." To appreciate the continued current of therapeutic experience for the therapist of whatever school or persuasion, is to deepen his relatedness to the patient, to spur his enthusiasm, to mitigate his disappointments, to temper his optimism and to humanize his work.

There is, moreover, a continuous thread of need which has shadowed the history of the human race and given rise to psychotherapeutic efforts. Each age has looked upon mental tension as the forerunner of dissolution of its social-psychological structure. Every age has groaned under increase in tension because of the increasing complexity of life. Today's statistics indicate acceleration in incidence of mental illness. According to Selective Service statistics, "one out of every 10 suffers from some form of mental disease." [1] More recent estimates indicate that in the United States 9,000,000 individuals suffer from psychoses, neuroses and forms of behavior disorder, as psychopathic personality; 3,800,000 from alcoholism; and 50,000 from addiction to narcotics. From the standpoint of disability and suffering, mental illness is a "major medical problem facing the profession today." [2] The cost of speed in living is commonly measured in increased mental illnesses. Yesterday, it was universally acknowledged that we lived in a neurotic, air-borne age; today, we have moved on from an atomic age to a space era. Yet, in 1878, Hack Tuke, a leading English psychiatrist, spoke with concern of "our railway age . . . [in which] injury is done by sacrificing mental quiet on the altar of haste." [3] Four decades earlier, Joseph Guislain, the Belgian psychiatrist, agreed that the "feverish pursuit of gain, and pleasure and great discussions upon political and social questions . . . kept society in Europe and America . . . [in] a half-intoxicating state of cerebral irritation." [4] And a century before that, an English physician, writing on nervousness, complained that

> the Wealth and Abundance of the Inhabitants . . . the sedentary Occupations of the better Sort (among whom this Evil mostly rages) and the Humour of

[1] National Committee for Mental Hygiene: Annual Report, 1947, p. 8.

[2] Editorial: Mental Health, J.A.M.A. 152:48, 1953.

[3] Tuke, D. H.: Insanity in Ancient and Modern Life, p. 182, London, Macmillan, 1878.

[4] Guislain, J.: Traité sur les phrénopathies, ou doctrine nouvelle des maladies mentales, Bruxelles, Etablissement Encyclo., 1833.

living in great, populous . . . Towns, have brought forth a Class and Set of Distempers . . . scarce known to our Ancestors . . . nor afflicting such NUMBERS . . . [as] these nervous Disorders.[5]

The life line of psychotherapeutic need promises to demonstrate its poignancy in every age.

ITS PRESENT SCOPE

Let us, for a moment, observe the extent of activity in the ephemeral "now." In this endeavor we immediately encounter a seemingly new phenomenon of the transformation of psychiatry, the Cinderella of Medicine.[6] The rejected Sister of Medicine has gained recognition: she has been fitted with the glass slipper and thus achieved queenly status. It is no longer accurate to speak of psychotherapy or psychiatry as a "coming thing." Within the medical profession, medical internists have appropriated the psychosomatic viewpoint. Surgeons and gynecologists are interested in psychological aspects of their work. Dermatologists and allergists daily see clinical evidences of psychological reflections in their patients. Obstetricians have resurrected hypnosis and other psychotherapeutic principles. Psychologists have invaded the field of mental therapy. Pediatricians have absorbed the findings of child psychiatry in their daily work.

Psychotherapy has broadened from a medical specialty to a point at which it spills over into community activities and becomes a part of international management: it engages the attention of the diplomat, the statesman, the business executive, the labor relations expert, the teacher, the government co-ordinator and the industrial engineer. A new social orientation has developed a need for laymen and professionals alike to improve our social relationships. It is this orientation toward human interrelatedness that has challenged those who practice psychotherapy. Not only the mentally ill person but the individual with emotional disturbances or minor personality distortions which may interfere with economic, marital or social life requires help. Psychiatry is now an integral part of the scheme and pattern of social-mindedness, and under the innocuous name of Human Relations it has seated itself firmly in the curricula of our colleges and secondary schools.

Widespread preoccupation with variants of social interaction, which necessarily includes the desire to reduce areas of human friction, i.e., psychotherapy, has been in response to stimuli stretching beyond the confines of

[5] Cheyne, George: The English Malady or a Treatise of Nervous Diseases of All Kinds, As Spleen, Vapours, Lowness of Spirits, Hypochondriacal, and Hysterical Distempers, London, G. Strahan, 1734.

[6] Salmon, T. W.: The Cinderella of medicine, a modern fairy story, M. J. & Rec. 134:253, 1931.

medicine. The changing face of polity within this country and throughout the world has advanced a new psychological format in which individual thinking is superseded by group thinking. One of the factors in this changing modality of thought and feeling is the apparent fact that the erstwhile durable institutions of freedom of individual action and movement, and complete economic independence in a free, competitive world, seem to be vanishing slowly but inexorably. For this reason and others the patterns of *group action* have become of primary concern. Appreciation of a common individual experience and common needs within the group has precipitated a greater interdependence in social living through recognition of the common heritage of human impulses and reactions. While *groupfeel* can be regarded as a natural evolutionary mode of social functioning growing out of a shrinking economic world, it can also be a result of ideologic change insidiously and rapidly rearranging our social lives. At all events, *groupfeel* and *groupact* contain practical and psychological elements which are rapidly becoming a prevailing mode in our psychic life. For these reasons psychotherapy has been pushed into many areas in daily life in which it was a stranger a decade or two ago.

These larger considerations lie in the foreground of the present status of mental healing as a discipline. The specific job of psychotherapeutics is still, in large part, focused on treating the individual patient, although recently group therapy has spread the canvas in a social direction. Because the methodologic slant and goals of psychiatry are gradually being absorbed by educators and social planners, and will probably be woven imperceptibly into our social fabric in the not too distant future, it would be well to outline the present scope of psychotherapeutic endeavors. The present activity, centering in vast numbers of mentally and emotionally ill, is tremendous.

Psychotherapy is a major aspect of the psychiatrist's work and will probably remain his chief concern. During the last two decades, however, ancillary groups, such as clinical psychologists, psychiatric social workers, psychiatric nurses, medical social workers and occupational, recreational, music, religious and biblio-therapists, have assumed a considerable share of this labor. At the same time, educators, rehabilitation workers, sociologists, welfare workers, personnel experts and public relations counselors also have entered the field of psychotherapy. To estimate the number of all these individuals would be very difficult, but, as a guide to such estimate, it is noteworthy that the American Psychiatric Association lists 7,125 members [7] in the United States and Canada. Perhaps a proportionate number exist in the rest of the world, including scores of psychiatrists and psycho-

[7] American Psychiatric Association, List of Fellows and Members, 1952-1953, New York, p. 140.

therapists not affiliated with official organizations. Psychiatrists and psychoanalysts (both medical and lay) are located in the main cities throughout the world—in Europe, South America, Asia and North America.[8] These individuals are active in private practice, state and provincial hospitals, Veterans or government hospitals and clinics, private clinics and sanitaria, general hospitals, psychiatric institutes, industrial plants, school systems (there are 550 psychiatrists active in universities in the United States [9]), military organizations, penal institutions, court clinics, mental-hygiene clinics operated on a city, county or state basis, family-welfare agencies, public and private and child-guidance clinics. It is a commonplace that medical practitioners the world over are involved in handling a vast number of mentally and emotionally ill persons who do not find their way into psychiatric hands.

Publicists are employed in advancing mental-hygiene concepts involving psychotherapy directly or indirectly in state, national and international associations. The Mental Health Section of the World Health Organization,[10] affiliated with United Nations, has brought ideas of mental hygiene to many backward areas of the world. The means used to disseminate information and attitudes on psychiatric subjects are the radio, television, pamphlets, books, newsletters, dramatic presentations, educational motion-picture films, news stories, magazine articles, posters, campaigns, lectures and adult-education workshops. Published material on all aspects of mental health attains astronomic dimensions yearly.

Religious leaders, who have intuitively played a psychotherapeutic role to their congregates for five thousand years, have extended their interest in therapy more specifically under the term *Pastoral Psychology*. There are other religious activities which carry therapeutic implications, such as church services, testimonials, confessionals, missions, novenas, prayer meetings, either self-inspired or led by religious leaders, evangelistic drives, etc. Shrines are still foci of mental healing. Organized churches, as the Christian Science Church, Unity, etc., devote themselves overtly to healing along metaphysical or philosophic lines. Fraternal organizations and service clubs exert a constant force for fellowship which is interpretable as indirect psychotherapy. Inspirational writers, religio-philosophic authors,[11] newspaper columnists, practical psychologists on the radio and the lecture platform, undoubtedly exert a psychotherapeutic force on their readers and

[8] World Federation for Mental Health: Annual Report, 1950, p. 5, London.
[9] Group for Advancement of Psychiatry, Role of Psychiatrists in Colleges and Universities, Report 17, September, 1950.
[10] World Federation for Mental Health: Annual Report, 1948-1949, p. 45, London.
[11] Exman, Eugene: Reading, writing and religion, Harper's Magazine 206:84, 1953.

auditors. Irregular practitioners of metaphysics, chromotherapy,[12] somnotherapy, herbal healing and dianetics, psychic science, science of mind, all of whom would deny the appellation of "irregular," are resorted to by many [13] for the healing of physical and mental troubles. And faith-healers who utilize "psychological," mystical or symbolic means for healing are legion.

Beyond those healers whose activities are defined by themselves and their clients, a large number of numerologists, patent-medicine vendors, fortunetellers, medicine men, gypsies, now, as in centuries past, dispense solace, advice and emotional support. Well-meaning friends, relatives, professional listeners, confidantes, athletic coaches, bartenders—all, in their various ways, engage in psychotherapy. Indeed, psychotherapy is everybody's business!

It is self-evident that, in a world moving toward the ideal of lessening human tensions and assuaging turbulent emotions, the opportunities and the needs for mental healing are staggering. Led by a changing social orientation, paced by increasing longevity and decreased infant mortality due to advances in biochemistry, physics and medicine, much of the focus of professional and lay interest in human beings can be identified with the endeavor called psychotherapy.

How did this multipolar activity called psychotherapy develop? Although there are problems enough to be solved in the present, our interest is in the evolution of mental healing. We will yield, therefore, to the compulsion and the necessities of beginning at the beginning, bearing in mind that the deeper we search, the less clear the trail becomes; the more we probe, the more speculation and interpretation replace clearly expressed and communicated information. A comprehensive statement of what has occurred in any human area requires calibration by the historian's warning that

> only a part of what was observed in the past was remembered by those who observed it; only a part of what was remembered was recorded; only a part of what was recorded has survived; only a part of what has survived has come to the historian's attention; only a part of what has come to their attention is credible; and only a part of what is credible has been grasped. . . .
>
> History as told . . . is only the historian's expressed part of the understood part of the credible part of the discovered part of history-as-recorded.[14]

[12] Life Science: On colour psycho-somatics, Cobham, Surrey, Inst. of Life Science, August, 1949.

[13] Steiner, L. R.: Where Do People Take Their Troubles?, New York, Internat. Univ. Press, 1949.

[14] Gottschalk, Louis: Understanding History: A Primer of Historical Method, p. 46, New York, Knopf, 1950.

PSYCHOLOGY OF THE HEALER

Psychotherapy, as art and science, has a most tangled history. The various methods of mental healing range over so wide an area of theory and empiricism, of physiologic fact and dramatic fantasy, as to appear completely unrelated to each other. It may be difficult to reconcile the efforts that we encounter of priests and kings, philosophers and neurologists, monks and physicians, psychiatrists and faith-healers, in this protracted evolution. Yet they are all united in a common derivation, held together by a common thread of purpose. This psychological thread is the wish to cure—the tenuous residue of narcissistic omnipotence—once unconsciously embedded in incantations and now understood but still carried in technics which utilize our operational knowledge of ego function. Psychiatrists, aware of this psychological factor, were forced to isolate the magical portion of the wish to heal from their manipulation of the laws of psychic function in healing.

The wish to heal is universal. Man has always been fascinated with the allegedly familiar terrain of his own mind. Its prejudices and hates, its angers and loves, its moods and dreamings, its impulses and sentiments, are so much a part of his reality as to make man and mind virtually synonymous. For the reason that every man is wedded almost from birth to his mental life, he feels instinctively that he is a psychologist on the tacit assumption that perpetual intimacy with the psychic apparatus provides the key to functional control of the abnormalities of that intricate organization.

Mental healing started as a self-curative process, moving by extension to others whose difficulties were recognized as familiar. Because the mind has a natural tendency toward repair of emotional injury, e.g., when due to deprivation or rejection, just as the body has powers of subduing an infection, mending a broken bone or recuperating from fatigue, everyone feels the magical power to direct this tendency. These automatic adaptive and balancing forces within the mind were the bases from which mental healing of the self unconsciously evolved and eventually became absorbed into a scientific discipline.

Psychotherapy could only come into being when our inner mental reactions became serious enough as not to yield to the magical wish. Then it was that more specific measures were devised. True, philosophy, religion and political science—for example, the overthrowing of the feudal state, the advent of individual freedom, etc.—aided the individual to face his emotional anguish. These institutions, civilization's contributions toward regulating mental distress in some measure, were utilizable solely by the few. Mental turmoil required a medicine more specific than the broad beneficence of religion, the leveling tranquillity of philosophy and the thinned-out benefits of political science. To accept solace from such institutions requires a tolerance beyond the range of the usual sufferer. It was inevitable that a personal psychotherapy should evolve, i.e., specific technics which would minister to the immediate cries for mental comfort.

The progression of mental-healing theories and methods followed an irregular, interdigitating pattern. Each method developed was effective in its time, yet each was superseded by another. In early times, healing was the province of sorcerers, medicine men and magi, who relied on a "scientific" magic closely related to the supernatural. The growth of this intermediation with the supernatural gave rise to a body of knowledge and a series of technics which contained in a crude way the effective principles of mental healing. Gradually, from this invocation of the supernatural for human aid, faith-healing developed, codified first by the pagan priest-caste in the form of amulets and mystic formulas, and then, to a degree, by organized religions in prayer and certain aspects of their theurgy. Faith-healing thus became closely identified with religion.

During these early periods, mental healing was not perceived as a distinct discipline or art. It was synonymous with and indistinguishable from "religion" in the sense of a series of activities pointing toward intercession with gods or the supernatural world generally. Indeed, ancient medicine itself was invested with a large share of interest in influencing the supernatural. One of the first regulating factors in medicine (and psychiatry) was the rationalism contributed by the philosophic genius of the Greeks. A second philosophic *Weltanschauung* which exerted a regulatory force in the evolution of mental healing was theistic religions, notably Christianity. Although other world religions of a nontheistic type [15] (as Buddhism) taught tranquillity through denial of human passions and (as Confucianism) emphasized the pursuit of truth, Christianity had a more specific effect on the ideology of Western civilization and, hence, on the evolution of psychotherapy in our culture.

Christianity, in its broad implications, was an institution which aided in the self-regulation of mind, body and soul. In its power and influence, the Church had an effect over a millennium of supplying the *only* organized technic of solace for mental anguish. In the main, this held until the sixteenth century, when the loosening of the authoritarian hold of the Church and the scientific Renaissance allowed for the entrance of a new factor in dealing with human feelings. This third factor was humanitarianism, which, until then, was generally enclosed within the vastness of the Church. To maintain a proper perspective, it should be realized that the majority of the world population had no concern with or appreciation of the influence of Greek philosophy or Judeo-Christian ethics on the evolution of psycho-

[15] Ducasse, C. J.: A Philosophical Scrutiny of Religion, p. 110, New York, Ronald, 1952.

therapy. For it is well to note again that psychotherapy as a definitive discipline did not exist even in the medieval period. It is only from our vantage point in time that these rudimentary yet powerful forces can be traced in the modern fabric of psychotherapy.

A fourth social force in the evolution we are sketching was the Reformation. Its significance resided in the freeing of the humanitarian spirit, until then a religion-bound function, and its availability to the masses who were otherwise denied its benefits. The remote effects of Deism, a philosophy that emphasized the goodness of God and the personal participation of the individual in religion, combined with economic-social pressures of the eighteenth century, pushed to the foreground the basic question of man's emotional and moral health. For these reasons the establishment of psychiatry and psychotherapy as specific disciplines may be said to date from the latter part of the eighteenth century.

This period is a nodal point in the evolution of psychotherapy. It is the point of confluence of the spirit of humanitarianism, the inventive genius of a few individuals and the fertile soil of social change. Social forces that allowed new technics and ideas to take root were of equal potency with those of the religiously derived human impulses and the acute observations of individual physicians. Social growth in the eighteenth century was doubly expressed by the revolutions epitomized in Deism and Unitarianism. The loosening of humanitarianism from its moorings in early religious systems allowed the people of the Western world, engrossed in wars, colonial conquests and industrial struggles, to attend to the relatively new idea of alleviation of mental illness.

Medicine came to grips with mental healing in the eighteenth and the nineteenth centuries. The entrance of physicians into mental healing occurred more by accident than by design, through the ill-fated Mesmer. Mesmer, discoverer of the nonexistent animal magnetism (from which hypnosis derived), is credited with being the first deliberate medical psychotherapist. As psychotherapy evolved from a polyglot medicine, psychology added its discoveries, organic neurology contributed its knowledge of the brain and the nervous system, and medicine was induced to extend its interest to the problems of the whole human individual.

PSYCHOLOGICAL FORCES IN HEALING

It has been indicated that the countless technics used in mental healing over the centuries appear unrelated to each other. Yet the actual forces utilized in bringing about changes in emotions or feelings are basically very few. It is a truism that although the technics for mental healing have often involved *doing* something to the sufferer, the medium through which a mental cure is achieved is the psychological apparatus of the *recipient*.

Whether mental healing is applied through magic, prayer, medicine or psychological analysis, the essential mechanics involved are those of penetration of the patient's feelings, thoughts and attitudes by an external influence and the patient's absorption of this influence.

The obvious fact that the patient's psyche is the battleground on which the struggle for mental health is fought was not always in the foreground of attention. Only in comparatively recent years have the reactions of the patient's ego, the vital partner in a mental-healing relationship, and the intricate relations between patient and physician been studied. Scientific psychotherapists work with these interpersonal forces within healer and patient with knowledge aforethought, in contrast with their lineal antecedents, the magi and the shamans, who wrought their cures chiefly through their own prescience. In effect, knowledge of the conscious and the unconscious interreactions between patient and healer have made a science of psychotherapy.

There now arises the question of the nature of the psychic forces interacting between healer and patient which bring about the therapeutic result. More is known of these forces and which ego-functions in the patient are involved in the alleviation of a mental symptom than the mechanisms by which they produce results. The fundamental problem of why the patient foregoes a psychic or a somatic expression of an emotional conflict or gives up an immature mode of adjustment is predominantly one of social values, of philosophy rather than psychology. In large part the relinquishing of a symptom relates to ethical values consciously or unconsciously imparted by the therapist and his society to the patient. The redirection of unconscious energy, until then absorbed in an emotional conflict, into a channel governed by limitations which reality has set for gratification of human needs implies, necessarily, a philosophic value-judgment. This knotty point is beyond the concern of this volume, which is dedicated to tracing the operation of psychological forces in mental healing throughout the centuries. We may, however, scrutinize as closely as possible the nature of the basic psychic forces involved in psychotherapy and attempt to formulate them.

The first such irreducible element in mental healing is *magic,* both in point of historical precedence and in terms of primitiveness of level within the personality. Magic, in therapy, has its most immediate reflection in healing through supernaturalism and occultism, but it is often an unconscious ingredient of any psychotherapy from the standpoint of the patient. The second is *faith,* expressed directly in religious belief and indirectly in modern man's reliance on principles of scientific medicine. The third is the *adaptive tendencies* of the human organism represented in the integrative and the adaptive capacities of the ego as it mediates between the requirements of society and the instincts within the individual. The force of adaptation is basic to treatment which effects a permanent change in the personality of the patient or permanent eradication of the symptom treated, or even impermanent relinquishment of a pattern of thought or behavior. The fourth element is that of the *intellect,* which aids in the integrative activities of the ego. Psychotherapy which operates through appeals to the reason utilizes the intelligence directly; however, almost no form of mental healing completely avoids the intelligence. It is obvious also that the psychic forces described are overlapping and interdependent in effective action of any form of psychotherapy. The appreciation by the therapist and the conscious or the unconscious manipulation or use of these forces in the patient are what distinguish scientific psychotherapy from its more intuitive predecessors. These modalities, these irreducible quanta, resident in every human being and in every patient, constitute in the last analysis the roots of mental healing. Further consideration of their operation in psychotherapy seems indicated.

Magic was an essential aspect of healing in antiquity and among nonliterate groups, as it is characteristic of primitive thinking in general. Reliance on magical thinking is still abundantly present in those deeper layers of our minds subject to fantasy and out of control of the reasonable ego. In the healing arts the influence of unconscious magical thinking within the patient in relation to the effect of medicines, injections and the like is immediately obvious, as every physician and every pharmacist are aware from daily experience. Magic is the infantile wish of the human race for accomplishment of the impossible; its universal presence depends less on proof of previous successes than on an ineradicable human wish. Belief in magic is uncritical, since its premises are extremely improbable. As Ducasse points out in his lucid discussion:

> Magic, like engineering, is application of theory to practice for the production of desired results. The difference is . . . that its theoretical premises are false, whereas those of engineering, i.e. of applied science, are true. . . . In the case of engineering [the premises] are fruits of the imagination controlled by experiment, induction, and empirical verification; whereas, in the case of magic, the premises come out of the uncontrolled imagination.[16]

Magic is, therefore, an attitude within the recipient who hopes for results, no matter how improbable. By definition the positive accomplishments of magic are destined never to be solved by the recipient, for when the premises on which magic is based are explained rationally it ceases to be magic.

It should be noted that there is a psychological relation between magic and faith in that both appear to be derived from a wish for bounty conferred by an all-powerful figure or force. The effective force in magic is

[16] *Ibid.,* p. 64.

unknown, whereas faith is based on observable psychological phenomena. But there is another odd aspect of magic: it is subject to ambivalent attitudes on the part of recipient or witnessing persons. Although magic is rationally disbelieved and shunned as improbable, a demonstration of purported magic—for example, as entertainment—amuses and intrigues us. Our deeper acceptance of the possibility of magic hence is betrayed even while we search for reasons to deny it. Though magic obliterates time, space and reason, it does not ever entirely gain or lose credence as a natural possibility or impossibility.

In a psychological sense, *faith* can be thought of as an extension of magical wishing, with the important difference that in human experience its premises cannot be considered as illusory. Although it appears to rest on the same emotionally toned wish for bounty, faith, unlike magic, feeds upon belief and, one may say, upon proof. Faith requires mental work in the "faithful" for its consummation, whereas magic confers on the recipient the results of activity, having its origin beyond the ken of man. Faith is critical to some degree, since it is related to a body of impressive occurrences, world-accepted legends or historical precedents. Its possibilities of success increase with successes following acts of faith. Ducasse summarizes his analysis of religious faith:

> "Faith" then apparently means not only (a) very firm belief, either unsupported or insufficiently supported by evidence; but in addition either (b) that the content of the belief tends to be made true by the very act of believing it firmly; or (c) that the content of the belief is of such a nature that firm belief of it tends to have certain valuable results.[17]

Uniformly, faith is endowed with a positive polarity; he who is ambivalent about faith has none. It belongs to a higher plane of ego integration than magic. The expectancy of faith in faith-healing is based on happenings closer to probability than magic, and, hence, falls within the orbit of recognizable feelings. Healings from religious faith are impressive to the mind of modern man because of the sense of immediacy and personal participation which faith imparts. In early times, faith was undifferentiated from magic in healing. Indeed, when we say that magic is the primitive's "science," and by inference that of ancient man, we mean that he placed faith in his "magical science."

As will be seen in the following chapter, faith in healing was embodied in early periods in anthropomorphized figures such as amulets, holy talismans or heavenly bodies (the sun). The sacred object or its symbol (talisman) *was* the substance conferring the cure; faith was merely a *post hoc* explanation advanced by thinkers. The modality of faith assumed a markedly different aspect with its investment in a Superior Being. With the develop-

[17] *Ibid.*, p. 74.

ment of Judeo-Christian philosophy and the organization of a specific church or religion, a figure, whether of prophet, saint, Jehovah, the Christ or God, became the repository of faith. From the modality of religious feeling united to a venerated object, faith became extended to ideals, institutions or bodies of knowledge, as that of medicine.

The third underlying force in psychotherapy is the *adaptive potential* of the human mind. This can be described as the amalgam of all those strivings, drives (both conscious and unconscious) that push the organism to accept, exploit, reject or modify its environment. It is an energy system utilizing the body and the mind for its expression. This statement brings us face to face with the extremely difficult problem of identifying psychic energy as it is represented in mental function. Psychoanalysts, starting with Freud, have been greatly concerned as to the actual biologic basis of instinctual energy which undergoes vicissitudes that emerge as neurotic symptoms. The instinct itself is regarded as a "primary life force . . . which arises through complex modifications in the course of both phylogenetic and ontogenetic development." [18] Instinctive energy thus coincides with adaptive energy whose effect we can see and measure, although we cannot isolate the force itself, as in the case of electricity. The question, What is mental energy?, remains at bottom the question, What is life? Biologists state that life depends upon continued metabolism in the body cells by which living matter "evades decay" [19] and at the same time utilizes energy from outside sources. Stated in another way, "Body chemistry energizes human behavior, forming from bio-physical processes . . . needs, cravings and patterns of activity of the body as a unit." [20]

For the purpose of understanding the forces active in psychotherapy, we may say that the potential for adaptation is rooted in the psychobiologic matrix of the human organism and expressed in the maturation pattern as it develops from infancy. Maturation involves physical and mental growth; in the latter, the bundle of impulses, needs and ideas becomes consolidated into a psychic structure called ego or self. The ego responds in its growth to internal physiologic pressures or to instinctual (id) tensions or to social experiences imposed by the world.

Adaptation to the physical environment in the animal kingdom is the evolutional precursor of adaptation in the mental sphere. The primate's adjustment to a hostile environment by arboreal living is of the same order of activity as man's character traits, attitudes or reaction-formations developed as a defense against social or emotional dangers. What is called mind

[18] Szasz, T. S.: On the psychoanalytic theory of instincts, Psychoanalyt. Quart. 21:25, 1952.
[19] Schrödinger, E.: What Is Life?, New York, Macmillan, 1945.
[20] Kubie, L. S.: Some implications for psychoanalysis of modern concepts of the organization of the brain, Psychoanalyt. Quart. 22:21, 1953.

and intelligence can be looked upon as an organized pattern of adaptation to a complicated sociopsychological existence. As long as man has existed he has exercised his adaptive powers, first in developing fire and implements, and then through increasingly intricate social and political institutions and technologic advances. In this sense, man's adaptive tendencies, which are brought into play in psychotherapy, provide the physiopsychological energy for the therapeutic interraction between patient and physician.

Of the psychic elements under discussion, the fourth, *intelligence,* is the most pervasive in human development. Noyes, in one comprehensive statement, has indicated the evolutionary psychobiologic background of intelligence, "The adaptive behavior of lower animals, even of protozoa, merges insensibly into the more highly adaptive, so-called 'intelligent' behavior of man." [21]

In the history of psychotherapy, great reliance has always been placed upon intelligence and the will directed as curative factors. Speaking generally, during the nineteenth century and before, the will and the intellect were considered to be the most important therapeutic agents in ordering people's adjustment and aiding their reintegration. As the attitude gained ground in the last half century that instinctive strivings and unconscious drives determined selection of intellectual direction and even conscious content, the importance of intelligence, as exploited in psychotherapy, has been minimized or even depreciated. This attitude emphasizes that the intellect, as part of the ego organization, is relatively weak in the face of the stream of unconscious impulses that constantly bombard it. Still, in spite of the power derived from release of repressed emotions and rechannelized unconscious impulses in the psychological relationship which is called the therapeutic process, the final influence is wielded by the *intellectual* and the *adaptive* functions.

What underlies the patient's ability to follow the therapist in his wish to relieve the sufferer is ultimately an undefinable alteration in psychic energy. Whether through faith, psychological impact, development of insight, persuasion, suggestion, emotional catharsis, the uncovering of unconscious forces, electric shock or neurosurgery, we must assume that a change in psychic energy disposition causes the patient to modify his "abnormal" formations in favor of more realistically based and more satisfying behavior. This adaptation to new reactions occurs through the mediation of an assumed physicochemical change and/or emotional situation—the transference relationship which is a displacement of infantile feelings and attitudes to the healer. Such a reaction may occur in a flash, so to speak, in sudden cures, as at a shrine or through faith in a physician, or gradually after a process of "working through" in a prolonged analysis where uncon-

[21] Noyes, A. P.: Modern Clinical Psychiatry, ed. 2, p. 27, Philadelphia, Saunders, 1939.

scious determinants of symptoms are slowly uncovered. Or it can occur with the aid of some medication or mechanical aid. At all events, it is through the transference that the relearning (i.e., adaptive) process occurs as discharges from old emotionally toned experiences release hitherto bound mental energies, which then become usable in the synthesis of new patterns of adaptation. The benefit in therapy is borne on the wings of transference, mediated through physiologic changes and subtly directed by the ideas, the values and the ideals of the healer and his society.

In brief, the factors entering into the process of healing through mental means include the primitive sense of magic, an aspect of faith displaced to the therapist and a re-enactment of infantile feelings within the transference situation. At the same time, the adaptive tendencies of the individual, following an unknown change in psychic energy disposition, become available to the ego. Guided by intelligence and reality demands, relearning, or what is called adaptation, occurs. These factors operate in various degrees, in concurrent or irregular manner, insensibly or overtly, in all mental healing. They are the silent forces at work, the psychic roots of mental healing. They will never be found absent from man's multifarious attempts over the centuries to rid himself of the anguish of mental pain.

2

Magic, Faith and Rationalism

No one can say when the attention of prehistoric man was consciously deflected from physical suffering to psychological pain—when he looked beyond the ache of a torn muscle to the existence of mental torment. Primitive man was threatened by injury and destruction on all sides; pain had to be accepted as a prerequisite of life. In a blind, hit-or-miss fashion the cave man found gums that soothed his bleeding flesh, and infusions of berries or leaves that eased his pain. As Victor Robinson [22] has reconstructed it:

> Early man moistened his bruises with saliva, he extracted the thorns which lodged in his flesh, he used a pointed stick to dig sandfleas from his skin, he put leaves or mud or clay on his wounds, he tasted herbs and some he spat out and some he swallowed, he was rubbed or stroked when in pain, his broken bones were splinted with branches.

Anthropologists estimate that about one hundred thousand years have elapsed since paleolithic man prowled the earth in the first glacial period. It would be mere speculation to speak of a mind of man in that incredible time. Yet it is in the prehistoric world that evidence, which can be broadly interpreted as psychological, may be found in therapeutic activities. Bits of human skull from trephining that date back to the paleolithic period (the Stone Age) have been uncovered. These presumably were used as amulets. It is highly probable that teeth of animals, snake's vertebrae and bits of bone found in the pouches carried by medicine men in the Stone and the Bronze Ages (from 15,000 to 7,000 years ago) were similarly employed.

It is generally assumed that the world known to us as "mental" was, in early man, projected to the sphere of the supernatural. Careful study of drawings on cave walls in Europe has enabled Schmidt [23] to conclude that the man of the mesolithic period (about 10,000 B.C.) utilized a "magical law" which took precedence over chance and fate. This scholar found evidences of the awakening of "symbolic concepts," particularly those of

[22] Robinson, Victor: The Story of Medicine, p. 1, New York, Boni, 1931.
[23] Schmidt, R. R.: The Dawn of the Human Mind, translated by R. A. S. Macalister, p. 210, London, Sidgwick & Jackson, 1936.

magic, which the sorcerer used for all human activities in that early time. The magical world and the supernatural world, areas which are roughly synonymous, were the repository of all that prehistoric man could not understand in terms of everyday life. In Goldenweiser's [24] words, supernaturalism was to the primitive a "world view . . . for in the realm of supernaturalism the wish and idea became objective realities." In this supernatural world lay a power generally identified as *mana,* a force distinct from physical power which grew crops, avenged enemies and healed the ill. The occurrence of *mana,* the supernatural force studied by Codrington among the Melanesians,[25] and analogous to *manitou* among the Algonquin Indians, *wakonda* among the Sioux and so on, can be considered the basis of a type of primordial religion.[26] Primitive man of our time period (the Melanesians) believe that a supernatural power, *mana,* "effects everything which is beyond the power of men, outside the common processes of nature." Codrington relates that a stone can possess *mana* if, when placed in the soil, it causes crops to grow abundantly; a successful warrior has *mana,* and the wizard who cured diseases possessed the power of *mana.*

The power of *mana,* being more abundant in the successful wizard, may well have been consolidated in him, passed on to his heirs or apprentices, slowly emerging as a body of knowledge useful to divining weather, casting spells, undoing mischief and healing the physically sick and the mentally distraught. With the primitive, so with early man; it can easily be imagined that the psychopathic, the epileptic and the eccentric among them were acknowledged to be in touch with the world of spirits and to share their suprahuman powers. Indeed, many a medicine man among living primitive races, says Frazer, "owes his place in society to strength or weakness of mind." And the medicine man and the conjuror-physician were apparently not slow to capitalize on their peculiarities. The wizard or shaman of preliterate groups was not, in the words of Opler, "a credulous dupe of his own supernaturalistic claims." [27] The Apache shaman was far from an inspired automaton, but rather "a circumspect and careful worker, a good judge of his fellowmen and of the ills to which humankind is heir." The prehistoric, as well as the primitive, medicine man undoubtedly added native psychological wit to magical science in his utilization of supernatural forces in healing.

The growth of religion, if one may speak in general terms, from its crude origins in reliance on supernatural powers such as were resident in *mana*

[24] Goldenweiser, Alexander: Early Civilization, p. 133, New York, Knopf, 1922.
[25] Codrington, R. H.: The Melanesians, p. 119, Oxford, Clarendon Press, 1891.
[26] Marett, R. R.: The Threshold of Religion, ed. 2, p. 97, New York, Macmillan, 1914.
[27] Opler, M. E.: Some points of comparison and contrast between the treatment of functional disorders by Apache shamans and modern psychiatric practice, Am. J. Psychiat. 92:1371, 1936.

and anthropomorphism, to theism in its generic sense and varied present forms,[28] did not dissipate the close connection between religion and magic. Magi were relied upon to dispense the benefits of magical science, as real to the primitive as the biophysical science is to us, and to minister to non-naturalistic needs of their people. In time they restricted their numbers by association and training, forming a special group credited with a supernatural power over disease and the affairs of men. The magician-priests kept their heritage as a tradition. Healing through magic and the priestly practice of intermediation with the supernatural became secret arts, closely related to a status of divinity. Castiglioni,[29] the medical historian, concluded that the medicine of "Mesopotamia which is perhaps the most ancient of which we have any clear knowledge . . . was dominated by magical concepts and priestly practice." Similarly, according to Japanese tradition,[30] the gods who created the islands of Japan gave birth to Amaterasu, Goddess of Light, ancestor of all the rulers of Japan, who in turn gave birth to a physician, Suku-na-biko, the giver of charms against evil spirits.

The ordinary man ceded his interest in healing and in cosmic problems to the priests and the magicians, who by tradition and through knowledge were in close contact with divinity. Moreover, the function of propitiating primitive gods and conferring benefits on ailing man was actively assumed by medicine men and priest-physicians. Through a gradual extension of this role, humanity's suffering was broadly accepted by the priest-physician as his proper responsibility. Mental healing and the religious spirit were inextricably mixed in their psychological origins. The healing arts have never lost their overtones of magic and supernaturality in the inner experience of the patient. For modern man, as for the preliterate, to heal is to assume the role of some great, extrahuman being, to partake of the larger spirit that religion has caught and structured into specific faiths.

THERAPY BY AMULET

Magic, faith and rationalism can be demonstrated likewise in the first medical records uncovered in Mesopotamia and Egypt, whose beginnings were lost in antiquity even when the Greek historian Herodotus wrote of them in 480 B.C. Fragmentary medical writings about Imhotep the Egyptian physician (3000 B.C.), in the Ebers papyrus or the Babylonian Code of Hammurabi (almost 2000 B.C.), contained a mixture of sober advice and magic, detailed measures for driving out demons, and prescriptions for the

[28] Ducasse, C. J.: A Philosophical Scrutiny of Religion, p. 63, New York, Ronald, 1952.

[29] Castiglioni, Arturo: A History of Medicine, translated from the Italian and edited by E. B. Krumbhaar, ed. 2, New York, Knopf, 1947.

[30] Veith, Ilza: Ancient Japanese Medicine, Ciba Symposia, Summit, N. J., 2:1191, February-March, 1950.

use of opium and olive oil. The magic of ancient Egypt, derived from religious practices, seems to have been important in ordering the emotional life as apart from treatment of mental disturbance. Foretelling the future through dreams during temple sleep was an attempt to discover the will of the gods, in order to act in accordance with that will.[31] Nevertheless, there is an observable absence of references in the earliest inscriptions to treatment of mental illness as such.

Psychiatry of the early Egyptians, comparable with that of other ancient peoples, was conceived in terms of spirit possession. Celestial bodies, the stars and sacred animals (the crocodile, the hyena or the bull) were worshiped in part for their power to defeat the evil spirits responsible for disease. Frequently, a replica of the animal, or even a symbol of it in the form of an amulet, achieved the potency for good thought to reside in the original object. In the amulet the healing and the protective principles of warding off the effect of potentially destructive evil spirits were available distant from the body of the holy object. Amulets and charms incorporated the magical power of sacred animals which could either destroy or save its worshipers. Like the totem, which represented a feared object that embodied the ambivalent feelings of hate and veneration of the worshiper, the amulet bore destructive and rewarding, i.e., health-giving, properties. Gradually the *beneficent* aspect of the amulet emerged to be employed in vanquishing the other "evil" spirits causing disease. Freud,[32] in his study of totem and taboo, has shown how the demons of the primitive world were "but the projection of primitive man's emotional impulses," just as the phobias of the neurotic sufferer are ideational projections defending against unconscious fears within the patient. The power to do evil, displaced to the outside world in the form of demons, was in reality the power to do evil within one's self. Protection against demons afforded by the amulet represented a solution for the repressed conflict within the supplicant between good and evil. The sacred amulet carried both magical power and ethical properties in proportion to the demon's investment in malevolence.

All the properties of an unconscious wish—its disregard of reality, timelessness, unchecked power—participate in the magical power conferred by a charm,[33] whether for good or evil. Among present-day primitive tribes, sorcerers believe that they can kill an enemy merely by stabbing a certain tree known to contain his soul. In medieval times, the magician John of Nottingham, allegedly with the aid of the devil, killed a courtier by stabbing his effigy made in wax. We have only to look at the custom of burning

[31] Murray, M. A.: The Splendour That Was Egypt, p. 217, New York, Philosophical Library, Inc., 1949.

[32] Freud, Sigmund: "Totem and Taboo," *in* The Basic Writings of Sigmund Freud, p. 878, Modern Library, New York, Random, 1938.

[33] Thorndike, Lynn: A History of Magic and Experimental Science, Vol. 2, New York, Macmillan, 1923.

political enemies in effigy or burning proscribed books in public to observe the credence given the magic wish. In a similar way, counter-fetishes or counter-charms were believed to block "action at a distance." The so-called "doctrine of signatures," which appeared during medieval times in the medicine of Paracelsus,[34] contained this principle. Each disease had its special "signature," and the application of a proper choice of fetish would result in cure of a given illness.

Not only did charms protect the individual from evil, but they protected a community from it. The phylacteries of the ancient Hebrews appear originally to have been amulets which warded off evil,[35] and were kept in a temple or the market place for the benefit of the community. The Greeks had numerous talismans, as had the Romans and the early Christians who used phylacteries. The scapular worn today by devout Catholics as a charm against unexpected danger embodies a similar psychological principle. Early medical history is replete with prescriptions for amulets and charms in prevention and cure of dread diseases. In the healing arts the object that carried the plea for help varied; the magic wish ever remained.

Mystic words of an ancient tongue, such as Greek or Hebrew, added the weight of venerable authority to the evil-dispensing properties of amulets. In time some physicians, originally priests, used words and phrases to the exclusion of other types of therapy; it was this tendency that developed the healers by the "word." The mysterious power of the "word" was represented in ancient cabalistic philosophy which hoped to find the key to the universe, the secret beyond the secrets of revelation.[36] The kabbalah (cabala), a sect of mystical Jews, and Christian Gnostics both furthered an alphabetical and numerical mysticism in which the mysterious power of the twenty-two letters of the Hebrew alphabet would furnish the key to eternal transcendence. The "Heavenly Alphabet" was an implement of divine powers, in "which every wall is removed from the spiritual eye." [37] This was the meaning that Cornelius Agrippa (1486?-1535), an otherwise enlightened medieval scholar, attributed to knowing the true pronunciation of the name "Jehovah." Such a person "had the world in his mouth." [38]

The vehicles of magic and faith in healing gradually underwent a transformation from totem figures to amulets, from precious objects to cabalistic words and numbers, from the demon-dispelling agate to the three "Egyptian

[34] Paracelsus: The Hermetic and Alchemical Writings of Philippus Aureolus Theophrastus Bombastus Paracelsus von Hohenheim, translated by A. E. Waite, New York, Theosophical Pub., 1894.

[35] Snowman, J.: A Short History of Talmudic Medicine, London, Bale, 1935.

[36] Kastein, Josef: History and Destiny of the Jews, translated by Huntley Paterson, New York, Viking, 1933.

[37] Ginzburg, Louis: "Cabala," *in* Jewish Encyclopedia, Vol. 3, p. 456, New York, Funk, 1907.

[38] Thorndike, Lynn: The Place of Magic in the Intellectual History of Europe, p. 21, New York, Columbia, 1925.

Days." Healing methods followed ritual in utilizing the symbolic and mystic numbers one, three, five and seven. The circumspect handling of the magic number three persisted in medicine through the Middle Ages as an inviolable law handed down from antiquity. To witness a passage in one of the "Anglo-Saxon Leechdoms," [39] "There are three days in the year which we call *Aegyptiaci,* that is, in our tongue, dangerous days; in which by no means, for no occasion, neither man's nor beasts' blood must be diminished." The venerable Bede, in his *Medesyns Approbate for Mortal Sekeness,* counseled, "[Whoever] of mankynde letteth hyme blode upon any of these iii dayes he shall be dede withynne five days nexte that followyn. These be iii forbode dayes." Indeed, the psychological undercurrent in medical practice to comparatively modern times was intimately related to the Pythagorean philosophy of numbers. There were four varieties of bodily humors (blood, phlegm, yellow bile, black bile), four natural elements (fire, air, earth and water); there were critical days in a disease and three forbidden days. Concoctions were given three times, prayers said over the patient seven times on seven days, ad infinitum. Numbers themselves were amulets against evil, and the modern physician who prescribes medicine three times a day combines his rational technics with the eternal power of the triad. For the mystical relations of numbers to things, numbers being the essence of things in Pythagorean metaphysics, allowed the priests of Memphis to say, "The science of numbers and the art of will power are the two keys of magic: they open up all the gates of the universe." [40]

It would not be in accord with the disordered time sequences in the development of psychotherapy to state that the magical therapeutic power deposited in objects—amulets or even numbers—passed directly to religious faith. Actually, magic faith and science were concurrent forces in mental healing. The passage of magical investment from a corporeal substance to an immaterial or ideational object, and thence to a spiritual ideal, was a gradual, almost imperceptible, transformation. The facts are, however, that purification of faith as a curative force moved from its lodgment in amulets and numbers to its representation in a divine figure with the advent of Christianity. In spite of retrogressions, progressions and intermixture of tendencies, it seems apparent that over a two-thousand-year period the civilized world in its healing methods replaced magic by faith, and faith by science.

[39] Payne, J. F.: English Medicine in Anglo-Saxon Times, Fitzpatrick Lectures for 1903, Oxford, Clarendon Press, 1904.

[40] A Group of Students: Pythagoras, ed. 2, p. 27, Chicago, Theosophical Press, 1925.

FAITH-HEALING AND HERBALS

The modification of faith-healing stimulated by the spread of Christianity in the Western world consisted in a refinement of the vehicle of faith. Jesus taught that faith alone was enough: "Thy faith hath made thee whole." [41] Although Jesus also healed with the Word—"He cast out the spirits with his Word" [42]—healing by direct faith was an even further simplification of psychotherapy beyond the various symbolic vehicles of healing. Revealed religion purified healing through faith by indicating that the "light of faith is a gift supernaturally bestowed upon the understanding" of man,[43] a "gratuitous" gift waiting only upon acceptance of God. For when Jesus healed:

> They brought unto him all sick people that were taken with divers diseases and torments, and those which were possessed with devils, and those which were lunatick, and those that had the palsy; and he healed them.[44]

he was using the faith of those who came to him. Centuries later this faith was recognized by scholastics as "an act of the intellect assenting to a Divine truth owing to the movement of the will, which is itself moved by the Grace of God" (St. Thomas). The purification of healing through faith in divinity occupied many centuries of Western life, awaiting in part the development of theology and in part a perception of a radical change in attitude toward mental life: in Mumford's words, "an assertion of the primacy of the person, and a shift from outer circumstances to inner values." [45]

Throughout this psychological transformation, the continuity of underlying magical influence active in faith-healing can be seen in the accessory technics used by early Christian healers. The laying on of hands, for example, was a healing tradition of great antiquity (Ebers papyrus), evolving apparently from the Oriental custom of treatment by massage with oil, water or saliva. This custom may have arisen from the use by Egyptians of aromatic oils for purposes of sensual stimulation.[46] In the Book of Mark [47] there is a description of the use of oil as a healing agent. The intermediary substance, oil or saliva, used by the ancient healer cemented the therapeutic bond between patient and priest-physician, since saliva (spittle) was an effective agent for breaking a charm or ward-

[41] Matt. 9:22.
[42] Matt. 8:16.
[43] "Faith," *in* Catholic Encyclopedia, Vol. 5, p. 756, New York, Appleton, 1909.
[44] Matt. 4:24.
[45] Mumford, Lewis: The Condition of Man, New York, Harcourt, 1944.
[46] Margetts, Edward L.: Personal communication.
[47] Mark 6:13.

ing off evil. The significance of the magical cleansing element in lustrum (spittle), acknowledged in antiquity, is seen in the Greek tragedy when King Oedipus proclaims the curse, "From fellowship of prayer or sacrifice or lustral rite is excommunicated." [48] Purification by water, oil or spittle (the lustral rite) is an expiatory act containing within it a healing connotation.

The adjuvant use of oil or water in early faith-healing has a deep psychological meaning beyond that of expiation and the cleansing of evil. In the dreams and the myths of almost all peoples, water often has the symbolic meaning of rebirth. Immersion in fluid means rebirth, and passage in death over water indicates the projected possibility of rebirth. The fascination of still bodies of water, Bonaparte [49] has pointed out, exerts a profound nostalgic appeal for human beings. It covers the anxieties of life and death by an unconscious yearning to return to the waters of the womb (mother). Bodies of water in dreams, folklore and poetry represent the mother in whom one found eternal peace as a child. The unconscious longing for peace is portrayed in the "inexpressible magic" of rebirth. The intermediary substance, water or oil, symbolizing the yearned-for mother, binds the sufferer to his faith, absorbing the magical wishes for eternal comfort present in the unconscious of every patient.

In the early days of Western Europe, healing through spiritual abstractions was mixed with pagan wizardry. The medical therapy of early Britain is illustrated in a poem "Lorica" (A.D. 830), studied by Singer,[50] to be used against "demons, all poisons, envy . . . and sudden death." It names each anatomic part, asking divine blessing and protection for each. To Singer it represented "classical science in last stage of degeneration."

Medical folklore, always popular, was rampant in Europe during the early Christian Era. The Church, set against this kind of therapy, insisted upon substituting exorcism for the magical formulas and herb concoctions of the leeches. Before the Norman invasion of England in A.D. 1066, leechdom was synonymous with medicine in Britain. The *Leech Book of Bald,*[51] one of the collections of folk medicine still extant, describes medical prescriptions for mental cases, for a "fiend, sick man or demoniac" which are in form a medley of herbal tradition, magic and faith:

[48] Sophocles: The Theban Plays, translated by E. F. Watling, p. 32, Harmondsworth, Middlesex, England, Penguin, 1947.

[49] Bonaparte, Marie: The Legend of the Unfathomable Waters, American Imago 4:20-31, 1946.

[50] Singer, C. J.: From Magic to Science; Essays on the Scientific Twilight, New York, Liveright, 1928.

[51] Cockayne, Rev. Oswald: Leechdoms, Wortcunning and Starcraft of Early England, being a collection of documents for the most part never before printed, illustrating the history of science in this country before the Norman Conquest, London, Longmans, 1864.

> When a devil possessed the man or controls him from within with disease: a spew drink or emetic, lupin, bishopwort, henbane, corpleek: pound these together, add ale for a liquid, let it stand for a night, add fifty bibcorns of cathartic grains and holy water—to be drunk out of a church bell.

Those espousing healing by faith alone had to battle the forces of native medical "science." Anglo-Saxon physicians, known as "leeches," developed an enormous list of medicaments, derived in large part from the "wise women" who occupied a role similar to that of the medicine man in earlier civilizations, but without his priestly attributes. The "wise women" had neither learning nor written precepts. They kept their pedestrian art alive from generation to generation through word of mouth. Gradually their herb recipes became interlarded with magic, bits of astrology, prayer and superstitious doggerel. Reviled by the learned of her generation, it was the "wise woman," nevertheless, to whom sufferers went when the advice and the physic of physician-leech were of no avail. Today, among some persons, a deep respect for the magic of grandmother's household remedies survives the barrage of scientific rationale in our generation.

Leechdom was finally subordinated when the higher clergy proclaimed that only the Church could work miraculous cures through the exorcising of devils from sufferers. But the appeal of the leech and his magic was strong, as was the combined appeal of religious ritual, magic and the royal healing touch. A medical treatise of the fourteenth century advises the making of a "cramp-ring" for the falling sickness (epilepsy) in imitation of the cramp-rings made of gold and silver largesse given by King Edward the Confessor and his successors. The ring, when formed of coins, was "hallowed" by the Plantagenet and the Tudor kings on Good Friday and given to supplicants for their curative value. The medical prescription, modernized somewhat, advises for the "Crampe":

> Take . . . on Gude Friday, at five parish churches, five of the first penyes that is offered at the crosse, of each church the first penye: then take them all and go before the crosse and say V. pater nosters in the worschip of fife wondes (of the crucified Jesus) and bear them on V days and say each day in the same wise . . . and then go make a ryng there without alloy of other metal, and write within Jasper, Batasar, Altrapa, and write without, c. nazarenus (Christ of Nazareth); and sithen take it fra the goldsmyth upon a Fridai, and say V. pater nosters as thu did before and use it alway afterward.[52]

As late as 1518, the College of Physicians in London agreed that rings consecrated by the King were charms against "Spasms"; amulets, against "slander and calumny."

The contamination of religious faith by magic, alchemy and leechdom in the first millennium was combated by the representatives of Rome, who

[52] Crawfurd, Raymond: "The Blessing of Cramp-Rings; a Chapter in the History of the Treatment of Epilepsy," *in* Studies in the History and Method of Science, edited by C. J. Singer, Vol. 1, Oxford, Clarendon Press, 1917.

prohibited the practice of all healing, except that of surgery by leeches. In earlier centuries, the Church encountered difficulties in stamping out belief in incantations, leechdom and, especially, pagan gods. Finally, it was forced to accede by incorporating heathen theology into Christian dogma, and some of the host of pagan spirits became the saints and the devils of organized religion. Satan did not take on his evil character and disease-producing properties until the Council of Toledo [53] in the fifth century authorized belief in the devil and hell. Evil, through the influence of the devil, was equated with madness, and the faith that healed was the faith that drove the devil from the unhappy lunatic. The devil and his technics—black magic, demon possession, incubi and succubi, witchcraft—whose depredations succumbed only to exorcism, invaded Western civilization. There was no cure but exorcism, no effective remedy other than faith.

The struggle between leechdom, the naturalistic medical magic of early Europe, and faith, for the health of the populace, is reflected in the statements of Christian apologists. Justin the Martyr [54] (in the second century of the Christian Era) explained:

> And now you can learn this from what is under your own observation. For numberless demoniacs throughout the whole world, and in your city, many of our Christian men exorcising them in the name of Jesus Christ . . . do heal, rendering helpless and driving the possessing demons out of the men, though they could not be cured by . . . those who used incantations and drugs.

The Church took full responsibility for exorcisms, and in so doing became the psychotherapists of the Dark and the Middle Ages.

NATURALISM IN MENTAL HEALING

The conglomerate mixture of ritual and mysticism that served for psychological healing in early civilizations eventually came under the rational influence of Hellenic culture. There had been earlier utilizations of rationalistic approaches to mental illness. The Judaic rules of personal and social hygiene indirectly tended to affect man's mental and physical health. As early as 1140 B.C., the Chinese maintained institutions for the insane, who were cared for until recovery took place. Ancient Hindu physicians (1400 B.C.) described the forms of insanity and prescribed "kindness and consideration" [55] as treatment. But the earliest beginnings of a planned or

[53] Coulauge, Louis: The Life of the Devil, translated by S. H. Guest, New York, Knopf, 1930.

[54] Justin the Martyr, Saint: The Apologies of Justin Martyr, Tertullian and Minucius Felix in Defense of the Christian Religion, etc., translated from the originals with notes (about 200 B.C.) by William Reeves, Vol. 1, London, Churchill, 1717.

[55] Whitwell, J. R.: Historical Notes on Psychiatry (Early Times—End of 16th Century), p. 7, London, Lewis, 1936.

"conscious" psychotherapy could be said to start with the Greeks contemporaneously with the emergence of Greek philosophy.[56] The great Hippocrates and his school approached mental illness as a natural phenomenon calmly, objectively, free of superstition.

Nevertheless, Greeks of the Homeric and the Periclean Ages were not universally "naturalistic" in their views of mental diseases. In the main, the Greek masses inherited from Asia and northern Africa the conception prevalent in pre-Hellenic times that mental disease was due to infestation by swarms of malignant spirits. On the other hand, the literate Greek of classic times considered madness a visitation from the gods or due to the malevolence of the Furies (the three goddesses of vengeance). The insane were often treated with humorous latitude, as judged from the Greek comedies.[57] Diphilus wrote a comedy entitled *Those Treated with Hellebore,* and Horace also ridiculed the reputed omnipotence of hellebore, a plant which had been recommended by the ancient physicians as the panacea for mental disease. Other poets entertained the notion that insanity was a sickness sent by angry Olympian gods as moral censure punishing the wrongdoings of men. The plays of Sophocles dealt fairly often with god-sent madness.

The cult of priest-physicians, who made the legendary Aesculapius their god, practiced a "rationalistic supernaturalism." [58] This did not mean a belief in magic but an empiricism influenced by religious ideas. "If nature is divine, plants [medicines] are divine" (Herophilus). The art of medicine could be rational within the framework of divinity. The gods aided the sufferer through "divine sleep, divine feasts, the sacred performances." [59] In this sense, Greek healing was a mid-point between pure supernaturalism and rationality, liberally sprinkled with respect for the healing power of the gods. Temples erected to the god, called Aesculapia (Asklepieia), were situated on high hills or near springs whose waters had medicinal values. Here the sons of Aesculapius utilized physical means to cure disease through rest, dietetics, massage, baths, exercise and a hygienic life. Patients were bathed and massaged by skilled attendants, and a type of mental suggestion called "incubation" was used.

The patient, having entered the temple or the halls especially built for incubation, lay down on the floor on a pallet. In these impressive surroundings, the god Asclepius revealed himself directly to everyone who

[56] Castiglioni, Arturo: *Op. cit.,* p. 129.

[57] Jelliffe, S. E.: Notes on the History of Psychiatry, 15 papers dealing with Graeco-Roman psychiatry, Alienist and Neurologist, February, 1910, to February, 1917.

[58] Edelstein, Ludwig: Greek medicine in its relation to religion and magic, Bull. Hist. Med. 5:201, 1937.

[59] Magnus, Hugo: Superstition in Medicine, translated from the German and edited by J. L. Salinger, New York, Funk, 1905.

needed his help.[60] The god was seen by the incubant in a dream, whereupon the patient entered into personal contact with him, and he proceeded to heal the disease brought to his attention or advised a treatment to be followed. Sometimes ventriloquism on the part of the priest-attendants aided the patient's spirit to converse with his Aesculapian god.

Diagnosis through interpretation of dreams apparently has a long history in antiquity, as does "temple sleep." In general, dreams were relied on to divine the nature of an illness and to foretell the future. Freud, who twenty centuries later penetratingly turned his attention to the psychological meaning of dreams, points out that interpretation of dreams through associations was freely utilized by Artemidoros of Daldianus, but that the interpretation was through the associations of the *interpreter,* not the patient.[61] An inscription on stone tablets discovered at Epidaurus relates a case history of an incubation treatment:

> Agestratos suffered from insomnia on account of headaches. As soon as he came to the *abaton* he fell asleep and had a dream. He thought that the god cured him of his headache and, making him stand up, taught him wrestling. When day came he departed cured, and after a short time he competed at the Nemean games and was victor in wrestling.[62]

Therapeutic dream oracles were frequently resorted to by priests in the Greco-Roman period. On the other hand, the relation between supernaturalism and dreaming was not regarded seriously by some philosophers: Socrates wrote, "To regard dreams seriously is absurd: they are the confused results of indigestion." [63] And Cicero [64] stated:

> There is no imaginable thing too absurd, too involved or too abnormal for us to dream about it.
>
> How, then, is it possible for us either to remember this countless and effort-changing mass of visions or to observe and record the subsequent results?

Tricks, miracles and "bare-faced quackery" notwithstanding, the physicians associated with the Asclepian temples developed a naturalistic attitude toward disease, including mental afflictions. Although there is a question as to whether the physicians of Hippocrates' time followed the priestly operations of the Aesclepiadiae,[65] Hippocrates, the Father of Medicine, is

60 Edelstein, E. J., and Edelstein, Ludwig: Asclepius, Vol. 2, Baltimore, Johns Hopkins Press, 1945.

61 Freud, Sigmund: The Interpretation of Dreams, translated by A. A. Brill, p. 107, New York, Macmillan, 1933.

62 Guthrie, Douglas: A History of Medicine, p. 44, Philadelphia, Lippincott, 1946.

63 Allbutt, Sir T. C.: Greek Medicine in Rome, Fitzpatrick Lectures, 1909-1910, p. 40, London, Macmillan, 1921.

64 Cicero: De Senectute, de Ami citia et de Divinatione, Book 2, 71, p. 533, translated by W. A. Falconer, Cambridge, Mass., Harvard, 1938.

65 Withington, E. T.: "The Aesclepiadiae and the Priests of Asclepius," *in* Studies in the History and Method of Science, edited by C. J. Singer, Vol. 2, Oxford, Clarendon Press, 1921.

believed to have worked at one of these temples of health, the temple at Cos. The most celebrated physician of the ancient world, Hippocrates inveighed against "charms, amulets and other such vulgarity." His collected works, *Corpus Hippocraticum* (considered by some the work of several men), contain the foundation stones of modern medicine [66] and the earliest unmodified statement of naturalism in medicine, "It is nature itself that finds the way; though untaught and uninstructed, it does what is proper" (Epidemics VI, 5). Discontented with the supernaturalism that passed for medical theory in his time, the Father of Medicine insisted that disease should be looked upon as arising from bodily (natural) sources. With regard to the disease "called Sacred" (epilepsy), Hippocrates wrote:

> It appears to me to be nowise more divine nor more sacred than other disease, but has a natural cause from which it originates like other affections. Men regard its nature and cause as divine from ignorance and wonder, because it is not at all like to other diseases.

The writings of Hippocrates exerted a lasting effect in removing religious influence from medicine, but not until centuries after his death. Even Galen, most prominent physician of the Roman world and a physiologist of scientific status, still thought in terms of supernatural healing and regarded the cure as essentially divine "even when it gave divine sanction to human methods." [67] Hippocrates contributed a high moral tone to the therapeutic aspect of medicine. Though his clinical observations were more medical than psychiatric, his influence proved to be significant in the evolution of psychiatric thinking. In effect, Hippocrates laid the ground for its readmission within the purview of clinical medicine. For example, hysteria was shrewdly considered by him to be due to the movement of the womb (hysteron) throughout the body. He antedated by two thousand years the modern findings of the place of sexuality in the neurosis. Although Hippocrates prescribed the traditional tight bandage around the abdomen for hysterical paroxysms, with fumigation by warm vapors conveyed through a funnel into the vagina, he astutely advised as a more practical remedy for hysteria "to indulge the intentions of nature and to light the torch of Hymen."

Mental disease as a natural problem did not escape the attention of the Greek psychologist-philosophers. Plato suggested that mental disorder was partly somatic, partly moral and partly divine in origin, "caused by 1, the result of love, 2, the result of great trouble, 3, from the Muses," and offered an essentially sensible therapy. The curative effects of words, of "beautiful logic," was advised by Plato in the case of one Charmides who

[66] Adams, Francis: The Genuine Works of Hippocrates, translated from the Greek, Vols. 1 and 2, New York, Wood, 1886.
[67] Withington, E. T.: *Op. cit.*, p. 204.

had lately complained of a heaviness in his head. . . . Charmides asking me whether I knew of a remedy? I replied, it is a certain leaf, and a certain incantation in addition to medicine. . . . The soul is cured by certain incantations, and these incantations are beautiful reasons.[68]

The ever-present conflict between magic and occultism, as related to psychic activity, and the naturalistic approach of Greek physicians to mental phenomena followed the flow of classic culture to Rome. Roman patricians were forbidden by tradition to practice medicine, since it was regarded as a profession worthy only of slaves or foreigners.[69] New healing methods and concepts brought to Rome by Greek physicians were feared: Garrison quotes Pliny the elder's [70] complaining at the invasion of Greeklings (physicians) that Romans with their household gods for every disease had "got on for 600 years without doctors." If one abandoned domestic simples, herbals and religious observances, Pliny observed, the Greeks "would murder us by means of their Physicke." Such an exclusive and isolationist point of view allowed little room in ancient Rome for the development of a psychotherapeutic attitude.

Nevertheless, the naturalistic approach to mental disorders progressed among Latin-speaking physicians as enlightenment struggled with ignorance and neglect. Those Romans who followed the Greek authors dwelt on diet, diversion, rest and the need of overcoming the fears of the patient. Aulus Cornelius Celsus (25 B.C.-A.D. 50), who is said to have introduced the word "insania" (insanity) into medical literature, reported the treatment of phrenitis (delirium?) with herbs and restraint:

For phrenitis . . . it is proper to restrain with fetters those who are violent lest they harm themselves or others. . . . A less debatable point . . . bowels should be freely opened and after lapse of one day, head should be shaved and warmth applied by means of water in which some verbena has been boiled, finally head and nose kept wet with rose-water, and rue bruised in vinegar applied to nostrils. There are two herbs of great value in these cases . . . nightshade and pellitory, head being wet all over with the mixed juices expressed from them. . . . [For] sleep . . . it is a good thing to apply to the head an ointment of saffron and iris which acts as calmative of mind. . . . [If] sleep does not come . . . should be given draught of poppy and henbane, others place mandrake apples under the pillow, others apply either amoms or sycamine tears to the forehead.[71]

By the time of Celsus' writings, Greek attitudes toward mental diseases had been accepted. In his classic *De Medicina,*[72] Celsus, who was apparently not a physician but, in Garrison's words, a *private litterateur,* ex-

[68] Whitwell, J. R.: *Op. cit.,* p. 55.
[69] Castiglioni, Arturo: *Op. cit.,* p. 203.
[70] Garrison, F. H.: An Introduction to the History of Medicine, ed. 3, p. 96, Philadelphia, Saunders, 1921.
[71] Whitwell, J. R.: *Op. cit.,* p. 160.
[72] Celsus: De Medicina, English translation by W. G. Spencer, Loeb Classical Lib., Book 3, p. 289, Cambridge, Mass., Harvard, 1935.

haustively covered the psychiatry of the first century. Here he matter-of-factly states: "I shall begin with insanity, and first that form of it which is both acute and found in fever. The Greeks call it phrenesis." His therapy was symptomatic and reminiscent of that of the early nineteenth century. Celsus' treatment of psychoses showed a practicality, a naturalism and a directness that, although not profound, made it a model for treatment of the insane for centuries. Spencer's translation indicates that for

> depression . . . rubbing twice a day is to be adopted; if the patient is strong, frequent exercise as well: vomiting on an empty stomach. . . . In addition to the above: the motions are to be kept very soft, causes of fright excluded, good hope rather put forward; entertainment sought by story-telling, and by games, especially by those with which the patient was wont to be attracted when sane; work of his, if there is any, should be praised, and set out before his eyes; his depression should be gently reproved as being without cause; he should have it pointed out to him now and again how in the very things which trouble him there may be cause of rejoicing rather than of solicitude.

In face of more delusional or chronic situations, however, the same frustrated feelings experienced by alienists of more recent date assailed Celsus and his compatriots:

> If however, it is the mind that deceives the madman, he is best treated by certain tortures. When he says or does anything wrong, he is to be coerced by starvation, fetters and flogging. He is to be forced both to fix his attention and to learn something and to memorize it; for thus . . . little by little he will be forced by fear to consider what he is doing. . . . To be thoroughly frightened is beneficial in this illness and so, in general, is anything which thoroughly agitates the spirit. For it is possible that some change may be effected when the mind has been withdrawn from its previous state. It also makes a difference, whether from time to time without cause the patient laughs, or is sad and dejected: for the hilarity of madness is better treated by those terrors I have mentioned.

The Greco-Roman writers seemed to unite on the middle ground of logical persuasion for their mental cases. Aretaeus, the Cappadocian (in the second century of the Christian Era),[73] recognized that one has to deal with different basic peculiarities in each patient:

> It is better to agree with some than to oppose them; those who will not eat are to be placed among those who eat; the educated should be forced to read and repeat what they learned.

Analogies, bland deceptions and suggestions were employed to free patients from their groundless fears. A patient who feared imminent ruin and starvation was told each day that he had come upon a rich heritage. One case, imputed to Philodotus, of a woman who believed that she had a snake in her stomach, was cured of her delusion by slipping a snake unnoticed into a vessel into which she vomited.

[73] Whitwell, J. R.: *Op. cit.*, p. 160.

This enlightened therapy of the Greco-Roman writers was not universally applied. It was only in relatively few instances that the advanced Hippocratic medicine was available to sufferers other than patricians. The descriptions in recorded medical writings most probably represent the high points in practice of the day. For the most part, mental suggestion, completely disguised in salves and philtres of the "wise women," salve dealers, army surgeons, professional poisoners and drug peddlers, was accepted therapy of the time.

PSYCHOTHERAPY OF THE SCHOOLS

In the early Christian Era, Hippocratic medicine had become a fixed tradition, the "Rational" system of medicine of which Galen (in the second century of the Christian Era) was the acknowledged champion. The early Christian Era witnessed considerable development in naturalistic medicine, and with it the inevitable theories. Groups arose, each with its varying explanation of diseases: the Empirics, the Methodists, the Pneumatists, the Eclectics and the Dogmatists.[74] Disease was considered to result from the pneuma or airy spirit, the humours or constriction of solid particles in the body. Some (the Eclectics) neglected medical theory entirely and treated only the symptoms as they arose in patients. The Hippocratic theory of the four humours, under the dogmatic espousal of Galen, became the guide for all physicians until the Renaissance. To this humoural theory, Galen added the concept of the *pneuma* or spirit which invaded every part of the body, the active cause of disease: in the nervous system, the *pneuma* became "animal spirits," in the liver, "natural spirits," and so on. A concomitant of this elaborate theorizing was the development of an equally complicated materia medica with herbals for every condition from which man suffered. These were the "galenicals" to which textbooks of medicine referred in the last generation. The authority of Galen's eclectic-school pronouncements was so pervasive, as his ideas were copied from generation to generation, that twelve centuries after his death in A.D. 200, Paracelsus, who sought to overthrow Galen's shadow in therapeutics in favor of his own mineral medications, was forced into medical ostracism.

What were the characteristic attitudes toward healing the mentally ill in this period? Roman civilization, spreading through a large part of Western Europe, had stamped the "dead-level respectability of Roman commerce and law" [75] on the cultural life of the continent. Militarily and politically the Romans were supreme, their feats of engineering outstanding, their orators and writers vitalizing. Latin authors dealt with many aspects of

[74] Garrison, F. H.: *Op. cit.*, p. 106.
[75] Murphy, Gardner: Historical Introduction to Modern Psychology, p. 10, New York, Harcourt, 1949.

medicolegal problems, with epidemiology, sanitation, nutrition, hygiene; philosophers wrote on morals, the ethics of man and his political institutions. But psychotherapy as a predominant medical interest was nonexistent. It was not until pride in Roman efficiency softened and the Roman Empire began to crumble, and paganism gave way to Christianity (A.D. 392), that traces of a humane spirit toward the mentally distraught appeared. The zeal of the early Christians, spreading doctrines of poverty, obedience and charity, paved the way for acceptance of the monastic tradition of humility and humaneness. The spirit which subserves interest in psychological matters is not that which underlies military conquest and expansion of trade. The Early Church, which "fitted admirably into the psychological perspective of the age," [76] nurtured the tradition that came to be identified with mental healing. This significant factor in the history of psychotherapy will be discussed in a following section.

We note at this point that with the fall of the Roman Empire, leadership in medical matters passed to Constantinople. Here, Greek medicine was kept alive, and the flourishing Arabians made progress in surgery, pharmacy and the companion sciences astronomy, mathematics and botany. The effect of Mohammedan, Persian and Jewish influences on medicine in the so-called "Arabic" period was noteworthy throughout the Dark Ages. Names like Avicenna (A.D. 980-1036) and Maimonides (A.D. 1135-1204) are prominent in the writings of that period. Maimonides wrote in opposition to magic and astrology. He believed in the close relationship between mental and physical health, recognizing the importance of mental hygiene.[77] Garrison [78] makes the point that while Western Europe was still trifling with charms, amulets and relics in their faith-healing, "many of the Jewish and Mohammedan physicians were beginning to look upon these things with a certain secret contempt." Hospitals in Cairo developed into specialized centers; the Arabians were much ahead of their contemporaries in Western Europe in their treatment of the insane. Still, the analytic turn of mind of the Oriental physicians did not develop a rational psychotherapy in that era. Magic as a technic for healing remained prominent in medical practice, and the majority of Jewish and Arabian physicians conducted their practice not unlike spiritualists or astrologists.

During the first millennium the doctrines of the Early Church, which taught that the aim of life hinged on a mystical and eventual reunion with God, exerted another effect on the development of mental healing. By accenting forbearance to pain and the mutability of earthly pursuits, the

[76] Barnes, H. E., and David, Henry: The History of Western Civilization, Vol. 1, p. 392, New York, Harcourt, 1935.

[77] Macht, D. I.: Moses Maimonides, physician and scientist, Bull. Hist. Med. 3:585, 1935.

[78] Garrison, F. H.: *Op. cit.*, p. 128.

Church retarded the progress of medical investigation throughout the Dark Ages and later. Though this is true, it is also true that the responsibilities and the dangers confronting man as he contemplated his soul—his relation to God, his guilt, needs for renunciation and efforts at salvation—did bring into focus those psychological deflections akin to disturbances now recognized as nervous afflictions. In this light, the sense of immediacy surrounding the earthly and heavenly fate of man's soul, which characterized the religious spirit of the Dark Ages, imparted an impetus to a future psychotherapy. This urgency for mental ease, to be sure, was an undifferentiated antecedent of modern psychotherapy, since its rallying point was faith in the institutions and the figures of early Christianity. Yet Neoplatonism, woven into early religious attitudes which fostered contempt for the world and liberation of the soul through asceticism, eventually brought the sickness of the soul out of the penumbra of medical neglect.

The advent of the Christian Era brought other social-cultural influences which had important repercussions for the story of mental healing. One was the development of the hospital with its tradition of humanitarianism; another was the renewal of faith and a tendency toward the negation of body ills as the antidote to a frustrating and materialistic world. The leaven of faith spreading throughout Europe indirectly redounded to the benefit of sufferers among the masses. It was not the purpose of the Early Church to cure mental illnesses. But its insistence on following Christian doctrines of patience and pity, of absolution of guilt through acceptance of grace, and elevation of the value of the human soul in union with God's, set in motion a spirit which was insensibly transmuted into an emotional soil that nourished an evolving psychotherapy.

MEDIEVAL FAITH-HEALING

A survey of the evolution of psychological healing has disclosed several forces at work in the ancient world up to the early Christian Era. The first was the force of primitive supernaturalism, in which magic was interspersed with incantations. The second was the enlightenment of the Greeks, wherein mental phenomena tended to be regarded by Hippocratic physicians as a natural occurrence. The third force, growing out of the primitive practice of fetishes and amulets, extended into faith-healing through organized theology. Christianity helped to crystallize man's reliance on an omnipotent *Mana* or Spirit into the pure culture of faith-healing. This healing force, discovered and organized and exploited by the Church of Rome, was the most significant contribution to mental healing in the Western world until the rise of psychological science in the eighteenth century.

The tangled strands of psychotherapy seemed largely to come to a focus during the Middle Ages in faith-healing. The masses were ignorant, medical knowledge was inexact, experimental science scarcely lifted its head. In the absence of science, faith was an all-powerful weapon, even as in its presence faith must be an ally. Under the leadership of the Church, faith became a ubiquitous force. The Church's position as molder of social consciousness in the medieval period is well epitomized by Worcester and McComb: [79]

> Religion, knowledge, science, art, philosophy, and even the chief pleasures of life, were in her keeping. When people went to the theatre it was to witness the mysteries of the Christian religion. When they traveled, it was to go on a pilgrimage to Christ's tomb. From the cradle to the grave, on week-days and Sundays, the Church surrounded human life.

For this leadership the Church exacted the price of implicit obedience. In healing, as well as in other aspects of contemporary activity, faith in the Church played a dominant role. But although the Church relied upon faith to guide and influence the masses, there were others who wished to wave this potent wand.

The absence of controlled medical practice in medieval days left the field of healing open to all those who could obtain the public ear. Moreover, there was no unity of medical opinion or practice: Arabian medicine did not grow, and Galenic physicians refused to budge from the texts of Galen, the "True Physition." In this confusion, the art of healing was the open prey of "itinerant tooth-drawers and prittle-prattling barbers." The medical act of 1511 in England, promulgated by Henry VIII, was aimed against a "grete multitude of ignorant persons . . . common artificers, smyths, wevers and women [who] boldly take upon them grete curis [cures] . . . in which they partely use socery and whichcrafte" [80] and partly medicine of a noisome type. The barbarities of therapy among "tinkers, tooth-drawers, horse gelders and horse leechers" need not be detailed. A supply of leechdoms and a taste for showmanship sufficed to embark one on a healer's career. The public was warned by *The Anatomyes of the True Physition and Counterfeit Montebanks* (London, 1602) to be wary of the following self-appointed physicians:

> Runagate Jews, the cut-throats and robbers of Christians, slowbellied monks, who have made escape from their cloisters, simoniacal and perjured shavelings, busy Sir John Lack-Latins, thrasonical and unlettered chemists, shifting and outcast pettifoggers, lightheaded and trivial druggers and apothecaries, sunshunning mechanics, stage-players, jugglers, peddlers, prittle-prattling barbers, filthy graziers, curious bath-keepers, common shifters and cogging cavaliers, bragging soldiers, lazy clowns, one-eyed or lamed fencers, toothless and tattling old wives . . .

[79] Worcester, Elwood, McComb, Samuel, and Coriat, I. H.: Religion and Medicine, the Moral Control of Nervous Disorders, New York, Moffat, 1908.

[80] Lawrence, R. M.: Primitive Psycho-therapy and Quackery, New York, Houghton, 1910.

Against this band of "dolts, idiots and buzzards," men like Burton[81] mourned, "All the world knows that there is no virtue in charms, &c., but a strong conceit and opinion alone . . . which takes away the cause of the malady from the parts affected."

One of the sources from which these "haters of all good learning" drew their *materia medica* was alchemy, the chemical science of the Middle Ages. Alchemists, intrigued by the search for the elixir that would confer everlasting life, and for the secret formula that would transmute lead to gold, drifted off into mysticism. In their dimly lit laboratories they detached themselves from any practical quest and delved into secrets which lay just beyond the veil. They came to be regarded as magicians whose murky solutions contained the answer to life's riddles. Magic and divination crept into the practice of alchemy. The secrets of the "wise women" were mixed with those of alchemy and necromancy to form black magic which was the life-stuff of the charlatan's practices.

Through the itinerant physician Paracelsus, alchemy was brought into medieval healing. Theophrastus Bombastus von Hohenheim, called Paracelsus (1443-1541),[82] was a vivid figure of his time, "half-genius and half rogue." Alone, he all but transformed the complexion of medical treatment in medieval times and after. He dared to lecture in the vernacular German, taking the results of his thought and experiments directly to the people. Paracelsus insisted that only minerals such as sulfur, lead, mercury, iron and other chemical compounds of proved activity were to be used in medical treatment, in place of the innocuous roots, herbs, extracts and tinctures of the traditional school of Galen. Bombastic in speech and positive to the point of vituperation, Paracelsus demolished the authoritarianism of medieval physicians:

> By what right, I ask, can that sausage stuffer (the Galenic physician) and that sordid concocter of the pharmacopeia give himself out as a dispenser. . . . If you would put aside these your incapacities and would examine . . . how the stars rule diseases and health, then . . . you would learn that your whole foundation amounted to nothing but fantasy and private opinion.

He insisted that iron received its magnetic power from the heavenly bodies and that the

> "Arcanum of the heavens" ruled human destinies as it ruled health. . . . Luna leads the brain. What relates to the spleen flows thither by means of Saturn. . . . So, too, kidneys are governed by Venus, the liver by Jupiter, the bile by Mars.

Paracelsus and the alchemists subtly displaced faith in healing from divinity to minerals through a "universal spirit" that affected the body of

[81] Burton, Robert: The Anatomy of Melancholy, London, Bell, 1896.
[82] Paracelsus: *Op. cit.*

man by changing his chemistry and (magnetically) polarizing him.[83] The mixture of ancient astrology and inorganic chemistry introduced by Paracelsus into medical therapy had a remote effect on the development of psychotherapy. Three centuries later, Mesmer unwittingly opened the way for tapping healing psychological forces within man himself in postulating that celestial bodies acted through a magnetic force on man.

MONARCHS AND FAITH-HEALING

But if the power of faith-healing was exploited by lowly quacks in medieval times, it was also freely accepted by monarchs. For generations the healing touch was regarded as the property of kings. English kings since Edward the Confessor, as well as European monarchs, Clovis the Frank in the fifth century and Henry IV and Louis IX in later years, enjoyed "the king's touch." The English kings chiefly exercised their power on scrofula (the king's evil), but some extended their activity to all types of illnesses and all manner of patients. In the *Parliamentary Journal* for July 2, 1660, there is an entry:

> His sacred majesty, on Monday last, touched 250, in the banqueting house; among whom, when his majesty was delivering the gold, one shuffled himself in, out of an hope of profit, which had not been stroked.

The practice of the king's touch faded with the removal of the Stuart line from the British throne, but a worthy successor arose in the figure of the commoner, Valentine Greatrakes.[84] Greatrakes, a veteran of Cromwell's army in retirement in the country, was seized one day with an inspiration to heal. The stroker explained how he became aware of

> an impulse, or a strange persuasion in my own mind (of which I am not able to give any rational account to another) which . . . suggested to me that there was bestowed on me a gift of curing king's evil.

Greatrakes was astounded no less than his patients at his success. Stimulated, he continued treating "the Ague . . . and . . . the Falling sickness," delighted to see the "pains slip and fly from place to place until they did run out." The procedure consisted of stroking the skin gently or vigorously while saying, "God Almighty heal and strengthen you for Jesus' sake." Greatrakes claimed that under energetic massage even the most malignant evil spirit would vanish and the devil would go "like a well bred dog." Greatrakes, the "Irish stroaker," became a national figure. A con-

[83] Bertrand, Alexander: Du magnétisme animal en France, p. 13, Paris, Baillière, 1826.

[84] Greatrakes: A Brief Account of Mr. Valentine Greatrakes and Divers of the Strange Cures by Him Lately Performed . . . Written by himself in a letter addressed to the Hon. Robert Boyle, Esq., for J. Starkey, London, 1666.

temporary minister witnessed Greatrake's healing. He recounted having seen cured "twenty several persons in Fits of the Falling-sickness or Convulsions, or Hysterical Passion (for I am not wise enough to distinguish them)." Several times he was investigated and discredited, but his kingly bearing and faith in his "gift of God" carried him to popular acclaim.

The significance of Greatrakes was not in the success of his stroking, or in the fact that he served as the progenitor of a long line of digital healers, but that he demonstrated that healing could be accomplished also by commoners. Greatrakes healed by faith without benefit of clerical ordination, medical knowledge or regal lineage. The masses that followed him and helped him gain phenomenal success regarded him as "even a greater miracle worker than King Charles himself"; they transposed their faith in healing from king to commoner. Psychotherapy henceforth could be dispensed by physicians and laymen as well as by kings and priests. The populace did not grasp this distinction so clearly. They considered Greatrakes, as he considered himself, at least divinely inspired. But the power which Greatrakes achieved was lent him in part by the mass mind. His successor, John Leverett, who inherited the "manual exercise," found the work difficult without the divine aura which surrounded Greatrakes. Leverett declared that after touching thirty or forty persons a day he "felt so much goodness go out of him that he was fatigued as if he had been digging eight roods of ground."

Here, in this transposition of faith from sovereign to subject, was a nodal point in the development of faith-healing. It was a visible phase in the investment of the psychotherapist with powers accepted almost universally as the attributes of divinity.

The displacement of faith-healing from kings and priests to laymen proceeded haltingly during the medieval period, achieving its full flowering during the Renaissance. In the interim, healing remained in religious hands. One of the fruitful sources of healing through faith was that of relics and shrines. Bones of the saints, pieces of the cross that bore the Saviour, shriveled bits of skin kept in parchment, and splinters of wood from chapels sanctified by the presence of a saint were discovered on every hand in the Holy Land by the Crusaders. The healing touch and the power to work miracles which Jesus bequeathed to his disciples and the early saints became invested in relics and shrines. The institution of shrines, maintaining its power in every generation, carried tremendous authority in medieval days.

The spirit of the shrine is timeless. It carries more than a message of mere healing; it bears the flood of spirituality that characterizes all religions and envelops its true believers. Few are immune from the aura of hope and peace that pervades the healing shrine. The devout lose themselves and their troubles easily in their adoration. The disbeliever finds his resistance softened through identification with believers who immerse themselves in the "oceanic feeling" of oneness. The ethic of kindliness, humility and mercy taught by churchmen [85] flowed from the shrine as well as from their scholastic theology. The modern hospital system, brought into existence by the Crusaders, epitomized this experience in the tradition of humane treatment of mental patients.

MENTAL HEALING IN THE MONASTERY

The medieval hospital movement was initiated in 1198 by Pope Innocent III. Monastic medicine flourished in such hospitals as that established by the Knights of St. John on the Island of Rhodes (1311) in days of the Crusades. Nursing groups were established in hospitals along the route to the Holy Land through France, Switzerland, Italy, in the eleventh, the twelfth and the thirteenth centuries. Within their walls, religious orders brought tranquillity and humaneness, piety and tenderness, to their charges. Because madmen and simples, uncared for by any organized group, roamed the highways, the butt of derision or neglect, the monasteries manned by religious orders assumed the burden of the maniacal or the feeble-minded patient. One of the first hospitals devoted to mental patients exclusively was the colony established in Gheel, Belgium, in the thirteenth century. The colony plan was a step forward in the treatment of mental patients, since it stressed other than purely custodial features.

The colony at Gheel centered in a shrine to St. Dymphna. According to the legend, Dymphna was the daughter of a pagan Irish king about the year A.D. 600. Influenced by her mother, a devout Catholic, Dymphna had decided to consecrate her life to God. Upon the death of her mother, the King proposed incestuous marriage to his daughter. She fled to the Continent, and, when she refused to yield, he slew her in insane rage. Because she had triumphed over the incestuous desires of a father made mad by demons, she became the saint of those with mental maladies. On the spot where Dymphna fell an infirmary and a church were erected. Patients were brought there to receive benefits from the relics of St. Dymphna contained in the hospital. Some patients remained at the shrine, being boarded out to peasants in the neighborhood. Retarded children, left for a longer while, were given work in the fields and the households under the benevolent guidance of the country folk and the healing influence of the spirit of St. Dymphna. In this way the "colony" plan or "boarding-out system" for treating defectives evolved and is in active existence today.[86]

[85] Durant, Will: The Age of Faith, A History of Medieval Civilization, Vol. 4, A.D. 325-1300, pp. 74-76, New York, Simon & Schuster, 1950.
[86] Kilgour, A. J.: Colony Gheel, Am. J. Psychiat. 92:959, 1936.

The monastic tradition of treatment through loving care and gentleness was particularly applicable to mental cases. The early hospitals conducted by The Sisters of the Society of Hospitalers did not attempt any physical treatment, principally because of injunctions by the Holy See against monks' engaging in healing by worldly means. These "sick houses" provided good food, rest and spiritual calm for their patients in an atmosphere of humility and service. But there is other evidence to show that the management of mental cases rested on a spirit of humanitarianism. The connotation of "barbarousness" commonly associated with the Dark Ages is not entirely merited, at least in the management of mental cases. Evidence from the early French romances reflects the tradition of humaneness and a realistic conception of mental disease. Study of this literature, Wright comments,[87] reveals the notion of curability of insanity through physical and mental means with little mention of demonology. In England, one of the Arthurian legends which details the story of Sir Launcelot's madness [88] is a reflection of the practical handling of madmen in the Dark Ages.

The story relates that hard upon a precipitating emotional shock, Sir Launcelot became mad and exiled himself from his customary haunts. While wandering in a forest, he was found by Sir Bliaunt and his aid, a dwarf, who conveyed him to the castle:

> And so they took . . . Sir Launcelot . . . to the castle; and then they bound his hands and his feet, and gave him good meals and good drink, and brought him back again to his strength and his fairness; but in his wits they could not bring him again, nor to know himself. Thus Sir Launcelot was there more than a year and a half.

Subsequently, Launcelot wandered off, returning to the forest and by "adventure came into the city of Corbin, where Dame Elaine was that had borne Galahad, Sir Launcelot's son." As was the custom, the wandering madman was reviled by the youths of the town:

> And so when he was entered into the town, he ran through the town into the castle, and then all the young men of the city ran after Sir Launcelot, and there they threw turfs at him, and gave him many said strokes; and, as Sir Launcelot might reach any of them, he threw them, so that they would never more come into his hands; for of some he break their legs, and some their arms, and so fled into the castle. And then came out knights and squires for to rescue Sir Launcelot, and when they beheld him, and looked upon his person, they thought they saw never so goodly a man; and when they saw so many wounds upon him, they all deemed that he had been a man of worship. And they then ordained clothes unto his body, and straw underneath him, and a little house, and then every day they would throw him meat, and set him drink; but there were few or none that would bring meat to his hands.

[87] Wright, E. A.: Medieval attitudes towards mental illness, Bull. Hist. Med. 7:352, 1939.

[88] Malory, Sir Thomas: The Arthurian Tales, from the text edition of 1634, R. B. Anderson, Editor-in-Chief, London, Norroena Society, 1906.

The kindness of Launcelot's rescuers required a complement of magic and faith for his eventual recovery. The resolution of the case occurred, so the story relates, when Dame Brisen applied an enchantment:

"Sir," said Dame Brisen, "we must be wise and ware how we deal with him, for this knight is out of his mind; and if that we awake him rudely, what he will do we all know not, but ye shall abide, and I shall throw such an enchantment on him, that he shall not awake within the space of an hour."

and a priest wrought a miracle through faith:

. . . and so they bear him into a tower, and so into the chamber, where as was the holy vessel of Sancgreal; and, by force, Sir Launcelot was laid by that holy vessel. And then there came a holy man and uncovered the vessel; and so, by miracle, and by virtue of that holy vessel, Sir Launcelot was all healed and recovered.

Naturalistic treatment attitudes toward the insane reflected in these Arthurian legends are mirrored in the historic work of a Franciscan monk, Bartholomeus Anglicus. Bartholomew, professor of theology at Magdeburg and later serving in England, was the author of a nineteen-volume encyclopedia called *De Proprietatibus Rerum* (Of the Nature of Things). Written on parchment in 1275, it had the distinction of being printed by Caxton himself; later it was translated into many languages and became one of the first to be widely published after the invention of printing. It had a tremendous vogue, especially among the clergy, being used as a household manual by those who were called upon to give counsel in medical as well as in spiritual affairs.

The seventh book of Bartholomew's *De Proprietatibus,* which dealt with mental illnesses, was most probably based on current knowledge and practice.[89] One is struck by the reasonableness of the viewpoint expressed and the restrained treatment prescribed, considering the therapy accorded "frenzied" patients several centuries later by medical men. Treatment recommended by Bartholomew [90] noted that

the diet shall be full scarce as crumbs of bread oft washed in vinegar and that he be well controlled or be bound in a dark place. He [the madman] should not see many people nor should he be shown pictures for they will probably make his state worse. All those about him should be required to be still and silent and they must not answer his nice [foolish] words. . . . The most important thing is to secure sleep for him and for this ointment and balming [use of balsams] applied to the head may be effective.

[89] Thorndike, Lynn: A History of Magic and Experimental Science, p. 406.

[90] Bartholomeus, Anglicus: De Proprietatibus Rerum, Book 7, on Medicine, translated and annotated with an Introductory Essay by J. J. Walsh, Vol. 40, Froben Press, October to December, 1933. (A parchment manuscript is in the library of the Academy of Medicine, New York, dated 1360, entitled: "De Proprietatibus Rerum," Libri XVIII, Opus Theologicum et Philosophicum, by Bartholomei Anglici, Ordanis Frere Minorum.)

For the melancholics he counseled:

> The medicine [treatment] of them is that they be bound that they hurt not themselves and other men and such patients must be refreshed and comforted and withdrawn from cause of any matter of busy thoughts and they must be gladded with instruments of music and some deal be occupied.

There was little of magic and no hint of demonology in the writings of Bartholomew on mental illnesses. With the hysteria of witchcraft seething around him, and ecclesiastic authorities and lawmakers putting demented, deluded witches to the rack, Bartholomew and his fellow monks and nuns plodded on, nursing, observing, helping patients by methods singularly like those used in modern hospitals.

The psychological cross-currents of the medieval period, as they affected the evolution of psychiatry, can be seen in contrasting the attitude of the inquisitors toward witches and heretics and that of the monks who treated the insane in the monastery. The inquisitors were originally drawn from the Franciscan and the Dominican Orders [91] and sent to aid the local courts in adjudicating cases, for example, of "Sorcery, Satanism and apostasy," for which crimes the secular court usually decreed death. Inquisitorial interest was predominately in heretics and the political implications of Satanism, which Summers in 1928 declared was identical with the "absolutism of any revolutionary of today . . . [of] Lenin, Trotsky, Zinoviev and their fellows." Later, the Church, through its inquisitorial representatives, increased its activity beyond that of apostates, hoping to quell the plan of witches and their black leader to destroy the true Church and set the standard of Satan on high.

The psychological trend of the time was against the investigation of the psychic life of the mischievous or heretical "witch." There seems little doubt that these individuals, perhaps unconsciously bound to an ancient pagan cult,[92] were acting out their rebelliousness through hysterical mechanisms, dissociation, projection, denial, hallucinatory experiences and delusional constructs, for young maidens, otherwise described as adjusted and personable, who suddenly embraced the Satanic belief to such a degree that, as they faced execution, they "set up a very loud Laughter, calling for the Devil to come and help them in such a Blasphemous manner, as is not fit to Mention,"[93] could be reasonably diagnosed as seriously disturbed individuals. The astounding extent of psychopathology among the alleged witches, as judged from contemporary records, was not the concern of monks who functioned as mental healers in monasteries. That, in 1408,

[91] Summers, Montague: Malleus Maleficarum, Introduction, p. xvii, London, John Rodker, 1928.
[92] Murray, M. A.: The Witch-Cult in Western Europe, A Study in Anthropology, Oxford, Clarendon Press, 1921.
[93] *Ibid.*, p. 26.

young women confessed their contentment and satisfaction at attending the devil's sabbat (witches' convocation) before a French investigator from Lorraine and retained their inner composure, even pleasure, as they approached the gibbet, and that, in 1590, two witches executed in North Berwick "dyed very Stuburn, and Refractory without any Remorse or seeming Terror of Conscience," was a matter more of judicial righteous anger and astonishment than medicopsychological concern.

For witchcraft was the outstanding abnormality of medieval days. In spite of the fact that the "science of theology [in the thirteenth century] was the medieval dash into reason," [94] it was unable to recognize the mass delusion of witchcraft. Its psychological influence was profound, for it functioned through a perversion of faith. Faith, at first a defense against insecurity and a support for the human ego, became the basis for intolerance. Under the banner of a demonologic ideology, the faith that healed changed into an all-consuming need to destroy those who disbelieved. Witchcraft turned the Christian ethic of patience, humility and mercy into a weapon of aggression against those who were mentally unable to believe or willfully rebellious of belief. The force of the crusade against the Evil One and his minions fell largely on the mentally ill of the medieval period, and witchcraft became the unwitting cause of a setback in the development of a rational psychotherapy which persisted for three centuries.

[94] Durant, Will: *Op. cit.*, p. 983.

3

Witchcraft and Psychotherapy

The panorama of witchcraft is of significance in a total view of the history of psychiatry chiefly because it illustrates the operation of a psychological-cultural mode on functions of the human mind. In the modern sense, witchcraft was neither the psychiatry of medievalism nor the psychotherapy of that period. It was, however, a phase in man's adaptation to certain psychological realities. It encompassed a complex group of observances, ideas and beliefs which sought to control behavior patterns that now lie within the area which the psychological sciences claim as their interest. But we cannot forget that witchcraft was essentially a political and a social problem for those churchmen and jurists who were most vitally concerned. It is quite probable that Murray has correctly analyzed the essential nature of witchcraft as an organized cult having its roots in the folk religion of prehistoric Europe,[95] a view which for Montague Summers is a "fundamental mistake," since only the "trained theologian can adequately treat the subject, not an anthropologist." [96] It is not improbable also that demonology and the witch-creed stood upon a curious, yet understandable, world view—the antithesis of Christianity. The *inverted religion* which Ducasse calls Satany (from a Hebrew word *satan* meaning adversary or enemy) stands upon the same degree of possibility this author points out, as does theism: "The theistic and the satanistic hypotheses are, from the standpoint of logic and evidence, exactly on a par." [97] Satanism, like Christianity, had its attendant divine figures, symbols and rituals; its "black" magic instead of miracles, its destructive aims in place of saving virtues, its evil ethic rather than a guiding principle of truth and goodness. It is conceivable that those who embraced it were "mental cases" by a social definition of adjustment. Just as the nonconformist communist in a democracy may be

[95] Murray, M. A.: The Witch-Cult in Western Europe, A Study in Anthropology, p. 10, Oxford, Clarendon Press, 1921.

[96] Summers, Montague: The History of Witchcraft and Demonology, p. 45, London, Kegan Paul, Trench, Trubner & Co. Ltd., 1926.

[97] Ducasse, C. J.: A Philosophical Scrutiny of Religion, p. 205, New York, Ronald, 1952.

considered "abnormal or socially perverted," the nonconformist capitalist in a totalitarian country "abnormal," so the Satanist is regarded as universally wicked. Murray asks the question why the witch could not die for her cause just as the Christian martyr perished for his in earlier centuries, or, one may add, as the modern patriot is willing to die for his nation and the principles in which he believes.

THE PSYCHOLOGY OF WITCH-CREED

In effect, the witch in medieval days was antiauthoritarian and nonconformist in the same sense that the antisocial person in our society is both individually rebellious and united in a community of similar spirits, a gang or an underworld group, who are dedicated to acting contrary to accepted standards.[98] Undoubtedly self-confessed witches were suggestible, as are hysterics; dissociated and hallucinating, as are schizophrenics; autistic, delusional and paranoid, as are some psychotic persons; and dedicated to an antisocial ethos, as is the psychopath. And in the same manner they utilized those mental dynamics both in fantasy and in behavior which are set in motion when such persons encounter extreme ego pressure. If one can understand witchcraft in these terms, he can agree with Kittredge that the "witch-creed is the heritage of the human race." For some it was a psychological refuge; for those who sought to root it out, a psychological morass. For the latter it was an outgrowth of the age-old practice of imputing abnormal, evil, hurtful or inexplicable occurrences to Satan or his human converts, the witches. Demonology answers a deep psychological need in all human beings. The supernatural was the primitive's road to understanding the mysteries of Nature, and retreat to demonology the explanation of myriad perverse impulses lying within the human mind. Demons are as necessary a part of the mystical and the unconscious thinking of peoples as are their protectors—the angels. The witch is the graphic embodiment of deep infantile fears as the angel is the symbolic figure of goodness and security. Fairy stories and childhood phobias with their mutual evil witches and good fairies share the function of coping with unconscious fears. In medieval days, witchcraft in a formalized way channeled off expressions of primitive fears just as fairy tales nowadays express childhood anxieties in dramatic story form.

The devil satisfied a deep need in mankind. On him was heaped all the "badness" of this world. Theologians taught that Lucifer and his fallen angels, driven from Heaven, were dedicated to evil from the start. Moreover, the devil could work magic and change his form in the twinkling of an eye, invade people, turn into an animal, carry his evil-doing into every

[98] Bromberg, Walter: Crime and the Mind, An Outline of Psychiatric Criminology, Chap. 5, Philadelphia, Lippincott, 1948.

cranny of God's world. This magic aspect of the devil made of him a formidable foe. The works of the exorcising churchmen appeared all the more miraculous in this light. The arch enemy of the race was, and is, tireless in his efforts to undo good, as Lewis so charmingly described recently.[99] The early Christian fathers saw their duty clearly. Humanity had to be preserved from these "thousand demons to the right and ten thousand to the left." A malevolent angel, Tertullian [100] insisted, was in constant attendance upon every person, and only the most energetic Christian action could combat its evil influence. Demons, according to Origen, writing in the third century of the Christian Era, produce disease, famine, unfruitfulness, corruption in the air, pestilence. They hover concealed in clouds in the lower atmosphere; they are attracted by blood and incense which the heathen offers to them as gods. In the cosmology of Satanism do we not see one bracket of the eternal antimonies—good and evil, God and devil, love and hate, cruelty and mercy, sin and virtue, flux and reflux, attraction and repulsion?

The science of witchcraft of the medieval period was a discipline that strove to explain wrongdoing, madness, senility, impotence, hysterical and psychopathic symptoms, in terms of demon possession. The saints and the clerics of the medieval period gave form to the illusion of witchcraft; their management of the possessed gave substance to their psychotherapy. Although the primary interest of the Church was the salvation of souls from enslavement by Satan and his demons, the Church managed to fan the embers of the pagan witch-creed into the roaring flames of witchcraft.

Indirectly, the sanction of witchcraft by the organized church deflected attention from the study of abnormalities of the mental life. What we know to be the symptoms of neurosis and hysteria, or designate as delusions and hallucinations, or diagnose as sexual deviation, were known to the learned inquisitors as the manifestations of the influence of Satan. To consider mental aberrations the result of natural processes was heresy. Generally, it is thought that only the ignorant and suggestible element in the medieval population believed in witchcraft. This is far from the truth. Belief in witches and the evil intent of the devil was common among men of learning and intelligence. Kings, priests, lawyers, judges, noblemen, scholars, artists —all believed firmly in this gigantic delusion: among them stood Lord Bacon, Sir Walter Raleigh, Sir Thomas Browne, Matthew Hale and so on.[101] Consider a world where belief in witches was as widespread as the belief in science is today and we can appreciate why the intellects of the

[99] Lewis, C. S.: Screwtape Letters, New York, Macmillan, 1943.

[100] Tertullianus, Quintus Sept. Flor.: Apologetic and Practical Treatises, edited by Rev. C. Dodgson, Oxford, Library of Fathers, 1854.

[101] Murray, M. A.: *Op. cit.*, p. 10.

Renaissance did not turn against the mass-illusion with more insistent voices.

In spite of occasional skeptics, the main emotional trend of the time was in the direction of supernaturalism. For magic was the science of the medievalists. Cornelius Agrippa wrote, "Magic is the acme of all philosophy"[102] (in this context, philosophy also meant science), and Thorndike[103] remarked that thirteenth-century scholars could not "keep magic out of science or science out of magic." Such a man as the Bishop of Paris, William of Auvergne (1180-1249), showed the attitude commonly adopted toward demonology by learned men of the thirteenth century by complaining[104] that medical men deny the presence of demon possession or incubi, claiming that mental illnesses are due to vapors (disease)!

Early churchmen fought the malevolent demons for more than fourteen centuries. In A.D. 563, the Council of Braga decreed that anyone who believed in the virtue of the devil to create thunder and lightning, tempests and droughts, let him be "anathema," or if anyone believed in the influence of stars on the body and the soul of man, "let him be anathema also." Saint Augustine, in the fifth century, wrote: "All diseases of Christians are to be ascribed to these demons. Chiefly do they torment fresh-baptized Christians, yea, even the guiltless newborn infants."

The reformer, Martin Luther, declared that the devil "stirs up arguments and quarrels, arms the murderer against his brother, urges rebellion, foments war, brings to birth storms, hail and diseases," and the Witchcraft Act of 1735 in England, based on the alleged offense of "trafficking with the devil," is still in force.[105]

In medieval days there were strong emotional reasons for the widespread acceptance of witchcraft. Life for the peasant masses was circumscribed. Their physical existence belonged to the feudal master, their spiritual being was entrusted to the Church. But their fantasy life was uncontrolled, and folklore, fairy tales and witches' stories became outlets for the peasants' fantasy. The gigantic fallacy of the Covenant of Satan, the flying cult of Diana and the thousand oddities of witchcraft had the stamp of reality.

HEALING BY EXORCISM

Healing by exorcism had been restricted to saints and bishops from the fourth century onward. As the number of demons increased on every hand, as was evident by their miserable activity, the supply of exorcists increased.

[102] Thorndike, L.: A History of Magic and Experimental Science, Vol. 2, p. 25, New York, Macmillan, 1923.
[103] *Ibid.*, p. 978.
[104] *Ibid.*, p. 360.
[105] San Francisco Chronicle, February 6, 1949: London—In Britain witches are still a fact.

Lower churchmen attempted exorcism with varying results. Rival groups made much of their successes. To witness, the story of the Lutheran minister who, in 1584, was mocked by a demon he was unable to exorcise from a good-wife of his town. After many attempts a Catholic exorcist succeeded in delivering her, to the delight of the Catholic commentators. Protestant ecclesiastics naturally quoted many cases to counterbalance this one.

The medical use of witchcraft developed into an art and science. Clinical cases [106] were reported extensively describing the interrogation of the devil and technics of exorcism. Signs of possession were detailed for the benefit of medical men and jurists.[107] Exorcists apparently were not above using a little trickery in their deliverance of witches. Ventriloquism was an important aid to the monks in making vivid their conversations with demons. From an accredited medieval authority comes the report of a conversation during an exorcism performed by a prominent bishop. The devil claimed that possession of his victim was accidental in this case. "It was not my fault," said the devil; "I was simply sitting on a lettuce leaf when she came along and ate it."

A corollary of the art of exorcism was the theory of satanic domination. The important discovery was made that the devil had a regular technic for enamoring and seducing his followers. The pact of Satan and the coven were in time uncovered. The Convention (coven) of the Sabbat, the midnight meeting of witches with their master, was believed implicitly by many. Each witch who testified confirmed the details. The activities of the coven and the pact constituted irrefutable legal proof of witchcraft to the satisfaction of the most meticulous.

The Witches' Sabbat or Coven was a ceremony in which Satan at intervals renewed his compact with the witches, binding them to eternal evil. The witches, walking or flying through the air, were met in a group by the devil on some lonely moor, where they indicated their allegiance to him by stories of their wickedness, depravity and psychosexual perversion. The coven was sealed by the "reverential kiss, *osculum infame* . . . on the Devil's fundament." [108] The details, described in medieval writings,[109] were of a frenzy of bestiality, whipped up and given direction by the devil, who, besieged by palpitating, quivering witches, seized them to satisfy his carnal lust. Accounts relate that the witches stood "waving their bellies" in a most sensuous dance, writhing in sexual torment and delight, while

[106] Wickwar, J. W.: Witchcraft and the Black Art, A Book Dealing with the Psychology and Folklore of the Witches, New York, McBride, 1926.

[107] Garcon, Maurice, and Vinchon, Jean: The Devil, An Historical, Critical and Medical Study, translated by S. H. Guest, New York, Dutton, 1930.

[108] Summers, Montague: *Op. cit.,* p. 137.

[109] Ferguson, Ian: The Philosophy of Witchcraft, New York, Appleton, 1925.
Olliver, C. W.: An Analysis of Magic and Witchcraft, London, Rider, 1928.

the fever grew to intense proportions and the wind of terror "froze their naked bodies."

Orgies of perversion and unspeakable cruelty, frenzies of undisguised sadomasochism, were imputed by common consent to the Prince of Evil. Magistrates and theologians were moved by the evidence, zealous to show the witch as she really was:

> an evil liver; a social pest and parasite, the devotee of a loathly and obscene creed; an adept at poisoning, blackmail, and other creeping crimes; a member of a powerful secret organization inimical to Church and State; a blasphemer in word and deed; swaying the villagers by terror and superstition; a charlatan and a quack sometimes; a bawd; an abortionist; the dark counsellor of lewd court ladies and adulterous gallants; a minister to vice and inconceivable corruption; battening upon the filth and foulest passions of the age.[110]

Summers, protagonist of the world of spiritism and witchcraft, joins the witch-hunt with fervor; in 1926 he writes that "the cycle of time has had its revenge, and this rationalistic superstition is dying fast." [111] The amazing spread of the delusion was aided by the suggestibility of hysterical witches themselves during trials for witchcraft. Witches on trial in France, Germany, England, Scotland and Italy responded uniformly to the queries regarding what happened at the Sabbat. An occasional figure like Montaigne saw the real complexion of the thing. He saw that in reality witches were mentally deficient, insane or highly suggestible individuals, and that the inquisitors were sadistic, aggressive zealots. "I would," said Montaigne, "rather have ordered hellebore for them [witches] than hemlock."

THE DIAGNOSTIC PROBLEM

As records of cases of witchcraft accumulated, learned doctors hastened to publish their experiences, hoping to assist others in the diagnosing of the possessed. Sammarinus, in his treatise on exorcism, states that the symptoms which, for a theologian, denote a demoniac are:

1. If he feigns to be mad, and the strength and size of his body continually grow and augment.
2. If he speaks in a language, be it Greek, Latin or any other, which he has never learnt.
3. If he becomes dumb, deaf, insane, blind, which are the signs contained in Holy Scripture.

The signs for physicians indicating possession were no less numerous or less precise. Here are those enumerated by Baptiste Codronchus: [112]

[110] Summers, Montague: *Op. cit.*, p. xiv.
[111] *Ibid.*, p. ix.
[112] Garcon, Maurice, and Vinchon, Jean: *Op. cit.*, p. 82.

1. If the disease is such that the doctors cannot discover or diagnose it.
2. If he loses his appetite, and vomits whatever meat he has taken; if his stomach is as if narrowed and drawn in, and if there seems to him to be some mysterious heavy thing inside himself.
3. If he becomes impotent in the arts of Venus.
4. If he feels a great lack of strength throughout his whole body, with extreme languor. If he feels stupid in his mind, and takes pleasure in uttering stupidities and idiocies, as do melancholics.

A final diagnostic sign was the Devil's Mark or Witch's Mark, otherwise known as the Stigmata Diaboli. These were blemishes on the skin indicating points of contact with Satan. A medical authority of the 1700's describes the mark as

sometimes like a blew spot, or a little tate, or reid spots, like flea biting; sometimes also the flesh is sunk in, and hollow, and this is put in secret places, as among the hair of the head, or eye-brows, within the lips, under the arm-pits, and in the most secret parts of the body.[113]

Proof of the stigmata could be obtained by a common technic reported in 1610 by French doctors in a case:

We, the undersigned doctors and surgeons . . . observed three little marks, not very different in colour from the natural skin. When we pierced this with a needle to the depth of two fingers breadth he felt no pain, nor did any blood or other humour exude from the incision.[114]

The church authorities felt the need of an authoritative work which would set down rules and regulations for the discovery, the apprehension and the conviction of witches and sorcerers throughout the Christian world. The need was met by the work known as the *Malleus Maleficarum,* or *The Witches' Hammer,*[115] by Fr. Henry Kramer and Fr. James Sprenger, of the Order of Preachers, which appeared in Latin in 1484, accompanied by a laudatory papal bull of Pope Innocent VIII. For two centuries this book was the bible of the inquisitors.

The papal bull authorizing the work of the inquisitors Kramer and Sprenger tells in measured phrases the need for their work:

THE BULL OF INNOCENT VIII

Innocent, Bishop, Servant of the servants of God, for an eternal remembrance.

Desiring with the most heartfelt anxiety, even as Our Apostleship requires that the Catholic Faith should especially in this Our day increase and flourish

[113] Summers, Montague: *Op. cit.*, p. 70.
[114] *Ibid.*, p. 72.
[115] Kramer, Henry, and Sprenger, James: Malleus Maleficarum, translated by the Rev. Montague Summers from the edition of 1489, "The Hammer of Witches which destroyeth Witches and their heresy as with a two-edged sword by Fr. Henry Kramer and Fr. James Sprenger, of the Order of Preachers, Inquisitors," with introduction and notes, London, Rodker, 1928.

everywhere, and that all heretical depravity should be driven far from the frontiers and bournes of the Faithful. . . .

It had indeed lately come to Our ears, not without inflicting Us with bitter sorrow, that in some parts of Northern Germany as well as in the provinces, townships, territories, and dioceses of Mainz, Cologne, Treves, Salzburg and Bremen, many persons of both sexes, unmindful of their own salvation and straying from the Catholic Faith, have abandoned themselves to devils, Incubi, Succubi, and by their incantations, spells, conjurations and other accursed charms and crafts, enormities and horrid offenses, have slain infants yet in the mother's womb as also the offspring of cattle, have blasted produce of the earth . . . afflict and torment men and women . . . hinder men from performing the sexual act and women from conceiving.

Our dear sons, Henry Kramer and James Sprenger, Professors of Theology, of the Orders of Friars Preachers, have been by Letters Apostolic delegated as Inquisitors of these heretical pravities. . . .

Wherefore We, as is Our duty, being wholly desirous of removing all hindrances and obstacles by which the good work of the Inquisitors may be let and tarded . . . (that the Inquisitors may be not) molested or hindered by any authority whatsoever . . .

(Given at Rome, at S. Peter's, on the 9 December of the Year of the Incarnation of Our Lord one thousand four hundred and eighty-four . . .)

To the inquisitors, witchcraft was the creed of all who fought against established order, who sought to blight fairness, who undermined religious institutions and, as Summers says, "set on high the red standard of revolution." The Church had to fight not only defections in its ranks and ward off the attacks of those few sincere souls whose protestations would win them the name of atheists or agnostics, but also those who nurtured subversive ideas against the state. Philosophers and thinkers of the day who spoke for the abolition of private property and the overthrow of monarchies, or who dreamt of the destruction of the feudal system, were fair game for the inquisitors. They, like the religious heretics, belonged to the hosts of the devil, their souls given over to the powers of darkness and obstructionism. It is against these that Summers speaks when he says:

In fact, heresy was one huge revolutionary body exploiting its forces through a hundred different channels and having as its object chaos and destruction. . . . The teachings of the Waldenses and the Albigenses, the Henricians, the Poor Men of Lyons . . . were in reality the same dark fraternity just as the Third International, the Anarchists, the Nihilists and the Bolsheviks are in every sense, save the mere label, entirely identical.[116]

This attitude toward political thought extended naturally toward other abnormal aspects of human behavior, including mental illnesses. The *Malleus Maleficarum* gave the approbation of authority to the idea that demon-possession was the cause of mental as well as all other types of human disturbances.

[116] Summers, Montague: *Op. cit.*, p. xviii.

The book, *Malleus Maleficarum,* is divided into three parts. The first part answers the question of the existence of witches through devious argumentation, chiefly based on the Scriptures, the canons and the works of the scholastics, St. Thomas, St. Augustine and numerous medieval theologians. The authors dispose of the obvious objection that witchcraft and magic are self-delusions or products of the imagination. Only God can change man, and, since the Almighty with His permission allows devils to exist, therefore devils actually change, inhabit and possess man. The tome goes on carefully to define the acts to be considered those of witchcraft, telling how to handle witnesses, how to controvert the arguments of laymen, how to obtain confessions or, failing that, force an acceptance through torture.

Throughout the whole volume, and indeed the whole of medieval demonology, runs the idea that women are closely allied to sin, the devil and witchcraft. The Church argued from the doctrine of primal sin that it was to the devil's advantage to encourage carnal pleasures. The female sex was a natural ally to concupiscence. The authors of the *Malleus Maleficarum* affirm:

> All witchcraft comes from carnal lust, which is in women insatiable. (See Proverbs XXX: There are three things that are never satisfied, yea, a fourth thing which says not, It is enough; that is the mouth of the womb.) Wherefore for the sake of fulfilling their lusts they consort even with devils.

In the section entitled "Remedies Prescribed for Those Who Are Bewitched by the Limitation of the Generative Power," is found:

> Although far more women are witches than men, as shown in the first part of the work, yet men are more often bewitched than women and the reason for this resides in the fact that God allows the devil more power over the venereal act through which the original sin is handed down than other human actions.

The misogynic tone of demonology rested on a characteristic medieval attitude toward women, which Havelock Ellis points out was expressed in the aphorism, "Woman is a temple built over a sewer." It is small wonder that half-crazed witches, buoyed by an intense masochism and in consonance with the prevailing value-judgment toward women, freely related their phantasmagoria. Consider the case of

> a young girl witch who had been converted, whose aunt also had been burned in the diocese of Strasburg. And she added that she had become a witch by the method in which her aunt had first tried to seduce her.
>
> For one day her aunt ordered her to go upstairs with her, and at her command to go into a room where she found fifteen young men clothed in green garments after the manner of German knights. And her aunt said to her: Choose whom you wish from these young men, and I will give him to you, and he will take you for his wife. And when she said she did not wish for any

of them, she was sorely beaten and at last consented, and was initiated according to the aforesaid ceremony. She said also that she was often transported by night with her aunt over vast distances, even from Strasburg to Cologne.[117]

or the following case report:

> Another, named Walpurgis, was notorious for her power of preserving silence, and used to teach other women how to achieve a like quality of silence by cooking their first-born sons in an oven. Many such examples are to our hand.[118]

or the confession of still another, who stated to the inquisitor that she could be transported to the coven either in imagination or bodily:

> For if they do not wish to be bodily transferred, but want to know all that is being done in a meeting of their companions, then they observe the following procedure. In the name of all the devils, they lie down to sleep on their left side, and then a sort of bluish vapour comes from their mouth, through which they can clearly see what is happening.[119]

WITCH-HUNTING, A MEDICOLEGAL SCIENCE

Under the impetus of *The Witches' Hammer,* witch-finding in the sixteenth and the seventeenth centuries passed from an art to a medicolegal science. Early editions of the *Malleus Maleficarum* were printed in miniature form so that "inquisitors might carry it in their pockets and read it under the table." [120] The inquisitorial boards were composed of clergymen, judges, professors, men of standing, learned in the science of witchcraft. Their opinions were authoritative and final; their technics of witch-hunting and torture were the approved legal procedure of the day. Sir Thomas Browne, author of the famous *Religio Medici* (1643), when questioned by the Judge, laid down the proposal as an accepted scientific fact "that the Devil in such cases did work upon the Bodies of Men and Women, upon a Natural Foundation to stir up, and excite such humours super-abounding in their Bodies to a great excess." [121]

Judges were called upon to pass sentence on witches in great numbers. A French judge boasted that he had burned eight hundred women in sixteen years on the bench; six hundred were burned during the administration of a bishop in Bamberg. The Inquisition, originated by the Church of Rome, was carried along by Protestant churches in Great Britain and Germany.

[117] Kramer and Sprenger: *Op. cit.,* p. 100.
[118] *Ibid.,* p. 102.
[119] *Ibid.,* p. 108.
[120] Withington, E. T.: "Dr. John Weyer and the Witch Mania," *in* Studies in the History and Method of Science, p. 201, edited by C. J. Singer, Oxford, Clarendon Press, 1917.
[121] Kittredge, G. L.: Witchcraft in Old and New England, p. 334, Cambridge, Mass., Harvard, 1928.

The foot-crushing by the Spanish boot, torture on the rack and immersion in cold water were not aimed at the witch but at the evil spirit imprisoned within the subject's body. The purpose of torture was to drive the demon out of the subject's body until he came forth admitting defeat. Medical records of the medieval period explain how baffling illnesses were cleared up in the most unexpected manner by the willingness of a devil to admit he was plaguing the body of the patient. A case attributed to the great surgeon, Ambrose Paré, one of the most rational physicians of medieval times, illustrates the literalness with which the devil was regarded as the cause of mental and physical disease. The doctor had been called to attend a young nobleman who

> had convulsions which involved different parts of his body such as the left arm, or the right, or on occasion only a single finger, one loin or both, or his spine, and then his whole body would become so suddenly convulsed and disturbed that four servants would have difficulty in keeping him in bed. His brain, however, was in no way agitated or tormented, his speech was free, his mind was not confused, and his sensations, particularly in the regions of the convulsions, remained intact. . . .
>
> At the end of the third month it was discovered that it was the devil who was the cause of the malady. This was learned from a statement made by the devil himself, speaking through the lips of the patient in profuse Greek and Latin. . . .
>
> This devil, forced to talk frankly by means of religious services and exorcisms, stated that he was a spirit. . . . He was then interrogated as to what kind of spirit he was, and by what means and by virtue of what authority he tormented the young nobleman. . . . [He] stated that he was relegated to the body of our patient by someone whose name he did not want to give, that he entered it through the patient's feet and went up to the level of the brain, and that he would leave the patient also through the latter's feet but not until the day set by previous agreement. . . .[122]

Communications with possessing demons sometimes were reported as long colloquies between demon and exorcist, and sometimes as peremptory commands, accompanied by prayer, "Depart, O Satan, from him," during the exorcism, or "Accursed Devil, hear thy doom . . . depart with thy works from this servant" of the Lord.[123] The abundant demonologic art of medievalism often pictures devils departing from the mouth and other parts of the body. In view of the devil's declamation in the above-quoted case by Paré, that he would leave through the patient's feet, it is interesting to read the description of exorcism by a Fiji Islander, as reported by a missionary, Rev. L. Fison (circa 1870): [124]

[122] Zilboorg, G.: The Medical Man and the Witch During the Renaissance, Vol. 2 of Publications of the Institute of the History of Medicine, pp. 84-87, Baltimore, Johns Hopkins Press, 1935. (Zilboorg has found this same case quoted by other medievalists.)

[123] Kramer and Sprenger: *Op. cit.,* p. 183.

[124] Codrington, R. H.: The Melanesians, p. 198, Oxford, Clarendon Press, 1891.

He passed his hands over the patient's body till he detected the spirit by a peculiar fluttering sensation in his finger ends. He then endeavored to bring it down to one of the extremities, a foot or hand. Much patience and care were required, because the spirits are very cunning.

The medicine man continued:

When you have got the demon into a leg or an arm which you can grasp with your fingers, you must take care or he will escape you. . . . But when you have drawn him down to a finger or a toe, you must pull him out with a sudden jerk, and throw him away, and blow after him lest he should return.

With the onset of the Protestant Reformation, demonology experienced an increase in intensity. Both Lutheranism and Calvinism retained an authoritarian and damning attitude in relation to the problem of evil and the witches who produced evil. We need only to look at the Salem witch epidemic [125] in New England and the severity of the Scottish Kirk of the seventeenth century toward witches to note how the devil, who encouraged sin and wrongdoing, was combated.

A case celebrated in the annals of the Scottish courts and quoted from the book *Daemonologie,*[126] by King James I, illustrates the sober legal and medical technic of witch-finding during the Reformation. It concerns one Geillis Duncane, a maid who was seen going out of her master's house nightly for the purpose of performing miracles for the benefit of the neighbors. Her master, suspecting that she was involved with the devil, examined and tormented her by "binding and wrinching her head with a corde," without result as far as confession was concerned. She was then brought before proper authorities and examined in the presence of the King. After a diligent search the examiners found the mark of the devil in her "fore crag or foreparte of her throate." At this Geillis confessed, accusing Agnes Sampson and others of teaching her to have traffic with the devil. The King's counselors examined Agnes Sampson for marks on her body indicating contact with the devil. After careful search the devil's mark was found on her external genitals. This was irrefutable evidence, since it was established that the devil, when he makes a pact with his subjects, binds it by licking them with his "tung" in some "privy" part.

During the reign of Queen Elizabeth, fear of witchcraft was rampant. Bishop Jewel, in preaching a sermon, warned the Queen:

It may please Your Grace to understand that witches and sorcerers within these few last years are marvelously increased. . . . Your Grace's subjects

[125] Kittredge, G. L.: *Op. cit.*, p. 334.

[126] King James I.: Daemonologie (1597). Contains also "Newes from Scotland declaring the Damnable Life and Death of Doctor Fian, a notable Sorcerer who was burned at Edenbrough in January last (1591)," London, John Lane, and New York, Dutton, 1924.

pine away, even unto death; their color fadeth; their flesh rotteth; their speech is benumbed; their senses bereft.

In 1581, a law was passed that any witch "prophesying how long her Majesty shall live" shall be judged as a felon and "shall suffer paynes of deathe as a felon." [127]

WITCHCRAFT AND MEDICAL PRACTICE

While the devil held dominion over the insane, influences were stirring that were eventually to dissolve the mass-delusion of witchcraft. The liberal atmosphere of the Renaissance, the stimulus to individual thought and experiment during the sixteenth and the seventeenth centuries, provided the background for dissolution of the grand illusion. Increased activities in mathematical and astronomical sciences, in literature, architecture, philosophy, exploration and colonization, all indicated the new spirit which had one reflection in a reorientation of implicit medieval reliance on supernaturalism. The Protestant Reformation was similarly a strong force in this liberation. Still, the loosening of church authoritarianism, the emphasis of a personalized worship of God and the increased "difficulty in ecclesiastical repression of intellectual freedom" [128] consequent on the Reformation undoubtedly helped the demise of witchcraft as a psychological phenomenon. The Protestant affirmation of individualism, the doctrine of "private judgment" (Lewis Mumford) and recourse to the conscience as the final arbiter in spiritual matters were added indications of the released rationalism which gave modern psychiatry its opportunity for early growth.

What was medicine's role in the loosening of demonology's clutch on psychiatric thought? Medicine was starting its emancipation from Galenical medicinals and disputations during the sixteenth and the seventeenth centuries, but it had not yet touched the field of mental illnesses. Advances in anatomy and the discovery of the microscope were helping medicine to move toward physiology. The action of the heart was being understood, the chemistry of digestion analyzed, optical mechanics and the function of the lens studied, respiratory activity and the exchange of gases in the lungs worked out. Discoveries in astronomy, physics and chemistry were impelling medical practice in a more empirical direction. The great physicians of that period in Great Britain—Willis, Harvey and Sydenham—and on the Continent—Van Helmont and Father Kircher—were examining patients, describing clinical conditions and making the observations on which

[127] Summers, Montague: *Op. cit.*, p. xxi.
[128] Barnes, H. E., and David, Henry: The History of Western Civilization, Vol. 1, p. 866, New York, Harcourt, 1935.

modern clinical medicine is built. The seventeenth century improved medicine through two other factors of importance—the scientific society and periodic literature.[129] The universities, well established by this time, were making medical men into scholars and gentlemen. Surgeons were elevated from their status as barbers or camp followers.

The greatest stimulus to the evolution of a scientific medicine was undoubtedly the invention of the printing press. A half century after the first books were written, articles and tomes came from the presses in increasing numbers. Heinrich Laehr [130] uncovered the fact that, from 1459 to 1800, fifteen thousand authors wrote articles on philosophy, medicine, psychology, forensic medicine, psychiatry and neurology. By analyzing the enormous compilation by Laehr, one may see the increasing interest in neuropsychiatric subjects. This bibliography, of course, does not include the thousands of tracts, pamphlets and letters which were written on all aspects of magic, faith-healing, demonology, etc. Thus, in the fifteenth century, about six items on neuropsychiatric treatment appeared; in the sixteenth century, this number had increased to 250 items; in the seventeenth century, 1,800 items appeared; and in the eighteenth century the number had increased to 3,000 items. The range of interest in psychiatric symptomatology is matched only by the complexity of treatments offered. All the prescriptions of the ancients with their commentaries added during fifteen hundred years were copied and recopied in the medical works of European writers of the sixteenth and the seventeenth centuries. To these were added the findings of demonologists, interspersed with old wives' tales, philosophic theories and herb lore in one conglomerate therapeutic mixture. For example, in Ronsseus' *Miscellanea* s. epist. med (1618), the subheadings were:

Of Mania; Therapy of Mania; A Fall Heals Mania; Daemonomania; Practices do not Rectify so-called Second Nature (Habits); Fornication brings about a Disease Manifested in Deadly Convulsions in Several Districts of Luneburg; Hydrophobia; Hydrocephalus; Tabes Dorsalis . . .

The impression of conglomerateness disturbing to a modern reader illustrates the width of interest and the necessity for the practical handling of numerous psychiatric and neurologic problems confronting the Renaissance physician. Let us glance at *Opera Omnia,* by Thomas Willis, a professor at Oxford in 1660, whose name still lives in neurology for his discovery of the Circle of Willis. The table of contents of his work, as noted by Laehr, reads as follows:

[129] Garrison, F. H.: An Introduction to the History of Medicine, ed. 3, p. 281, Philadelphia, Saunders, 1921.

[130] Laehr, Heinrich: Die Literatur der Psychiatre, Neurologie und Psychologie von 1459-1799, Akademie der Wissenschaften zu Berlin, Berlin, Reimer, 1900.

Of the Convulsive Diseases; Pathological Affect of Hysteria; Of the Mind of Brutes; Manifestations of the Physiological and Pathological Aspects as Melancholia, Mania, and Stupidities and Imbecility; Anatomy of the Brain; Chemical Theories; Recommendation of Diversion in Melancholia; Occupational Therapy including Mathematics and Chemistry; Change of Location; Farming; Ought not to be Left to Themselves; Beatings and Chains for Maniacs only in Institutions; Imbecility Depends Mostly on Changes in the Brain . . .

Or let us glance at the more garish work of Karl F. Paullini, called *Flagellum Salutis* (1698), whose table of contents follows:

Strange tales how by beatings all kinds of incurable cases have been easily and quickly cured; In the new editions has been added miraculous cures by music (F. E. Neidter); Life has been prolonged up to 115 years by the breath of young girls (F. H. Cohauser, Stuttgart); Deals with the usefulness of voluntary beatings in many diseases of the head; Beatings in melancholia; in frenzy; in paralysis; in epilepsy; in facial expression of feebleminded; in hardness of hearing; in toothache; in dumbness; hysterical crying; in nymphomania; sleepwalking . . .

Still, there were fresh voices and clear minds that cut through this welter of confusion. George Baglivi,[131] a prominent Italian physician, in his well-known *Practice of Physic,* boldly states:

I can scarce express what influence the physician's words have upon the patient's life, and how much they sway the fancy; for a physician that has his tongue well hung, and is master of the art of perswading, fastens . . . such a vertue upon his remedies and raises the faith and hopes of the patient . . . that sometimes he masters difficult diseases with the silliest remedies.

While this medical activity was in progress, psychology was slowly moving from its scholastic position, rooted in Aristotle and St. Augustine and amplified by Thomas Aquinas, into the fields of associationism and sensationalism. Other problems in psychology, such as that of perception, the relation of body and soul (mind), the problem of memory, etc., were analyzed. An experimental, empirical view of the mind that wished to observe mental phenomena directly replaced the union of Aristotelian psychology and scholastic philosophy. As the wish to observe mental processes grew, supernaturalism gradually came under the influence of the attitude of reality-testing. Still, through these centuries, psychiatry as a body of knowledge and psychotherapy as a scientific attitude toward alleviating mental illness had not yet come into being. Astrology, cabalistic medicine and the newly born doctrine of the Rosicrucians, though ridiculed by Congreve the playwright, were accepted by physicians and laymen alike. Popular medicine remained steeped in paganism or witchcraft in the seventeenth century to the detriment of the mentally ill.

[131] Baglivi, George: The Practice of Physick Reduced to the Ancient Way of Observations, p. 189. Written in Latin, Rome, 1696. Printed in London, 1704.

THE DECLINE OF WITCHCRAFT

The years of the Renaissance showed signs of forthcoming disintegration of witchcraft. Opposition developed from both an antichurch attitude and the trend toward naturalistic explanations. The printing press was spreading ideas and opinions at a much more rapid rate than was possible in the days of the copyists; education was less the sole privilege of the clergy and the nobility. Skepticism became more prevalent; people ventured to discuss witchcraft with some freedom. Those who upheld witchcraft were forced more and more to take cognizance of dissenting voices. In the preamble to King James's *Daemonologie* one catches a panicky note:

> The fearful aboundinge at this time in this countrie of these detestable slaves of the Devill, the Witches or enchanters, hath moved me . . . to dispatch in post, this following treatise . . . against the damnable opinions of two principally in our age . . . the one called SCOT, an Englishman, is not ashamed in publike print to deny, that ther can be such a thing as Witchcraft. . . . The other called VVIERVS, a German Phisition, sets out a publick apologie for al these craftes-folkes.[132]

Still, men could not easily speak against that which the Church and monarchs supported wholeheartedly. It required intellectual courage and honesty for men like Reginald Scot to attack openly belief in witchcraft. In his *Discoverie of Witchcraft,*[133] published in 1584, the Squire from Kent declared:

> The common people have beene so assotted and bewitched, with whatsoever poets have feigned of witchcraft, either in earnest, in jest, or else in derision; and with whatsoever lowd liers and couseners [swindlers] . . . that they thinke it heresie to doubt in anie part of the matter; speciallie bicause they find this word witchcraft expressed in the scriptures.

The significance of Scot's book for psychiatry resides in his insistence upon natural explanations for the weird self-confessed experiences of witches. He collected examples of mysteries attributed to witches, and showed by logic and scientific, philosophic and even theologic argument that they could all be explained on naturalistic grounds. In place of the torture chamber, what these bedeviled, starved, ignorant suspects needed was "physick, food and necessaries." Scot's views were attacked on all sides. Even Montague Summers, the twentieth-century witchfinder, expresses his belated contempt of Scot's work by saying, "[He] covers his atheism with the thinnest of ear and in fact wholly and essentially denies the supernatural."

[132] King James I: *Op. cit.*

[133] Scot, Reginald: The Discoverie of Witchcraft, with an introduction by the Rev. Montague Summers, reprinted by John Rodker, Suffolk, 1930.

An area explored by Scot was that of the theory of incubi and succubi which loomed large in the transformation of psychosis and neurosis into the work of Satan and his demons. Incubus was the name given to the male demon who visited women at night, forcing them into sexual congress against their will, while succubus was a female spirit who visited men for a similar purpose. Incubi and succubi were accounted to be the cause of night terrors, violent dreams and nightmares. The incubus caused a sensation of weight on the chest, difficulty in breathing, terror and a feeling of strangulation in sleeping persons, especially women, presumably due to the weight of the devil on the body of the sleeper. The incubus was regarded as a demon with a material body. It was believed, for reasons not difficult to understand, that the incubi particularly chose virgins and virtuous women to molest but did not cavil at the good-wife. The authors of *Malleus Maleficarum,* discussing a case of "Phantom pregnancy," blame incubi for the nocturnal activities that produced such diseases:

> At times also women think they have been made pregnant by an Incubus, and their bellies grow to an enormous size; but when the time of parturition comes, their swelling is relieved by no more than the explosion of a great quantity of wind. . . . And it is very easy for the devil to cause these and even greater disorders in the stomach.

But to Scot these explanations were cloaks for lechery, a deception fed to an ignorant and trusting populace to gloss over the amours of young (and older) adventurers. Thus Scot in exposing

> Bishop Sylvanus, his lecherie opened and covered againe, how maides having yellow haire are most combred with Incubus, how married men are bewitched to use other men's wives, and to refuse their own . . .

relates the case of an incubus that came to a lady's bedside and made "hot loove unto hir." The lady being offended cried out loudly, and the company came and found the incubus under her bed in the likeness of Bishop Sylvanus. The defamation of Sylvanus continued until one day this infamy was purged by a devil who made a confession at the tomb of St. Jerome. Scot's caustic comment on this tale is, "Oh excellent peace of witchcraft or cousening * wrought by Sylvanus!"

Troublesome incubi, although occasionally discovered to be youths bent on erotic adventures, were more often recognized as demons lying with married women even while their husbands were abed with them. Chaucer seems to have caught the humor of the situation when he writes in the *Wife of Bath:*

> Women may go saufly up and doun,
> In every bush, or under every tree;

* "Cousening" is an obsolete term meaning to cheat in a petty way.

There is noon other incubus but hee,
And he ne wol doon hem but dishonour.[134]

Later students of the nightmare, however, feel that the evidence is sufficient to believe that the "Witch . . . represents in the main an exteriorization of the repressed sexual conflicts of women." Ernest Jones, the English psychoanalyst, goes on to say that the nightmare

consists of an imaginary fulfilment of certain repressed wishes for sexual intercourse, especially with the parents. The beliefs in question are evidently determined by attempts to ward off the sense of guilt accompanying these wishes (i.e., by projecting them on to the Incubus) . . .[135]

Witchcraft apparently gave weight and substance to anxiety dreams or nightmares by imputing them to actual forms of incubi and succubi. The treatment prescribed by physicians was exorcism.

Details of sexual congress between the devil and his devotees are numerous in the recordings of the period, and the psychopathology of the sexual life, induced by demons, is fully expounded in the *Malleus Maleficarum* and other texts. One difficult symptom was that of impotence, for which an ingenious theory was advanced, namely, that of "Glamor." A glamor was a devil in the form of a man but so transformed as to be without his natural sexual organs. In this state of deprivation the glamor would replace the intended victim without the latter's knowledge. The victim, turned into a sexless being, needed only to find someone who would exorcise the demon to regain his virility. Parenthetically, it is interesting to note how the original castrative meaning of "glamor" has been displaced through the intermediate meaning of "deceptive allure" to the present connotation of "exciting, stimulating or colorful." A case of glamor is reported by Kramer and Sprenger: [136]

A certain young man had an intrigue with a girl. Wishing to leave her, he lost his member; that is to say, some glamor was cast over it so that he could see or touch nothing but his smooth body. In his worry over this he went to a tavern to drink wine: and . . . got into conversation with another woman who was there, and told her the cause of his sadness, explaining everything and demonstrating in his body that it was so. The woman was astute, and asked whether he suspected anyone; and when he named such a one, . . . she said: "If persuasion is not enough, you must use some violence, to induce her to restore to you your health." So in the evening the young man watched the way . . . the witch was in the habit of going, and, finding her, prayed her to restore him the health of his body. And when she maintained that she was innocent and knew nothing about it, he fell upon her, and winding a towel tightly around her neck, choked her, saying: "Unless you give me back my health,

[134] Chaucer, Geoffrey: "The Tale of the Wyf of Bathe," *in* The Works of Geoffrey Chaucer, edited by W. W. Skeat, ed. 2, Vol. 4, p. 345, Oxford Univ. Press, 1900.
[135] Jones, Ernest: On the Nightmare, p. 97, London, Hogarth, 1931. (Am. ed. published by Liveright, New York)
[136] Kramer and Sprenger: *Op. cit.*, p. 119.

you shall die at my hands." Then she, being unable to cry out, and with her face already swelling and growing black, said: "Let me go, and I will heal you." The young man then relaxed the pressure of the towel, and the witch touched him with her hand between the thighs, saying: "Now, you have what you desire." And the young man, as he afterwards said, plainly felt, before he had verified it by looking or touching, that his member had been restored to him by the mere touch of the witch.

The authors warn, however, that the male organ was taken away "not indeed by actually despoiling the human body of it, but by concealing it with some glamor."

Reginald Scot was not a physician, and he was more concerned with the injustices done suspected witches during the trials in inquisitorial courts than in understanding the psychological basis for witchcraft. For the law, far more than medicine, held the fate of demonologic psychopathology in its iron control. Besides Scot, there were other disbelievers in the universe of demons. Paracelsus had supplied an ingenious explanation to the incubus legend: [137]

Incubi are male, *succubae* female creatures. They are the outgrowths of an intense and lewd imagination of men and women, formed of the semen of those who commit the unnatural sin of Onan. . . . This semen, born from imagination, may be taken away by spirits that wander about by night, and that may carry it to a place where they may hatch it out.

Father Kircher, in the seventeenth century, insisted that either the possessed were the victims of mental derangement or the inquisitors were the victims of delusions.

Another iconoclast was Cornelius Agrippa von Nettesheim (1486-1535), who was earlier a strong advocate of magic. Later he became a rugged defender of sanity in the malignant disease of demonology. Hated and persecuted by his colleagues for his attack on the delusion of witchcraft, Agrippa, in his mature years, wrote a volume, *On the Uncertainty and Vanity of All Sciences* (*i.e., Occultism and Magic*), decrying witchcraft and magic, and declaring that their advocacy would benefit neither science, the Church nor the state. While advocate of the city of Metz, Agrippa was able to put some of his convictions into practice. At one time he vanquished a particularly cruel judge, the Inquisitor Savini, and Agrippa's pupils hailed his triumph with delight. One Brennon wrote him: "All the poor women who were in prison are free and those who fled [the city] have returned. Savini sits in his monastery cell biting his nails and does not care to go out." [138] Eventually the monks of Metz accused him of belonging to the devil and of inviting the Master of Hell into his rooms. He was arrested twice and finally forced to flee to Grenoble.

137 Paracelsus: De Morbis Invisibilus. *Quoted by* Pachter, H. M.: Magic into Science, The Story of Paracelsus, p. 74, New York, Schuman, 1951.

138 Scot, Reginald: *Op. cit.*

WIERUS (WEYER) THE GERMAN "PHISITION"

The second of the two whose "damnable" opinions caused King James I so much vexation was Johann Wierus (Wier, Weyer) (1515-1576), born in Germany, a student of medicine under the preceptorship of Cornelius Agrippa. Although widely interested in philosophy and the classics, Weyer devoted himself to the practice of medicine throughout his life. His great work, *De Praestigiis Daemonum* [139] (1563), is a volume in which he lays open with prophetic psychiatric insight the fallacies of demonology. Weyer's work was of great significance, a veritable landmark in the history of psychiatry; numerous editions appeared up to 1581.[140] He was both attacked by the Church and acclaimed by his followers for two centuries after the publication of his work. Bodin, a scholar of proportions, particularly castigated Weyer as one who "armed himself against God" and was skeptical at the evidence of "the most notorious of existing facts." [141] Montague Summers retained the vigor of his attack on disbelievers when he dubbed Weyer's work that of a "natural skeptic, a man without imagination, an ineffective little soul, a myopic squireen."

Weyer, a gentle physician and a loyal churchman, could and did lash out at the corrupt and slothful practice he witnessed about him.[142] His zeal, unlike Scot's, which was that of the reformer, arose from seasoned clinical observation and the desire to find the "shining truth" in an age of darkness. From experience he wrote that priests and monks

> are, in the main, ignorant and bold. (The good and pious ones which I hold in high esteem, I except.) They claim to understand the healing art and they lie to those who seek help that their sicknesses are derived from witchery . . . and the ignorant and clumsy physicians blame all sicknesses which they are unable to cure or which they have treated wrongly, on witchery.[143]

Johann Weyer's method of study was that of clinical science. His practice was to search out cases of demon-possession and investigate, taking notes on every aspect of the phenomena. He did not speculate, he studied patients. Hence his views have a freshness and a freedom from emotional bias rare in Weyer's day. Weyer insisted on *individualization* of cases. People should not be "molded in accordance with one definite

[139] Wiero, Joanne: De Praestigiis Daemonum et Incantationibus, ac Veneficiis, Libri V, 1563 (translations by Zilboorg and Binz).

[140] Zilboorg, Gregory, and Henry, G. W.: A History of Medical Psychology, pp. 200 et seq., New York, Norton, 1941.

[141] Lecky, W. E. H.: History of the Rise and Influence of the Spirit of Rationalism in Europe, Vol. I, p. 109, New York, Appleton, 1866.

[142] Binz, Carl: Doctor Johann Weyer, ein rheinischer Arzt der erste Bekampfer des Hexenwahns, ed. 2, Berlin, Hirschwald, 1896.

[143] *Ibid.*

model, as is the custom of many inept people, liars, impostors and various other grand masters of superstition and impiety." [144] Weyer's plea that the patient be regarded as an individual heralded a medical psychology which three centuries later regarded patients as individuals with an emotional life and a set of reactions specific unto themselves. Weyer introduced a practical, clinical attitude, presaging the perception of individual differences and individual emotional needs.

Weyer's system of treatment for the possessed is summarized in his works. He cautioned the physician who believed the patient to be possessed to examine him carefully in body and spirit. If the body were at first freed from demons, then more attention could be given to the physical aspect of healing. Weyer counseled (at this point he apologized for going counter to the Church) that the possessed first be taught about the deceptions of the demon. Official prayers are to be said for them. Fasting is effective, because "if you are full of food and lazy, the demon has a special likeness for you." Alms should be given according to the patient's means. Every person was to be treated individually. In cases of impotence he advised the patient first to consult a doctor "to see if there is any other natural reason." If the cause is deeper, he should wait for three years until he considered it a reason for divorce. During this time he should give alms eagerly, should pray and make contrition, but should not fast. From his carefully observed cases Weyer deduced principles of treatment that are fundamentally sound.

Notions of demonology did not obscure Weyer's understanding of his cases. For example, when he dealt with the incubus question, he explained it as a nightmare due to the combined effects of indigestion and imagination:

> What is called Incubus is nothing than the condition which you call in this country "mare" and in England nightmare. . . . Why should not melancholic women, when they are lying on their backs asleep, once in a while imagine and assert that they were raped by an evil spirit? [145]

Consider Weyer's management of the case of a monk convinced that he was possessed by a succubus, treated successfully without resort to exorcism. Dr. Weyer wrote:

> This priest consulted me because every night an attractive woman came to him as a frightening, oppressive nightmare. He had gone to a monk and to an old woman to get advice, but without success. I succeeded, after a short time, in explaining his sickness to him and was able to discharge him with the prospects of recovery.[146]

[144] *Ibid.*
[145] Modified after Zilboorg, G.: *Op. cit.*
[146] Binz: *Op. cit.*

Yet Weyer was hooted down except by a few. For, as Binz says, "Weyer was talking like a rational human being to the inmates of a gigantic insane asylum, and undoubtedly with the same success."

Persistent, gentle, clear-headed, Weyer paved the way for a clinical psychiatry. Zilboorg, who "discovered" Weyer's importance in the history of psychiatry recently, with justice calls him the "first psychiatrist." [147] Only patient investigation and unbiased judgment could have allowed him to solve, according to psychiatric principles, cases which the medieval world accepted as due to demons. He described the case of a sixteen-year-old girl who suffered the common complaint that the devil put cloth, nails and needles in her stomach "when her head was turned and her eyes were averted." Weyer relates the case: [148]

> Her father told me that she had often brought such objects up out of her stomach. But this piece of cloth was moistened by only a little saliva, and not by chyme, which it should have been, as this was shortly after lunch. Shortly before, I witnessed how Satan made her roll her eyes, squeeze her hands tightly, and clamp her mouth. The father and the bystanders reported that the woman's mouth could be opened only if the sign of the cross were made. I opened both without this, only through trust in God. I certainly do not mean to say anything against the cross, but only against its mis-use. When I asked the girl if she knew the author of her sickness, she named a respectable woman who, along with her mother and two other women were locked up in prison for witchcraft. A few weeks later, they were released. The whole uproar had started, when the girl, on account of a natural, but allegedly witch-bourne belly ache, bought (and drank) holy water from a priest or the sexton of the town of Amersfort. These are the consequences, when men turn away from God and from the natural means which God lends to men, and turn to things which nourish the erroneous belief in witches.

Weyer was a man of genuine religiosity. He did not deny the devil, but, like Paracelsus, cautioned accepting at face value fanciful powers accredited to Satan. In the dedication of his volume he wrote: [149]

> To you, Prince, I dedicate the fruit of my thought . . . that rather their imagination—inflamed by the demons in a way not understandable to us makes them only fancy that they have caused all sorts of evil. For when the entire manner of action is laid on the scales, and the implements therefore examined with careful scrutiny . . .

For his careful scrutiny Weyer was placed on the Index Librorum Prohibitorum, which meant that "not only *De Praestigiis Daemonum,* but all his other writings were forbidden." [150]

[147] Zilboorg, G.: *Op. cit.,* p. 205.
[148] Binz: *Op. cit.,* p. 45.
[149] Zilboorg, G.: *Op. cit.,* p. 119.
[150] *Ibid.,* p. 192.

ENCROACHMENT OF LIBERAL THOUGHT ON WITCHCRAFT

Another prominent man of the seventeenth century who spoke out against the wholesale illusion of witchcraft was Father Spee, a German monk. In 1623, Spee published a volume in which he denounced the prejudice-ridden magistrates of Germany and France. Starting in the traditional manner with the affirmation of belief in witches, Spee, his profession of faith made, was able then to demonstrate the absurdities of the doctrine of demonology. With admirable candor he said, "We who have to do with such people in prisons and have examined them often and carefully (not to say curiously), have sometimes found our minds perplexed." In an anonymous entry in a volume, *Cautio Criminalis* (1631), the monk was less circumspect. Here he pleaded: [151]

> Why do you search so diligently for sorcerers? I will show you at once where they are. Take the Capuchins, the Jesuits, all the religious orders, and torture them—they will confess. If some deny, repeat it a few times—they will confess. Should a few still be obstinate, exorcise them, shave them, only keep on torturing—they will give in. If you want more, take the Canons, the Doctors, the Bishops of the Church—they will confess. . . . If you want still more, I will torture you and then you me. I will confess the crimes you will have confessed and so we shall all be sorcerers together.

Father Spee's interest was chiefly in the legalities centering in the reality of confessions by witches. What he did, in effect, was to point out to the inquisitors that a wizard or a witch under trial must necessarily be suggestible. And therein he hit upon a vital point in the psychology of witch-making. A wizard on trial, besieged by questions, hammered at, grilled for hours, taken to the rack, grilled again and then taken back to the torture chamber, all the while being adjured to tell the truth, prayed at, shouted at, derided, mocked, was not a fit subject to give correct testimony. But with the inquisitors and judges of those times, acquiescence after torture of such a person was used as a point of evidence legally. The "swim test," in which a subject was considered innocent if she drowned and subject to torture as a witch if she survived, was held just by the established law.

Reginald Scot, Father Spee and Adam Tanner in turn pointed out the absurdity of rules of evidence used against witches. Father Spee was joined by other members of the German church in urging that doctors and theologians should be consulted before the judiciary took steps in prosecuting cases of witchcraft. In the late 1600's, Robert Burton, divine turned psychiatrist, satirized the "cunning men and witches" who claimed a "St. Catherine's Wheel printed in the roof of the mouth" as proof of their

[151] Withington, E. T.: *Op. cit.*, p. 204.

satanic association.[152] The St. Catherine's wheel, an instrument of torture, characterized by spikes projecting from a wheel's circumference, was so named in memory of the Saint's martyrdom. The "cunning men" and witches, appropriating the place of wise women in providing therapy through enchantment, were castigated by Burton: "Tis a common practice of some men to go first to a witch, and then to a physician; if one cannot, the other shall; if they cannot bend Heaven, they will try Hell." [153] Doubt was arising on all sides as to the validity of self-confession among witches and the ubiquity of witches and the devil's ability to cause disease by possession.

Witchcraft was also decried from a moral point of view. Men began to sense that the ignominy associated with witches was but a reflection of their own emotions. The writers of a play, *The Witch of Edmonton*,[154] put this into their character's mouth:

> Why should the envious world
> Throw all their scandalous malice upon me?
> 'Cause I am poor, deform'd, and ignorant,
> And like a bow buckled and bent together
> By some more strong in mischiefs than myself?

Early in the eighteenth century, liberalists of France entered upon a campaign of mockery of witchcraft. They thrust the rapiers of their wit at it, puncturing the bombastic conceit of the clergy and subduing the glee of the witch-pursuing mob. The Encyclopedists, Voltaire, Rousseau and other French writers, insisted again and again that belief in witchcraft was a "species of madness." The subtle influence of the Age of Reason was extending itself.

The agreement of the judiciary to employ doctors in witchcraft trials was a forward step. Still, it was difficult for physicians to accept a rational for a "revealed" cause of mental disorder. In spite of the introduction in the eighteenth century of the inductive method of thought into scientific work generally, mental conditions, especially mystifying hysterical seizures, were still thought of as caused by the devil or other "spiritual" agency. Century-old prejudices were not to be laid aside so easily. As late as 1769, Professor Cullen, a leader of medical thought in Great Britain, had to caution the readers of his *First Lines of Physick* [155] that "we do not allow that there is any true demonomania. . . . In my opinion the species [of

[152] Burton, Robert: Anatomy of Melancholy, p. 382, edited by Floyd Dell and Paul Jordan-Smith, New York, Tudor, 1927.

[153] *Ibid.*, p. 383.

[154] Dekker, Thomas: Dramatic Works, Vol. 4, p. 365, London, John Pearson, 1873. (Originally published in 1868.)

[155] Cullen, William: First Lines of the Practice of Physic, Edinburgh, Creech, 1779-1784.

demonomania] . . . are melancholy or mania, feigned diseases or diseases falsely lived by spectators."

A note reminiscent of the "glamors" of the *Malleus Maleficarum* creeps into his discussion of nervous ailments when Cullen writes, "Anaphrodisia magica is a fictitious species." Still, Robert Whytt, a contemporary of Cullen's, adopts a less reverential tone in discussing "the incubus or nightmare": [156] "I shall just remark that a plethora, as well as other causes may so affect the nerves of the stomach as to give rise to the incubus."

While many were accepting the advances of medicine and natural science, there were some who mourned the passing of witchcraft. John Wesley said in 1768: "It is true that the English have given up all . . . witches. I am sorry for it. . . . Giving up witchcraft is in effect giving up the bible."

In the light of these conflicting pronouncements, it is questionable whether Lecky is entirely justified in saying that Scot "exercised no appreciable influence," and that Weyer might have waited for the "gradual insensible yet profound modification of habits of thought due to progress of civilization." [157]

In our exploration of the currents of mental healing, the digression into witchcraft was forced upon us by an odd psychological turn of events. Until the seventeenth century, demonology was the psychological modality within which certain mental aberrations were perceived. Even if the examination and the disposition of witches were universally aimed at the salvation of society from evil, and in no way consciously turned toward the problem of treating individual mental patients, it still occupies a significant place in the history of mental healing. In a way not always demonstrable, the emotional energies bent on detecting and punishing witches can be conceived as being identical with those energies which during the late Reformation period spurred humanitarian enterprises. These are the ambivalent tendencies expressed in society's handling of larger sociopsychological problems. Humanitarianism in public dealings with criminals and the insane during the eighteenth century betrayed the reactive aspect of feelings of hate toward malefactors of a century or two earlier. In the history of Western civilization the social conscience frequently has expressed alternate aggressive and restituting or compensatory impulses toward vexing or challenging psychological occurrences; the urge to destroy is succeeded by the equally strong wish to re-create. Demonology, with its legal institution of witchcraft, and humanitarianism were opposite sides of the same emotional medal.

[156] Whytt, Robert: Observations on the Nature, Causes and Cure of those Disorders Commonly called Nervous, Hypochondriac or Hysteric, ed. 3, Edinburgh, Balfour, 1767.

[157] Withington, E. T.: *Op. cit.*, p. 223.

How does this notion bear on the psychology of psychotherapy? In the first place, the psychic forces described in the first chapter as forming the roots of mental healing were also involved in witchcraft. The processes of primitive *magic* and of *faith* were part and parcel of the demonology pandemic. Another irreducible element of mental healing, the *intellect*, was also involved in witchcraft as clerics and philosophers sought by logical use of arbitrary postulates, arising from a revealed religion, to account reasonably for the effect of Satan on the human organism. For example, Thorndike [158] states that William, Bishop of Paris, was puzzled as to how far demons were outside human power and within God's as he strove to understand how disorders imputed to incubi were not really due to vapors (disease) as medical men insisted. The final factor developed in the discussion of the forces of mental healing, namely, the *integrative capacity of the ego*, enters less obviously into the phenomenology of witchcraft when compared with that of mental healing. Since demonology was imposed upon people from without, through authority, one might expect rejection of its tenets. But a closer scrutiny of this situation sheds light on the ego participation in witchcraft. This consisted in a tolerance to physical pain and cruelty developed in the collective ego of medieval man not dissimilar to the tolerance to disease, deformity, bizarre anomalies, devastating epidemics and early death which was common in the prebacteriologic age of medicine. Disfigurement, amputations, burnings, etc., were apparently accepted as unchangeable elements of life, the price of psychological maladjustment.[159]

Demonology was a way station in society's adaptation to its psychological problems as interest in man's soul passed from ecclesiastical to secular hands. Before the vicissitudes of the soul (mind) in health and disease ceased to be the exclusive concern of the ecclesiastics and became the domain of philosophers and natural scientists, a phase of resistance, a psychological upheaval, occurred. In the main, the effect of pressures on man's soul could not be directly translated into naturalistic terms by medieval man, for he was born and lived within a theological frame of reference. It is understandable that the observable effects of adverse emotional tensions were conceived in supernatural terms; that emotional trauma, frustration, restriction and deprivation, reduced outlet for psychic energies, anxiety, projections and shrinkage of the ego were displaced onto Satan and his witches. The cosmology of Satanism contained a satisfactory explanation for the manifestations of evil and "sin" on the body and the mind of man and in his social behavior. For this cosmology had a realistic structure and meaning; it was a screen on which to visualize cause and effect in human behavior. Witches and devils during the centuries up to the Renais-

[158] Thorndike, L.: *Op. cit.*, p. 380.
[159] Huxley, Aldous: The Devils of Loudun, New York, Harper, 1952.

sance were not psychological distortions; they were palpable perverse elements in a social world, given shape and idealized form by the Church.

Broadly speaking, the Age of Reason in the eighteenth century provided the base-line from which emotional disturbances could be viewed in terms of natural occurrences as far as knowledge allowed, permitting a nonsupernatural concept of cause and effect in human activity. It was then that concern with the substance and the content of witchcraft passed from clerical to medical hands. The transition was slow and uncertain. For in the 1690's Cotton Mather [160] viewed with alarm the invasion of New England by the Invisible World, "Another Wo that may be Look'd for is, the Devil being let Loose in preternatural Operations . . . perhaps in Possessions and Obsessions," while Robert Burton,[161] seventy years earlier, stated that only to the "prepared bosom" of the physician-friend could the melancholic patient profitably confide his troubles.

160 Mather, Cotton: On Witchcraft, Being the Wonders of the Invisible World. . . . First published in Boston in Oct. 1692 and Now Reprinted with Additional Matter and Old Wood-Cuts for the Library of the Fantastic and Curious. Mt. Vernon, New York, Peter Pauper Press, 1951.

161 Evans, Bergen, and Mohr, G.: The Psychiatry of Robert Burton, p. 89, New York, Columbia, 1944.

4

Medicine Enters Mental Healing

The demise of the cult of Satanism occurred during the early years of the eighteenth century. The psychological reorientation which paved the way for considering "possessed" individuals as "insane" was spurred by a growing curiosity about natural events and a softening of the accepted sadistic atmosphere common in earlier centuries. As Lecky put it: "The old theological measure of probability completely disappeared . . . replaced by a shrewd secular common sense. The statements of the witches were pronounced intrinsically incredible." [162]

Political and social upheavals of the century sharpened the use of intellect in matters up to then neglected or attributed to unknowable or unapproachable forces. The intellectualism and humanitarianism of the "admirable eighteenth century" provided a background for the evolution of modern psychotherapy. The token spirits of the Age of Reason, not the least of which was skepticism toward revealed religion, combined with the rise of a clinical sense among medical men to constitute the chief factors making for the entrance of medicine into mental healing. The wish for intellectual liberty and for tolerance, which occupied thinkers in England and on the Continent, was a pervasive spirit forming an invisible matrix of opinion that was intimately related to the union of medicine and psychotherapy.

INTELLECTUALISM, FORERUNNER OF PSYCHOTHERAPY

Among literate persons and in civilized areas, ideas attained a new validity and mobility. In Europe, Adam Smith the economist, Goethe the universal genius, Pestalozzi the pioneer in modern education, Beccaria a penal reformer, Rousseau, Montesquieu—all wrote, conversed, argued and pleaded for the right of man to improve his lot by the application of civilization's accumulated knowledge. The intellectual ferment of the century

[162] Lecky, W. E. H.: History of the Rise and Influence of the Spirit of Rationalism in Europe, Vol. 1, p. 111, New York, Appleton, 1866.

was most apparent among the aristocracy, in whose salons philosophers (this term included scientists and social reformers) expounded their views and disseminated knowledge, receiving adulation in return. But preoccupation with issues of the day, with the validity of revelation, of miracles, of tolerance for deistic ideas or even atheism, of skepticism of ten centuries of dogma, did not remain the exclusive property of one class or one nation. English Deism and rationalism were hailed in France, Voltaire's skepticism was admired in England, Holland's tolerance of religious differences was adumbrated in the American colonies. While Voltaire cried, "Your study is Man, that labyrinth you explore," the Quakers in England astonished "all Christendom by behaving like Christians." [163] The spirit of humanitarianism, which had energized truly religious persons and gentle philosophers who sought for man a better life on earth, epitomized an age that opened the way for Pinel's liberation of the insane in France and Tuke's humanizing of asylum treatment in England.

The tone of intellectualism is easily demonstrated in mid-century France, where publication of the French Encyclopedia comprising thirty-five volumes in the 1750's symbolized, as well as any other single event, the humanizing effort which characterized the period. As Voltaire [164] wrote in the Prospectus announcing the Encyclopedia:

> The last age has put the present in a condition to assemble into one body and to transmit to posterity, to be by them delivered down to remoter ages, the sacred repository of all the arts and all the sciences, all of them pushed as far as human industry can go.

It was in the Parisian salons that the flower of European society, alert to new trends, including the significant thinking of early psychologists, discussed the implications of skepticism and rationalism. The associationism of Hobbes and Locke, the empiricism of the English philosophers turned psychologists, were discussed avidly. Condillac's formulation that sensation passed through the sense organs to result in higher mental forms attracted much attention. A salon chronicler described how Mme Necker, mother of Baroness de Staël, vivaciously discussed recent theories of sensation with M. Diderot, the French encyclopedist:

> "M. Diderot," Madam Necker said, "Did you not tell me that it was possible to explain thought by the succession of sensations?" . . . Answered M. Diderot, "All nature is nothing but a series of progressive sensations; the stone feels, but very feebly; the plant feels more than the stone, the oyster feels more than the plant, and so on till I reach man. Weak sensations leave no trace of themselves behind. The light impress of my finger on a hard body could not

[163] Durant, Will: The Story of Philosophy, p. 226, New York, Simon & Schuster, Inc., 1926.

[164] Mowat, R. B.: The Age of Reason, p. 36, Boston, Houghton, 1934.

be preserved, but stronger sensations do actually produce a remembrance—remembrance which is nothing other than thought."[165]

There is general agreement that scientific discoveries of the seventeenth century, in combination with a "free play of mind" (Shaftesbury) in matters of religion, formed an antisupernatural climate of opinion.[166] The *honnête homme,* the man of clear perceptions and unfettered thinking, became the "man of parts and sense . . . the moral norm of the age." Sainte-Beuve,[167] a friend of Mme de Staël, caught the sprightly tone of a society which had provided the intellectual's haven, as he tells in his memoirs of a salon conversation, ". . . these two holding the magic racquets of the discussion, and sending back to each other, for hours at a time, without ever missing, the ball of a thousand related thoughts."

This new norm, spreading through many ramifications—philosophic, physiologic, political—imperceptibly allowed the "free play of mind" to settle on an appreciation of the mind and its vagaries. The stimulus toward doing good works rested on a basic religious spirit: eighteenth-century religion was a religion of humanity.[168]

The English Deists, who conceived of God as a benevolent being, as opposed to the orthodox picture of a severe, condemning judge, were much admired in France; their ideas were eagerly and secretly discussed in the Parisian salons.[169] The Earl of Shaftesbury, in defining an urbane and a tolerant Deity, "matched," comments Barnes, "that of a typical English gentleman of the eighteenth century."[170] Deism or "natural religion" formed the philosophic background for the French and the American revolutions, since a benevolent God was primarily concerned with men's happiness in the "now." The doctrine that "all men were created equal" and entitled to "liberty and equality" followed from the deistic position. Humanitarianism encompassed the wish to improve social relations, and hence conferred sanction on emotional and social problems as worthy of attention. Although Deism often led to atheism among intellectuals, the force behind social reforms retained the positive vigor derived from an accepting God. Human aspiration was pointed more toward laying a groundwork for a better posterity than for securing one's salvation. The cultural force of humanitarianism as the precursor of the movement which made the twentieth

[165] *Ibid.,* p. 222.

[166] Willey, Basil: The Eighteenth Century Background, p. 75, New York, Columbia, 1941.

[167] Sainte-Beuve: "Portraits de femmes (1845)," *in* Mowat: *Op. cit.,* p. 224.

[168] Becker, C. L.: The Heavenly City of the Eighteenth-Century Philosophers, New Haven, Conn., Yale, 1932.

[169] Seignobos, Charles: The Rise of European Civilization, translated by C. A. Phillips, p. 304, New York, Knopf, 1938.

[170] Barnes, H. E.: The History of Western Civilization, Vol. 2, p. 178, New York, Harcourt, 1935.

century alive to the human worth of the mentally ill cannot be underestimated.

The fact that many tracts were written anonymously on the Continent, that studies of religion and politics took the form of satire and "inquiries," indicates that tolerance was still an uncommon attitude, not yet a political reality. For the illiterate masses, interest in philosophy and science lay in the unvisualizable future. Unknown to them, the social and intellectual forces we are outlining were destined to lay a groundwork for the eventuality of a psychological century with direct implications for the insane and the nervous who struggled in their half-world of suffering and neglect.

It was inevitable that interest should pass from religious criticism to philosophy and later to psychology and neurology. Emanuel Swedenborg, the Swedish scientist-mystic, "resolved, cost what it may, to trace out the nature of the human soul," [171] delved into the anatomy of the cortical substance. This search for the soul led him to the modern concept that "brain activity is combined activity of individual (cortical) cells. The cerebral cortex is the seat of soul." [172] Search for the place of abode of the "soul" with its neurologic connotations was still distant from everyday medical interest. We shall see later how a rudimentary neurology struggled with these questions as the school of "neuropathology" developed in the latter part of the eighteenth century. But clinical medicine was too unevenly developed in the eighteenth century to nurture a union between humanitarianism and medical science in regard to mental disease. Lack of conformity in the theory of medical treatment, antagonisms growing out of ignorance, were characteristic. Weikard,[173] a German, wrote in his autobiography of the state of medicine in mid-century:

> What confusion when we regard the therapy of different nations! The French bleed, use enemas, astringents, purges, water, always want to dilute. The English give salts and herbs, minerals. . . . The Viennese praise their new remedies, the good effects of which the other sons of Aesculapius never can confirm. The other Germans mill about, try first this and that, and in therapy do as they do in other things, imitate and admire the foreigner. . . . Almost every province, every university has its own routine. Where shall an impartial physician seek his information?

THE AGE OF MEDICAL SYSTEMS

The eighteenth century has been called the Age of Systems. Medicine followed Linnaeus (1707-1778), the Swedish physician and botanist who

[171] Swedenborg, Emanuel: The Soul, or, Rational Psychology, translated by F. Sewall, ed. 3, New York, New Church Board, 1887.

[172] ——: Encyclopædia Britannica, ed. 13, Vol. 21, p. 653, 1945.

[173] Weikard, M. A.: Autobiography, 1784. *Quoted in* Robinson, Victor: The Story of Medicine, p. 335, New York, Boni, 1931.

revolutionized biologic science by suggesting a classification of animals and plants based on similarities of structure or function. In the same period, Cuvier, the father of paleontology, brought order into the science of comparative zoology. De Sauvages[174] (1706-1767), a prominent clinician, classified diseases, following Linnaeus, into 10 classes, 295 genera and 24,000 species. The encyclopedic fervor exemplified by the French Encyclopedists was both a product and an indicator of intellectual activity of the eighteenth century. Leaders in medicine were immersed in classifying the body of medical knowledge which had been accumulating. The urge for cataloguing the bewildering array of human illnesses developed as a reaction to the spotty medical knowledge of earlier centuries and fitted the psychological trend of the time—to recount and capitalize the gains "made by civilization prior to the Industrial Age."[175]

Classificatory interest was not the sole area of activity among medical men. Scientific physiology, stemming earlier from the alchemist's work in organic chemistry and enlisting the discoveries of oxygen, nitrogen and hydrogen and their chemical interreactions in the living body, had long appropriated chemistry within itself. The basis of modern medicine was being written in experiments by Lavoisier (1775), who demonstrated the combustion of oxygen in respiration. Investigations of the basic function of muscle irritability made by von Haller, the regeneration of nerve tracts (Spallanzani), Volta's use of electricity in inducing muscular contractions and the early analysis of types of skulls (Blumenbach) were fundamental findings that bore directly on the infant field of neurology and indirectly on the embryonic science of psychiatry. The nature of the nerve impulse, the difference between sensory and motor impulses mediated by the nerves of the body, led to speculation concerning the role of the nervous system in physical illness.

Significant for the field of psychotherapy was the thinking centering on the "motions . . . in the animal economy," which we may identify as nerve impulses.[176] Movement of nerve impulses was thought by Cullen to underlie all disease. As will be described later, Cullen upheld the "neurosis" theory of disease. Explanations of many illnesses, otherwise obscure in their etiology, as gout, were conceived in terms of "neuroses" or nerve diseases. Cullen's definition of neurosis as "those affections of sense or motion . . . which do not depend upon topical affection of organs but upon general affection of the nervous system"[177] demonstrates the influ-

[174] Garrison: An Introduction to the History of Medicine, ed. 3, p. 318, Philadelphia, Saunders, 1921.

[175] Mowat: *Op. cit.*, p. 18.

[176] Riese, Walther: An outline of a history of ideas in neurology, Bull. Hist. Med. 23:111, 1949.

[177] Cullen, William: First Lines of the Practice of Physic, Edinburgh, Creech, 1779-1784.

ence of neurophysiology on neuropsychiatric thinking of this period. William Cullen, whose position as professor of physic at the University of Edinburgh made him an influential figure, wrote a book [178] entitled *Nosology, or a Systematic Arrangement of Diseases by Classes, Orders, Genera and Species.* He divided diseases into several main classes—fevers, neuroses, cachexias, local disorders. Characteristically, he included also vesania (insanity) and oneirodynia (painful dreams, i.e., incubus and somnambulism).

Theoreticians in medicine, principally teachers, were hard put to it to bring understanding to this strange field of neuroses, i.e., diseases without "topical affections." In his discussion of hysterical convulsions, Cullen touched on the emotional and sexual phase of the problem. He perceived that

> it [hysteria] affects the barren more than the breeding woman, and therefore frequently young widows. . . . It occurs in those females who are liable to the nymphomania; and the nosologists [diagnosticians] have properly enough marked one of the varieties of this disease by the title Hysteria libidinosa.[179]

Professor Cullen recognized the relationship, which the Greeks perceived centuries earlier, of hysterical disturbances in the emotional and the sexual life of the patient. He accepted the Hippocratic theory that hysteria was due to a displacement of the ovary. "In what manner," Cullen wrote, "the uterus and in particular the ovaria . . . rise upwards to the brain so as to cause convulsions . . . I cannot explain." Their obeisance made to the Father of Medicine, physicians of Cullen's time preferred to treat hysteria with evil-tasting medicine and indulgent benevolence rather than to probe into the emotional or the sexual life of the patient. The renowned Sydenham prescribed for hysteria: [180] "Let eight ounces of Blood be taken away. Apply Plaister of Galbanum to the Navel. Next A.M. Two drams cochia the greater, cafloreum powder 2 grains, Balsam of Peru, 3 drops, etc."

The struggle to account for inexplicable nervous symptoms continued for decades. Cullen, of whom Pinel wrote,[181] "One English nosologist, Cullen, made sound remarks on the specific character of the delirious mania . . . but . . . [also] futile explanations and gratuitous theories," nevertheless

[178] Cullen, William: Nosology, or a Systematic Arrangement of Diseases by Classes, Orders, Genera and Species with the Distinguishing Characteristics of Each and Outlines of the System of Sauvages, Linnaeus, Vogel, Sagar and Macbride, translated from the original Latin, 1769, London, Bell, Bradfut & Murray, 1810.

[179] *Ibid.*

[180] Dr. Sydenham's Compleat Method of Curing Almost All Diseases, abridged and translated from Latin, ed. 5, p. 6, London, Horne & Parker, 1713.

[181] The Psychiatry of Pinel, Raymond de Saussure, Ciba Symposia, Vol. 11, No. 5, p. 1233, summer, 1950.

was not entirely unaware of the need for a psychology in psychiatry.[182] "I must take notice," Cullen remarks, in the Introduction of his text,

> that to many of you I may appear to deal in Metaphysics; . . . in so far as some analysis of the faculties of the human mind, some account of its general operations is to be so called. I employ Metaphysics because every physiologist has employed them; they have been employed to corrupt and destroy Physiology to a great degree.

Psychology (metaphysics) beckoned students of neurosis in their clinical studies. Consider the suggestion of a French physician who, in studying the confusing symptom of nymphomania, pointed out that "one of the principal points to which a physician ought to attach himself is the study of the effects of the imagination" [183] in obscure illnesses of women. For imagination was "the mother of the greater part of the passions and of their excesses" that eventuated in the disease nymphomania. This condition, incidentally, was in actuality a broad category; as reconstructed from de Bienville's description, it was a combination of puberty longings, adult libidinal sensations, masturbation, leukorrhea, endocervicitis, vulvovaginitis, depression, schizophrenia and psychopathic behavior patterns. More than a century was to pass before the acute clinical perceptions of the nineteenth-century psychiatrists were to separate the effects of emotional morbidity from accompanying somatic pathologic processes.

THE LUNATICK

Let us turn from the consulting rooms of the medical man to the madhouses of the eighteenth century where the insane lay entombed. The emotional force of philosophic and political enlightenment that exploded in the French Revolution also led to emancipation of the insane from their virtual incarceration. All the forces of "natural" religion (Deism), Reason and increased recognition of the Rights of Man pressed for better treatment of Europe's "lunaticks." In and through the attrition of these cultural-psychological forces, physicians gradually became an integral part of the group which finally lifted the dark shadow from the insane.

The "lunatick" houses of the eighteenth century were still dark, foul-smelling dens. A description of Salpêtrière in 1787 by Robin reads:

> Patients massed in fours or more in narrow cells; a dirty sack of straw, with vermin crawling through; rats running in troops by night, eating the clothes,

[182] Thompson, John: An Account of the Life, Lectures and Writings of William Cullen, M.D., Vol. 1, p. 260, Edinburgh, Blackwood, and London, Cadell Strand, 1832.

[183] de Bienville, J. D. T.: Nymphomania, or A Dissertation Concerning the Furor Uterinus, translated from the French by E. S. Wilmot, London, J. Bew, 1775.

the bread, and in time, the flesh of the patients . . . poisoned in their insanity worse than before . . . the more delicate perished in little heaps.[184]

Bethlehem Hospital, in London, was characteristic of the few special institutions for the insane in Europe. In the New World, the State of Virginia established in 1773[185] the first hospital exclusively for "Persons of Unsound Mind" at Williamsburg, where, although chains were used, the atmosphere was more humane than on the Continent. Nevertheless, the story of Bedlam illustrates the status of custodial treatment of the insane up to 1800. Bethlehem, commonly called "Bedlam," was a general hospital established in 1247,[186] which, about the fourteenth century, came to be used exclusively for the insane. The inmates of Bedlam, known as Bedlamites, were composed of lesser criminals of many types, prostitutes, vagrants, beggars and the feeble-minded, in addition to the insane. In time, Bedlam came to be known as a place for punishment of shiftless ne'er-do-wells rather than a hospital offering help. Hogarth's famous portrayal of "The Rake's Progress" shows his descent to ultimate degradation in Bedlam. Unlike the quiet monasteries of earlier days which cared for the insane in kindness and humility, Bedlam became a circus operated for the profit of the wardens. Londoners went of a Sunday afternoon to titter at the madmen on the payment of one shilling.

Demonstration of lunatics as performers purveyed to an unconscious prejudice on the part of society. The lunatic belonged forever to some other world, his mind was irretrievably perverted, stamped by the Evil One with the mark of sin, damned forever. Hogarth's pictures show the large moral element which ran through prevailing notions of mental disease. The lunatic, like the criminal, had left the company of human, righteous individuals; insanity was the price of lechery and tippling. Luna, the moon, was his guiding light, and he dwelt in the "night side" of nature. Mass feelings toward madmen were still tinged with the feeling-tone of witchcraft, and the psychological background which allowed for neglect and cruelty in the management of the insane derived from unconscious but strongly toned social prejudices.

Control of patients in institutions such as Bethlehem passed from the hands of the religious into those of wardens. The early monastic tradition of mercy and loving care for the insane had been carried on by the novices of St. Jean de Dieu and the Order of St. Francis in Europe during the

[184] Robin: Nouvelles de médecin et de chirurgie, A Description of Salpêtrière, p. 107, 1787.

[185] Shryock, R. H.: "The Beginnings: From Colonial Days to the Foundation of the American Psychiatric Association," *in* One Hundred Years of American Psychiatry, p. 16, New York, Columbia, 1944.

[186] O'Donoghue, E. G.: The Story of Bethlehem Hospital from Its Foundation in 1247, London, Unwin, 1914, and New York, Dutton, 1915.

Renaissance and later. St. Vincent de Paul [187] founded the Maison de St. Lazarus in Paris in 1632. One of the figures that perpetuated the tradition of "warmth and consideration" for the insane was Juan Luis Vives, Spanish-born philosopher and educator. A prolific writer, Vives wrote in criticism of scholastic psychology, scoring St. Augustine, among others, for his involved argument and accent on the "soul" as a subject of psychological consideration. "What the soul is, is of no concern for us to know. What its manifestations are, is of great importance." [188] His heresy earned him the position of being suspect, but his practical organization of public relief and insane asylums in France (*circa* 1530) won him acclaim. Noting that the insane and the poor tended to be herded together in workhouses, Vives, in a work called *De Subventione Pauperum* (1526) (The Support of Paupers), called attention to the need not only of their separation but of courteous treatment and the benefits of "enlightenment and instruction" [189] for the insane. An associate of Erasmus and Thomas More, Vives, while in England as lecturer at Oxford, functioned as a molder of empirical psychology during the Renaissance.[190] His predominance in the development of psychology was matched by a practical interest in administration of asylums for the insane during a period when the lunatic was a subhuman spectacle, the cross which society had to bear.

By the beginning of the eighteenth century, activities in the care of the insane by monkish physicians decreased as the social problem of insanity forced municipalities and state governments to place paupers and the mentally ill under the control of lay overseers. The separation of these two groups was a constant administrative problem for those who wished to see justice done; for the calloused overseer, no problem existed. It was noted as an accomplishment, in the time of Vincent de Paul, that inmates whose behavior needed correction, "correctionnaires," were separated from the lunatics. From correction and punishment to care, from exorcism to medical treatment, from neglect to concern, the historical orbit passing from social recrimination to humaneness and back crossed and recrossed the horizons of the insane.

THE THERAPEUTIC BATTLEFIELD

With this gradual change in stewardship came a reorientation of the philosophy of treatment. Management, in the form of punishment, designed

[187] de Saussure, Raymond: Philippe Pinel and the Reform of the Insane Asylums, Ciba Symposia, Vol. 11, No. 5, p. 1222, summer, 1950.

[188] Vives, J. L.: Encyclopædia Britannica, ed. 13, Vol. 23, p. 227, 1945.

[189] Peze, Louise: Les précurseurs de Pinel en France, Thèse de Paris, Paris, L. Arnette, 1922. Jean Louis Vives (1526), "De Subventione Pauperum."

[190] Zilboorg, Gregory, and Henry, G. W.: A History of Medical Psychology, pp. 180 et seq., New York, Norton, 1941.

to calm the madman or to prevent anticipated rages, replaced humanity. Wardens, with the cruelty born of fear and an honest wish to achieve a result, chained, beat and bled these unhappy creatures. Physicians who advised the wardens were under the same defensive influence, masquerading as a therapeutic wish. Cullen, for example, counseled restraint for the safety of the patient and the diminution of excitement. This authority suggested a "constant impression of fear . . . [exerted on the patient] . . . by those in attendance." "Stripes and blows about the body" were advisable, except when the patient did not understand the reason, for then they became "a wanton barbarity." Cullen's feelings were somewhat mixed, since he advised that the "persons who hit should be upon other occasions the bestowers of every indulgence and gratification that is admissable, never however neglecting to employ their awe when their indulgence should have led to any abuse."

In similar vein, John Battie,[191] another English specialist, in his *Treatise on Madness* suggests that reliance is to be placed on the "sagacity of the physician" in treatment. If the excitement did not subside of itself, recourse should be had to the "unaccountably narcotick virtue of the poppy [opium]." If these failed, time-tested methods were relied on, as witness the advice, "Body pain may be excited to purpose and without the least danger. Beating is often serviceable." Battie prescribed "blisters and caustics and rough cathartick" in disturbed patients, to cause pain and discomfort, and hence reduction in excitement. His book demonstrated flashes of insight and a leaning toward scientific thinking, mixed with gropings through a speculative haze and sadistic feelings toward madmen.

If his therapy was positive, Battie's theory of mental disease, on which it was based, was obscure. His involved argument utilized syllogisms of logic rather than information based on observation. But he, no more than his colleagues, groped in an enigmatic field wherein nerves were regarded as carriers of "sensation" and insanity as due to disordered "sensations." Battie wrote:

> From whence we may collect that madness with respect to its cause is distinguishable into two species; the first is solely owing to an internal disorder of the nervous substance being indeed in like manner disordered, but disordered *ab extra:* and therefore is chiefly to be attributed to some remote and accidental cause. The first species until a better name can be found may be called *Original,* the second may be called *Consequential Madness.*

The therapeutic attitude of physicians and wardens alternated between the sadism of punishing treatment and the guilt for having used it. Like despairing parents, physicians did not know whether to apply censure or gentleness to their erring children. Each physician accused the other of

[191] Battie, John: Treatise on Madness, London, Whiston & White, 1758.

ignorance. Battie became involved in several bitter controversies, particularly with Dr. John Monro, then medical superintendent of Bethlehem Hospital. Battie had deplored in his treatise the fact that the public treatment of mental patients was in the hands of "quacks and certain gentlemen (wardens, etc.)." At the same time, Battie, who represented the private-hospital physician, had written a series of papers in which he outlined a very fanciful theory of treatment and management. Dr. Monro, as physician to Bedlam, took violent exception to his writings. In vigorous language, Monro objected to Battie's use of "bleeding, blisters, rough cathartics, the gum and foetid anti-hystericks, opium, mineral waters, cold bathing, vomits." "If these general methods are applied without judgement or discretion," he added, "common sense will at once join with madness and reject them too." While Monro and his fellow workers at Bedlam were beginning to see the need of training attendants to understand their charges, Monro insisted that he "never thought of reading lectures on a subject that could be understood no otherwise than by personal observations." Scornfully he pointed out that Battie's book contained "30 pages of medication, against two pages, which were adorned, on management."

The controversy continued until Battie, a physician with a large London practice, was haled before a House of Commons committee investigating the regulation of madhouses. Monro was on the investigating committee, and the evidence which he elicited from Battie contributed to the drafting of the Bill of 1774 which brought private mental institutions within the regulation of the state.

This bill was a step forward. Until then, persons treating mental patients were without any social responsibility. The public hospitals housing the pauper insane, such as the Salpêtrière in Paris and Bedlam in London, were fortunate in having physicians present to supervise treatment occasionally. The almshouses and smaller asylums depended on a routine which was dictated once in ten years by a physician who was on contract for a period of time. Since insanity was still considered to be a unitary disease, change in the treatment was unnecessary. The routine followed at the Bethlehem Hospital consisted in free bleeding in April and October with plentiful administration of purges and "vomits" through the month of May. All physicians agreed that treatment of the intestinal tract was important in mental cure.

Other routines recommended for raving maniacs were the scarifying and the bleeding of the scalp. The skin was blistered in order to overcome one of the basic causes of insanity, "over-determination of blood to the head." The apologetic apothecary of Bethlehem Hospital, Haslam,[192] with a candor not restricted by medical tradition, reports of the practice of vomiting

[192] Haslam, John: Observations on Insanity, with Practical Remarks on the Disease, and an Account of the Morbid Appearances on Dissection, London, 1798.

patients "frequently and severely: I am sorry that it is not in my power to speak of it favorably." Haslam, for one, did not like the attitude of the gaping crowds who paid for an opportunity to see the howling madmen and chained idiots. He wrote of the need for human understanding of the patient and fair treatment: "It should be the object of the practitioner to remove . . . disease rather than irritate and torment the sufferer." To Haslam, the idea that the mental patient should be beaten for whatever salutary effect it might have appeared ridiculous. "If the patient be so far deprived of understanding why he is punished, such correction, setting aside its cruelty, is manifestly absurd."

The treatment of the insane, a subject on the periphery of medical attention, received impetus through judicial inquiries in England toward the end of the eighteenth century. The recurrent attacks of insanity suffered by King George III and the controversies regarding treatment given by his physicians [193] stimulated much debate. Over the winter of 1788-1789, England was without a ruler. Guttmacher notes that "instead of being seated on his throne, . . . [King George] was much of the time confined in a strait-jacket." [194] Unable to secure results from medication, Doctor Munro, an outstanding practitioner in the field of mental diseases in England, was summoned. Further consultations brought Sir George Baker and Dr. Heberden, who recommended blistering the King's shaved scalp. Advice poured in from the four corners of the world. One advocated "communicating the Itch" to the royal patient. Another recommended the ingestion of the blood of an ass, to which the brains of a ram were to be added.[195] Finally, Dr. Francis Willis, clergyman turned psychiatrist, was called in. From the first, Doctor Willis showed skill in handling his patient. He employed a combination of leniency and firmness for which he was deservedly renowned.

The House of Commons, aroused that His Majesty did not seem to improve under his advisors, held an investigation as to King George's ability to attend Parliament. During the hearings in January, 1789, a bitter controversy broke out between mentors Warren and Willis as to the need for force in subduing the King during his delirious period. Warren made the statement that he would rather have persons of common sense, such as nurses, attend the King than men who purported to be mental specialists. Willis countered that his royal patient would recover, and that "as a rule" his patients recovered if they were brought to him within three months of the onset of the illness. The committee investigating deemed that the report of the hearings "must be published immediately in the public interest." The psychiatric controversy occasioned by Willis' use of restraints raged

[193] Guttmacher, M. S.: America's Last King, New York, Scribner, 1941.
[194] *Ibid.*, p. 188.
[195] *Ibid.*, p. 205.

for years, having the virtue of focusing attention on the efficiency or the lack of it of drastic treatment for madmen.

In spite of his use of strait jackets, the skills which Willis possessed in handling mental cases should have given him, comments Wilson, "a larger place in the history of mankind than he has yet received." [196] His ability to lay aside "all false pretences, all petty vexations, all unnecessary restraints" [197] presaged the inauguration of the moral treatment of insanity.

For decades the struggle continued between coercion and force on one hand and kindness and personal attention on the other. The latter part of the eighteenth century was the nodal point at which the forces of humanitarianism and political emancipation met the bankruptcy of medical science to heal the mentally distraught. Alert, rational, politically conscious and mechanistically minded, the eighteenth century nurtured the humanitarian management of the insane, thus forging another weapon in the perpetual fight against social sadism. It was the nodal point that turned the tide against misidentifying the insane with evil and identifying them with humanity. This period of medical history ranks high with the era a century later that established the bacteriologic cause of disease and the earlier period that gave the world anesthesia.

The dawn of a new attitude toward the mental patient was at hand in the closing years of the eighteenth century when Philippe Pinel, defying custom and tradition, struck the irons from his insane wards at Bicêtre, in France. History usually accords Pinel the honor of having drawn aside the curtain, but the Italian, Vincenzio Chiarugi, freed the insane from their chains at the Bonifazio Asylum, in Florence, ten years before Pinel entered Bicêtre. Although Livi,[198] in championing Chiarugi's claim for historical honor, complained that "the French, a fervid, enterprising race . . . aspire to primacy in everything," the fact is that both men share the glory of emancipating the buried insane, for their acts virtually set in motion a new department of human endeavor.

PINEL THE LIBERATOR

A shy, retiring man, Dr. Philippe Pinel had "found his way" acting as physician for the insane in Dr. Belhomme's sanitarium in Paris.[199] In the second year of the French Revolution, Pinel called upon his friends, asking for support for a new project which would apply to the insane the practice

[196] Wilson, P. W.: William Pitt, the Younger, pp. 184, 185, Garden City, N. Y., Doubleday, 1930.

[197] *Ibid.*

[198] Workman, Joseph: Life of Chiarugi, a translation of a letter by Livi (September, 1864), Alienist & Neurologist 3:93, 1882.

[199] Semelaigne, René: Les grands aliénistes français, Vol. 1, p. 31, Paris, Stein & Neil, 1894.

of humaneness about which Marat and Danton were thundering in the National Assembly. Why not give to those miserable creatures the benefits of Liberty and Equality? Thouret, Commissioner of Public Safety in 1793, and Cabanis, physician to Mirabeau, were staunchly in favor of enlightenment. But Thouret was a realist; earlier, acting for the Faculty of Medicine, he had upheld science in denouncing Franz Mesmer when he sought official sanction for his "animal magnetism," remarking that Mesmer's universal treatment was "an illusion which cannot be excused in an enlightened age." Apparently Cabanis and Thouret were impressed by Pinel's plan, for, in their role of Administrators of the Hospitals of Paris, they granted his request and appointed him physician to the lunatic asylum of the Bicêtre in August, 1793. As a bespectacled, tongue-tied young student, Pinel, appearing before Thouret, prefect of the Faculty of Medicine, had sought the prize for an essay answering the question, "Give the best ways of effectively treating the insane." But Pinel was destined to answer in a way that his professors little dreamed.

Pinel, appointment in hand, approached Couthon, the prison-commission member of the Paris Commune, and explained his proposal. Couthon, a hardened warden, listened impatiently to the doctor. "Why not," he satirically suggested, "proceed to the *zoo* and liberate the lions and tigers?" Pinel persisted and finally Couthon agreed. They entered the halls; at the sound of three hundred maniacs screaming and clanking their chains, Couthon drew back. "Citizen," he said to Pinel, "are not you yourself crazy that you would free these beasts?" Pinel replied, "I am convinced that the *people* are not incurable if they can have air and liberty." [200] Entering the cell of an English captain who was believed to be particularly dangerous because he had once killed an attendant with a blow from his manacles, Pinel called the attendants and ordered the fetters struck. The old man tried to walk; he could not. He had been in chains for forty years. After many attempts he tottered from his dark cell to the corridor, where he could see the sky. "Ah," he cried, "how beautiful!" The second to be released was a drunkard, Chevigne by name. For ten years he had been in chains. His mind disordered, combative and surly, he was considered incurable. Pinel went to him, took off the iron anklets and handcuffs. The vicious sot stood up, and, with a courtly flourish, bowed to Pinel. He became a model of good conduct and in time was released.

Pinel passed on among his newly acquired charges, encouraging one, talking to another. He unleashed some from stone posts in which anklets and chains were riveted, removed patients from dungeons, some of whom had lain there on filthy straw mats for years. He dosed his patients with a new kind of medicine, a medicine mentioned nowhere in the treatises

[200] *Ibid.*, p. 42.

read by the doctors of the 1790's. This new drug was kindness. Skeptical Couthon could not believe his eyes. "Citizen," he said sharply to Pinel, "I will visit you in the Bicêtre tomorrow and woe to you if you have deceived us and concealed enemies of the people among thy madmen." The enemies of the people were not to be found in the asylum; only a friend was there.

With what Semelaigne describes as "superior practical sense," Pinel brought order into the administration. Later he was given charge of the Salpêtrière, where he continued "piling up his great store of ideas." [201] Slowly and methodically Pinel built up a clinical psychiatry [202] and a theory and practice of psychotherapy.

The success of his venture and the radical nature of his ideas attracted attention throughout Europe. When Pinel's *Treatise on Insanity* was published in London in 1806, the translator, Dr. D. D. Davis, observed that in distinction to most treatises, which were "advertisements of lunatic establishments under the superintendence of their respective authors," Pinel's book was the work of an "enlightened foreigner." The great contribution of Pinel and his followers was the recognition that an insane person was not another kind of being, but simply a human being with an illness, with which physicians, without loss of dignity, could grapple.

For maniacal fury Pinel recommended the "bland arts of conciliation or the tone of irresistible authority pronouncing an irreversible mandate." Violence was absolutely forbidden. In its place Pinel substituted the burden of humane management on the shoulders of the physicians whose "many great qualities both of mind and body . . . are necessary in order to meet the endless difficulties and exigences" of the maniac's situation. Pinel impressed an idea of great significance on his confreres by insisting that the physician must be a man in whom kindness and humanity predominated. Such a physician must be able to project himself into the situation of the patient. He put considerable store in the ability of hospital superintendents to command respect through voice and manner. Moral persuasion, Pinel said, is better than threat and force, and the forceful personality of the physician is the greatest factor in success.

The second edition of Pinel's *Treatise* stressed the extension of the moral treatment to the hospital as a human unit: [203]

> One of the principal rules in a well-regulated hospital is to have a central authority who shall decide without appeal, having the sole control over both

[201] *Ibid.*, p. 51.

[202] Pinel, Philippe: A treatise on insanity in which are contained the principles of a new and more practical nosology of maniacal disorders than has yet been offered the public, exemplified by numerous and accurate historical relations of cases from the authors of public and private practice, with plates illustrative of craneology, of maniacs and idiots, translated from the French, Sheffield, England, 1806.

[203] ——: Traité médico-philosophique sur l'aliénation mentale, 1809, ed. 2. *Quoted in* Galt, J. M.: The Treatment of Insanity, New York, Harper, 1846.

domestics and patients, and being never interfered with either by any other officer or by the friends of the patients. I am opposed, for many reasons, to blows as a means of cure; which measure has been in constant use; . . . and which was used by a farmer in Scotland, who worked patients sent to him as beasts of burden, and who was famous for the cure of insanity. Blows are incompatible with the character of the French nation, and would rather suit those who had been always slaves.

THE QUAKER INFLUENCE

In England, a similar development was taking root, initiated by William Tuke, a tea merchant. Inflamed by the ill-treatment of a mental case which came to his attention, Tuke, in 1796, induced the Society of Friends, of which he was a member, to organize a retreat under his supervision in York. William Tuke proposed to treat cases on the basis of the humane religious spirit of Quakerism. Mental patients, he felt, were like children, inaccessible to the ordinary motives of fear or honor, but, as children, they required to be taught and encouraged. The regimen established featured medical treatment with "moral therapy, encouragement and judicious kindness," in addition to suitable work for convalescing mental patients. And the retreat featured the innovation of a physician in charge of the patients.

The initiation and the development of the York Retreat was a direct reflection of the Quaker conception of closeness to God which meant unity with the brotherhood of man. The Society of Friends as a religious group was founded on a view of man's contact with the spirit of God as an immediate experience—a personal response to an Inner Light. The Quakers have been "the most practical mystics the world has ever seen." [204] George Fox, the founder of the Society, fought the idea of excessive punishment of criminals in the eighteenth century, and the Society has since been identified with humanitarian projects. Nevertheless, William Tuke had considerable opposition to overcome in putting his ideas into action. His fellow members protested, and even Tuke's wife [205] pleaded with him against the project, "William, thou hast had many children of thy brain, but this will prove an idiot." [206]

The first report published by the York Retreat proclaimed that the hospital was not operated as a prison, as was the contemporary institution in London, Bedlam, but embodied the "idea of a rural farm." Not a physician himself, Tuke insisted that "bleeding, blisters, seatons, evacuants

[204] Comfort, W. W.: Just Among Friends, The Quaker Way of Life, p. 9, Philadelphia, Blakiston, 1945.

[205] The Retreat, York, Addresses Given During the 150th Anniversary Celebrations, William Sessions, York, Ebor Press, 1946.

[206] Mennell, R. O.: Personal communication, Kenley, Surrey, England, February, 1943.

. . . appear too inefficacious to deserve the appellation as remedies." He observed "how much was to be done by moral means and how little by any known medical means" in the relief of mental patients. Physicians also noted that after the acute maniacal excitement was over in many of their cases, patients responded to a regimen of encouragement, kindliness and routine work. William Tuke's work was carried on by his grandson, Samuel Tuke, author of a widely read book on the Retreat.[207] The York Retreat supported, managed and lived in by "the family," became a mecca for observers from the Continent and America. Independently of Pinel, the Tukes brought to their patients a true moral management, "the little nameless unremembered acts of kindness and of love." [208]

Yet, while the leaders who have been singled out were exerting pressure for a better treatment of mentally disturbed patients, the average medical practitioner neglected or avoided his mental charges or treated them as purely medical problems. The embryo field of psychiatry and the new moral treatment concerned them little. If these principles were known by the general run of physicians, they were not reflected in their day-by-day management of nervous patients. Doctors were also apparently unaware of the emerging philosophic and psychological trends which were to shape a neurology and psychiatry in the nineteenth century. The associationism of Hartley and Hume which led to empiricism and the detailed study of sensation, the faculty psychology based on Christian Wolff's ideas (1734) and developed by many to a high point in the first half of the nineteenth century, had not yet been incorporated into a science of mental therapy. Although associationism, in a sense, "made" psychology a scientific field, it did not contribute directly to psychotherapeutic methods for a century. Nor did faculty psychology, except as it was diverted into Gall's phrenology, contribute even indirectly to the field of psychotherapy. Philosophic idealism (Kant), with its spurring of intellectual pursuits and focusing on the mind, on individual inner life, needs and values, initially did not bring stimulation to the psychotherapeutic discipline. The specific influence of these eighteenth-century trends on psychotherapy operated only after a prolonged time-lag and through the uniquely unrelated efforts of Mesmer, Gall, Tuke, Pinel, Rush, Bell, Magendie and a host of neurologists, physicians, experimenters, practical philosophers and mystics.

The generalizations given above as to the influence on psychotherapy of philosophic-psychological trends suffer as do all generalizations from the presence of exceptions. Stimulated by the direction of political and philosophic inquiry of the time, there were men who thought deeply on the

[207] Tuke, Samuel: Description of the Retreat in the Institution in York, for Insane Persons of the Society of Friends, Containing an Account of Its Origin and Progress and Means of Treatment and Statement of Cases, York, England, 1813.

[208] The Retreat, York: *Op. cit.*, p. 24.

relation of mind and society, and body and mind. The physicist Lichtenberg,[209] a friend of Kant about whom Goethe wrote, "We can use Lichtenberg's writings as the most marvelous divining-rod; where he makes a joke, a problem lies hidden," wrote in 1769:

> There are certainly just as many, if not more, people imaginatively sick as there are those who are really sick. There are just as many people, if not more, imaginatively sane as there are people who are really sane.

In spite of Lichtenberg's cynicism:

> There is hardly in the world a stranger ware than books. Printed by people who don't understand them; bought by people who don't understand them; bound, reviewed and read by people who don't understand them; and even written by people who don't understand them.

there was a spirit of optimism in the social atmosphere, during the Age of Enlightenment reflected in utterances of men of education and good will, which was indirectly related to a psychotherapeutic attitude. Consider a statement discovered in a church in Gotha, Germany (1784), which proclaimed a cause for rejoicing:

> Our age occupies the happiest period of the eighteenth century. Emperors, kings, and princes humanely descend from their dreaded heights, despise pomp and splendor, become the fathers, friends, and confidants of their people. Religion rends its priestly garb and appears in its divine essence. Enlightenment makes great strides. Thousands of our brothers and sisters, who formerly lived in sanctified inactivity, are given back to the state. Sectarian hatred and persecution for conscience' sake are vanishing. Love of man and freedom of thought are gaining the supremacy. The arts and sciences are flourishing, and our gaze is penetrating deeply into the workshop of nature. Handicraftsmen as well as artists are reaching perfection, useful knowledge is growing among all classes. Here you have a faithful description of our times.[210]

But since these concepts were still expressed in philosophic and social terms, unassimilated concretely into medicine or early psychiatry, we can agree that medicine had scarcely entered the field of psychotherapy by the last two decades of the eighteenth century.

The effect of a rudimentary clinical psychology and neurology on modern psychotherapy can be more easily stated than traced at this point in our narrative, and it can be stated most clearly in terms of individual medical leaders. Such a one was the illustrious American physician, Benjamin Rush. At the time that Rush was active, surgery and medicine had progressed in the Colonies in close relation to European concepts. But psychiatry undeveloped in the States was virtually catapulted to medical

[209] Loewenberg, R. D.: A review of Georg Christoph Lichtenberg, ETC 1:102, 103, winter, 1943-1944.

[210] Randall, J. H., Jr.: The Making of the Modern Mind, A Survey of the Intellectual Background of the Present Age, rev. ed., p. 384, Boston, Houghton, 1940.

attention by the vigorous, embattled, moralizing yet scientific man who became the Father of American Psychiatry.

FATHER OF AMERICAN PSYCHIATRY

Rush, who had been a student under Cullen in Edinburgh, Scotland, was appointed to the Pennsylvania Hospital in Philadelphia in 1783. He soon became impressed by the needs of patients "afflicted by madness" and agitated for the erection of a separate building for the insane at the Pennsylvania Hospital, insisting that the mad should be the "first objects" of a physician's attention.[211] In 1792, the Legislature appropriated $15,000 for this building. For thirty years as practitioner and teacher of medicine, Rush studied and treated the insane, exhorting his fellow physicians to strive to "lessen a portion of some of the greatest evils of human life." In 1812, his observations were gathered into a textbook on psychiatry [212] which stood as the American authority on mental disease until the 1880's.

Rush's contribution to psychotherapy was consonant with his personality and intellectual vigor. He brought a physician's concentration and a sincere, although formal and moralistic, attitude toward the private mental patient. Rush, who considered himself essentially a doctor and, therefore, always right, did not hesitate to use drastic therapy on mental patients with an assurance that was irksome to his colleagues and embarrassing to his commentators.

Subscribing to the theory that "the cause of madness is seated primarily in the blood vessels of the brain," Rush was admittedly an ardent blood-letter. Since "overcharging" the brain with blood was the cause of mental disease, relief was obtained by depleting the body of blood to the point of causing faintness and debility. Bleeding was carried out vigorously; an average of 20 to 40 ounces (600 to 1,200 cc.) of blood was let per treatment. Commenting on the technical problem of having the patient stand during blood-letting to induce fainting more quickly, Rush recommended keeping the patient in an erect posture for 24 hours at a time. Taking his cue from a method of taming refractory horses in England, "by first impounding them . . . and then keeping them from lying down or sleeping by thrusting sharp pointed nails into their bodies for two or three days and nights," Rush saw the same advantages of keeping madmen awake in a standing posture, "for four and twenty hours, but by different and more lenient means." This would fatigue the muscles and "the debility thus induced in those muscles would attract morbid excitement from the brain,

[211] Goodman, N. G.: Benjamin Rush, Physician and Citizen, Philadelphia, Univ. Penn. Press, 1934.

[212] Rush, Benjamin: Medical Inquiries and Observations upon the Diseases of the Mind, p. 9, Philadelphia, Kimber & Richardson, 1812.

and thereby relieve the disease." Having reduced the action of the blood vessels "to a par of debility of the nervous system," he proceeded in workmanlike fashion to stimulate the body with diet, alcoholic beverages, emetics, bitters, alkaline salts, asafetida, tar infused in water and garlic and the "noble" medicine, laudanum. This was followed by a routine of baths, massage, exercise, with perhaps blistering and cupping.

In Rush's hands the theory of depletion and stimulation was advanced with more vigor, though with no more persistence, than was common among good psychiatrists of the period. Many physicians had worked on the problem of mental stimulation for "torpid" cases. For example, Dr. Cox,[213] of London, secured mental stimulation through the action of a "rotator." This was an ingenious device consisting of a cage moved by a set of pulleys which rotated the patient to the point of nausea and prostration. Cox reported a case of a furious maniac who was treated for eight days, rotation lasting six minutes each treatment. The first day the patient became pale and was carried to bed, where he slept. The next day rotation lasted four minutes, followed by prostration. The next day he refused to eat and was rotated four minutes again. "He had abundant vomiting," the notes read, but seemed more calm; after further treatment the patient was finally "reduced of his mania." Even Christian Reil [214] had invented a movable wheel which operated like a squirrel cage, "the least motion making the patient toss about," thus forcing him "to repose." Good medical opinion, as summarized by John Galt, recommended rotation (1) as a means of coercion, (2) in mania, (3) in monomania for sluggishness. These stimulating apparatuses were used in alternation with immobilizing devices. An interesting piece of equipment used for "repression" of maniacs consisted of an osier cage the length of a man with a mattress on bottom and a lid at the head, in which the patient was completely immobilized without chance of self-injury.

Rush's own machine, the gyrator, for "torpid madness" and the tranquilizing chair for maniacal states were simply applications of generally accepted principles. In common with Cox's "rotator" [215] the gyrator subjected the patient to rotary motion so as to give a centrifugal direction of the blood toward the brain until nausea, vertigo and perspiration were produced. The tranquilizer was a chair in which the patient was strapped at the ankles, the wrist, across the chest and the abdomen, his head being confined in a wooden box. Rush invented the tranquilizing chair in reaction to the "mad shirt" or strait-waistcoat which did not allow for bleeding. In Rush's treatment, the patient in the tranquilizing chair was bled until his

[213] Cox, J. M.: Practical Observations on Insanity, London, C. & R. Baldwin, 1806.
[214] Galt, J. M.: The Treatment of Insanity, p. 181, New York, Harper, 1846.
[215] Overholser, Winfred: Cox and Trotter, Two Psychiatric Precursors of Benjamin Rush, Address, Vidonian Club, New York, October 27, 1951.

reason returned or his pulse diminished. The original description of the apparatus,[216] with line drawing, was accompanied by the report of case, A. D., whose pulse was 96 strokes to the minute when he was placed in the tranquilizer:

> Upon examining him an hour after I found the pulse diminished in frequency 6 strokes. Upon the 2nd hour the fullness diminished. By the 4th hour his pulse was nearly normal and the ferocious looks of the maniac were changed to an agreeable aspect.

The need for remedies acting through the medium of the mind, in contradistinction to equipment operating on the brain and its vascular structure, was not lost on Rush. In his lectures he urged that the attitude of the physician be fitted to the mood of the patient. In melancholia, one must be gentle. In mania, a different address was needed, for "the dread of the eye was early imposed on the beast in the field . . . tygre and mad bull all fly from it" and hence "a man deprived of his reason . . . is terrified or composed by the eye" of a sane man.[217] If a stern eye did not suffice, obedience could be secured by a firm voice and countenance of the physician, or through acts of justice or kindness. If this was not effective, pouring cold water under the coat sleeve, so that it might descend to the armpits and down the trunk of the body, was advised. If these methods of punishment "did not suffice," it would be proper to resort to the fear of death, and Rush quotes several cases in which fear of death was followed by mental improvement.

Another psychological technic used by Rush was based on the hoped-for "reflux action" of resentment and mortification to banish delusions from the minds of patients. A case is related of a patient who believed himself to be a plant and was persuaded that unless he were watered he would not live. He was treated daily by ablutions of water from the spout of a teapot. In reality, a friend was discharging his urine upon the patient's head, and in the "reflux" resentment and mortification of the incident, the patient was cured.[218]

PSYCHOLOGICAL THERAPY IN THE 1830'S

The impingement of strong emotion of terror and mortification on patients was a spectacular variant of the general theory that morbid preoccupations of the patient must be removed to allow free expression of basic

[216] Rush, Benjamin: Essays Literary, Moral and Philosophical, ed. 2, p. 183, Philadelphia, Bradford, 1806.
[217] *Ibid.*, p. 175.
[218] *Ibid.*, p. 110.

healthy trends. One statement of this theory, adapted by a phrenologist,[219] was "to regulate the exercise of the different powers of the mind, so as not to leave those which are naturally in excess in undisturbed sway over the rest." Driving morbid ideas from the patient's mind became a specific aim of psychiatric treatment; in the hands of some physicians, it consisted in a type of mental legerdemain calculated to outwit patients. A patient of Pinel who believed that his head had been cut off was cured after being forcibly exposed to view the head of one who had been guillotined. Rush recites the case of an opium addict treated by her physician who

> took a large snuff-box out of his pocket. She looked at it as if she wished for a pinch of snuff. The physician put it into her hands. Upon opening it, an artificial snake that had been coiled up in it, suddenly leaped upon her shoulder. She was convulsed with terror, and from that time left off the use of opium and rapidly recovered.[220]

As late as 1883, textbooks of psychiatry discussed the possibility of removing delusion by bringing external influences to bear. In an institution near Philadelphia, the superintendent occasionally fired a shot alongside mental patients in an attempt to free them of their delusions.[221]

The development of a therapy directed toward the "mind" was carried to an advanced point by an ingenious French physician, Leuret. His technic, a type of crude conditioning, forcibly repressed the expression of every insane or morbid idea by giving the patient a douche each time he uttered the delusion. Leuret combated passions by passions; he would place himself face to face with the patient, struggling with the latter's ideas, behavior and determination. If the patient was adamant, Leuret was doubly so. If the patient developed an ingenious delusional system, Leuret outdid him. He used pain as a "motive power" which banished evil and sought to replace morbid ideas by good. Convinced of Pinel and Esquirol's doctrine of acceptance and compassion for the insane, Leuret did not hesitate to enter into and combat the patients' inner mental struggle: "To passion, abuse and blows, oppose sangfroid and compassion." [222] Leuret's promise,[223] which he later modified, encompassed "the use of all methods that directly agitate the intelligence and emotions of the insane . . . without

219 Combe, Andrew: Observations on Mental Derangement, Being an Application of the Principles of Phrenology to the Elucidations of Causes, Symptoms, Nature and Treatment of Insanity, p. 277, Boston, Marsh, Capen & Lyon, 1834.

220 Rush, Benjamin: Medical Inquiries and Observations upon the Diseases of the Mind.

221 Spitzka, E. C.: Insanity; Its Classification, Diagnosis, and Treatment, p. 401, New York, Treat, 1883.

222 Leuret, Francis: Du traitement moral de la folie, Paris, Baillière, 1840.

223 ———: Biographical notice: *A Brièvre de Boismont gaz. Médicale de Paris,* Am. J. Insanity 8:361, 1852.

recourse to physical methods." His work represented a courageous and premature attempt to enter the chaotic terrain of the insane mind.

Pinel's influence, however, remained the most pervasive. His "moral" tradition was ably carried forward by his student, Esquirol. Faithfully propagating his master's program, Jean Etienne Dominique Esquirol, the moving spirit of the Salpêtrière, laid the foundation for French psychiatry admired the world over. Joining Pinel in condemning the "bath of surprise" and the abuse of blood-letting among the insane, Esquirol set the tone by stating, "One has to love the mentally sick in order to be worthy and capable of serving them." His text, *Des maladies mentales considérées sous les rapports médical, hygiénique et médicolegal,*[224] appearing in 1838, is considered the first modern treatise on clinical psychiatry. The calm, measured description of mental cases provided by Esquirol, his indefatigable efforts in behalf of the rights of the mentally ill as embodied in the Law of 1838 which he drafted,[225] contrasted with the drastic methods of treatment such as exemplified by purges, venesection or mechanical gyrators. The saneness of Esquirol's work contrasted also with such erratic attempts at influencing the insane as Cox's rotator, which Haslam called a "whimsical mode of treatment," or Cox's discussion of music therapy [226] with its effect on patients:

> Torpid patients—SCREECHES and YELLS, made in an apartment painted *Black* and *red* or *glaring* white . . . or an opposite state . . . patient to be placed in *airy* room, surrounded with *flowers breathing odours,* the walls colored *green* and the air agitated by softest harmony.

Wider acceptance of the "moral" treatment during the early decades of the nineteenth century brought a deeper appreciation of the difficulties of modifying a patient's "mind" and the importance of the instrument required—the physician himself. Gentleness and kindness, which the Tukes employed, sufficed only until a more abiding and pervasive relationship was set up between patient and physician. Pinel intuitively understood the doctor's part in the therapeutic process; his life-infusing calm, his warm interest, his deep humanity, were large factors in moral management. Others who followed sought with greater consciousness to achieve Pinel's benignity, for, after their heroic methods of gyration, rotation, venesection and purging were exhausted, physicians to the insane were acutely aware of the emotional drain occasioned by mental patients upon themselves. These physicians, in their efforts to carry further the burden they had assumed, gradually augmented the "moral" treatment, the business of supplying an

[224] Esquirol, J. E.: Mental Maladies, A Treatise on Insanity, translated by E. K. Hunt, Philadelphia, Lea & Blanchard, 1845.

[225] Amdur, M. K., and Messinger, E.: Jean Etienne Dominique Esquirol, Am. J. Psychiat. 96:129-135, 1939.

[226] Cox, J. M.: *Op. cit.,* p. 61.

atmosphere of love, by the more difficult task of modifying the patient's behavior and morbid ideas.

In the preceding century, exhortation, colored by a religious idealism, was thought to answer that need: as witness the therapeutic admonition of Jean Dumas [227] in his treatise on suicide, "Instinct and reason are the foremost means by which God makes his will known to us, proving that he wants us to preserve ourselves and not to destroy ourselves." In the nineteenth century, exhortation softened by a sobering recognition of the profundity of the problem was replaced to some degree by an attempt to control emotion at its primary source—the mind.

It is safe to say that there were few psychiatrists who did not ponder a method which would effectively influence the mad world of delusions and morbid passions otherwise than through venesection, purging and "agitation." Among others, Benjamin Rush, in the midst of his efforts to deplete his patients, thought in terms of a mental therapy. His recommendation to the managers of the Pennsylvania Hospital for a man "of education" who would superintend the "Lunaticks . . . to walk with them, converse with them, etc. in order to awaken and regulate their minds" [228] bespoke his insight in spite of his espousal of the "penetrating eye" which would overwhelm the madman and "arrest the thoughts as they arise." Other men also recognized the hopeless nature of such dramatic methods. Haslam,[229] the perspicacious director at Bethlehem who carried the title of "apothecary" to the hospital, complained that "carrying no thunder in my voice, nor lightning in my eye," he had to rely on knowing his patient's history, on a mild manner and a real interest in his patient's problems. Haslam disbelieved the arresting cure, the dramatic collapse of a mania, under the weight of a physician's personality. When he met such "gentlemen . . . gifted with this awful imposition of the eye . . . I have never been able to persuade them to practice this rare talent tête à tête with a furious lunatic." The notion of individual therapeutic contact was not entirely new; Rush's "man of education" had been foreshadowed (1677) by a suggestion to use a chaplain at Bethlehem Hospital who was to "pray with lunatics as are capable of it." [230] Undoubtedly also there was considerable personal contact with individual patients which was not dignified by the term psychotherapy or moral treatment.

Forty years of the moral treatment softened some of the expectations

227 Dumas, Jean: Traité du suicide, ou du meurtre volontaire de soi-même, Chap. 3, Amsterdam, D. J. Changuion, 1773.

228 Rush, Benjamin: The Autobiography, His Travels Through Life Together with his Commonplace Book, edited by G. W. Corner, Am. Philos. Soc., Princeton, 1948.

229 Haslam, John: Observations on Madness and Melancholy, ed. 2, London, J. Callow & G. Hayden, 1809.

230 Burrows, G. M.: Commentaries on the Causes, Forms, Symptoms and Treatment Moral and Medical of Insanity, London, Underwood, 1828.

of success hoped for by physicians to the insane. In 1835, Prichard[231] summarized the state of psychotherapy through moral means by stating the maxim that it is not well

> to direct the attention of patients to the subjects on which their illusions turn, or to oppose their unreasonable prejudices by argument, or contradiction. . . . It is better to excite interest in connection with things remote from the morbid train of thought.

The deliverance of mental patients from chains and fetters still left the problem of control and management a vital one. Translated into practical terms, kindness was recognized as the right of the patient, but "obedience is the ground of the physicians' management."[232] What Heinroth, the German authority, stated in restrained terms, another German, Dr. Teschallener, of Tyrol, put more realistically, "Kindness . . . is my right hand, as earnestness and severity are my left."[233]

The twin problems of restraint and application of the moral treatment gradually took precedence over specific medical treatment during the early decades of the nineteenth century. Reliance on blood-letting had faded, although nauseating and purging drugs were still used in quantities on mental patients. "Day-long" restraints, "surprise baths" wherein the patient, passing over a trap door, fell into a concealed tub of water, were still popular. Striking the maniacs with hand or club from time to time was utilized on the theory that the insane were insensible to pain or to physical discomfort. In spite of an occasional writer's statement that the introduction of moral management allows the discontinuance of "coercion by blows, stripes and chains," although sanctioned by the authority of Celsus and Cullen,[234] the use of force was common in asylum practice. The practical problem of violent behavior was met by mechanical appliances which had as their purpose a humane application of restraint, but which in our day appear to be far more cruel than was ever intended by the innovators.

Restraint in public institutions was accomplished by means of iron rings on ankles and wrists. Patients chained to the floor were considered put "into treatment" for the day and left to wallow in excrement. Other patients were washed with a broom and doused with cold water in the open courtyard. Deaths were falsified in the annual reports. Implements resembling medieval armor were openly in use and condoned by authority. The commissioners investigating the Lincoln Asylum (England) in 1820 came upon

[231] Prichard, J. C.: A Treatise on Insanity and Other Disorders Affecting the Mind, London, Sherwood, Gilbert & Piper, 1835.
[232] Earle, Pliny: Institutions for the insane in Prussia, Austria and Germany, Am. J. Insanity, Vol. 9, April, 1853.
[233] *Ibid.*, p. 326.
[234] Beck, T. R.: An Inaugural Dissertation on Insanity, pp. 27, 28, New York, 1811.

padded iron collars, heavy, cumbrous leathern muffs, belts with manacles, solid iron wrist-locks, jointed iron leg-locks or hobbles and the quarter-boots of Dr. Charlesworth, a well-thought-of man in insanity, to keep feet secured to foot-board.

From Rush's tranquilizing chair to Dr. Charlesworth's quarter-boot to the Utica crib or Aubanel's [235] restraining bed, the basic theory was relief of the patient from the destructive effects of his mania.

[235] Hamilton, S. W.: "The History of American Mental Hospitals," *in* One Hundred Years of American Psychiatry, p. 107, New York, Columbia, 1944.

5

The Era of Asylums

The gradual change in designation given institutions for mental cases in the early nineteenth century, from "madhouse" to "asylum," sheds light on society's acceptance of the new therapeutic attitude toward the insane. Although consummation of this attitude in terms of modern mental hygiene and medical psychology was not immediately achieved, the slow infiltration of the moral treatment over the decades lifted the insane from their position of obloquy and condemnation to that of being befriended and sheltered and finally treated as ill human beings. With this development of social conscience arose technical problems that exercised all the ingenuity that physicians who attended the insane could muster. These will be outlined in this chapter, as they exerted profound influences on the science of psychotherapy.

One of the early problems encountered by the asylum doctor was that of management. With the recognition that asylums and retreats could be adapted to treatment came the need for organization and administrative procedures. Even in the sixteenth century, monks of the 3rd order of St. Francis had developed detailed rules of administration [236] to replace the haphazard methods of centuries before, and, long before the Tukes, St. Vincent de Paul appreciated that organization and an ordered life were vital to the care of mental patients. Before Pinel introduced the notion of a central authority for a "well-regulated hospital," Louis XVI's Minister of Finance, Necker, in 1780 appointed Colombier and Doublet medical inspectors of insane asylums throughout France. In 1785, reforms were instituted in the organization of mental hospitals on the recommendation of the inspectors, but the reforms which *l'ancien régime* started to put into practice "were blocked by the Revolution."

In this spirit of administrative organization, Johann Christian Reil, a universal medical talent of his time, contributed the new viewpoint to Germany. In 1803, a work appeared by Dr. Reil, professor at the Univer-

[236] Peze, Louise: Les Précurseurs de Pinel en France, Thèse de Paris, Paris, L. Arnette, 1922.

sity of Halle, Germany, under the title *Rhapsodies on the Application of Mental Treatment to Insanity.*[237] Reil, an ophthalmologist and a neurologist of first rank, showed a strong grasp of problems of the mentally ill. He was one of the first to study the construction of mental hospitals and to urge the segregation of different types of insane cases. Although Reil rarely saw mental cases in his practice, and apparently did not have contact with an asylum, reasoning led him to make a strong plea for the medical consideration of mental patients.

The "new" theory that the insane were treatable encouraged the erection of many special institutions where the "curables" could be isolated from the "incurables." In Germany, under the leadership of Langermann, new asylums were built, or old ones remodeled, to accommodate the treatment needs of the "curables." During the first three decades of the century, public asylums in Saxony, Schleswig, Heidelberg, Prague, were built [238] for new patients, and older institutions were set aside for the incurable epileptics, idiots and dements. Against the abstruse discussion of the philosophy of insanity, the morbid psychology of the soul, etc., which was the preoccupation of German psychiatrists, the "English practice" of using asylums for treatment made headway.

French psychiatrists, following their Master, Pinel, turned asylums into hospitals. Bicêtre, Salpêtrière, in Paris, and Charenton, under Esquirol's direction, became the pivotal points for the elaboration of Pinel's ideas. As in England, the older asylums in France were rededicated to the newer methods of management.

In America, special institutions for the insane were rapidly becoming accomplished facts. General hospitals had been admitting mental cases for years. The Pennsylvania Hospital, Philadelphia, opened in February, 1752, had maintained an "insane department" [239] from the start as a prominent part of "this noble charity." In New York, in 1745, a building on the "precise spot where now stands City Hall" [240] received the sick, the indigent poor and "the maniac." In company with the Pennsylvania Hospital,[241] the New York Hospital, in New York City, utilized its basement for the mentally ill until thirty years later (1821), when the trustees established the Bloomingdale Asylum as a separate institution for the insane.

[237] Boldt, Arnold: On the Position and Meaning of Rhapsodies on the Application of Psychic Methods of Treatment to the Insane of Johann Christian Reil in the History of Psychiatry, Abh. zur Geschichte der Med. und der Naturalwissenschaft, Vol. 12, 1936.

[238] Griesinger, W.: Mental Pathology and Therapeutics, translated by C. L. Robertson and J. Rutherford, ed. 2, New York, Wood, 1867 and 1882.

[239] Kirkbride, T. S.: A sketch of the history, buildings and organization of the Pennsylvania Hospital for the Insane, Am. J. Insanity 2:97, 1845.

[240] Miscellaneous, Am. J. Insanity 1:287, 1845.

[241] Hamilton, S. W.: "The History of American Mental Hospitals," *in* One Hundred Years of American Psychiatry, pp. 73 et seq., New York, Columbia, 1944.

The first state (colonial) hospital for the insane was opened at Williamsburg, Virginia, in 1773.

The stimulus of the Quakers' work in England spurred private philanthropists to open the Friends Asylum in Frankford, Pennsylvania (1817), the McLean Asylum in Boston (1818), and the Hartford Retreat, Connecticut (1824). During the third and the fourth decades of the century, state and private hospitals for the insane increased perceptibly in number in the United States.[242]

THE STRUGGLE OVER RESTRAINT

Except for the "moral treatment" which was under study by physicians, hospital treatment was still such as to arouse public ire. In England, parliamentary inquiries were authorized in 1815, again in 1840, and later. Especially revolting were the disclosures that attended the House of Commons investigation of 1815. William Tuke, founder of the York Retreat, then an octogenarian, was active and influential in this parliamentary inquiry.[243] Stories of rat bites, of amputation from frost bite, of fettering lunatics continuously in iron collars and iron waistband, until then rumors, emerged as fact from testimony of witnesses. In spite of investigations, little was accomplished to relieve these deplorable conditions. A new technic was needed to supply a practical answer to the old problem of restraint.

The answer came in the nonrestraint system initiated by Gardner Hill, house surgeon at the Lincoln Asylum. When Dr. Hill went to Lincoln in 1829, the quarter-boot was in use. This was a device which secured the patient's feet to the end of the bed in an upright position. The patient was then securely strapped in for the night *after* a day of restraint treatment. The object of this procedure was, said Dr. Charlesworth, "not punishment but security." Hill, in constant contact with the patients, wondered whether restraint was at all necessary. Universal practice in asylums seemed to imply that it was, for few asylum superintendents questioned the use of restraint.

Hill, experimenting with different types of cases, found that restraint could be safely dispensed with for most patients. In nine years at Lincoln Asylum he was able to reduce the restraint hours from 20,423 per year to none (for a period of 16 months), this while the hospital almost doubled its roll of patients. This was, Hill wrote modestly, "the first frank statement . . . laid before the British public."[244] The medical fraternity was up in arms at this unnecessary idealism. The editors of the *Lancet* reminded the profession that "restraint forms the very basis on which sound

[242] *Ibid.*

[243] Personal communication from Robert O. Mennell, great-great-great-grandson of William Tuke, Kenley, Surrey, February 11, 1943.

[244] Hill, R. G.: Modern treatment of the insane (letter), Lancet, p. 355, Sept. 21, 1850.

treatment of lunatics is founded." A responsible authority criticized Hill's idea that restraint is never justified for the insane: "The curious opinion . . . is more remarkable for its *rashness* even than its *boldness*." The nonrestraint system was attacked as a "wild scheme of a philanthropic visionary;" "a breaking of the sixth commandment;" "the attempt of a candidate for popular applause," etc. Undaunted, Dr. Hill continued his methods of nonrestraint.

Soon others followed his example. In 1839, at the Hanwell Asylum,[245,246] Dr. John Conolly discarded mechanical restraints completely. And while the orthodox continued to mutter about Hill's "mania," and Moreau de Tours caustically remarked that it was "an idea entirely Britannic," and hence impractical, the more thoughtful physicians embraced Hill's and Conolly's technics.

The principle of nonrestraint was the natural consequence of Pinel's emancipation of the insane from their fetters. But the wall of defensiveness against admitting the insane person into the circle of human beings was not easily dissolved. The notion that the insane could not be treated without restraint was one with the idea that the insane belonged to another, perhaps lower, order of beings. For proof, it was pointed out that they required stronger doses of drugs, were insensible to pain and, like the "mad bull," were susceptible of being stared into submission. The strength of this prejudice was reinforced by practical considerations. In many asylums there were not enough trustworthy attendants to be given the privilege of using manual restraint when necessary in place of mechanical restraint. Besides, there were suicidal patients who needed control; there was the general view that "moral restraint" was insufficient for "liberty-loving Americans," and so on. Dr. Isaac Ray [247] declined to abolish restraints on the grounds that "the abolition of mechanical restraint meant merely the substitution of another form of coercion—'manual restraint' or force exercised at the hands of attendants—which was hardly more desirable."

Theoretical considerations in resolving the place of the insane in the genealogic tree of mankind also prevented physicians from adopting Hill's and Conolly's practices. Griesinger, in the second edition of his text, admitted that his inner wish for reform had been influenced by the "adverse opinions of German psychologists," [248] but that he felt we could now "pursue the new system fearlessly." The unspoken principle that insanity, a violent deviation from normality, required violent means for its correc-

[245] Conolly, John: An Inquiry Concerning the Indications of Insanity, with Suggestions for the Better Protection and Care of the Insane, London, John Taylor, 1830.

[246] ———: The Treatment of the Insane Without Mechanical Restraints, London, Smith Elder, 1856.

[247] Deutsch, Albert: The Mentally Ill in America, ed. 2, Chap. 11, New York, Columbia, 1949.

[248] Griesinger: *Op. cit.*, p. 350.

tion was almost as ineradicable as the unconscious hostile wish that lay behind it.

In spite of the reasonableness of the nonrestraint principle and the marked improvement in patients which physicians using it could demonstrate, the question was intensively discussed in the medical literature for almost fifty years. In America, as an example, the problem exercised the Association of Medical Superintendents of American Institutions for the Insane (now the American Psychiatric Association) from their initial meeting in 1844, when a resolution was passed upholding the use of restraint. Thirty years later, at the meeting of 1874,[249] discussion on the subject raged on. The great majority of psychiatrists over this period recognized the occasional need for restraint, but in general practiced it sparingly. As late as 1885, Hack Tuke [250] observed in his exhaustive survey of American institutions that American psychiatrists such as Dr. John P. Gray were "stout defenders of mechanical restraint, including the crib-bed," and that among British superintendents the teachings of Hill and Conolly were held rather as "pious opinion" than invariable rule.

In the private hospitals of the period, particularly those which received their stimulus from the Quakers, the situation admittedly was different. Here the moral treatment was almost universal. On admission patients were immediately put "under treatment." This meant medication three times a day, purgatives and baths and sometimes outdoor recreation, frequently work, amusements in the form of lectures or concerts in the evening. Under Dr. Kirkbride's aegis at the Pennsylvania Hospital for the Insane, a routine was established by waking the patients at a quarter after five in the winter and a quarter to five in the summer, the attendants unlocking the doors and giving "the patients a kind greeting." [251] After medicine was distributed, the patients breakfasted and the physician spoke to each patient. Then there were walks in the garden, occupational activity and, after tea, reading, visits by the physicians, lectures or entertainment. Restraint was still used for difficult patients, but the greatest reliance was placed on the presence and the kindliness of the physician who acted as paterfamilias. Religious services were frequent, and occupational therapy in the form of suitable work was constantly advocated and pressed.

At another American sanitarium, the Hartford Retreat, which opened its doors in 1824, the personalized influence of Dr. Eli Todd made moral management a living reality. Nonrestraint, kindness and employment were the principal measures used; but the most effective of these remedies was

[249] Bunker, H. A., *in* Hamilton, S. W.: One Hundred Years of American Psychiatry, p. 201, New York, Columbia, 1944.

[250] Tuke, Hack: The Insane in the United States and Canada, London, Lewis, 1885.

[251] Bond, E. D.: Dr. Kirkbride and His Mental Hospital, p. 56, Philadelphia, Lippincott, 1947.

Dr. Todd himself. Warmly interested in his patients, "Father," as many called him,[252] walked, talked and dined with his charges. Night after night he would bring out his violin or flute and play for the patients as they gathered round him. The ordinariness of the retreat environment, its patterning after the best of family life and its kindly paternalism were factors that recalled many patients from a life of chronic mental illness.

The direct application of moral treatment with its corollaries, nonrestraint and benign management of the insane "mind," was not reflected, however, in treatment given the pauper insane. These unfortunates interred in asylums for the incurable or in almshouses and jails were still subjected to chains, violence, blood-letting and neglect. The actual stimulus for the spread of humane treatment to a larger number of patients came from philanthropic and inspired citizens in America and on the Continent, even more than from the few leaders among the medical profession who constituted the modernist vanguard. The most effective of these lay persons was Dorothea Lynde Dix, a New England schoolteacher, who, single-handed, galvanized the torpid, crushed legislative opposition and vanquished public indifference toward the erection of adequate institutions for the insane during the mid-century. The story of Miss Dix's activity, covering a period of twenty-five years, is a saga of raw courage and idealism in the service of human betterment.

DOROTHEA DIX, MILITANT REFORMER

On a visit to an East Cambridge jail in 1841, Miss Dix came upon a few lunatics housed among the criminals. She protested to the jailor that no stoves were provided for the insane inmates on this blustery spring day. The jailor gave the stock answer that the insane were insensible to cold.[253] Her Puritan conscience aroused, Miss Dix vowed to investigate this shocking situation; systematically she visited every jail and almshouse in Massachusetts during the next two years. As a commentator remarked,[254] "The jailor who refused fire for patients thought he was dealing with a woman, not with destiny." The horrors she witnessed moved her to dedicate herself to their alleviation:

> Cages, chains and whip, strong heavy chain [hanging] from an iron collar which invests neck . . . band of iron one inch wide around the neck with a six foot chain . . . hands restrained by clavis and belt of iron . . . and to each wrist united by a padlock in a cell six feet by eight feet by eight feet, patients were chained up all night.

252 Winkler, J. K., and Bromberg, Walter: Mind Explorers, pp. 88 et seq., New York, Reynal & Hitchcock, 1939.

253 Tiffany, Francis: Life of Dorothea Lynde Dix, Boston, Houghton, 1890.

254 Beach, S. C.: Daughters of the Puritans, p. 142, Boston, Am. Unitarian A., 1906.

As a result of this inspection, Miss Dix sent a vivid memorandum [255] to the Massachusetts legislature. It began: "I shall be obliged to speak with great plainness, and to reveal many things revolting to the taste and from which my woman's nature shrinks. . . . But truth is the highest consideration," and, after thirty pages of a report, painstakingly gathered, of revolting conditions that she had encountered, ended: "Gentlemen, I commit to you this sacred cause. Your action upon this subject will affect the present and future conditions of hundreds and of thousands."

The Memorial produced a sensation in Boston; many attacked her, while others, including Dr. Luther V. Bell, of the McLean Asylum, came to her support. The result was the passage of a bill for relief of overcrowded conditions in the Worcester State Lunatic Hospital.

From New England Miss Dix traveled to New Jersey, and thence north and south and west, investigating and studying in minute detail the condition of patients. She badgered legislatures to appropriate money for State insane asylums. Through sheer will she battered the unwilling asylum superintendents into allowing her to inspect their buildings and, by direct appeal to State legislatures, forced them to give decent medical care to their charges. It was the influence of Dorothea Dix that added medical men to the staffs of many institutions in the States. By 1847 she had visited 18 penitentiaries, 300 county jails and houses of correction, and 500 almshouses. It was through her personal activity that she founded or enlarged 32 mental hospitals, among them the Government Hospital for the Insane at Washington, D. C., now St. Elizabeths Hospital.[256]

Her success in state after state was phenomenal. Finally, in 1848, Miss Dix conceived the idea of urging the Government to cede public land to the states, the sale of which was to be earmarked for improvement of the care of the insane. Her plan, encompassed in a bill that finally passed both houses of Congress, called for the setting aside of 12,225,000 acres [257] "from the many hundreds of millions of public lands." So vigorously and successfully had Miss Dix fought that had it not been for President Pierce's veto on "constitutional and States' rights" grounds, the bill would have become law in 1850 and the revolutionary principle that the insane are "wards of the nation" would have become established. This inspired scheme was attacked in many quarters. The *Boston Medical and Surgical Journal* [258] commented that "to create a mammoth hospital . . . would soon become an instrument with adroit, designing politicians for disturbing the

[255] Dix, Dorothea L.: Memorial to the Legislature of Massachusetts on Behalf of the Insane, Old South Leaflets, Vol. 6, No. 148, p. 489, Old South Meeting House, Boston, Directors of the Old South Work, 1843.

[256] Overholser, Winfred: Dorothea Lynde Dix, a note, Bull. Hist. Med. 9:210, 1941.

[257] Deutsch: *Op. cit.*, Chap. 9, pp. 175 et seq.

[258] Memorial of D. L. Dix, praying of Congress a grant of land for the relief and support of the indigent curable and incurable insane, Am. J. Insanity 5:286, 1849.

peace of the country." This was manifestly not her plan, but the complaints that the states might "slide off" their patients to the Federal Government was a compelling one. Nevertheless, psychiatrists recognized the vitality of her attack. As early as 1853 the Association of Superintendents resolved that "this association regards with continued admiration and unabated interest, the benevolent and unwearied efforts of Miss Dix." [259]

The major work in the States accomplished, Miss Dix subsequently traveled to Scotland and England, where, with the same bold strokes, she stormed parliamentary halls, leading the movement to examine conditions in private and in state asylums. She spent the next two years traveling all over Europe—in Italy, France, Russia, Holland, Turkey and Scandinavia—inspecting institutions with an evangelical zeal. When she returned to her native land, the results of her efforts were partly apparent in the series of state asylums stretching from Maine to Illinois. What she had accomplished virtually was to lift the insane out of jails and almshouses and place them within asylum walls.

In spite of the consecration of Miss Dix and the increasing interest in mental diseases by the mid-century, the verdict of the ages, "Once insane, always insane," hung like an albatross round the necks of the mentally ill, a tombstone for their hopes. The dark shadow of supernaturality in mental illness had not been universally dispelled. The attitude arising from the unconscious linking of insanity and demonology was deeply intrenched; yet early in the century a reaction of optimism had punctured the gloom surrounding the incurability of the insane. Deutsch has called this reaction the "Cult of Curability." [260] It was characterized by a rising tide of optimism concerning the curability of the insane on the part of heads of asylums and physicians. This enthusiasm proved later to be unsupported by the facts, but it provided a crude beginning for a changed social attitude toward insanity which, a century later, flowered into a mental hygiene movement.

INSANITY BECOMES CURABLE

One factor behind the Cult of Curability was the rediscovery by the profession that insanity was a disease and hence within the scope of medical practice. This was evidenced by the increasing stream of publications on the subject. In addition to treatises mentioned in this chapter, journals devoted to mental disturbances appeared: the first, in 1805, was *Archiv für Gemüths- und Nervenkrankheiten,* by A. S. Winkelman; [261] the second,

[259] Association of Superintendents: Resolution on Dorothea Dix, Am. J. Insanity 10:87, 1853.

[260] Deutsch: *Op. cit.,* Chap. 8.

[261] Amdur, M. K.: The dawn of psychiatric journalism, Am. J. Psychiat. 100:205, 1943.

established by Christian Reil the same year, *Magazin für psychische Heilkunde.* Other German journals appeared, as the *Magazin für die philosophische, medizinische und gerichtliche Seelenkunde* (1829), which became the *Archiv für Psychologie für Ärzte und Juristen* (1883). The *Annales Médico-Légales* in French was published in 1842, and the *American Journal of Insanity* (predecessor of the *American Journal of Psychiatry*) was founded in 1844. English psychiatrists brought out the *Asylum Journal of Mental Science* in 1854.

The spread of the gospel of moral management, which rendered madmen tractable and the frenzied approachable, further spurred physicians to reconsider the dictum that the mind was a sacrosanct area. Finally, medicine's appreciation that the diseased mind, like other diseased organs, could be studied, a view stimulated by the German school, which, under the domination of cellular pathology (Virchow) had laid a cornerstone for clinical medicine, reduced interest in metaphysics and led to adoption of an organic approach to mental disease. A spokesman for this orientation, Griesinger, whose text on psychiatry appeared originally in 1845,[262] stated, "The brain alone can be the seat of . . . abnormal mental action." As Sigerist remarks, the organic view of the German school developed "a psychiatry without psyche." [263]

The change in attitude which underlay the Cult of Curability was consummated relatively rapidly. Whereas insanity was commonly considered an "awful visitation from Heaven and that no human agency can reverse the judgement by which it was inflicted," [264] the therapeutic approach now became positive. The contrast between Rush's statement in his *Treatise on the Mind* ("In entering upon the subject of the following Inquiries and Observations, I feel as if I were about to tread on consecrated ground." [265]) and Burrows' summary ("Few popular errors have been more prejudicial . . . than that insanity is commonly incurable." [266]) sounded the new note of optimism.

Statistical treatment of mental cases seems to have received its impetus from Willis' statement, made during a House of Commons' Committee hearing on King George's illness (January, 1789), that of patients placed under his care "within 3 months after the attack, nine out of ten recovered." This bare numerical report was considered amateurish by most physicians in lunacy. Haslam, of Bethlehem Hospital, called the statement

[262] Griesinger: *Op. cit.*

[263] Sigerist, H. E.: "Psychiatry in Europe at the Middle of the Nineteenth Century," *in* One Hundred Years of American Psychiatry, New York, Columbia, 1944.

[264] Deutsch: *Op. cit.,* p. 137.

[265] Rush, Benjamin: Medical Inquiries and Observations upon the Diseases of the Mind, ed. 2, Philadelphia, Richardson, 1818.

[266] Burrows, G. M.: Commentaries on the Causes, Forms, Symptoms and Treatment Moral and Medical of Insanity, p. 507, London, Underwood, 1828.

"bold, unprecedented." [267] But the inspired Willis continued to cure patients in his private hospital in Lincoln. Slowly he gained adherents, who, digging into published reports of asylums, emerged with a new perception of the improvement possibility of madness. Burrows,[268] reporting some years later (1820) on a series of figures collected from 21 asylums in Britain, 8 in France and 1 in Italy, was glad to note that the recovery rate varied from 39 to 43 per cent. He demonstrated further that there was a yet higher proportion of recoveries of recent cases in "private lunatic houses." Agreeing that Willis' finding of "8 in 10, or even 6 in 7 recent cases credibly" reported recovered was sound, Burrows stated that 81 per cent of patients in his own "House (verified under oath)" recovered, including those in a state of "fatuity, idiocy and epilepsy." Considering recent cases only, he claimed 91 per cent cures. In his later work, Burrows [269] confirmed his earlier claims, but expressed prophetic insight in tempering his enthusiasm in saying that "there must be a revolution of public opinions respecting insanity as a human malady . . . before that point of excellence will be attained, which is within reach." Against those who sat "with hopeless apathy" [270] among their insane patients, doing little but restraining them, private-asylum physicians came forward with figures of cures that dazzled the imagination.

This trend, curiously, was tremendously stimulated by a British author-traveler, Captain Basil Hall, whose travel books were widely read. An indefatigable tourist, Hall visited the Hartford Retreat in Connecticut, where Dr. Eli Todd, superintendent, "gladly communicated his plans, and showed us over every part of this noble establishment—a model, I venture to say, from which any country might take instruction." [271] The remarkable assertion by Captain Hall contained in the Report of Visiting Physicians that Todd cured 91.3 per cent of all recent cases during the year 1826 (21 out of 23 recent cases) was read with incredulity in England; especially Hall's further comment that "at two most 'ancient and celebrated institutions' of same kind in Great Britain, the percentage of recent cases cured was 25.5 per cent." [272] Until then, Todd and the Retreat had been practically unknown. Todd's figures of cures astounded the world, and all eyes turned toward Hartford, while every private institution in the United States set out to copy Todd's methods and improve his figures.

[267] Willis, Francis: A Treatise on Mental Derangements, Gulstonian Lectures for May, 1822, London, Longman, Hurst, 1823.
[268] Burrows: "An Inquiry into Certain Errors Relative to Insanity," *in* Rush: *Op. cit.*
[269] ——: Commentaries on the Causes, Forms, Symptoms and Treatment Moral and Medical of Insanity, p. 533.
[270] Willis, Francis: *Op. cit.*
[271] Hall, Capt. Basil: Travels in North America in the Years 1827 and 1828, Edinburgh, Cadell, 1829.
[272] *Ibid.*, Vol. 2, p. 194.

Turning to their records in an effort to emulate Dr. Todd's successful management, hospital superintendents discovered that they also could report high percentages of cures. Dr. Samuel Woodward, superintendent of the State Lunatic Hospital at Worcester, which opened in 1833, reported 82¼ per cent recoveries for the first year of operation.[273] Later reports showed increasing successes: in the 1836 report, 84 per cent recoveries, and in 1837, 89 per cent recoveries of "recent cases" were announced. In reviewing his cases for a five-year period, Dr. Woodward admitted that if the deaths and those cases left in the hospital (not yet cured) were subtracted, "we should increase the percentage to 94." The record established by Dr. Woodward of 91.42 per cent of cures of recent cases (1840) was soon to be eclipsed by Dr. John M. Galt, of the Eastern Asylum, at Williamsburg, Virginia, who, in 1842, announced 92.3 per cent recoveries. Finally, the following year, the ultimate of 100 per cent recoveries was promulgated by Dr. William Awl, superintendent of the Ohio Lunatic Asylum at Columbus!

The best psychiatrists of the period believed that insanity had been brought under control. European authorities, such as Guislain in Belgium, reported that "of 227 offering probabilities of cure, 191 achieved notable improvement, or 84 per cent." [274] Men of the stature of Luther V. Bell, of the McLean Asylum, wrote (1840 report) that "the records justify the declaration that *all cases*, certainly recent—recover under a fair trial." Arraignment of early psychiatrists for their "deficiency of modesty," [275] as Earle put it, is not justified, for the onrush of sentiment favored the Cult of Curability. Dr. Amariah Brigham, eminent head of the Utica State Hospital and a *moderado* in Earle's opinion, stated "that no fact relating to insanity appears better established than the general certainty of curing it in its early stage." New hope for the cure of the insane, derived from mounting statistical successes, stimulated the building of more asylums. Convinced that the millennium had been reached, legislative committees urged the construction of more state hospitals.[276] These, in turn, proved the thesis of curability by providing the material for more statistics.

The inevitable counterreaction soon set in against the doctored statistics. Dr. Isaac Ray, superintendent of the Maine Insane Asylum, asked some pointed questions in 1849 concerning the criteria of "recovery" of "recent" cases, of borderline states, and of the validity of medical statistics in general.[277] Perhaps the early discharges were due to impatient friends. How

[273] Earle, Pliny: The Curability of Insanity, A Series of Studies, pp. 22 et seq., Philadelphia, Lippincott, 1887.

[274] Guislain, J.: Traité sur les phrénopathies, ou doctrine nouvelle des maladies mentales, Bruxelles, Etablissement Encyclo., 1833, p. 352.

[275] Earle, Pliny: *Op. cit.*, p. 27.

[276] Deutsch: *Op. cit.*, p. 193.

[277] Ray, Isaac: The statistics of insane hospitals, Am. J. Insanity 6:23, 1849.

can one judge recovery in periodic insanity? Can one elucidate "moral conduct of man, or his propensities" by statistics? Gradually, the leading medical superintendents of the asylums in America began to modify their therapeutic optimism as their mathematical analyses improved. In a decade, the reported cures dropped to 48 per cent (State Hospital, Maine, 1850), and within two decades, cures of recent cases tumbled to between 30 and 40 per cent. Dr. Thurnam, of the York Retreat in England, summed up the situation in 1845 by concluding:

> In round numbers, of ten persons attacked by insanity, five recover, and five die, sooner or later during the attack. Of the five who recover, not more than two remain well during the rest of their lives: the other three sustain subsequent attacks.[278]

The pendulum was swinging to the opposite pole. Dr. Luther Bell so reversed himself that he wrote in 1857, "I have come to the conclusion that when a man once becomes insane he is about used up for this world."

Analysis of the statistical difficulties culminated in a series of studies by Pliny Earle, extending from 1876 to 1885, which effectively called a halt to the Cult of Curability. Earle pointed to cases that had been tabulated as "recovered" each time they had been readmitted to a given institution during one year. One patient had been recorded as recovered in one asylum or another as often as forty-six times during her lifetime! For example, he showed that of 92 recoveries of "repeaters" presented in a report of the Worcester Hospital, only four were *permanent* recoveries when followed some years later, and two of these were readmitted after his survey was completed.[279] No less serious were errors in criteria of recency of illness, of the "personal equation" (charitably called the observer's "own temperament") in favor of his own cases, and the practice of estimating percentages of cures based on those discharged to those admitted rather than to the total hospital population. One can readily side with Earle when he said of his work, "It is not presumptuous to claim that [my work] greatly modified the aspect of insanity as a curable condition."

The curious phenomenon, during the early decades of the century, of mounting statistics indicating increasing numbers of patients cured is imputed by Albert Deutsch[280] to several factors: The artless, irresponsible methods of collecting statistics; perpetuation by heads of institutions of a fallacy that they knew to be incorrect; confusion surrounding the terms *recent* and *recovered*. The accuracy of this analysis is undeniable; nevertheless, there is perceptible a psychological factor in the background of the curability boom. This was the slow dissolution of congealed hostility

[278] Thurnam, John: Observations and Essays on Statistics of Insanity, York, 1845.
[279] Earle, Pliny: *Op. cit.*, p. 12.
[280] Deutsch: *Op. cit.*, p. 148.

toward madmen, which had been bound into a prejudice that insanity was irreversible, and its replacement by an equally intense, though opposing, feeling of benevolence and optimism.

THE ASYLUM ACHIEVES STATUS

The tide of curability had practical consequences. Insanity tended to be recognized earlier, and asylum resources were utilized with increasing frequency for hundreds of hitherto neglected patients. On one point there was general agreement: The earlier a person "attacked with insanity" was placed under treatment, the greater was the prospect of recovery. Another consequence was the determination of leading alienists throughout the world to establish a reliable method of calculating statistics of mental patients and the results of treatment. In 1867, the International Congress of Alienists appointed a committee to set up a reliable system to be used by the various superintendents of asylums. The commission was composed of distinguished men: Bucknill, of England; Falret, of Bicêtre; Griesinger, of Berlin; Lombroso, of Pavia; Pujadas, of Spain; Tuke, of Great Britain; and so on. The report was prefaced by the statement that "it is no longer doubtful to any one that the numeric method may be usefully applied to the study of mental diseases." [281] The growing experience of psychiatrists and the apparently growing number of insane created a salutary reciprocal reaction between the public and the profession. The result of this can best be gauged by a series of propositions voted as resolutions by the Association of Medical Superintendents of American Institutions for the Insane at their annual meetings from 1844 to 1875. Written by Thomas Kirkbride and Isaac Ray, they represent a Magna Carta, whose basic tenets the modern hospital continues to observe as a guide:

1. Insanity is a disease—to which everyone is liable.
2. Properly and promptly treated, it is about as curable as most other serious diseases.
3. In a great majority of cases it is better and more successfully treated in well-organized institutions than at home.
4. It is humanity, economy and expediency for every state to make ample and good provision for all its insane.
5. The best hospital—best built, best arranged and best managed—is always cheapest in the end.

6-9. Hospitals should be plain, in good taste and well ventilated.

10. A proper classification is indispensable.

11-13. Overcrowding is an evil of serious magnitude.

14. Abundant means for occupation and amusement should be provided.
15. As little restraint as possible should be used.
16. The insane should never be kept in almshouses or in penal institutions.

[281] A project of a system of statistics, Am. J. Insanity **26**:49, 1869.

17. Insane criminals should not be treated in ordinary state hospitals.

18-20. There should be a qualified physician in undivided charge of each hospital. He should be responsible to a board of trustees of high personal character and without political motives.[282]

The recognition of the need for asylum for large numbers of insane still housed in county almshouses brought with it practical building problems. Construction became a subject of importance for medical superintendents the world over. One of the founders of the American Psychiatric Association, Dr. Thomas Kirkbride, was a pioneer in this [283] important field. His propositions for construction of hospitals embodied his plans. These later were published as a book, *On Hospitals*, which remained until recently the bible for architects of state institutions. Kirkbride worked out in the greatest detail the familiar central building with extended wings, ground location, ventilation, heating, air space, water supply and so on. His plan to provide maximum air and sunshine for each patient, so commonplace now, was revolutionary then. Kirkbride put his whole philosophy of humane management of the insane into brick and stone, in plumbing, kitchens, fireproofing, water lines, and in constant attention to these details. The preoccupation of medical superintendents with inducing legislatures to adopt modifications of Kirkbride's plan led to the charge that the former were no more than wardens. Later in the century, these superintendents were to be attacked on the score of isolation from their medical brethren and of their concern with construction and management. But practical problems, which meant in actuality therapeutic problems, were more pressing. As increasing numbers of mental cases poured in on hospital superintendents, mass domiciliary care became the immediate duty of the state hospital staff. The trend toward state care [284] of pauper insane, previously herded in county jails and almshouses, and the segregation of chronic, incurable cases posed taxing medical, sanitary and housekeeping problems for hospital superintendents. State care, attained after a severe struggle, enlarged the potentialities and the responsibilities of the state hospital and reduced the intrusion of politicians and legislators. Such innovations as the cottage system, a renascence of the colony plan in vogue at Gheel, Belgium, since the fourteenth century, had to be reconciled with Kirkbride's construction propositions which formed a "set of cast iron rules" [285] to which hospital men adhered. Questions as to the size of asylums,[286] as to physical or

[282] Bond, E. D.: *Op. cit.*, pp. 107, 108. Collected from Am. J. Insanity, 1851-1876.

[283] Kirkbride, T. S.: Remarks on the construction, organization and general arrangements of a hospital for the insane, Am. J. Insanity 2:1, 1854.

[284] Deutsch: *Op. cit.* Chaps. 12 and 13 give full treatment of this historical development.

[285] Hurd, H. M., et al.: The Institutional Care of the Insane in the United States and Canada, Vol. I, p. 207, Baltimore, Johns Hopkins Press, 1916.

[286] Editorial: Large and small asylums, Lancet, p. 163, Jan. 27, 1883.

chemical restraints, the type of assistants, custody versus treatment, cried for solution.

PROGRESS THROUGH CHAOS

Progress in treatment was positive but slow. By mid-century, Bucknill, reviewing Conolly's book on nonrestraint, could say, "The altered state of feeling now prevalent among civilized nations, in regard to the infliction of pain . . . would have rendered old inhumanities of the mad-house even without abolition of restraint." [287] Physical aspects of insanity were treated consistently. "Supporting treatment," in which each symptom was medicated individually,[288] came into favor. In time, supporting treatment broadened into "rest treatment," developing a rationale at the hands of neurologists like Weir Mitchell. But of mental factors in mental illness, little was known which could be attacked psychologically.

Medical records spoke of "jealousy, abusive husband, disappointed love, novel reading, blasted prospects" (Kirkbride).[289] Confusion of cause and effect, of symptom and etiology, was noted in listing the causes of mental disease as "tight lacing." The events in the life of patients were taken at their face value. In a Scottish asylum, reading "works of fancy," as well as "chagrin" and "politics," was considered "the apparent or supposed causes of insanity." [290] An English preacher "ascribed his insanity to the dull, flat and unvarying scenery of the neighborhood of Cambridge." [291] In 1879, Daniel Tuke, son of the enlightened Samuel Tuke, warned in his widely accepted textbook of the "haste of life" in "our railway age." [292] Disobedience of the laws of nature and hygiene, sexual excesses, were also warned against. However, these causes were not always taken at face value; Isaac Ray suggested that "many emotions set down as causes 'religious doubts,' 'anxiety' would often be more justly regarded as its effects." [293]

There were attempts to penetrate the veil surrounding the moral (emotional) factors underlying insanity. The French alienists, extending Pinel's moral treatment, agreed that mental illness resulted from "the action of the spirit upon itself." [294] They pointed to the cultural factor of civilization and

[287] Bucknill, J. C.: Book review of Conolly's *The Treatment of the Insane Without Mechanical Restraint*, J. Ment. Sc. **3**:253, 1857.
[288] Cowles, Edward: Progress in the care and treatment of the insane during the half-century, Am. J. Insanity **51**:10, 1894.
[289] Bond: *Op. cit.*
[290] The Philosophy of Insanity, By a Late Inmate of the Glasgow Royal Asylum for Lunatics at Gartnavel, with an introduction by Frieda Fromm-Reichmann, pp. 62 and 108, New York, Greenberg, 1947.
[291] Psychological gossip, Asylum J. Ment. Sc. **2**:338, 1856.
[292] Tuke, D. H.: Insanity in Ancient and Modern Life, p. 182, London, Macmillan, 1878.
[293] Ray, Isaac: *Op. cit.*, p. 43.
[294] Falret, J. P.: Des maladies mentales et des asiles d'aliénés, p. xii, Paris, Baillière, 1864.

the competitive spirit, "with defeat inevitable for most of the competitors" as Falret realistically put it, as responsible for the increased incidence of mental disease. Esquirol, following Pinel, stressed the nature of insanity as the response of human nature to life's injuries.[295] Esquirol pointed to the stress of the French Revolution, the changing life under the Industrial Revolution, etc., as the shaper of types of insanity. In the same vein Esquirol noted, "The English say, a republican or representative government, in giving play to all passions ought, other things being equal, to be more favorable to production of insanity." Place of origin seemed an undoubted factor; Great Britain was acknowledged to be a fruitful site where derangements of mind "may be considered almost endemical." [296] Recognition that mental illness represented a struggle of the healthy versus the sick tendencies within the patient [297] brought alienists closer, but not close enough, to the enigmatic cause of mental illness. Voices like those of Leuret and John Conolly pleaded for individualized treatment, an "improvement yet to be made." [298] In the main, however, the inner emotional life of the patient, his deepest doubts and anxieties, were left untouched in medical application of mental healing methods.

Without precise knowledge of the psychological movements of the warped mind, treatment could not be scientific in the sense of being reasonably predictive. Apart from scanty, uncritical information as to the causes of insanity, there was little agreement regarding diagnostic categories of mental cases. Alienists in one country spoke a different psychiatric language from that in another. The physician in active asylum practice found it difficult to assign his cases to the categories set up by each expert. The practical consequence was that before the turn of the century, patients were considered by the hospital doctor to be "either maniacal, melancholic or demented." [299] Diagnostic classifications were developed on an earlier psychological framework (disturbances of intellect, emotion and will), or on physiologic assumptions (anatomic brain changes, nutritional disturbances or intoxications) or on a symptomatic basis.

Clinical descriptions varied markedly: Frances Morel described *démence précoce,* while Kahlbaum and Hecker, in Germany, further differentiated such cases as catatonia and hebephrenia. The English held to

[295] Esquirol, J. E.: Mental Maladies, A Treatise on Insanity, translated by E. K. Hunt, p. 43, Philadelphia, Lea & Blanchard, 1845.

[296] Spurzheim, J. C.: Observations on the Deranged Manifestations of the Mind or Insanity, Am. ed. 1, with appendix by A. Brigham, Boston, Marsh, Capen & Lyon, 1833, Eng. ed., London, 1817.

[297] Falret: *Op. cit.,* p. liii.

[298] Conolly, John: The Treatment of the Insane Without Mechanical Restraints, p. 64.

[299] White, W. A.: Forty Years of Psychiatry, p. 17, New York, Nerv. and Ment. Dis. Monographs, 1933.

ideational insanity (Maudsley), whereas the French followed Esquirol's classification of monomania (partial ideational insanity). Many agreed with the diagnosis chronic mania, but some called it chronic delusional insanity, or even chronic melancholia, or, again *folie systématisée*. Falret, in France, delimited circular insanity (*folie circulaire*) when mania alternated with melancholia, whilst Maudsley complained that "there has been in France an ambition to discover a new variety of insanity and to coin a new name for it." The German authors brought hypochondria and melancholia under depression, and acute mania and monomania together under conditions of exaltation. In addition to this bewildering array of diagnostic entities, specific diseases, as phthisical, postconnubial, anemic, diabetic [300] insanities, were described. The Italians followed Morselli, who placed mania, melancholia and catatonia under phrenopathies, although Tanzi states that they also adhered to Krafft-Ebing's classification of delusional insanity (monomania) under the psychical degenerative states, while melancholia was classified under the psychoneuroses!

By the end of the century, the tangled threads of psychiatric nosology were sorted out and arranged in orderly groups by Kraepelin. Adopting the "life-history" idea,[301] Kraepelin united the multifarious cross-sectional pictures of mental illnesses into meaningful concepts which had a history, a course and a prognosis, if not an etiology. His concepts of dementia praecox, manic-depressive insanity, organic states, morbid personalities, etc.,[302] provided a solid foundation for a clinical psychiatry. His diagnostic innovations were, as Zilboorg puts it, "the natural culmination of a generation of efforts in France and Germany." [303] Kraepelin's work, though not directly related to treatment theories or procedures, opened up the world of insanity which, until then, was so conceptually unwieldy as to discourage the making of preliminary hypotheses which necessarily precede the evolution of new methods of therapy.

Gradually Kraepelin's achievements strengthened the profession's grasp on the inchoate world of insanity. In 1883, Spitzka wrote that the "day is past when the asylum physician can content himself with such a classification as: mania, melancholia, amentia and general paresis." [304] Although some diehards complained that Spitzka was a "weak echo of a class of

[300] Henderson, D. K., and Gillespie, R. D.: Classification, Chap. 2, *in* A Text-Book of Psychiatry, ed. 3, New York, Oxford, 1932.
[301] Jelliffe, S. E.: Some historical phases of the manic-depressive synthesis, A. Research Nerv. & Ment. Dis., Annual Meeting, December, 1930.
[302] Diefendorf, A. R.: Clinical Psychiatry, abstracted and adapted from the 7th German edition of Kraepelin's *Lehrbuch der Psychiatrie,* ed. 2, New York, Macmillan, 1907.
[303] Zilboorg and Henry: A History of Medical Psychology, p. 458, New York, Norton, 1941.
[304] Spitzka: Insanity; Its Classification, Diagnosis, and Treatment, p. 129, New York, Treat, 1883.

modern crazy German pagans, who are trying . . . to break down all the safe guards of our Christian civilization" with their probing of every area of human mentality, psychiatry had indeed become a branch of established clinical medicine with the opening of the twentieth century. The cystallization of psychiatric conditions around the concept of the "life history," the new meaning given diverse symptoms now viewed as mental illnesses or characteristic mental reactions, helped to change the lunatic asylum into the mental hospital. It represented a metamorphosis of the connotation of "retreat" or "asylum" to that of hospital. Modern psychiatry gathered up the loose ends of lunacy and deposited them in the hands of trained physicians. Manias, melancholias, delusions and depressions became problems in human disease, not oddities of mental derangement.

6

The Return of Faith-Healing

The gradual intrusion of a clinical viewpoint into asylum practice helped to provide a firm foundation on which to construct psychiatry. During the last quarter of the nineteenth century, insights derived from laboratory study of diseased brain and nerve tissue, combined with clinical clarification of mental states, burgeoned a polyglot field into a scientific discipline. These new viewpoints contributed a note of objectivity to the mental sciences which extended later to an analysis of the hitherto relatively unexplored world of the patient's emotional life. One source of this evolutionary development was neurology. As will be seen in a later chapter, neurology's scrutiny of nervous-system physiology and pathology provided an impetus for the exploration and the illumination of man's instinctive and emotional life. The entrance of medical disciplines into mental healing did not immediately revolutionize medical attitudes toward the mentally ill. Nor did it bring to physicians that objectively based analysis of subjective phenomena characteristic of present-day dynamic psychotherapy.

There was still a goodly portion of faith and more than a hint of magical thinking in medical treatment of the mentally ill. Simultaneously, rationalism began to emerge in approaches to mental healing. In this emergence, the strongest conscious element was intellectualism, observable in technics aimed at modifying emotions by ideas or supplanting unhealthy notions by moral precepts. The psychotherapy, or mental therapeutics as it was called, of the prepsychological era was formalistic and rather thin ideationally, save for its accent on humanitarianism. The fruitful concept of the human being as a reacting organism, under the varied influences of its remote and current environment, had not yet been developed. The revolution in biologic thinking following Darwinism was to find its way into psychological and psychiatric concepts within the century and thus open up a psychological horizon of magnificent scope and wide practical implications.

While science was setting in motion an objective and later evolutionary view of human life through its researches in biology, pathology and chemistry, the more rudimentary modalities of mental healing—magic and faith

—continued to thrive. And in the inexplicable way in which human events fail to follow obvious surface causes, mystic healers like Mesmer paved the way for scientific psychotherapy while a neurologic science like Gall's craniology eventuated into the charlatanry of phrenology. Mental healing is a jungle in which magic and science are tightly intertwined, first one root then the other appearing on the surface, and neither fasciculus ever completely lost from view. It is not astonishing, therefore, that during that nodal point, the eighteenth century, when "Reason" underlay a revitalized medical science, faith-healing should recur in its mystic splendor. Now, however, the magic-worker was disguised as an animal magnetizer rather than as an alchemist; as a worker in electricity rather than as a ventriloquist in an Aesculapian temple, or as a wise woman with her leeches and herbs. The retreat to magic recurs again and again through the life of mankind, as it does with the individual. Reason and primitive emotion struggle side by side in society as they do in the individual human being. Though faith-healing is ever present, magic-healing rises to a sharp historical focus from time to time through the person of one more dramatically or more spiritually stirred. This is the nodal significance to the history of psychotherapy of Mesmer's founding of animal magnetism, which, though derided as irrational, precipitated the long unfolding of hypnotherapy.

EIGHTEENTH-CENTURY CHARLATANS

Mesmer was merely one of a large company of scientific magicians who purveyed to the credulity and the magic-worship of the eighteenth-century public. The bustling technology of the period aided in supplying a scientific matrix on which the mystic wishes of the populace could feed. The discovery that static electricity could be conducted (Gray, 1729), stored in the ingenious Leyden jar (Musschenbroek, 1746) and plucked from the heavens to be discharged upon the earth (Franklin, 1752) caught public imagination. Advances in magnetism, optics, mechanics and electric experiments were grist alike for the mills of the scientist and the charlatan. The devotional fervor of the masses acclaimed its new heroes and thronged to witness the illusory marvels of the quacks. Men like Cagliostro,[305] who prescribed "extract of Saturn," Weisleder, the "Moon Doctor," Schuppach, the Swiss "mountain doctor," who shocked his patients with electricity, and Perkins with his metallic tractors—all charmed the throngs of the aristocracy and the third estate. A mythology surrounded magnetism and electricity, and Mesmer, Graham, Perkins and Cagliostro became its divinities. While Wiegleb [306] attacked the forces of superstition in twenty vol-

[305] de Francesco, Grete: The Power of the Charlatan, translated from the German by Miriam Beard, pp. 188 et seq., New Haven, Conn., Yale, 1939.
[306] *Ibid.*, p. 234.

umes, and Franklin said,[307] "Quacks were the greatest liars in the world, except their patients," thousands used Elisha Perkins' "tractoration" for their distressing pains.

Inspired by the famous observation of Professor Galvani that a muscular twitch occurred in a frog's leg when touched with pieces of metal, Doctor Perkins concluded that two such pieces of metal could be used to cure bodily pain. Doctor Perkins, a founder of the Connecticut Medical Society,[308] announced his discovery in 1796. Traveling through the eastern states, he introduced his patented tractors, one iron, the other copper, which drew pain from limbs with miraculous ease. In the same year the Connecticut Medical Society voted that the doctor whose methods were "gleaned up from the miserable remains of 'animal magnetism' " be expelled from the Society. But Perkins' magnets, now made of gold and silver, spread in popularity. George Washington bought one for family use. The tractors were obtainable in a "neat Red Morocco Case . . . for five guineas the set." [309] Doctor Perkins died believing that he had come upon a great natural secret. His son Benjamin, a graduate of Yale, carried on his work in London at the Perkinean Institute with the condemnation of the Royal Medical Society ringing in his ears.

The practice of tractoration spread to the Continent. Its adherents, including physicians who obtained marvelous cures with the tractors, prophesied that they would displace the family physician, make medicine unnecessary and revolutionize the art of healing. Surgeon Rafn, in Germany,[310] reported his personal experience with intractable rheumatic pain:

> I determined to try the effects of Dr. Perkins Metallic Tractors. The application was made . . . at a time when my pain was very violent. After having operated with them for 5 or 6 minutes . . . the pain disappeared entirely, and I have not felt any since.

Eventually it was proved by Dr. Haygarth,[311] in England, that tractors made of wood or lead or tobacco pipe produced the same miraculous cures as were accomplished through the gold and the silver tractors sold by Perkins. The boom collapsed. Perkinism, as Holmes wrote, "perished by an easy and natural process."

The public, taught by the Age of Enlightenment to deride witchcraft, was intrigued by electricity and "animal magnetism." From this fascination with magnetism, quacks like James Graham drew their sustenance. As a

[307] Van Doren, Carl: Benjamin Franklin, p. 770, New York, Viking, 1938.
[308] Perkins, Elisha: *In* Dictionary of American Biography, Vol. 14, p. 466, New York, Scribner, 1934.
[309] Perkins' Patent Metallic Tractors, London, George Cooke, 1800.
[310] Perkins, B. D.: Experiments with the Metallic Tractors in . . . Various Topical Diseases, translated by Charles Kampfmuller, London, Herboldt & Rafn, 1799.
[311] Holmes, O. W.: Medical Essays, Homeopathy and Its Kindred Delusions, Boston, Houghton, 1895.

youth, Graham—bold and a rogue by any measure—had studied at Edinburgh University, leaving, by common agreement between his professors and himself, long before taking his degree. When he met the stimulating Franklin in Paris, Graham conceived the idea from Franklin's experiments with lightning that electrical stimulation could cure disease. Styling himself John Graham, O.W.L. (O Wonderful Love!), he opened his Temple of Health in London in 1779. In this gaudy showplace he held forth, promising to "dissipate melancholy and mitigate extravagant gaiety" with "electricity communicated by magnetized baths." In this Templum Aesculapium Sacrum, adorned with magnets and electrical devices, set upon forty pillars of glass, flanked by marble statues, bathed by intoxicating incense, the Celestial Magnetico-Electrico Bed held out a promise of rejuvenation to the jaded coxcombs of London. Graham, the Barnum of his time, thundered: "In this tremendous edifice, are combined or singly dispensed the irresistible, and salubrious influences of electricity."

With a public prepared for scientific marvels, it is readily understandable that when Franz Anton Mesmer announced his "animal magnetism" to be a cure for nervous ailments, his garden in the Landestrasse overflowed with patients and his name became a by-word in the coffee houses of Vienna. Mesmer belonged to a stirring era, but his inspiration came from the past. From the vantage point of later developments, Mesmer made a fatal scientific error; he constructed a hypothesis first and spent his life trying to fit the facts to his theory. What started as scientific theory became, for a period of years, banal sensationalism. As will be discussed in a later chapter, Mesmer loosed a new and fascinating force which was eagerly seized upon by an impressionable public. Following his "discovery" of a subtle magnetic fluid that passed from the stars to human beings and produced crises, convulsions and other impressive changes in patients, magnetic societies and amateur "magnetizers" were active everywhere. One of these, Marquis de Puysegur, an eccentric member of a noble family in France, continued the experiments, discovering phenomena that reoriented the subject completely. It was de Puysegur who discovered that somnambulism could follow the magnetic influence upon patients. One of the Marquis' subjects, under magnetization, went into a peaceful sleep instead of a convulsion, which had routinely been achieved by Mesmer. During this state he showed unusual clarity of thought, whereas ordinarily he had been known as a dull fellow. De Puysegur was astounded that he could avoid the painful contortions of the crisis and put his patients to sleep; he was even more impressed that people in a somnambulistic state developed the properties of clairvoyance. Dull peasants became mentally alert and could even foretell events or understand things ordinarily obscure to them. Somnambulists made medical diagnoses in other patients brought before them and foretold the future. The magnetizer of the 1820's merely brought his patient before a competent somnambulist and waited for the diagnosis. From a contemporary report comes an account of a puzzling case reputedly solved by a Doctor Clapier through a clairvoyant whom the doctor had magnetized.

The idea of clairvoyance in a somnambulist caught the fancy of the Romantic Era. Poets, clergymen, physicians and popularizers practiced and extolled mesmerism.[312] Romanticists recognized in somnambulism and clairvoyance the entrance to a new world of sensationalism. Mesmerism was pitched to new heights, claiming what Gall claimed for phrenology, "Truth though opposed by the philosophy of Ages." [313] Lay magnetizers, spiritists and mediums reaffirmed that somnambulists, during the crisis, could "penetrate to the furtherest horizons of life." In Europe and America, magnetizers, table-turners and somnambulists were rampant; magnetism was almost universally accepted. The Vatican, in a letter from the Holy Office (June, 1840),[314] condoned the use of magnetism, "provided it does not tend to an illicit end or one which may be evil." But as spiritism and clairvoyance threatened to get out of bounds, the Vatican interdicted the use of magnetism (1847) and condemned as heretical "those who profess to see things which are invisible . . . or apply purely physical principles to things which are in reality supernatural." Finally, in 1856, an Encyclical letter warned the clergy of the errors and the dangers of magnetism.

Magnetism remained in relative social disrepute until two medical men, Braid and Elliotson, again revived the smoldering science in the 1840's. Through the neurohypnotic experiments of James Braid, a stolid practitioner of Manchester, and John Elliotson, the iconoclastic professor at University College, London, hypnotism derived both its name and a modicum of physiologic respectability. The slow mastery of the phenomena of induced sleep, occupying several decades, will be dealt with in a subsequent chapter. Here, however, we will deal with a new expression of science-turned-faith—phrenology, which became fused with mesmerism in the minds of its enthusiastic but uncritical devotees.

THE FLOWERING OF PHRENOLOGY

Phrenology had its beginnings in the precise anatomic work of Franz Gall, a Viennese physician. The scientific beginnings of phrenology, known as craniology, will also be discussed subsequently. Early craniology was based on the study of skulls of criminals, of insane people and idiots. The

[312] Townshend, C. H.: Facts in Mesmerism with Reasons for a Dispassionate Inquiry into It, ed. 2, London, H. Baillière, 1844.
[313] The Zoist, a journal devoted to cerebral physiology and mesmerism, London, 1843.
[314] Surbled, Georges: Hypnotism, *in* Catholic Encyclopedia, Vol. VII, p. 609, New York, Encyclopedia Press, 1913.

result of Gall's researches represented a primitive type of constitutional psychiatry. As Spurzheim, his associate, put it,[315] "Configuration and organic constitution proclaim innate disposition and capacities of action." When to the early constitutional psychiatry was added a "phrenological mode of considering cerebral organization," Gall felt he had enriched medicine by indicating how dominance or inferiority of the various mental faculties and sentiments could be accurately gauged, how "determinate characters" could be outlined and powers of the brain projected to the outside world for all to see and comprehend. Organs of the brain and specific mental functions were plotted on the skull with care and conviction. In a later chapter Gall's contribution to neurology will be outlined. It should be noted at this point, however, that phrenology, as it was evolving from craniology, maintained a reputable medical position for a time. Dr. Elliotson lectured before the Phrenological Society (1823) on a celebrated murderer, a "poor wretch . . . [whose] bumps of amativeness, destructiveness, acquisitiveness" were overdeveloped. And the *Lancet*[316] noted that Dr. Willis was preparing to give a series of lectures on phrenology, which it was hoped "would include the dissection of the brain according to Gall's system."

Whilst Gall was a scientist, Spurzheim, his Boswell, developed into a publicist. Together they lectured and traveled, basking in the sun of public acclaim. A correspondent from the *Birmingham Journal* wrote from Paris, "This man is the greatest moral philosopher [psychologist] that Europe has produced;" but the *Edinburgh Review* set down the whole doctrine taught by "these two modern peripatetics as a piece of thorough quackery."

As Gall's social successes mounted, his scientific standing became murky. While Parisians took Gall and his "organic" descriptions to their hearts, Pinel became engaged in an academic quarrel with Gall concerning the seat of insanity. A contemporary journalist wrote, "Great indeed was the ardor excited among Parisians by the presence of the men, who . . . could tell their fortunes by their heads," but Pinel insisted on hearing from Gall how exaggeration of the various faculties of the brain could cause insanity when, for example, the hypochondriac's disorder was in the nerves of his stomach. At the same time, the lectures by Gall and Spurzheim at the Athénée Royale were oversubscribed, and fashionable gentlemen had their "physiognomies" engraved on their snuffboxes.

The physiognomy fad had a scientific beginning not dissimilar to that of phrenology. A Swiss theologian, Johann Casper Lavater, on the intuitive feeling that "all passive and active movements, . . . all traits whereby the suffering or acting man can be immediately perceived—all this is the object

[315] Spurzheim, J. C.: Phrenology in Connection with the Study of Physiognomy, London, Treuttel, Wortz & Richter, 1826.
[316] Lancet Notes: Phrenology 2:182, Feb. 8, 1824.

of physiognomy," developed a science quite in line with today's constitutional psychiatry.[317] Lavater published four volumes called *Fragments on Physiognomy* (1775-1778), which were enhanced later by technics for measuring silhouettes of physiognomies. Instruments were invented for measuring the brow, the outline of the face and the head, etc., hoping in this way to analyze psychosomatic reactions and characterologic structure. As Loewenberg points out, physiognomy, although criticized by some scientists of the 1780's, was brought into disrepute "by irresponsible popularizations."

With Spurzheim's coinage of the term *phrenology* in 1814, craniologic concepts subsided as a subject of medical interest. Parisian wits lampooned the plodding Viennese doctor; Villers wrote, "At one time everybody . . . was trembling for its head and fearing to put it in Dr. Gall's cabinet." The medical fraternity were increasingly brusque with Gall's bumps and knobs which underlay propensities, sentiments and faculties. The Institute scientists rejected him. Gall retired to work on his opus magnum,[318] and Spurzheim moved on to England to carry the phrenologic science to greater heights of popularity.

The shift from craniology to phrenology brought a shift in interest from the correlation of mental capacity and brain architecture to a doctrine which combined anatomic pretensions and moral principles. In England, phrenology and its champions Spurzheim and Combe became the toast of the intelligentsia. George Eliot, whose success as a novelist was attributed by Combe (her teacher and England's foremost phrenologist) to the phrenological philosophy she absorbed, had her propensities gauged at regular intervals and "never found them wanting." "I am pronounced," she wrote to a friend, "to possess a large organ of 'adhesiveness,' a still larger one of 'firmness' and as large of 'conscientiousness.' "[319] Because physiognomy and phrenology were mixed in the popular mind, this "science" ran through the charlatan's mill. Fowler and Wells, the New York phrenologic publishers, featured in their 1881 catalogue:[320]

The New Physiognomy

Reduced to $3.00

Beautiful	Faces	Homely
Benevolent	Faces	Miserly
Honest	Faces	Knavish
Thoughtful	Faces	Blank
Good	Faces	Bad

How to Study

All Kinds of Faces

Still, the study of the face as an indicator of the psychic life within did not entirely remain in the hands of irresponsible individuals. Among his other interests, William James had a hobby of collecting photographs to study the human physiognomy,[321] which he called his "anthropologic collection." The influence of phrenology on the popular mind was so widespread that the Church was forced to make a pronouncement against it. Combe's book, *The Constitution of Man,* was said to be on household bookshelves that held nothing more than the Bible and Pilgrim's Progress. Even clear-headed Edinburgh took phrenology to its bosom, although the *Edinburgh Review,* with Scottish frugality, complained that the organ of "philoprogenitiveness . . . was a word it couldn't spare another day to write."

From England Spurzheim traveled to America. Although Pope Pius VII excommunicated those who preached phrenology, and the Parisian authorities forbade Spurzheim to lecture further in France, America welcomed the prophet of the key to human character. Huge audiences turned out to hear him in New York, Philadelphia and Boston. The president of the American Phrenological Society, Dr. Capen, welcomed Spurzheim's "feasting presence . . . full of light." The America of the 1830's called the discoverer of phrenology to mental institutions, schools, churches, where he lectured, demonstrated and observed. Americans, in what George Seldes called the "stammering century," absorbed phrenology as they did every evangelistic preachment that came their way. When Spurzheim died in 1832 in Boston, the populace reacted as if it were a national catastrophe. "The decease of Spurzheim," wrote Dr. Capen, "cast a gloom over the city not to be described."

Phrenology flourished in America. Educationalists hoped to utilize phrenologic diagnoses to remodel school curricula and "to improve the race." The Albany Female Academy in 1843 resolved through its grateful trustees [322] "that phrenology, as taught by Mr. Grimes . . . is useful in everyday intercourse with society . . . that it is destined to become useful in legislation, and in the government of children in families and in schools." Physicians utilized its predictive diagnostic aid in managing insane patients.

[317] *Quoted in* Loewenberg, R. D.: The significance of the obvious, an 18th century controversy on psychosomatic principles, Bull. Hist. Med. **10**:666, 1941.

[318] Gall, F.: Anatomie et physiologie du système nerveux en général et du cerveau en particulier, Paris, 1810-1819.

[319] Eliot, George: Life As Related in Her Letters and Journals, edited by J. W. Cross, Vol. I, p. 78, New York, Harper, 1884.

[320] The Phrenological Journal, New York, Fowler & Wells, 1881.

[321] Perry, R. B.: The Thought and Character of William James, Cambridge, Harvard, 1948.

[322] Grimes, S. J.: The Mysteries of the Head and Heart Explained, An Improved System of Phrenology, p. 355, Chicago, W. B. Keen, Cooke & Co., 1875.

A phrenologically trained psychiatrist, Andrew Combe [323] counseled, could keep his "temper calm and unruffled" by plotting the patient's propensities preliminarily, "Perceiving in the maniac's rage the blind outpourings of excited Destructiveness . . . the physician can allay the storm . . . by merely addressing himself . . . to the patient's moral nature."

Opportunists tilled the phrenologic ground assiduously. Matters of interpersonal relationships were solved on the basis of diagnoses of propensities and sentiments. Orson Fowler, under the slogan of "Natural Waists or No Wives," wrote a book applying phrenology to the "Selections of Companions for Life." One must watch the propensities, for "if Hope be large in the husband, but small in the wife, he magnifies prospects . . . whilst she, especially if Cautioness be large, looks at them in a directly opposite light, she fearing . . . he rejoicing." [324]

The publishing firm of Fowler and Wells, New York, developed the *American Phrenological Journal,* the Phrenological Museum and the American Institute of Phrenology to a point of financial success. In their *Journal* they ask subscribers: "Could you have spent it [your money] to better advantage? That is, could you have derived from other disbursement of it, a greater amount of HAPPINESS?" [325]

PHRENOLOGY AND FAITH-HEALING

Since the unit characteristics or propensities of combativeness, amativeness, veneration and many others could be demonstrated qualitatively if not quantitatively in the subject, it was not far to the assumption that these organs could be influenced by mesmeric control. Stanley Grimes, self-styled leader of phrenology in this country, introduced the concept of *phrenomagnetism* in 1845.[326] Utilizing mystic terms not unlike those of Mesmer, Grimes spoke of an *etherium* which pervaded all matter, including phrenologic bumps themselves. By pressing a skull protuberance which he assumed to be responsible for the mesmerizing "propensity," he was able to invoke mesmeric trances directly. The clear-thinking James Braid accepted phrenomagnetism early in his hypnotic work, although he later recanted this hybrid science emphatically.[327] By hypnotizing a subject and stimulat-

[323] Combe, Andrew: Observations on Mental Derangement, Being an Application of the Principles of Phrenology to the Elucidations of Causes, Symptoms, Nature and Treatment of Insanity, Boston, Marsh, Capen & Lyon, 1834.

[324] Fowler, O. S.: Matrimony or Phrenology and Physiology Applied to the Selection of Companions for Life, New York, Fowler & Wells, 1847.

[325] American Phrenological Journal, Vol. 1847.

[326] Grimes, S. J.: Etherology of the Philosophy of Mesmerism and Phrenology, Including a New Philosophy of Sleep and of Consciousness, with a Review of the Pretentions of Neurology and Phreno-Magnetism, New York, Saxton & Miles, 1845.

[327] Braid, James: Experimental inquiry to determine whether hypnotic manifestations can be adduced in proof of phrenology, M. Times, London 2:184, 1845.

ing the phrenologic organs, Braid demonstrated the "phrenological sway during hypnotism" and the close connection between the sister sciences of phrenology and mesmerism. One of his cases,[328] a Miss S., "an entire skeptic," became readily hypnotized when Braid touched her organ of veneration:

> The moment "veneration" was touched, her features assumed the peculiar expression of that feeling, the hands were clasped, she sank on her knees in the attitude of the most devout adoration; combined with "hope," the features were illuminated, and beamed with a feeling of ecstasy, and when "ideality" was added, the ecstasy was so extreme as scarcely to be supportable. On changing the point of contact to "firmness," she instantly arose, and stood with an attitude of defiance; "self-esteem," flounced about with the utmost self-importance; the "love of approbation" was painted to the greatest perfection; "imitation" imitated accurately everything done or spoken in any language; "friendship and adhesiveness," clasped hold of me; and by stimulating "combativeness," she struck out with the arm of the side on which combativeness had been touched.

The union of mesmerism with other cerebral manifestations continued to excite scientific investigators and amateur magnetizers alike. Phrenology and mesmerism, odylic force [329] (a luminous expression of the chemical current which ran along the nerves from the brain) and magnetization, hypnotism and "propagation of nerve influx," were marriages of hasty theory and observable phenomena. But while the scientific workers grappled with imponderable explanations of the marvels that they witnessed, kneading them dry of logical meaning and slowly rejecting them, the irregular practitioners of mental healing clung to their effluvial doctrines. Phrenomagnetism and the theory of od (odylic force) remained in the lexicon of mesmeric faith-healers, and, though both have fallen into desuetude, the spirit of the former survives in the side show and the latter in the Ouija board. Similarly, Dods' School of Electrical Psychology,[330] based on the proposition that "electricity is the connecting link between mind and inert matter," attracted much attention in 1840. John B. Dods, in discovering the true nature of mesmerism, attracted enough attention to warrant an invitation to lecture on his findings before a senatorial committee (1850) composed, among others, of H. Clay, Daniel Webster and Sam Houston. His science was taught to "thousands." Dods proudly stated, "Gentlemen *ten* dollars for tuition, ladies *five*."

Pseudoscientific innovators who rode on the coattails of medical inves-

[328] Braid, James: Neurypnology, or, The Rationale of Nervous Sleep Considered in Relation to Animal Magnetism, illustrated by numerous cases of relief and cure of disease, London, Churchill, 1843.

[329] Reichenbach, von, K. L.: Reichenbach's Letters on Od and Magnetism (1852), translated by F. D. O'Byrne, London, Hutchinson, 1928.

[330] Dods, J. B.: The Philosophy of Electrical Psychology, New York, Fowler & Wells, 1850.

tigators spoke a strange tongue, a patois of romantic idealism, physical science and always some admixture of magic. Sober minds, linking hypnotism to the irregular groups, became impatient of these attempts to unite spiritualism with psychology. But hypnotism, the Hydra-headed creature, was not yet scotched; nor did belief in magic or yearning for its miracles cease to motivate the search for methods of mental healing. As Walsh [331] remarks, but without offering an explanation, "The recurrence of attention to it [hypnosis] in each succeeding generation is one of the most interesting phenomena in the history of the use of the mind to influence the body."

The newly honored science of physics, from which arose magnetization (hypnosis), electricity and odylic effluvium, contributed material for the "scientific" faith-healers, while metaphysical neoreligions provided substance for those faith-healers with no scientific pretensions. The particular trend of the latter-day faith-healers that distinguished the nineteenth century was their neoreligious affiliation. These were faith-healers who were anchored to a personal religion, an identification with deity, or to a subjectivized psychology which borrowed phrases and ideas from the then current stage of psychological science. Some who exploited a faith based on spiritual identifications struck intuitively at the core of emotional causes of illness, touching off hidden wells of healing power. From healer they moved to the status of prophet, soon tumbling from this lofty position under the slow inroads of realism and a psychological science which tested empathy in the crucible of emotional realities.

It is this type of prescient temperament which predominated among the latter-day faith-healers. There were some, like the Rev. Mr. Dowie, fanatical, overzealous, visionary, who perished. Others, like Mary Baker Eddy, their ideas having attained practical meaning, have flourished. The mainspring in each was faith, faith in the capacity of man to understand and utilize the living, therapeutic essence of religion.

The trend toward faith-healing through neoreligions, so characteristic of the nineteenth century, has not diminished materially in our own. Perhaps there are cultural-social reasons for this. Religious faith as a healing force, with the exception of shrines such as Lourdes, in France, or Ste. Anne de Beaupré, in Quebec, did not maintain the same social and religious significance that it did in the days of the Holy Crusades. Faith in earlier times was almost entirely an attribute of religion. Faith-healing in latter days was, and is, mediated through transcendental philosophy and physical science. The cultural-social institutions in which trust is placed change with the times; physics, biologic chemistry, electronics, psychology and the precision of modern clinical medicine now are the repositories of that psychological force which is the effective core of faith-healing. Though

[331] Walsh, J. J.: Psychotherapy, *in* Catholic Encyclopedia, Vol. XII, p. 550, New York, Appleton, 1911.

religion is not psychotherapy, it functioned as such for two millennia in the Western world. For about two centuries the faith that heals has been displaced by the material sciences and by a personalized philosophic psychology.

Perhaps the explanation of this displacement of faith lies in the truth that man's wish for magical results is never lost. The magic reality of childhood becomes, for adults, an unconscious reality. The hard-pressed ego, the censor of irrationality, is constantly required to comb magical elements from the psychological matrix of each newly coined system of mental healing. For the history of psychotherapy this seemingly eternal intrusion of magic in mental healing is no less fascinating than the equally eternal quest to extract psychological or physiologic forces from faith-healing.

LATTER-DAY FAITH-HEALERS

The people of the United States in the 1800's were a hard-headed, earthy group, eminently practical yet capable of deep spirituality. The genius of Early America resided in its capacity for physical hardship and a simultaneous seeking for things of the spirit. Perhaps because Americans were less dominated by the authoritarian overtones of organized religion, more experimental in their tendencies and less intellectually bound to European formalism, they easily embraced the faith-healing arising from newly formed religions. Although this tendency is present among other peoples in Europe, particularly in northern Europe, for purposes of illustrating the derivation and the expansion of latter-day faith-healers this development will be traced chiefly as it pertains to the American scene.

Revivalism was in the ascendancy in the 1820's. In part, it was a reaction to the Age of Reason, the repressive puritanism of Colonial America and the need of intellectual and emotional nutriment for hungry minds. Frontiersmen were as eager for the rough country evangelists as were the Brahmins of Boston for the transcendental philosophy of Emerson and the Concord group. The spiritual revival that passed over into spiritualism was vigorous and gusty. Emotional strivings, brought to a "high plane of experience" [332] by Evangelist Charles Finney, self-styled "Brigadier-General of Jesus Christ," resulted in trance states as he exhorted his audiences to "Agonize, I tell you!"

On a more contained level these emotional upheavings were channeled into numberless reform movements. The Abolitionists were clamoring for the end of slavery; temperance societies demanded the prohibition of alcohol and tobacco; the Oneida colony, established by John Noyes the Perfectionist, strove for a practical embodiment of the communist plan

[332] Finney, C. G.: *In* Dictionary of American Biography, Vol. VI, p. 394.

of life; and socialism, imported from France through Fourier, was to be based on "The Principles of a True Organization of Society." Everywhere the "crust of Puritanism broke, and from its fiery core came new idealisms and strange fantastic religions." [333] In 1840, Emerson wrote: "We are all a little wild here, with numberless projects of social reform. Not a reading man but has a draft of a new community in his waistcoat pocket." [334]

Though much of this spirit was directed into poetic intellectualism and transcendentalism which stated,[335] "The mind properly stirred and lifted could go direct by intuition to the sources of absolute truth," a considerable portion of it was expressed in phrenology, odic psychology, mesmerism and clairvoyance. The model of the Byronic American, the "American romantic rebel, even down to studying language reform and animal magnetism," [336] sparked and sustained the trend toward a spiritualism that "improved the mind, increased its power and healed earthly woes."

The philosophic leaven at work in America stemmed from the idealism of Kant and Hegel, flowering into transcendentalism. The central notion of these philosophies was molded to the idea that the human mind and soul were emanations from God, inhabiting the body for the period of life. Reunion with God, the mystic return to God, was the supreme conclusion of life. Moreover, it meant a reflection of perfectionism and a life of triumph over matter, which itself was imperfection. Disease cannot occur in a perfect God world in which life flowed indestructibly through all beings back to its supreme source. Such a philosophy shaped a plan for mental and physical life, for a religion and for a philosophy of mental healing. To raise human beings to divine stature rather than to debase them in groveling before a vindictive God, to "hitch your wagon to a star," to attain the ineffable union with God, became the aim of transcendental philosophy. Those who absorbed these concepts felt buoyant. To transform houses of common clay in which they dwelt into divine habitations became the guiding principle of New Thought, theosophy and numerous shades of religious healing groups. Borrowing from Buddhism, the proponents of New Thought propounded, "All that we are is the result of what we have thought!" And Emerson exclaimed, "Never name sickness!" [337] In this state of intoxication, diseases became immaterial, pathology a chimera, emotions a dross of an unspiritual intellect, and psychological science unnecessary.

Faith-healers, riding the tide, rediscovered mind cures through hypno-

[333] Canby, H. S.: Thoreau, p. xiv, Boston, Houghton, 1939.
[334] Emerson: Works, Vol. X.
[335] Canby: *Op. cit.*, p. 84.
[336] Hale, W. H.: Horace Greeley, Voice of the People, p. 92, New York, Harper, 1950.
[337] Brooks, V. W.: New England: Indian Summer, 1865-1915, p. 335, New York, Dutton, 1940.

tism and the magic of spiritualistic séances. The Fox sisters of Rochester, N. Y., for example, had startled the country with their "spirit rappings." Communicating with the great spirits of the ages through these rappings, they obtained directions for healing their clients of obscure or chronic illnesses. Cases that had passed through the hands of physicians unbenefited went to the Fox sisters. The new movement started by them enveloped the country. Sober-minded folk were alarmed at the shift toward spiritualism. Mary D. Wellcome, in 1860, in a tract exposing the spiritualism of Dods and Davis, noted that there were already 1,537,000 persons who were spiritualists in the United States alone, and that 150,000 "are from our own loved Maine."

At another point in the spectrum of latter-day faith-healers came self-appointed healers who sought to represent within themselves the healing power of divine faith. Among the garish examples of this group were Dowie and Schlatter, messiahs and prophets. The Rev. James Alexander Dowie, an Australian, received the revelation that he was the reincarnation of the Prophet Elijah. Arriving in the United States in 1888,[338] he traveled through the country preaching the advent of salvation. Organizing the Christian Catholic Church in Zion City, Illinois, he developed a community along theocratic lines which, among other things, prohibited the presence of physicians. Besides the title of a second Elijah, Dowie claimed the power of healing through prayer and the laying on of hands. Well organized and lashed by his domination, Dowie's hosts, in 1903, moved on to New York to convert and heal the unenlightened millions of the metropolis. His blatant manner cost him followers, and an ensuing scandal soon dissolved Dowie's kingdom.

Francis Schlatter belonged to the same tragicomic group of inspired healers who traveled along the Mississippi and through the Southwest as public healers a half century ago. He appeared in Denver, reporting that he had undergone a forty-day fast and was the carrier of the divine power of healing by touch, transmitted from Jesus through the sovereigns of Europe to him. Thousands flocked to him. Schlatter conceived the idea of extending his operations by sending out through the mail, to those who needed aid, handkerchiefs which had been touched by him. The federal postal authorities felt that the extension of his power through the mails was fraudulent and summarily acted on this decision.

Inspired healers rose and fell, taking their places in a never-ending stream of psychologists, physiologists, health experts and seers. Some ephemeral healers utilized a newly discovered physiologic fact, as in the case of Horace Fletcher, the food faddist. Fletcher pinned his faith on the healing properties of uncooked cellulose in raw vegetables, espousing veg-

[338] Dowie, J. A.: *in* Dictionary of American Biography, Vol. V, p. 413, 1943.

etarianism, which was advanced as a reaction to the heavy consumption of meat during Victorian days. He developed the idea that slow, thorough mastication added enormous value and energy to food. If chewed properly, Fletcher claimed, only one twentieth of what was ordinarily consumed was needed. From nature's storehouse a new source of energy was available, which he claimed would be reflected in mental and physical well-being. Fletcherism became a household word, almost a new creed. William James, the psychologist, tried it for three months and gave it up because "it nearly killed me." And preceding Fletcher was Dr. Sylvester Graham, promoter of vegetarianism, open windows and cold baths. Young men, like Horace Greeley, the crusading editor of the *New York Tribune,* who lived at Dr. Graham's "Diet-reform" hotel on Chatham Street, New York, during his youth,[339] succumbed to the new reform. Similar psychotherapeutic systems attached themselves to other dietary ideas; during the middle of the century bread pills enjoyed high repute because of their curative power. The healing power of the sun shining through blue glass, in the hands of General Pleasanton, became a popular curative method about 1870. Thousands sat exposed to the sun with blue glass interposed; physicians prescribed it for debilitated patients, not daring to resist the pressure of socially approved magic.

To detail every derivative of physiologic-psychological-inspirational school of mental healing would be merely to repeat the basic principle of yearning for magic projected to an indifferent object or idea, embellished often with an artificial, confusing terminology. Each year witnessed a new "psychic" science, arising like the phoenix from the ashes of the last. The despair of medical lobbies and a short-lived boon to publishers, their sponsors came and went like itinerant healers of an earlier period. All were based on an attempt, not always conscious, to pragmatize idealism, to do something about an accepted philosophy which had as its theme the vulgate expression, "The power of mind over matter." The transcendental philosophy of nineteenth-century America was practical. When Thoreau wrote, "The fickle person is he . . . who has not an ancient wisdom for a life-time but a new prudence every hour," [340] he meant seriously to find a way for salvation of the individual, for a better use of his life. A sense of practicalness, an American confidence that all religious truths were not exhausted and "the distrust of the expert, rationalized into a democratic axiom during the Jacksonian era, . . . deeply ingrained in the American character" [341] were the factors that stimulated the flood of religio-philosophic healing systems during the nineteenth century.

[339] Hale, W. H.: *Op. cit.,* p. 25.
[340] *Quoted in* Canby: *Op. cit.,* p. 186.
[341] Commager, H. S.: The American Mind, p. 12, New Haven, Conn., Yale, 1950.

TRANSCENDENTALISM AND THE BEGINNINGS OF CHRISTIAN SCIENCE

The tendency for publication of indefensible systems like John Bunyon Campbell's "Spirit Vitapathy," or "Christolution," by C. R. Edwards, began slowly to be matched by maturer movements such as embodied in New Thought and other idealistic quasi religions. Gradually the atmosphere surrounding the development of spiritual healing systems became respectable, and the Chautauqua spirit receded. Elements borrowed from psychology, such as were crudely inherent in mesmerism or magnetization, were gradually relinquished. Spiritualism, united with slight deviations from denominational religions and with the addition of Hindu esotericism, became the background for faith-healing systems. Starting with an attempt to derive a practical benefit in terms of happiness, a workable philosophy of life or relief from despondency, these mind-cure systems spiraled into neoreligions, anchored in Christian theology and in idealistic hope. From theosophy [342, 343] to Christian Science, faith-healing underwent a renascence in the latter half of the nineteenth century. Although neurologists fumed at the new classification of "Christopaths," explaining them as due to a "brain [that] strained by the trials of life or disease . . . seeks relief in study of the Scriptures . . . [and] insomnia and neuratrophia and cerebrasthenia hasten the fatal denouement and the Christopath is evolved," [344] they drew adherents by the thousands. Of the schools of mental healing derived indirectly from transcendentalism, Christian Science, founded by Mrs. Mary Baker Eddy, far eclipsed the others in attaining a continued success. Mrs. Eddy was a product of the spiritualistic and pious atmosphere of New England. Attuned by a sensitive personality to receive the benefits of magnetism from Phineas Quimby, she transformed his "Science of Health" into a religion, a cosmology and a method of psychotherapy.

The story of their first meeting in 1862 in his consulting parlor is given varying treatment. According to a neutral reconstruction of the scene, Quimby proceeded to talk over the patient's problems along religious-healing lines, after preliminary magnetic passes and rubbing the head. Apparently Mrs. Eddy, who was then Mrs. Patterson, underwent prompt improvement, and her enthusiastic interest in his cure gratified Quimby, for he agreed to teach her his "Science." For several weeks Mrs. Eddy studied and discussed with him the "truth which he opposes to the error of giving intelligence to matter." From the standpoint of an official biog-

[342] Besant, Annie: Esoteric Christianity, or, The Lesser Mysteries, New York, John Lane, 1901.

[343] Encyclopædia Britannica, Vol. 22, p. 69.

[344] Hughes, C. H.: Christopathy and Christian Science (so called), Alienist & Neurologist **20**:611, 1899.

rapher, the meeting had a totally different aspect. The patient had come prepared with a philosophy of healing, interpreting the cure as the accomplishment of "Quimby's mediatorship between herself and God:"[345]

> She had come to Quimby prepared to find him a saint who healed by virtue of his religious wisdom, and as soon as she met him she completed her mental picture, endowing him with her own faith. Thus the hypnotist had actually nothing to do with it.

Quimby, with little background in science or letters, had learned hypnotism from Charles Poyen, a French mesmerist, in 1838. Soon Quimby's exhibitions of magnetization established a sound local reputation. His piercing black eyes "possessed the power of looking at an object even without winking for a length of time."[346] Like other magnetizers of the period, Quimby moved into medical fields. In 1843, a Dr. Wheelock wrote to a prominent city physician in Portland, Maine, of his success in operating on a nasal polyp in a woman whom Quimby had magnetized. "I operated for 4 to 5 minutes," wrote the physician, "the patient did not show the slightest pain. . . . Mr. Q. is an intelligent gentleman and worthy of the utmost confidence."

Utilizing a clairvoyant who "read" diagnoses to him, Quimby performed healing miracles.[347] An eyewitness states:

> He took a man that had a lame shoulder. It was partially out of joint. He worked upon it and the man said there was no pain in it. This astonished them. This afternoon the man went about his work as well as ever. . . . [Mr. Quimby] took a man out of the audience (a perfect stranger to him) and effected a cure on his arm. The man had not been able to raise it up for two years and in a few minutes he was able to raise his arm up to his head, and moved it around free from pain.

Presently he dispensed with magnetization, finding that he could influence the patient's mind directly by demonstrating that disease was "deranged state of mind" imparted to patients through words that assumed tangible form. If disease is merely belief, one can attend directly to the mind and banish belief in disease. While he worked with his partly persuasive and partly exhortative method, Quimby conceived the notion that his discoveries pointed the way to an understanding of how Christ had healed. Under the stimulus of this idea he wrote ten volumes in longhand,

[345] Wilbur, Sibyl: The Life of Mary Baker Eddy, ed. 4, p. 87, Boston, Christian Science Publishing Society, 1938.

[346] Quimby, P. P.: The Quimby Manuscripts, Showing the Discovery of Spiritual Healing and the Origin of Christian Science, edited by H. W. Dresser, p. 31, New York, Crowell, 1921.

[347] *Ibid.*, p. 24.

the now famous Quimby manuscript,[348] claimed by Wilbur to be "absolutely hypothetical" and a plagiarism.[349]

In spite of errors in grammar and logic, Quimby's writings had a common-sense flavor that, if the premises were admitted, could easily have swayed his multitudinous neurotic patients. For several years his rooms in Portland, Maine, were crowded with patients from all parts of New England. Some he treated through letters, but most through his head-stroking and his transcendental semantic monologue: [350]

> If I (as a typical doctor) tell you that you have congestion of the lungs I impart my belief to you by a deposit of matter in the form of words. . . . If you eat my belief it goes to form a disease. . . . Like its author, my belief grows, comes forth and at last takes the form of a pressure across the chest. . . . All this is very simple when you know what caused it.

The official biographer of Mary Baker Eddy, intent apparently on freeing Quimby from any claim of originality for the system of Christian Science healing, calls him a "blundering and stumbling reasoner . . . an unconscious hypnotizer." According to this version, after the first treatment, which, it is said, was given by stroking Mrs. Eddy's head, shoulders and back, Mrs. Eddy said to Quimby,[351] " 'It is not magnetism that does this work, doctor,' she declared. 'You have no need to touch me, nor disorder my hair with your mesmeric passes.' " " 'What then do you think does the healing?' he asked." "Your knowledge of God's law, your understanding of the truth which Christ brought into the world and which had been lost for ages." What heals, she told him, was the "God in you" that works through man. At the time of her conversion, however, Mrs. Eddy had naught but reverence for her teacher.

Some considered Quimby a quack, but few could deny his sincerity of purpose and success. His political creed was unassailable; as pointed out by the *Portland Advertiser* in 1860, "Dr. is a strong union man: as soon cure a sick rattlesnake as a sick rebel." [352] Some hailed him with such fervor that Quimby at one time published an essay called "A Defense Against Making Myself Equal with Christ." His perceptions were remarkable: "A person may perceive feelings of another by simply sitting near by and rendering himself receptive—no mesmerism necessary. Higher spirit—is God spirit and healing is Christ's method." [353] As he grew older, Quimby, imbued with the idea that he had rediscovered the universal technic for healing disease, pressed his son George and a Mrs. Dresser into service as disciples to carry on his works and spread his doc-

[348] *Ibid.*
[349] Wilbur: *Op. cit.*, p. 95.
[350] Quimby: *Op. cit.*, p. 40.
[351] Wilbur: *Op. cit.*, p. 88.
[352] Quimby: *Op. cit.*, p. 96.
[353] *Ibid.*, p. 51.

trines, but overshadowing these was the vigor of his pupil, then Mrs. Patterson.

The life of Mrs. Mary Baker Glover Patterson Eddy has been subject both to deification by disciples and to the cold objectivity of unsympathetic critics. But for the drive of her ego and insistence on practicality, she would have lived and died a nervous, sickly woman whose life of suffering would have been interspersed by periods of mystical poesy and flashes of religious inspiration.

THE FOUNDER OF CHRISTIAN SCIENCE

Mary Ann Morse Baker was born in 1821 in New Hampshire. Her mother died early under the strain of the unremitting cares of a New England farm; her father was a religious man, uncompromising in his code of ethics, permitting only the tenets of the church to be the guide of conduct in his home. In this circumscribed life-setting, the Bible was the chief source of intellectual food. Mary was a precocious child; biographers call her a poetic, moody child, astounding the church elders by her understanding of Christ and her piety. Extremely nervous in her early years, Dr. Ladd, the family physician,[354] described her symptoms as those of hysteria "mingled with bad temper," which he found were treatable by suggestion. Later her husband recommended that she be taken for treatment to one of the itinerant mesmerists then active in New England.

Life for a young woman in those times was prosaic, with few outlets for one with an imaginative nature. The thought she carried in the recesses of her mind was that she was predestined for a nobler mission. The affair of the "Rochester rappings" by the Fox sisters stimulated Mrs. Glover (she had been married now) to interest herself in spiritualism, a subject for which she had always had a penchant. She discovered that she possessed considerable ability as a spiritualistic medium. But it was not until 1862 that her psychic predilections abruptly became a cogent philosophic system. For several years after her contact with Quimby she contemplated the influence of Christ's teachings, conducting her "solitary research"[355] and trying to understand Quimby's method, "the self-taught man walking wisdom's ways." Revelation attended Mrs. Patterson, for in 1866 she "discovered the Christ Science or divine laws of Life, Truth and Love and named my discovery Christian Science."[356]

By 1872, literally driven by want and a compulsiveness to communicate

[354] Dakin, E. F.: Mrs. Eddy; The Biography of a Virginal Mind, p. 9, New York, Scribner, 1929.

[355] Eddy, Mary Baker: Science and Health, with Key to the Scriptures, p. 109, Boston, Stewart, 1917. From authorized version of 1875.

[356] *Ibid.*, p. 107.

her discoveries, she had written notes and Bible commentaries called "The Science of Man by which the Sick are Healed, Embracing Questions and Answers in Moral Science, Arranged for the Learner by Mrs. Mary Baker Glover." During this period her manuscripts were changing through many laborious rewritings, so what was at first called "Extracts of Dr. P. P. Quimby's writings" became "Christian Science Mind Healing," and, in 1875, "Science and Health, with Key to the Scriptures."

Accepting the Berkeleyan idealism that God is all, the world but a reflection of Divine Will, and Spirit the only true reality, she demonstrated that matter, which was not mind, could not exist. If matter did not exist, disease, carnality, sins and immorality did not exist. The application of the perception of God the infinite eternal Mind [357] was the Science of Christ, her discovery. "It teaches that matter is the falsity, not the fact of existence: that nerves, brain, stomach, lungs, and so forth have—as matter—no intelligence, life nor sensation." The purpose of Christian Science was not primarily one of physical healing, although acts of spiritual healing were demonstrable in the present as well as in Christ's time. The essential message was the recognition that man is "harmonious and eternal" when controlled by divine intelligence.[358]

The basis for Mrs. Eddy's therapeutic effectiveness resided in attaining the belief that if the concept of matter could be dispensed with as an illusion of "false materiality," disease would also vanish. "If the Scientist reaches his patient through divine love, the healing work will be accomplished at one visit, and the disease will vanish into its native nothingness like dew before the morning sunshine." [359] All other types of psychotherapy, indeed medical therapy, as mind cure, hypnotism, materia medica, etc., belonged to "mortal mind" and hence inherently "error." Particularly hypnotism (magnetism) earned Mrs. Eddy's condemnation, for while she was evolving the principle of Christian Science she had found herself "hampered by the theories of Quimby" [360] and the effects of "malicious animal magnetism." Freeing herself from this unseen power, which was equated with evil, allowed Mrs. Eddy to expunge manipulation from her healing system in 1872 and denounce it as without a scientific foundation, criminal, subtle, ubiquitous and enslaving. "How shall I treat malicious animal magnetism?," she wrote to her students. "This growing sin must now be dealt with as evil, and not as an evil-doer or personality. . . . but, met with Science, it can and will be mastered by Science." [361]

[357] *Ibid.*, p. 127.
[358] *Ibid.*, p. 184.
[359] *Ibid.*, p. 365.
[360] Powell, L. P.: Mary Baker Eddy, A Life-Size Portrait, p. 109, New York, Macmillan, 1950.
[361] Eddy, Mary Baker: Miscellaneous Writings, 1883-1896, p. 284, Boston, Stewart, 1917.

In 1881, she moved to Boston and established the Massachusetts Metaphysical College, in which "pathology, ontology, therapeutics, moral science, metaphysics, in their application to treatment of disease" were taught. Students, intoxicated with her doctrines, went there for instruction in metaphysical "obstetrics" and moral science. Her success grew; students propagated her methods throughout the world. Practitioners of Christian Science healing were located in many cities of Europe and the Orient. Some astonishing cures were reported through Mrs. Eddy's teachings. One such case, said to have been related by Mrs. Eddy to her classes, concerned a cripple whom she had healed merely by putting out her hand as he came to the side of a carriage in which she rode.[362] Healings of more specific type were reported by followers attesting to her spiritual power. A disciple recounts an eyewitness report: [363]

> On a certain occasion Mrs. Eddy, accompanied by a student, went to a furniture shop to select some chairs, where they were waited on by a man who was wearing a bandage over one eye. As they were being shown the chairs, Mrs. Eddy seemed so absorbed that she paid little attention to them, replying to a question as to which she liked best with the words, "Any that we can sit on." Later when the student reproached Mrs. Eddy with her lack of attention to the business in hand, she replied, "Could I think of chairs when the man was suffering?" When the student returned the next day to order the chairs, the salesman asked: "Who was that lady with you yesterday? I had an abscess on my eye and when she went out, I took the bandage off, and there was not a sign of it left."

The healer now bent all her energies toward developing the organization of her church. She established journals, wrote pamphlets, books and rules for the church services, and re-edited her textbook. Her organizational ability was close to genius. By 1890, students carrying on her work over the New World and the Old looked at Mrs. Eddy as a savior. Prestige, power, wealth, came to Mrs. Eddy. As Dakin points out, when most women are looking toward the grave, Mrs. Eddy was developing a religion and a healing movement that remade the lives and rechanneled the thoughts of millions.

The period from 1890 to 1910 witnessed the growth of the Christian Science Church numerically, politically, economically, financially. Its critics multiplied as anxiety covering the Christian Science "Trust" spread. Mark Twain,[364] writing in 1899, feared for the nation's future as the popularity of Christian Science reached its apogee:

> It is a reasonably safe guess that in America in 1920 there will be ten million Christian Scientists . . . that this will be trebled in 1930. . . . In 1920,

[362] Dakin: *Op. cit.*, p. 148.
[363] Tomlinson, I. C.: Twelve Years with Mary Baker Eddy, p. 53, Boston, Christian Science Publishing Society, 1945.
[364] Twain, Mark: Christian Science, p. 72, New York, Harper, 1907.

the Christian Scientists will be a political force, in 1930, politically formidable—to remain that permanently.[365]

Orthodox religious leaders, medical lobbies, became alarmed at the spread of the religion. Psychologists and clergymen studied its cases and theories. Public leaders were disturbed by its monetary power. Mark Twain, scornful of this financial interest, remarked:

> The Dollar is hunted down in all sorts of ways: the Christian Science Mother-Church and Bargain Counter in Boston peddles all kinds of spiritual wares to the faithful, on one condition . . . cash, cash in advance.[366]

Several lawsuits were entered against Mrs. Eddy, the most widely noted being that brought by her son and other relatives to have her declared incompetent to handle her funds. The trial became the occasion for a "conclusive investigation" of Mrs. Eddy by the *New York World* [367] for the satisfaction of its readers who were intrigued by the seer and her growing adherents. A lengthy court trial ended by an open vindication of her sanity and capacity to manage her affairs.

Eloquence, sympathy, scorn and derision re-echoed in the press and in the family magazines. But Mrs. Eddy maintained her serenity, extolled even more by her supporters. In her ivory tower at Concord, New Hampshire, she issued missives of inspiration to her followers and laid the ghost of "malicious animal magnetism." Augusta E. Stetson, the Leader's chief lieutenant before her excommunication in 1909, wrote: [368] "Victory has come at last. We have demonstrated the powerlessness of hypnotism, witchcraft and mental diabolism to overthrow the cause of Christian Science and the work of our beloved leader, Mrs. Eddy."

Although the way for acceptance of Mrs. Eddy's healing philosophy had been prepared by a half century of American transcendentalism, the strongest factor in her personal success was her dominating personality, its memory softened by the years. Throughout her life, she could abide no peer. In 1895, she "ordained" that the Bible and "Science and Health with Key to the Scriptures" be the pastor of all the churches of Christian Science "on this planet." This ordinance, she noted, "met with the universal approval and support of Christian Scientists." [369]

The cosmologic note, introduced by Mrs. Eddy as to her own place among mankind, leaves open several implications. An impartial psychological observer cannot help but be impressed that she, no less than other healers through the centuries, harbored a feeling of identification with

[365] *Ibid.*, p. 68.
[366] *Ibid.*, p. 68.
[367] Dakin: *Op. cit.*, p. 419.
[368] Stetson, A. E.: Reminiscences, Sermons and Correspondence, New York, Putnam, 1913.
[369] Eddy, Mary Baker: Miscellaneous Writings, p. 383.

Deity. This was shown when she said, "I have not sought leadership. Before the great problems that have been given to me, I have felt myself nothing. There has been a voice saying to me, 'Mary, take yourself out of the way and let God act through you.' " [370]

Although Mrs. Eddy referred to her extramortal position in such words as "I am alone in the world, more alone than a solitary star . . . although I lead and am obeyed by 300,000 people at this date," [371] she also disclaimed her deification in slightly ambiguous terms, "We shall claim no especial gifts from our divine origin." [372] In time, the pressure of projected omniscience from her followers to Mrs. Eddy, aided by a constant stream of external criticism, impelled her publicly to decree (1903) that the title "Mother" should be replaced by the designation "Leader" in its application to her.

In the role as founder and revered leader of a religion, Mrs. Eddy occupied a unique position. One can easily speculate that the emotional nurturance she provided her close associates was directly related to a religion oriented about a Mother-imago rather than a Father-imago. Whether she claimed a semidivine origin or felt she had interpreted Christ's words in a spirit of true metaphysics, Mrs. Eddy had so aroused a sense of spiritual completeness and fealty in her followers that the Rev. Irving Tomlinson was able to conclude his book (1945): [373]

> As the years pass, Mary Baker Eddy's true position will be more fully recognized and appreciated. As Jesus strove to turn the attention of his disciples away from his corporeality and to open their eyes to his real identity, so did Mrs. Eddy endeavor to turn the thought of her followers away from her personality and to reveal through her writings her true place in spiritual history.
> The real identity of God's messenger to this age will be unfolded as mankind seeks to understand it through a study of the Bible and her writings.

Others were more realistic in their appraisal of Mrs. Eddy's position in the cosmic order. An official spokesman, Emily M. Ramsay,[374] in answer to the question, "What has Mary Baker Eddy done for the world?," states:

> She has furnished us with a key by which we may enter into the heart of the Gospel teaching. She has cleared away the ignorance and superstition which through long centuries have hung about the words and works of our Lord.

In its present form, Christian Science does not give so strongly the impression of a matriarchal religion, although it is based exclusively on

[370] Tomlinson: *Op. cit.*, p. 124.
[371] Milmine, Georgine: Life of Mary Baker G. Eddy, p. 449, New York, Doubleday, 1909.
[372] Chr. Sc. J., Vol. 1, 1883.
[373] Tomlinson: *Op. cit.*, p. 219.
[374] Ramsay, E. M.: Christian Science and Its Discoverer, p. 111, Boston, Christian Science Publishing Society, 1923.

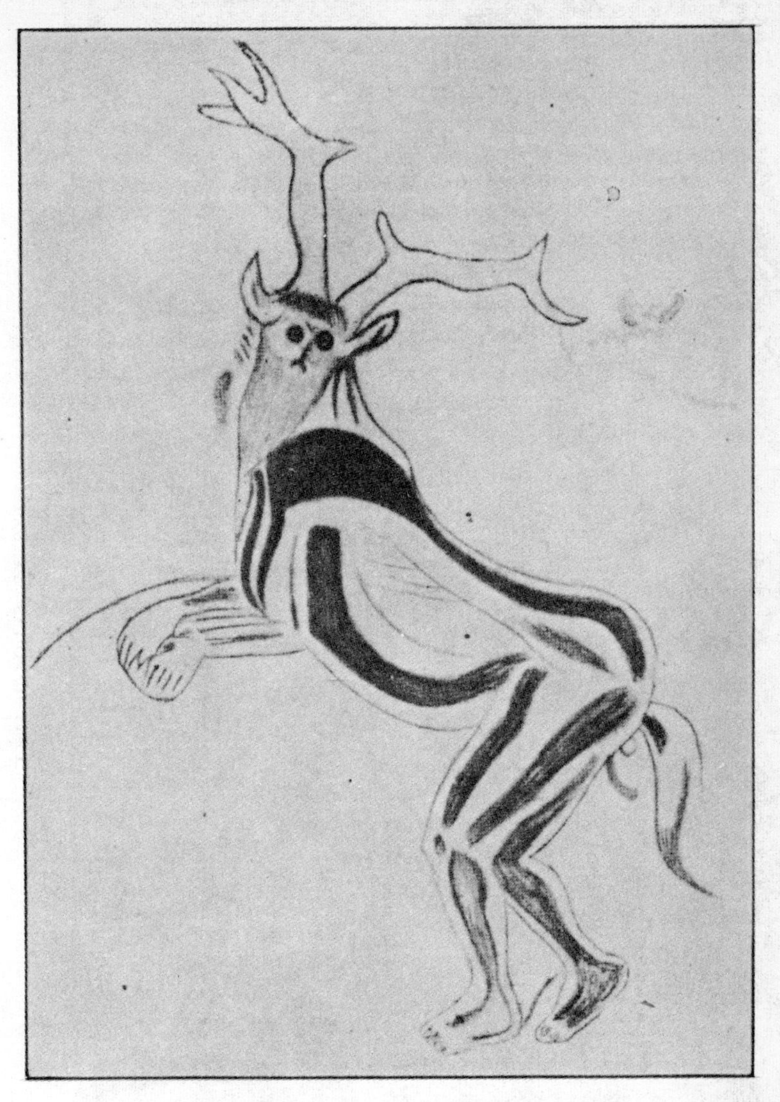

SORCERER DISGUISED AS AN ANIMAL

Mural Engraving Found in Cavern of Trois Frères at Ariège, France.

THE WITCHES' SABBATH

From *Deutsches Leben der Vergangenheit Atlas*, Vol. I.

St. Benedict Delivering a Cleric of a Demon

From *Les Démoniaques dans l'Art,* by J. M. Charcot and Paul Richer, Paris, 1887.

THE RAKE'S PROGRESS—BEDLAM

By William Hogarth. Courtesy of Metropolitan Museum of Art

Healing by Laying on of Hands
Valentine Greatrakes, the Irish "Stroaker"

BENJAMIN RUSH AS A YOUTHFUL PHYSICIAN (1768)

Painting at College of Physicians, Philadelphia, attributed to Benjamin West.

PINEL LIBERATING THE INSANE AT THE ASYLUM OF BICÊTRE

From *The Story of Bethlehem Hospital from Its Foundation in 1247*, by E. G. O'Donoghue, Unwin, London, 1914.

FRANZ ANTON MESMER

Courtesy New York Academy of Medicine.

WILLIAM TUKE

JEAN MARTIN CHARCOT

Courtesy of the Armed Forces Medical Library, Washington, D. C.

Dorothea Lynde Dix

Courtesy of *American Journal of Psychiatry*.

SILAS WEIR MITCHELL

Courtesy of *American Journal of Psychiatry.*

JOHN HUGHLINGS JACKSON

Courtesy of the Armed Forces Medical Library, Washington, D. C.

SIGMUND FREUD

Courtesy of the Armed Forces Medical Library, Washington, D. C.

Adolf Meyer

Paul F. Schilder

Mrs. Eddy's writings. Its principles are woven into an attitude toward health less doctrinaire and less revelatory. Individual problems are met by practitioners working with clients under the "conquering efficiency of courage, hope and trust." Moreover, the religious organization relies on secular leaders, not priests or ordained clergymen. Every "scientist" is able to heal; practitioners are those who devote their main activities to the work of healing.[375] But denial of the physical and of "knowing desire" in the attainment of perfection of thought, and hence of bodily health, derives from a repression of instinctive drives, variously interpreted as "evil," "animal magnetism" and medical unreality. The shrewdly divined mental healing principle that "the sick are terrified by their sick beliefs," which Mrs. Eddy culled from her study of philosophic idealism and from Quimby, proved to the world the therapeutic value of religious faith.

MIND CURE AND OCCULTISM

The Christian Science application of a faith in a personal, helpful God, as mediated through Jesus' example in works of healing, was part of a larger movement developing in America, and later in Europe, during the last half of the nineteenth century. The feeling that the old theology was too binding, that a liberal Christianity[376] had something to offer in the direction of practical help, was at the bottom of such movements as New Thought, Unity and Christian Science. The period of 1880 onward witnessed a sweep toward readjustments in Christianity. As Atkins[377] noted, people were requesting "illumination and spiritual deliverance along other than accepted lines of Christian redemption." Protest against the "old school medicine," the challenge of a psychology which recognized power in the "subconscious" mind, the influence of evolution and the "lure of the short cut,"[378] all combined to push the quest for religious aid against an engulfing national disease—neurasthenia. Christian Science, New Thought, mind-cure, "mental science" (dubbed the "Boston Craze"[379] in 1882), were movements that spread to include Oriental mysticism at one extremity and transcendentalism at the other. From Quimby's work in the 1860's, which denied the validity of disease except as a projection of men's ungodlike thinking, to the teachings of Unity and theosophy that man through God is divine in essence and can claim his freedom by thought, there lies the irregular evolutionary growth of a new attitude toward human mental frailty.

[375] *Ibid.*, p. 90.
[376] Dresser, H. W.: A History of the New Thought Movement, p. 153, New York, Crowell, 1919.
[377] Atkins, G. G.: Modern Religious Cults and Movements, New York, Revell, 1923.
[378] *Ibid.*
[379] Dresser: *Op. cit.*, p. 132.

The "mind-cure" groups gradually diverged in their evolution into two main streams: Those that clung to spirituality as their chief therapeutic weapon, and those that sought the aid of neurologic scientists who were studying personality dissociation as this phenomenon demonstrated the function of the subconscious mind. The former group encompassed New Thought, theosophy, Unity and the Ba'hai movements. These religio-philosophic systems do not practice mental healing directly, but are supportive of faith-healing as it arose from a sharing of perfection with a perpetually perfect Divine Universal Spirit. The latter group was exemplified by the Emmanuel movement, a religio-psychological healing method, the work of two clergymen and a psychiatrist. It was this branch of mind cure which became the precursor of modern pastoral psychiatry.

The main body of mind curers, however, asked less for guidance from psychopathology than from esoteric philosophies and Oriental mysticism. One of the main schools in New Thought was theosophy, built upon a doctrine espoused by a brotherhood of Mahatmas (Tibet).[380] This was an expression of Oriental philosophy which considered the body a "ductile instrument of intelligence" amenable to control through thought as it participated in the essence of divinity. From this general spiritualistic doctrine, theosophists dipped into the mystic explanations of Madame Blavatsky and Annie Besant. The latter described the effects of mental healing wherein the "irregular vibrations of the diseased person are so worked . . . as to accord with the regular vibrations of the healthy operator." [381] Even more esoteric is the Rosicrucian Fellowship, who claim their origin from a spiritual teacher in the thirteenth century bearing the symbolic name Christian Rosen Kreuz (Rose Cross). The solution of the mystery of man's evolution became the goal of the Rosicrucian Mystery School, and astrology its technical implement. Some Rosicrucian groups offer healing services [382] which, utilizing astral diagnosis and astropathology, have been carried to a point of incomprehensibility:

> The Silver Cord is grown anew in each life, that one part sprouts from the seed atom of the desire body in the great vortex of the liver, that the other part grows out of the seed atom of the dense body in the heart, completion of the Silver Cord marks the end of child-life, and from that time the solar energy which enters through the spleen and is tinted by refraction through the prismatic seed atom of the vital body located in the solar plexus. . . .

Though occultism, as a vehicle of faith, often strains credulity to the utmost, its practitioners and adherents are eternally active. In recent years

[380] Theosophy, Theosophical Societies, 1875 (started by Madame H. P. Blavatsky), *in* Encyclopædia Britannica, Vol. 22, p. 69.

[381] Besant, Annie: *Op. cit.*, p. 339.

[382] Heindel, Max: The Rosicrucian Cosmo-conception, or Mystic Christianity, ed. 18, p. 10, Oceanside, Calif., Rosicrucian Fellowship, Mt. Ecclesia, 1942.

Lee Steiner [383] has tracked down many of these psychotherapists in their counseling chambers, on the radio and the lecture platform. She estimates that from 15 to 20 million Americans are influenced by irregular practitioners of the healing art, and Seabrook's statement that "half the literate white population in the world today believe in witchcraft" [384] seems to be borne out by one reverend gentleman whom the author heard on the radio. As this man sold hallowed handkerchiefs to be sent through the mail, he claimed: "I lay hands on a cloth. . . . The healing power of God which I received four years ago is passed on to the cloth which I send to you."

During the decade following World War I, interest in New Thought in some quarters merged chaotically with a new-found fascination over the findings of psychoanalysis and modern psychology. Speakers and writers, often extravagant, uncritical and confused in their expositions of the new "personal" psychology,[385] were legion, their followers numbered in the thousands. Books which promised to revise the personality, which taught "Personal Magnetism," keyed to teach social success and increase the income,[386] flooded the market. With the rapid changes in economic and social conditions in the 1930's, expectation of limitless personality development and, with it, financial success, grew dimmer.[387] The trend moved away from a psychology that looked toward "peace, power and plenty," away from a misuse of psychological theory in amateur hands. Nevertheless, New Thought continued to gain followers, less on the basis of individual leaders inspired by therapeutic revelation than of a preoccupation with intriguing problems regarding the reality of the Spiritual Life and its palpable influence on the mind of man.

NEW THOUGHT HEALING MOVEMENTS

To return to the sounder New Thought healing movements, one may cite the Emmanuel movement as an example of a sincere and conscious use of spiritual participation for psychotherapeutic purposes. The Emmanuel movement was developed by a Boston minister, Elwood Worcester. In conversation with Dr. Weir Mitchell, the famed neurologist, he had been stirred to introduce the healing ministry of Jesus [388] through the same sug-

[383] Steiner, L. R.: Where Do People Take Their Troubles, New York, Internat. Univ. Press, 1945.

[384] Seabrook, William: Witchcraft, Its Power in the World Today, New York, Harcourt, 1940.

[385] Haddock, F. C.: The Personal Atmosphere, Ten Studies in Poise and Power, Auburndale, Mass., Power-book Lib., 1910.

[386] Carnegie, Dale: How to Win Friends and Influence People, New York, Simon & Schuster, Inc., 1937.

[387] Bromberg, Walter: The passing of personality, Current History, p. 271, June, 1935.

[388] Powell, L. P.: The Emmanuel Movement in a New England Town, p. 6, New York, Putnam, 1909.

gestive means which were proving effective in medical psychotherapy. He and his associate, the Rev. Mr. McComb, asked why this could not be done without "hurt to intelligent Christianity or to scientific medicine." Classes for treatment of functional nervous disorders, similar to those of Dr. J. H. Pratt with his tuberculous patients, were started in 1906 at the Emmanuel Church in Boston. As the movement spread it maintained close contact with neurologists and psychopathologists who were enunciating theories of subconscious mind function. The aim was to inculcate suggestions from the Scriptures in accordance with the principle that a temporary dissociation of the personality allowed ready acceptance of faith-laden ideas by the subconscious.[389] In this, the universality of suggestion as a mechanism operating through the subconscious was stressed. Proponents of the Emmanuel movement recognized hypnosis, suggestion and the persuasion method of Dubois as legitimate methods of psychotherapy; they added to these the stability and the calm which accompany the surrender to God as an act of faith.

Beyond faith and suggestion, the work of the Emmanuel movement emphasized the strengthening of the will. The words of Emerson, "The education of the will is the object of our existence," was the implied motto. The Emmanuel movement was essentially a "moral" treatment. As the patient improved under suggestion of the clergyman, he was taught to allow the idea that the physician and mental functions were proceeding according to natural laws to perfuse his mind and to strengthen his desire, or *will,* to be well. Against the strain and stress of daily life, religious feeling offered a serenity which would communicate itself (through the sympathetic nervous system) to the organs themselves. Faith gave a pervasive feeling of rightness, an aura of invincibility and a "sense of the transforming power of spiritual feeling" that spread like a wave, regenerating the life of a given individual. As one practitioner put it: "Is your life filled with pain? . . . God who dwelleth in me has no pain, nor is he sick." [390]

The conviction that a higher form of spiritual reality existed [391] and could be harnessed for healing was echoed in the teachings of American psychologists, particularly William James. That ideas and emotional excitement could "energize" a man and release inhibitions which habitually cut down his capacity for work and enjoyment, seemed self-evident to James.[392] To him the mind-cure movement was real, even though it in-

[389] Worcester, Elwood, McComb, Samuel, and Coriat, I. M.: Religion and Medicine, The Moral Control of Nervous Disorders, New York, Moffat, 1908.

[390] The Emmanuel Press, A Magazine Devoted to the Fine Art of Being Well, Berkeley, Calif., T. P. Boyd, August 12, p. 4.

[391] Worcester, Elwood, and McComb, Samuel: Body, Mind and Spirit, Boston, Jones, Marshall, 1931.

[392] James, William: The Energies of Men, New York, Holt, 1916.

curred the "enmity of the trades union wing" of the medical profession. During his periodic depressions James himself was benefited by mind curers. For his melancholia he felt:

> It is barely possible that the recovery may be due to a mind curer with whom I tried eighteen sittings. . . . I should like to get this woman into a lunatic asylum for two months, and have every case of chronic delusional insanity in the house tried by her. That would be a real test.[393]

James felt that as a "metaphysical hypothesis of the first importance" it "afforded an experimental approach to religion and constituted the only hopeful possibility of giving scientific support to a supernaturalistic faith." To the pragmatic philosopher-psychologist to whom all that mind experienced was valid material, the work of Freud and his pupils did not negate the value of faith-healing of the New Thought type. Regarding Freud's visit to America in 1909, James commented:

> I hope that Freud and his pupils will push their ideas to their utmost limits, so that we may learn what they are. They can't fail to throw light on human nature; but I confess that he made on me personally the impression of a man obsessed with fixed ideas. . . . A newspaper report of the congress said that Freud had condemned the American religious therapy (which has such extensive results) as very "dangerous" because so "unscientific." [394]

But James was only one psychologist who busied himself with a serious interest in mind cure. Others were, to understate the situation, dubious. Christian Science was dubbed neither Christian nor scientific; orthodox theologians found fault with the pragmatism of modern mind-healing which, emphasizing health of the body, left no room for the "necessity of a moral life." [395] But logic availed not against the practical value of spiritual help through mind-healing. In answer, the proponents of New Thought exclaimed with fine irony:

> Many are figuratively looking back over their collars to some ancient mountain to hear what God said to the race in its childhood, instead of looking up . . . to hear what God will say to the race in its manhood.[396]

The new alignment of Christian faith moved on to pastoral psychiatry, a controlled attempt to utilize emotional forces evoked by religious participation within a clinical atmosphere. Beyond the psychoanalytic study of the unconscious as it determined conscious attitudes and derivative neurotic symptoms, beyond explanations of religious feelings in psychological terms of human "needs" and dependencies, lay personal experiences, "some

[393] Perry, R. B.: *Op. cit.*
[394] *Ibid.*
[395] Bellwald, A. M.: Christian Science and the Catholic Faith, New York, Macmillan, 1922.
[396] The Emmanuel Press 1:12, April 12, 1912.

ways of coming to terms with existence [i.e., the complete spiritual and physical reality of the cosmos, which] . . . are healing and life-giving and transforming." [397] The real problems of reconciling religion and psychiatry in their common therapeutic goals engaged more and more attention from exponents in both fields. Both disciplines [398] taught methods for attaining serenity and peace of mind; both charged themselves with the task of resolving basic concepts of psychotherapy with correlative ones from the Christian doctrine of redemption and Judaic concept of the "revelation of God's working in history." [399,400] From a theological point of view the possibility arose that "inner conflict" could be incorporated in the doctrine of sin, and healing (trust and acceptance) in the doctrine of grace (Roberts).

PASTORAL PSYCHOLOGY

Clergymen, following Worcester, worked with psychiatrists in a clinical team or used clinical concepts in their counseling. A pioneer in this field, John Rathbone Oliver, an Episcopalian priest, had studied medicine and psychiatry to "diversify the spiritual reactions" [401] in his patient—petitioners who suffered from emotional problems. The field of pastoral counseling is distinct from faith-healing in its pure form. The particular function of pastoral psychiatry, which has developed in the last several decades, is to apply whatever remedial and preventive measures ministers of the gospel can contribute as they arise from a simultaneous use of the perceptions of modern psychiatry and the values of religious solace. These include [402] instruction, prayer, confession, persuasion, assurance, encouragement and suggestion. The method discussed by the Rev. Mr. Stolz starts with a series of relaxation treatments,[403] as developed by Edmund Jacobson, which release muscular and nervous tension. It is then suggested that a survey be made of the possibilities of aid through God, a God who is "a partner in our fortunes," a living reality. Finally, specific problems are thought through and a plan is developed to cope with them. More recently,[404] some clergymen have carried their counseling to the level of a psychoanalytically oriented procedure, with its roots in the use of faith as a therapeutic measure.

[397] Roberts, D. E.: Psychotherapy and a Christian View of Man, p. 76, New York, Scribner, 1950.
[398] Casey et al.: Faith and Psychopathology; A Symposium, Washington, D. C., American Psychiatric A. Meeting, May 18, 1948.
[399] Liebman, J. L.: Peace of Mind, New York, Simon & Schuster, Inc., 1946.
[400] Roberts: *Op. cit.*
[401] Oliver, J. R.: Psychiatry and Mental Health, p. 298, New York, Scribner, 1932.
[402] Stolz, K. R.: Pastoral Psychology, rev. ed., p. 255, New York, Abingdon-Cokesbury, 1941.
[403] *Ibid.*, p. 243.
[404] Pastoral Psychology, Great Neck, N. Y., Pulpit Digest Pub. Co., 1952.

Another technic is that used in such church clinics as New York's Marble Collegiate Church,[405] where neurotic, unhappy individuals are seen first by a psychiatrist, who evaluates the specific problem presented by the client. The client is referred to a psychologically oriented clergyman who uses prayer and Scriptures most suited to the psychic state to be treated. Working as a team, the psychiatrist demonstrates to the patient what his symptoms mean in terms of his emotional life, and the minister shows how prayer and faith taken from "the great medicine chest of the Christian faith" can restore balance to the patient's life. As Dr. Blanton writes:[406]

> Religion wells from the unconscious mind. It was and it remains an emotional experience; ordinary reason cannot be applied to it. Even the power of prayer depends to a large extent on the deep unconscious mind.

The church clinic deliberately introduces the view of psychiatry that tension, anxiety and unhappiness are symptomatic of emotional lack of balance and have a discoverable cause in the life history of the patient. Whereas earlier workers in the Emmanuel movement spoke of utilizing the subconscious as a repository of faith, now pastoral psychiatrists attempt to understand and remove the tension and the anxiety which prevent faith from being effective. Rationalizations are singled out, denials are faced and symptoms interpreted to the end that the patient who can then face his faults "become[s] able to receive the healing power of God." [407] Religious counseling of this soundly based type has become part of the service which an increasing number of psychiatrically educated ministers are offering their parishioners. Training for clinical pastoral service in mental hospitals has been organized through the efforts of the Rev. Anton T. Boisen.[408]

The progression of faith as a functional psychological modality, using first symbols, then religious abstractions and, finally, metaphysical constructs, as described in its therapeutic frame of reference, leaves out of consideration the ultimate nature of this force. Nor do we know specifically whether the actual ceding of power to a Divine Being, the surrender itself, or the fact that the supplicant believes his Deity will and can heal, is the motive force for successes in faith-healing. Professor Ducasse in his penetrating analysis of the philosophy of religion [409] has pointed out that the

405 Blanton, Smiley, and Peale, N. V.: Faith Is the Answer, New York, Prentice-Hall, 1941.

406 *Ibid.*, p. 48.

407 Peale, N. V., and Blanton, Smiley: The Art of Real Happiness, New York, Prentice-Hall, 1950.

408 Council for Clinical Training for Students of Theology, New York Annual Catalogue, 1952-1953.

409 Ducasse, C. J.: A Philosophical Scrutiny of Religion, p. 158, New York, Ronald, 1952.

efficacy of faith—for example, in prayer—depends on the belief that it will work, quite apart from the theistic hypothesis, i.e., that God is omnipotent. In this sense faith is effective whether related to a religion, to a scientific creed or to a set of ethical principles. Ducasse, in attempting to solve the therapeutic enigma of faith-healing, differentiates the act of faith-healing as

> being healed by God as a reward for believing in his existence and love, or being healed by God by the belief itself that God can and will heal, or being healed by the belief that one can be healed by believing that one is (or will be) healed.[410]

It seems apparent that the majority of faith-healing effects wrought by semiscientific workers or charlatans derived from the belief that healing was possible if one willed it, knowingly or otherwise, through the vehicle presented by the healer. On the other hand, the results achieved by faith-healers who invoke a theistic formula or rely on God's love directly are intimately dependent on the belief in God Himself and his essential attribute of goodness. The search for a final objective explanation of the workings of faith in terms of man's subjective responses or mechanisms has been unavailing. As a matter of psychological experience, faith-healing is no less effective or ubiquitous now than it was fifty centuries ago.

The growth of diverse religiophilosophic schools of thought or, more accurately, cults [411] represents a psychological movement of tremendous importance in our present era. It is nothing less than an urge for democratization in each man's relation to his inner and outer universe. Every man, in wishing to find sources of emotional strength that will help him to meet the pressures of life, seeks to understand, in his own terms, the cosmic power which he senses about him. Continued absorption with psychology on the part of the nonprofessional public is part of this process to democratize the distribution of sources of emotional power. As the priest-function of the mental healer slowly fades, the wish for individual participation in faith as one healing force asserts itself. Religion and psychiatry are both called upon to unlock their treasures and dispense their healing riches to an anxious society. A maturing public, expanding its familiarity with philosophy and the psychological and the social sciences, demands participation in the healing powers which a liberal religion and a practical psychiatry are unfolding. This is the meaning of the democratization of religion in its healing function, the diversification of sects and denominations in their search for a practical, i.e., healing, use of its verities. It is a return to those underlying social and personal motives in religion which the Early

[410] Ducasse, C. J.: Personal communication, 1953.

[411] Wach, Joachim: "Church, Denomination and Sect," Chap. 9 *in* Types of Religious Experience: Christian and Non-Christian, Univ. Chicago Press, 1951.

Church espoused, and which, in the opinion of some scholars,[412] was the rationale for the eventual growth of the dominant religion of the Western world.

Medical science, bound by a materialism directly related to an increasingly helpful technology, has been slow, in terms of the life of Western civilization, in reaching a clinical interest in the mental life. But man in a conflictful world cannot wait for a final solution of technical psychological problems or for the understanding that tedious scientific study brings. The sufferer yearns for relief, not in the hereafter but in the now. He cries for the touch of the hand that heals, the spirit that succors. Impatiently, but with eternal hope, humanity, like the prophet Jeremiah,[413] cries:

> Is there no balm in Gilead,
> Is there no physician there?

[412] Harnack, Adolf: The Mission and Expansion of Christianity in the First Three Centuries, translated by J. Moffatt, Chap. 2, Bk. 2, p. 121, New York, Putnam, 1904; "Luke the Physician," *in* New Testament Studies, translated by J. R. Wilkinson, New York, Putnam, 1907.

[413] Jeremiah 9:22.

7

The Neurologic Heritage

Up to this point we have traced the forces of mysticism, faith, humanitarianism and medicine as they formed the knotted skein of mental healing. We have seen the gap close between social-political pressures loosed by liberalizing influences in human affairs and medical management in asylums. Simultaneously we have observed how belief in, or willing submission to, a Universal Power approached, in its healing effects, psychological knowledge of the effect of suggestion. To be sure, medicine has always shown a time-lag, reviving ideas years and decades (even centuries) after they were a common heritage of intuitive thinkers or even common men and weaving them into usable clinical technics. Thus mysticism, passing through the hands of Mesmer and his detractors, evolved into the valuable method of hypnotism; faith, under the influence of transcendentalism, was fashioned by neoreligionists into a specific faith-healing technic; humanitarianism, spreading from a political philosophy of individual freedom to a credo for the care of the insane, was kneaded into "moral treatment" by physicians. So, also, a smoldering awareness of a deeper level of mind function, the unconscious, was lifted by a series of bold medical strokes to the position of a meaningful body of knowledge.

These mergers provided mental healing with substance and clinical form. But more insight was needed to make mental healing a tool of scientific dimensions which would be both realistic in psychological terms and predictable. This requirement was met by the evolution of a dynamic psychotherapy, which carried mental healing to a conceptual level and pointed the way to its attainment of the status of a scientific discipline. This progression will be discussed in later chapters. At this juncture we should note that neurology as a specialty within medicine was, in part, responsible for this latter development. The general concentration of interest on the mysteries of the nervous system was neurology's heritage to psychotherapy. More specifically, neurology, by its acceptance of "nervousness" (neurasthenia) as its legitimate concern, endowed psychiatry with this heritage.

The clinical science of neurology brought other influence to bear on psychotherapy's growth: one was an objective attitude toward nervous and mental symptoms; another was an evolutionary viewpoint most clearly contained in the broad field called psychobiology. That the mind possessed a phylogenetic and an ontogenetic history, that it was a correlate of nervous-system function and not a disembodied "soul," was the essence of the psychobiologic viewpoint. The notion that "all life is reaction,"[414] just as physical disease is reaction of tissues, drew its meaning initially from a minute knowledge of neuropathology wherein results of destruction of certain brain tissues were found to be identical with results of destruction of mental functions. Neurology in a circuitous way brought a psychobiologic viewpoint to the fore, paving the way for acceptance of a psychotherapeutic ideal in psychiatry. In so doing it appears to have circumvented psychology, whose early interest was in the very "soul" which neurology was to redefine. Psychology's later preoccupation with the "mind," which psychiatry appropriated in its efforts to understand function and malfunction, was equally side-stepped in the psychobiologic orientation which neurology bequeathed to psychiatry.

It may well be asked why psychology did not play a direct part in the evolution of psychotherapy. Did not psychology divorce itself from philosophy and theology during the nineteenth century and take up the taxing burden of experimental work with memory, attention, sensation, perception, reaction time, thus raising psychology to the proud level of a science? Did nothing come from the psychological departments of the universities of the world to give psychotherapy an instrument, a viewpoint or a logical basis for advances? The answer can be given in Moore's words that "American psychiatry had definitely turned its back on psychology and gone to neurology for information about the mind of man."[415] But the answer needs some modification, for matters of psychological concern were beginning to appear in clinical psychotherapy. Associationism was implicit in Freud's early (and late) analytic procedures and Jung's experiments on complexes. Moreover, introspectionism impliedly formed the mental furniture of every psychiatrist, and the essence of James's pragmatic attitude filtered through the various groups of mind curers and mental healers at end of the last century. Still physiologic psychology, pride of the German school (Wundt), and the variants of academic psychology, personalism, structuralism, functionalism, etc., had a negligible influence on the evolution of psychotherapy.

[414] Meyer, Adolf: A short sketch of the problems of psychiatry, Am. J. Insanity 53:538, 1896.

[415] Moore, T. V.: "A Century of Psychology in Relationship to American Psychiatry," *in* One Hundred Years of American Psychiatry, p. 447, New York, Columbia, 1944.

EARLY NEUROLOGIC INFLUENCES

There was, however, one aspect of physiologic psychology, Gall's craniology, which, in forging a liaison between neurology and faculty psychology, contributed to the evolution of psychotherapy. Gall's neuro-anatomy was accurate and scientific, but his studies of temperament and brain structure were catapulted into the discredited field of phrenology before they could be tested by clinicians or laboratory psychologists. At the time of Gall's early work (1796) the internal structure of the brain was unknown; it was considered to be a formless, pulpy mass. The nerve fibers were known to originate in the walls of the ventricles, united in some way by the spinal fluid. Soemmerring, a German authority,[416] and his contemporaries felt that the quantity of spinal fluid secreted was directly related to the degree of intelligence. But Gall, tracing the spinal fiber bundles into the brain, by the method of unfolding the layers of gray matter and separating the bundles of white matter, demonstrated the nervous system to have a design and, presumably, a meaning. He studied the differences in convolutions between the brains of animals and of human beings, and postulated differences in mental capacity in direct proportion to the quantity of convolutional (gray) matter. Gall was one of the first to demonstrate the paucity of cortex in idiots, accounting for their mental weakness. His contemporary, Christian Reil, is quoted as saying that Gall demonstrated in his dissections of the nervous system "more than I conceived a man could discover in the course of a long life."

From his conviction that higher mental functions were connected with convolutions of the cerebrum, Gall postulated that certain areas in the frontal lobes served specific functions, as arithmetic, music, language, etc. By comparing the internal concavities of the skull corresponding to the convexities of the brain substance, and noting the relative size of various areas or "organs" of the cortex, Gall pointed to organs of *courage, memory, observation, liberality, copulative urge* and so on.[417] Classifying hundreds of skulls in relation to the histories of temperament (behavior), character (personality function) and powers (intelligence) of their possessors, Gall felt that he had validated his findings. He used a series of unit functions in various degrees of dominance or deficiency to account for the infinite gradations of human behavior and disposition. These units were described as "PROPENSITIES, (Amativeness, Philo-progenitiveness, Concentrativeness, etc.), SENTIMENTS, Lower (Self-Esteem) and Superior (Benevolence, Veneration . . .) FACULTIES, Perception (Form, Size,

[416] Hollander, Bernard: In Commemoration of Francis J. Gall, Medical Press, London, July, 1928. Published by Ethnological Soc., London.
[417] Exposition de la doctrine physionomique du Docteur Gall, Paris, Heinrichs, 1804.

Weight . . . Language . . .), Reflective (Comparison, Causality . . .)."

Forbidden by the Emperor to continue his "blasphemous researches" on the brain in Vienna, Gall traveled to Germany and then to France, where, in 1808, he prepared an anatomic work for the Institute of France.[418] Neurologists were much impressed; Flourens, an experimentalist of cerebral physiology, stated, on viewing Gall's dissections, "It seemed to me that I had never seen that organ (the brain)."

Neuro-anatomy in Gall's hands constituted a step forward for a clinical neurology which, until the eighteenth century, had remained a curio of medicine. Spotted through two millennia of medical writings are records of astute clinical observation of epilepsy, cerebral hemorrhage, migraine and head injuries, and occasional experiments on the brain and the spinal cord of dogs, kittens or monkeys.[419] Herophilus, the Greek anatomist, it is reported, proved in his vivisections of criminals that nerves passed from the brain and the spinal cord to the muscles. Galen, by cutting the spinal cord of monkeys, showed that paralysis occurred on the opposite side of the body to the incision.[420] Many observations of clinical value in head injury, convulsions, paralyses, etc., over the centuries were loosely interwoven in neurologic writings with the philosophic problem of localizing the seat of the soul (mind) in the body—for example, in the pineal body. Meanwhile, during the sixteenth and the seventeenth centuries, earnest attempts were initiated to explain normal and abnormal phenomena in the body, couched in terms of action of the soul. Stahl, in the eighteenth century, had developed a doctrine (vitalism) which stated that the soul represented a life force, exerting its effect on the body in health and disease.

This neurophilosophic concept was furthered by the school of "neuropathology," at that time a derivative of vitalism. William Cullen, spokesman and mainspring of this school, pushed the notion of a governing or "moving" force as energizer of bodily processes; the moving force was, in terms of "neuropathology," the nervous impulses themselves. Cullen called nerve impulses "the prime mover in the animal oeconomy" and hence responsible for many diseases in the body. At the same time life itself was localized as a nervous system function by Cullen, "LIFE, as far as it is corporeal, . . . consists in the excitement of the nervous system, especially of the brain, which unites the different parts and forms them into a whole." Excitement of the nervous system was mediated through the nerves by "motion," which Cullen and his school considered to encompass

[418] Gall, F. J., and Spurzheim, J. C.: Recherches sur le système nerveux en général et sur celui du cerveau en particulier . . . , Paris, Schoell, 1809.

[419] Wechsler, I. S.: "Introduction to the History of Neurology," *in* A Textbook of Clinical Neurology, ed. 5, pp. 758 et seq., Philadelphia, Saunders, 1944.

[420] Garrison, F. H.: History of Medicine, ed. 3, pp. 94, 105, 317 et seq., Philadelphia, Saunders, 1921.

both "sentient (sensory) and nervous Power (motor)" impulses.[421] Translated into neurologic terms, the "motion" of the nervous system was conceived as a "subtle elastic fluid somehow connected with their medullary substance (the nerves)" . . . which vary in density and fulness in age and disease." [422] Furthermore, the changes in force of this fluid as it reached different parts of the body was termed by Cullen the "action or Energy of the Brain."

The significance of this type of thinking, which was overthrown as a valid pathology of bodily diseases by the cellular theory of Virchow during the nineteenth century, lay in a concern with the nervous system as the carrier of somatic and psychic activity. In a sense, psychosomatic medicine is a representation in modern dress of this older theory; a more distant derivative is the psychotherapeutic task of influencing somatic symptoms through analytic or other psychological means. Riese,[423] in a careful study of the growth of neurologic ideas, points out that the nervous system is still conceived of as an organ related to "movements and impressions . . . but with no permanent privilege with regard to other organs." The notion of a series of levels, a hierarchy within the nervous system, wherein the nervous tissue acts to integrate life processes within the body, was brought to attention later by Sherrington (1906). Hughlings Jackson, the great English neurologist, also gave form to the evolutionary concept in which higher cortical structures controlled lower functions, particularly those of movement. In other words, the physical (neural) basis for life was discussed in terms of "movements and impressions," thus making the problem of mental life a purely physiologic one. The complex problem of the physical basis for mental life, including thought, emotion and volition, has colored neurology's theoretical interests up to the present time.

The burden of this type of neurologic theory falls within clinical concepts of brain diseases, particularly convulsive seizures and motility disorders, but also has an implication for psychotherapy. The search for the medium through which a nerve force was exerted led to explanations which ranged from "subtle elastic fluid" to animal magnetism, electromagnetic fluid and the modern concept of electrical potential in the brain. Where physiologic forces do not suffice to explain the physics of life forces as *instinct* or *volition,* concepts such as *élan vital, instinct-drive, hormic psychology,* theory of *libido* have arisen as clinical tools to aid in understanding the structure and the development of nervous symptoms. The importance of theoretical considerations gains as more modern methods of

[421] Cullen, William: First Lines of the Practice of Physic, Edinburgh, W. Creech, ed. of 1779-1784.

[422] ——: A Treatise of the Materia Medica, Vol. 1, Edinburgh, Elliot, 1789.

[423] Riese, W.: An outline of a history of ideas in neurology, Bull. Hist. Med. 23:111, 1949.

therapy are encountered. Through this evolution, which will be alluded to in more detail later, one can see the thread uniting modern attempts to account for the normal and the abnormal mental life and Cullen's early preoccupation with a "nerve force" in the human body.

While theoretical explanations of nerve function were being advanced, clinical and descriptive neurology proceeded to disentangle a jungle of confusing symptoms and signs—headache, spasms, tics, paralyses, neuralgias, convulsions, muscular atrophies, chorea, rheumatic conditions, syncopes, vertigo, cramps, sciatica, etc.—to form disease entities that are valid today. From mid-century on, the tempo of neurologic, diagnostic studies and experimentation increased markedly in the medical centers of Continental Europe, Great Britain and America. The entire field of neurology was outlined from 1840 to 1900 by men whose names are eponyms of clinical syndromes: Sir Charles Bell, Magendie, Charcot, Broca, Duchenne, Hughlings Jackson, Erb, Romberg, Westphal, Wernicke, Marie, Strümpell, Wilson, Weir Mitchell, Sachs, and on for pages. The bibliography for this period is enormous: for example, no less than 286 meaningful articles and books on neurologic subjects (excluding "psychiatrik" items) were abstracted from the European literature for the year 1860.[424] It would add little to list the myriad contributors; suffice it to say that from this indefatigable labor arose a specialty, neurology, whose professors were assailed by a responsibility to minister to the thousands of cases of "nervous debility" and "spinal neurosis" that appeared on the medical scene.

THE NERVOUS PATIENT ATTAINS STATUS

The advent of the specialty of neurology raised the "nervous" patient to a status that demanded and received dignified recognition. Symptoms attributable to the brain and the spine standing upon an objective footing were subject to therapeutic enterprise. With increasing accent on nervous symptoms, hitherto impatiently dealt with by physicians, or treated by hypnotists or faith-healers, came a new series of descriptive terms. One reads of "nervous prostration, spinal irritation, spasmodic cerebral neurosis, brain fatigue, cerebral anemia." As medical men gladly relinquished their troublesome hysterics, neurologists accepted the burden. The picture offered by patients with "nervous exhaustion" presented so formidable an array of symptoms that one can readily appreciate with Weir Mitchell "the disgust with which the general practitioner encounters this malady [hysteria]." Beard's description of neurasthenia listed a complex bundle of symptoms that passed beyond hysteria in its involvement of the auto-

[424] Year-Book of Medicine, Surgery and the Allied Sciences, London, New Sydenham Soc., 1860.

nomic nervous system, the sexual sphere and mental function. Neurasthenics suffered from

> tenderness of scalp: dilated pupils: sick headache: pressure pain in head: irritable eye (asthenopis): noises in ears: atonic voices: concentration inability: irritability: hopelessness: morbid fear (anthro-phobo-claustro-phobias, etc.): blushing: insomnia: tenderness of teeth: dyspepsia: sweating and dryness of skin: spinal hyperesthesia: palpitations: spasms, dysphagia: exhaustion: neuralgias: sexual disabilities: yawning: impotence, spermatorrhea, etc.[425]

The functional disorder which Beard discovered seemed to be especially prevalent in America. The complexity of neurasthenia was analogous to, but not identical with, severe cases of hysteria which flooded German and French clinics. America's "hot-house educational system, . . . the rash, restless speculative character of our business enterprises," were the causes of this malady, according to Van Deusen,[426] who antedated Beard in his description of nervous exhaustion or neurasthenia. Neurasthenia implied the essentially subjective character of much "nervousness," and Beard saw clearly how foreign to the true problem posed by these cases was the average physician's approach.[427] That neurasthenia, as Van Deusen had also indicated, was a product of "our progress and refinement . . . among the indoor classes of civilized countries" was generally acknowledged, but Beard's discerning genius lay in lifting nervous exhaustion out of its diagnostic resting place to the level of a practical problem for neurologists. Hysteria also was attaining status as a functional, treatable condition in the clinic of Charcot and others in Europe, but neurasthenia as a concept bore the additional distinction by its name of indicating its neural and neurologic derivation. For decades neurasthenia became the diagnosis of fashion and "a household word" in America and Europe.

It may be surmised that the advent of a specialty of neurology stimulated recognition and increased incidence of states of nervous debility. The "genteel tradition" imposed upon women a set of values that found expression equally in the "charming invalid" of the Victorian period and the bizarre hysterics described by French neurologists. The moral education of women commenced with the doctrine, divinely sanctioned, that a boundary existed between "these two great divisions of mankind," male and female, and extended to the virtues of humility, patience and "loving deference" to their spouses. The emotions of women during the Victorian age

[425] Beard, G. M.: A Practical Treatise on Nervous Exhaustion (Neurasthenia), New York, Wood, 1880.

[426] Van Deusen, E. H.: Observations on a form of nervous prostration (neurasthenia) culminating in insanity, J. Insanity, p. 445, April, 1869. *See also* Bunker, H. A.: *In* One Hundred Years of American Psychiatry, Am. Psychiat. A., New York, Columbia, 1944.

[427] Beard, G. M.: Neurasthenia or nervous exhaustion, Boston M. & S. J. 3:217, April 29, 1869.

were arranged and ordered for them, and they were advised to accept these restrictions gracefully. Under such social limitations it is not strange that the sexual and aggressive drives of women required the circuitous route of hysteria for expression. An emancipated woman, writing in 1865, complained of the universal poor health of women, "In my immense circle of friends all over the union, I can't recall more than 10 married ladies born in this country who are sound, healthy and vigorous." [428] Beyond the dangers of the nuptial chamber, the rise of education among women brought its penalties. "I see breakdowns among women of 16 to 19 in female colleges, when the nervous system is so sensitive," wrote Weir Mitchell in a slender volume, *Wear and Tear,*[429] which was to serve as a warning of the neurologic cost of "restless" living. And, in agreement on the other side of the ocean, an eminent French physician said, "If your daughter reads novels at fifteen she will have hysteria at twenty."

Prior to the cultivation by neurologists of the somatic representations of emotional problems among women (interpreted in the main as results of nervous exhaustion), the secrets of "female weaknesses" remained in other domains. For physicians under the spell of a suppressive psychology were contemptuous of the wish to improve the ordained gynecologic lot of nineteenth-century women. Judge, for example, Professor Meig's pronouncement that the publications of Oliver Wendell Holmes, which warned that the spread of puerperal fever to women occurred through the carelessness of doctors, were the "jejune and fizenless dreamings of sophomore writers." [430] Well might Lydia Pinkham, whose "Greatest Medical Discovery Since the Dawn of History" brought relief to thousands of women suffering in silence, become the repository of clinical details of the causes of nervous debility. Jean Burton,[431] Pinkham's biographer, comments that the "Pinkham files were the nearest thing to a Kinsey Survey the era produced." But the ubiquitous hysterical illnesses were not confined solely to women. Charcot early pointed to hysterical symptoms among men, a view which was treated with ridicule when Freud, upon his return from Paris, remarked on this finding at the Vienna Medical Society.

In America, hints of the vulnerability of masculine nervous systems under stress to develop nervous exhaustión were crystallizing in the minds of American neurologists from their Civil War experiences.[432] Numerous

[428] Beecher, Catherine: Letters to the People on Health and Happiness. *Quoted in* Edes, R. T.: New England Invalid, Boston, Clapp, 1895.

[429] Mitchell, S. Weir: Wear and Tear, or, Hints for the Overworked, Philadelphia, Lippincott, 1871.

[430] Robinson, Victor: The Story of Medicine, p. 475, New York, Boni, 1931.

[431] Burton, Jean: Lydia Pinkham Is Her Name, New York, Farrar, Straus, 1949.

[432] Deutsch, Albert: "Military Psychiatry of the Civil War," *in* One Hundred Years of American Psychiatry, p. 367, Am. Psychiat. A., New York, Columbia, 1944.

psychiatric casualties observed by Surgeon General William Hammond, of the Union Army, and his confrères, Weir Mitchell and W. W. Keen, were both impressive and puzzling, particularly states of exhaustion in soldiers on the battlefield. These experiences [433] returned to Mitchell's mind when later, in civilian practice, he encountered cases of "brain-tire" and neurasthenia occurring under stress of business competition, "Railway Travelling" and a speeded-up social life. Just as Beard inveighed against the causes of American nervousness,[434] one of which he listed as "American Oratory," so Mitchell set out to remind his countrymen in down-to-earth language that brain fatigue and nervous exhaustion were preventable diseases susceptible to a hygienic regimen that eliminated, among other dietary evils, the "frying pan . . . which reigns supreme west of the Alleghanies." From *Wear and Tear,* Mitchell went on to describe his regimen in *Fat and Blood,*[435] a book that answered the therapeutic problems of hysteria and neurasthenia through the celebrated Rest Cure.

NEURASTHENIA AND THE REST CURE

The symptom of mental fatigue, Mitchell claimed, was essentially a misinterpretation of physical fatigue. For this reason he advised that "Dr. Diet and Dr. Quiet" be called in, that the indifference of medical men toward hysterics be supplanted by a patient, interested attitude. Undertreatment rather than overtreatment was advocated, the excitement surrounding the hysterics eliminated and encouragement through the force of the physician's personality tirelessly administered. A new element, interest in the personal side of the patient, an exceptional attitude at that time, presaging the modern doctor-patient relationship, was stressed by Mitchell. Though he realized that emotional involvements were basic factors in nervous breakdowns buried in the remote past, Mitchell, because of his "Philadelphia propriety," [436] embodied his psychosexual intuitions in fiction writings rather than in scientific papers. To the profession Mitchell described the technic of his Rest Cure clearly: The patient, said Mitchell, must be rebuilt and retrained. She must have rest, good food and, above all, isolation. There must be no contact with relatives. She must be removed from the morbid surroundings in which her illness had developed or flourished. Instead of being waited upon hand and foot by loved ones, pampered and catered to by nurses and attendants, the patient should have only one

[433] Mitchell, S. Weir: The evolution of the rest treatment, J. Nerv. & Ment. Dis. 31:368, 1904.
[434] Beard, G. M.: American Nervousness, Its Causes and Consequences, New York, Putnam, 1881.
[435] Mitchell, S. Weir: Fat and Blood, An Essay on the Treatment of Certain Forms of Neurasthenia and Hysteria, Philadelphia, Lippincott, 1877-1905.
[436] Earnest, E. P.: S. Weir Mitchell, Philadelphia, Univ. Penn. Press, 1950.

nurse, preferably one emotionally indifferent to the family. Mitchell understood very clearly how emotional contacts could retard the progress of a case, how the hysteric feeds upon the attention and the adulation she gets from those about her. Where shades had been drawn and silence preserved, the doctor day by day increased the light and the reading or other task.

The Rest Cure attained a rapid popularity throughout the medical world. From the 1880's to the period of suggestive therapeutics and the psychoanalytic infiltration into neuropsychiatric thinking, textbooks in the United States,[437] Great Britain,[438] Germany,[439] France and elsewhere advocated the Rest Cure. Many were impressed with the adjunctive methods, massage and the painstaking management of the patient. All agreed that the rest cure was an effective vehicle for moral treatment, although as early as 1888 Gowers warned that "rest in bed (without massage and electricity) will probably convert the patient into a helpless invalid." In time, the impermanence that attacks all methods of psychotherapy invaded Mitchell's Rest Cure. A commentary on this impermanence is seen in an American text [440] which stated in 1923 that "rest cures, massage, electricity . . . and such agents . . . have a place in therapy of the neuroses but it is a secondary one." Even the layman's fondness for the term so freely used thirty years ago has passed the way of all therapeutic flesh. But Mitchell's skillful handling of wasted muscles, tense nerves and gastric distress, and the strengthening of the hysteric's psychic resources, represented a landmark in neurology's heritage to psychotherapy.

To return to Beard and his newly discovered group of neurasthenics, we may observe that his therapeutic attack was generally medical in nature. The medical treatment offered by Beard was a continuation of the so-called "supporting treatment" [441] for the insane, itself a reaction to the earlier venesection and depletion procedures. Arsenic, caffeine, ergot for "congestion of the brain and cord," blisters, phosphates, chloral, belladonna, calomel, baths, were freely administered. In addition to this regimen honored by neurologists for eighty years, Beard added a serious consideration and an intensification of electrotherapy, already sporadically used since the eighteenth century. From the days of Benjamin Franklin, electricity had been recommended for stimulation of the nerves and improvement of blood

[437] Mills, C. K.: The Nervous System and Its Diseases, Philadelphia, Lippincott, 1898.

[438] Gowers, W. R.: A Manual of Diseases of the Nervous System, Vol. 2, London, Churchill, 1888.

[439] Oppenheim, H.: Diseases of the Nervous System, translated by E. E. Mayer (from 3rd German edition), Philadelphia, Lippincott, 1904.

[440] Jelliffe, S. E., and White, W. A.: Diseases of the Nervous System, ed. 4, p. 895, Philadelphia, Lea, 1923.

[441] Cowles, Edward: Progress in the care and treatment of the insane during the half-century, Am. J. Insanity 51:10, 1894.

circulation. Much experimentation [442] with electrical conductors, storers of static current (Leyden jar), faradic and galvanic current stimulated the introduction of electricity for hysterics and melancholics. John Wesley, in speaking of Lovett's electric-spark treatment, avowed that "more nervous disorders would be cured by this single remedy . . . than the whole Materia Medica." [443] As early as 1767, electricity was employed in English hospitals (Middlesex Hospital), and the following year Garrison notes [444] that an electric bath was advocated in another English hospital. Elaborate apparatuses for delivery of electric current to the head, for migraine, deafness and other nerve diseases, are described in the literature of Mesmer's time.[445] The names of Remak, in Germany, Gull, in England, and the indefatigable Duchenne, of Boulogne, are associated with widespread employment of electrical current for nervous patients in the first half of the nineteenth century.

When Beard espoused medical electricity for neurasthenics, enthusiasm for this treatment in neurologic disorders was high. His monograph on the subject, which covered 65 pages in the first edition, grew to a tome of 788 pages in the eighth edition.[446] In Europe, in this period, Wilhelm Erb, a leading German neurologist, developed electrotherapy to the point at which it became the mainstay of treatment of neurotics. It was of the highly regarded electrotherapy that Freud, years later, remarked that he found himself helpless with neurotic patients in the face of disappointments following its use. Variations appeared in the form of electrical vibrators (Granville's Percuteur) [447] and others, each with its proponents, intent on stimulating the "torpid centers." Treatment by electricity vied with hydrotherapy for neurasthenics. A German authority, more confident in baths than electrical current in the treatment of hysterics, recommended that "the calm waters of the Baltic are preferable for delicate, nervous constitutions, and the North Sea, with its stronger billows, may be recommended in torpid constitutions." [448] In general, stimulating therapy, hydrotherapy, electricity and the inevitable "tonic" were the mainstays of neurologic psychotherapy at the time.

[442] Stainbrook, Edward: The use of electricity in psychiatric treatment during the nineteenth century, Bull. Hist. Med. 22:156, 1948.

[443] Wesley, J.: The Desideratum, or, Electricity Made Plain and Useful by a Lover of Mankind and of Common Sense, London, 1759.

[444] Garrison: *Op. cit.*, p. 333.

[445] Grapengiesser, K. J. C.: Versuche den Galvanismus zur Heilung einiger Krankheiten anzuwenden, Berlin, 1801.

[446] Beard, G. M., and Rockwell, A. D.: Medical Use of Electricity, New York, Wood, 1867; Medical and Surgical Uses of Electricity, ed. 8, New York, Wood, 1892.

[447] Neurotherapy. Selections. Alienist & Neurologist 5:135, 1884.

[448] Rosenthal, M.: A Clinical Treatise on the Diseases of the Nervous System, translated by L. Putzel, Vol. 2, pp. 51 and 52, New York, Wood, 1879.

It was inevitable also that the doctrine of stimulation of torpid or exhausted nerve centers should appropriate a theoretical background from the vast amount of neuropathology that was being pursued. For Beard and Rockwell the current theory was acceptable, that nuclei of nerve cells shrank after exhaustion (or electrical excitation) and regained their normal appearance and activity after rest. The essential cause, derangement of nutrition of the nervous system through repeated toxic influences, became the point of attack for the rest cure and for the "total attack" of which Beard spoke in the management of neurasthenics. Each case, Beard advised, was a study in itself; mental treatment without medication was as ineffective as medication without a "mental method."

Perhaps the most significant contribution encompassed in the neurasthenic concept was the tolerant attitude which Beard fostered toward patients with nervous and sexual symptoms. His accomplishment in bringing sexual disturbances among men into relation with nervous diseases [449] constituted a major advance in a period when impotence or spermatorrhea was relegated to the genito-urinary surgeon or treated with dark moralism and subsequent neglect. The day had not passed when Philippe Ricord, the great Parisian venereologist, set the forlorn tone physicians employed toward men with venereal diseases, "We know when gonorrhea begins, but only God knows when it ends." [450] Ricord, whom Holmes called the "Voltaire of pelvic literature, a skeptic as to the morality of the race," [451] expressed the prevalent difficulty of medically treating gonorrhea and syphilis as well as the gingerly disdain with which sexual inadequacies in patients were met. Extension of the neurasthenic concept to sexual neurasthenia dispelled some of this gloom and offered an attitude of assurance and naturalness in sexual matters. Beard urged that seminal emissions and masturbation were not, as was commonly thought, diseases among unmarried men but evidences of exhaustion of one of the three great reflex irritation centers—brain, stomach and genital system. The cure was to "strengthen the constitution, advise them to live generously, work hard, keep brain and muscle active" and avoid excesses.

NEUROLOGY ABSORBS THE NEUROTIC

It cannot be said that neurologic interest in the symptomatic inadequacies of the sexual life of men, as reflected in neurasthenia, was the only fulcrum that opened the door to a serious consideration of sexual problems in neurosis. Other factors were operative. The question of general paresis

[449] Beard, G. M.: Sexual Neurasthenia, Its Hygiene, Causes, Symptoms and Treatment, edited by A. D. Rockwell, ed. 6, New York, Treat, 1905.
[450] Robinson, Victor: *Op. cit.*, p. 424.
[451] Holmes, Oliver Wendell: Medical Essays, Boston, Houghton, 1895.

and tabes in relation to syphilis was being actively studied: Krafft-Ebing published his *Psychopathia Sexualis;* Havelock Ellis, his studies on the *Psychology of Sex;* Freud was soon to bring out his views on sexuality in the neuroses. Reaction against the rigid formalism of Victorianism with its freer expression, in Zilboorg's words,[452] of the "*bête humaine* and the assertion of the lower instincts" was observable in literature and the *esprit de la fin du siècle.* Aberrations of sexuality, if still a hushed subject, achieved a position of tolerance in neurologic areas which was soon to be raised to one of clinical dignity. One must agree with Zilboorg that the intellectual climate of Europe forged by Ibsen, Shaw, Nietzsche and Zola helped to direct attention to the "inner man and his primordial drives." Nevertheless, neurologists like Erb,[453] who stressed the functional nature of sexual symptoms (partial impotence, premature ejaculation, etc.), and Beard, who recognized that sexual weaknesses were being misdiagnosed as "indigestion, oxaluria, imagination," were unquestionably early pioneers in the twentieth-century emancipation of sexuality. From the standpoint of psychotherapy, however, we note the faint tones of objectivity toward subjective symptoms in the attention paid sexual dysfunction in the neurasthenic and nervous exhaustion syndrome.

One consequence of the gradual absorption by neurologists into their practices of cases of functional nervous disease was to bring the insane closer to the doctor's office. Just as hypnotic and suggestive therapists moving into larger clinical fields encountered the obsessive, compulsive and phobic patient, so the neurologist dealt with a widening group of patients who would have been consigned to the asylum earlier as acute insanities. Bramwell, the English psychotherapist,[454] expressed the growing recognition on the part of practicing physicians of the number of mental cases that could be handled without recourse to the asylum. "Until I began hypnotic practise" (*circa* 1889), he wrote, "I had no conception of the number of people whose lives were made miserable by morbid ideas" (obsessions and phobias). The old question of home versus asylum treatment was being revived; opinion slowly veered away from the accepted conclusion that mental patients should be separated from their families and housed in asylums. The borderline between outright insanity and nervousness represented a problem that vexed administrators. One journalist inquirer found, in the case of a friend who had suffered for two years from

[452] Zilboorg, G., and Henry, G. W.: A History of Medical Psychology, p. 482, New York, Norton, 1941.
[453] Erb, W. H.: "Spinal Cord," *in* Cyclopedia of Medicine, Vol. 13, translated by Geoghegan, Schauffler, Lincoln and McCreery, New York, Wood, 1878.
[454] Bramwell, J. M.: Hypnotism, Its History, Practice and Theory, p. 436, London, Grant Richards, 1903.

nervous prostration and begged admission to an insane asylum, that she was not admitted until "she had become entirely a lunatic." [455]

A standard English text [456] (1879) concluded after thorough discussion of the subject that the physician should "write for the Private patient at home rather than the public asylum." Neurologists complained that asylums for most cases were the "worst possible thing"; asylum heads were equally dubious about neurologic skills. One author prefaced his advice by remarking archly that "not being the superintendent of a lunatic asylum, I have no business setting up as an authority on insanity," [457] while a more politic and hopeful editorialist [458] commented that "the practical doctor and the alienist are gradually coming into closer relationship."

The outcome of this running interprofessional conflict was to have important practical results for the entire field of psychotherapy. There is no doubt that superintendents of mental institutions were absorbed in administrative problems to the extent that cherished dreams of physician-alienists to bring individualized treatment to their patients remained pious wishes. The tremendous effort involved in inducing state legislatures to supplant haphazard county care for the insane by a state system attained only after a "severe struggle," [459,460] the absorption of psychiatrists in refining a confused mass of symptoms into diagnosable and understandable mental disorders, and the dull routine of asylum work kept therapeutic interest at a low ebb in institutions. In Europe, pathologic studies were going forward with vigor; Kraepelin, Wernicke, Krafft-Ebing, Kahlbaum, were striving to unite knowledge of brain pathology with clinical pictures of mental illness. But therapy did not keep pace with scientific activity. A distinguished contemporary, William A. White,[461] described the basic therapeutic principle of asylum practice in the 1890's by the statement that, aside from the intuitive individual, not infrequently an attendant, "violence was met by violence, hyperactivity was met by restraint, wakefulness was dealt with by hypnotics." There was hopefulness on every hand but little practical accomplishment. The plan to admit acute cases of insanity to general hospitals was still branded as "utopian," and the

455 Hammerton, C. R.: The Chautauquan, Treatment for Insanity, Vol. 14, p. 310, 1891.

456 Bucknill, J. C., and Tuke, D. H.: A Manual of Psychological Medicine, ed. 4, London, Churchill, 1879.

457 Hammond, W. A.: Treatise on Insanity, New York, Appleton, 1883.

458 Editorial, Remarks on insanity, J.A.M.A., p. 759, November 22, 1890.

459 Hurd, H. M., et al.: The Institutional Care of the Insane in the United States and Canada, Baltimore, Johns Hopkins Press, 1916.

460 Deutsch, Albert: The Mentally Ill in America, ed. 2, Chaps. 12 and 13, New York, Columbia, 1944.

461 White, W. A.: Forty Years of Psychiatry, p. 105, New York, Nerv. & Ment. Dis. Monographs, 1933.

Lancet [462] noted that the "notion with which a large number of alienists are honestly impressed" is that of incurability of the insane.

Yet neurologists were restive as they witnessed their brethren in the asylums disinterested in availing themselves of the advances of neuropathology and clinical and therapeutic neurology. The ivory-tower position of the alienist in the state hospital was more than a figure of speech to medical men generally. More and more practicing neurologists were faced with handling and advising not only neurasthenics and neurotics but also the insane. A merger of neurology and psychiatry was imminent.

THE MERGING OF NEUROLOGY AND PSYCHIATRY

In general, the situation in the asylum was in a state of "reasonable satisfaction." There was an interest in scientific psychiatry and a feeling of accomplishment when a patient was entered into an asylum. But this spurious sense of progress did not satisfy Weir Mitchell, dean of American neurologists. At the semicentennial meeting of the American Medico-Psychological Association (now American Psychiatric Association), 1894, invited to address the assembly, Mitchell invaded this complacency. His remarks turned out to be more than a scholarly communication for his fellow specialists; it was an attack on the isolation of psychiatrists in asylums and their remoteness from research on living problems in mental disease. He charged them with "scientific unproductiveness" and asked, "What is the matter? You have immense opportunities, and seriously, we ask you experts, what have you taught us of these 91,000 insane whom you see or treat?" [463] With causticness and vigor he assailed them, "Asylum life; there is despair in the name as there is in the idea." [464] Upbraiding the alienists, he said:

> You were the first of the specialists and you never came back into line. . . . You live out of range of critical shot . . . constituted almost a sect apart from our more vitalized existence. . . . We get as your contributions, odd little statements, reports of a case or two, a few useless pages of isolated post-mortem records. . . . I want to see not a mere well-worked, so-called model institution . . . where easily pleased managers come and go, the routine is perfect, and every one is satisfied, and the nice little reports describe the amusements, and the new dairy and the statistics are there, and we lament the death of our manager, Mr. Blank; the whole smug business is monotonously alike as your asylum corridors. . . . Where are your careful scientific reports; the earnest note of indignant appeal to your boards [of managers] and the world without; which should help you and will not?

[462] Editorial: Large and small asylums, Lancet 1:163, January 27, 1883.
[463] Mitchell, S. Weir: Address Before the 50th Annual Meeting of the American Medico-Psychological Association, Proc. Am. Med.-Psychol. A., Utica, N. Y., 1895.
[464] *Ibid.*, p. 101.

Spokesmen arose in defense against the incisive criticism and "hissing cautery." [465] of Mitchell's address, pointing to scientific work already in progress in several state hospitals. But Mitchell's insistence that the medical duties of a superintendent were inseparably bound up with his humanitarian, economic and executive duties aroused the profession. To Adolf Meyer, who came forth as the leader in the revitalization of therapy for the insane during the following decades, Mitchell's "burst of vision . . . was a spur" toward implementing the desired scientific attitude within state hospitals.[466]

Practical problems, such as recruiting staff members, interesting young men in the potentialities of psychiatry, demonstrating neuropathology and neurology in relation to mental cases, and stimulating philanthropic citizens and legislators to endow laboratories in mental hospitals, were the tasks to which Meyer dedicated himself. To bring the neurologist's therapeutic zeal to the asylum physician required a preparatory cultivation of psychiatric *morale,* a bringing together of diverse interests and a steady infusion of vitality. This was the contribution of Adolf Meyer, the young Swiss who, in establishing a pathologic laboratory in the Illinois Eastern Hospital for the Insane in 1893, started a career that was to carry the heritage of neurology to a high point of usefulness and nihilistic emancipation.

Inception of the post of pathologist on a state hospital staff was an innovation that augured well for scientific psychiatry in America. It had the smell of the lamp of science about it, contemplating postmortem examinations, lectures on anatomy, examination of brain tissues with exposure of the secrets of insanity. Meyer's first laboratory was in the morgue,[467] a "most unhygienic place for a laboratory;" there he worked out the pathology of cases of senile dementia, epilepsy, general paralysis, acute mania, demonstrating these to the staff. Under Illinois Governor Altgeld and Superintendent Clarke Gapen, Doctor Meyer's work seemed to give the lie to Mitchell's criticism of the asylum physician's unproductivity, for German authorities had sanctioned the view that the only legitimate research for the alienist was pathologic anatomy of the nervous system. But autopsies of insane patients proved disappointing; spectacular findings were often absent, often there were no findings at all to report. The pathologic studies that caused Nissl, German student of neurosyphilis, to remark that [468] "as soon as we agree to see in all mental derangements the clinical

[465] Reviews, Proc. Am. Med.-Psychol. A., 50th Meeting, Philadelphia, 1894, J. Ment. Sc. 42:172, January, 1896.

[466] Meyer, Adolf: Presidential address: 35 years of psychiatry in the United States and our present outlook, Am. J. Psychiat. 85:1, 1928.

[467] Pathological Report, Illinois Eastern Hospital for the Insane, Chicago, Blakely, 1896. John P. Altgeld, Governor, Adolf Meyer, Pathologist.

[468] Meyer, Adolf: A few trends in modern psychiatry, Psychol. Bull. 1:217, 1904. *Quotation by Nissl.*

expression of definite disease processes in the cortex, we remove the obstacle which makes impossible agreement among alienists," did not obtain in functional psychoses. Meyer ventured to look behind the tissue slides and the chemical analyses. A true medical study of the insane (the pathologist was expected to bring real medicine to the asylum) "must begin before the patient is dead," [469] he averred. In psychiatry this meant integration of a hospital about the patient as a person, his life story, aspirations and plans, home environment, mental and physical state; it meant that the scientific pathologist must enter a new field of leadership where young psychiatrists would be taught to unite the "medicine" of the patient with the story of the patient as a person. The neuropathologist of Kankakee, Illinois (later of Worcester and Ward's Island, N. Y.), was more impressed by the question a jury foreman asked after report of an autopsy, "And what did you find on the mind?," than with the "quasi-intoxication" of pathologists with the neuron theory. When Meyer brought living patients for study to the Pathologic Institute of the New York State Hospitals, whose head he became in 1902, he symbolized the vital use of neurology for psychiatry. When this organization became known as the Psychiatric Institute, the subtle change which Meyer had wrought in American neuropsychiatry became concretized.

THE EVOLUTION OF PSYCHOBIOLOGY

The growing familiarity of psychiatrists with the diagnostic labors of Kraepelin, Wernicke, later Bleuler and others, the work of neuropathologists of the early 1900's, brought no new therapeutic innovation to the mental hospital; only a deeper understanding resulted and, with it, a recognition of the enormous complexity of mental states. As enthusiasm for finding the ultimate answer to mental disease in pathology faded, a kind of hopelessness toward doing anything for chronic patients arose. To this attitude Meyer addressed himself with a practicality and a vision that were to find expression in two directions: one in mental hygiene as a wide social move to change attitudes toward insanity, and hence to prepare the ground for sowing therapeutic optimism; the other in an enlivening of clinical psychiatry through the principles of psychobiology. Against the attitude which some German psychiatrists expressed, that "the inner experience does not concern our natural science," Meyer contended that our interest should be in the *doing* aspect of mental life (as the psychiatrist studies it) not in the *being*.[470] Description of a disordered mental process tells what

[469] Meyer, Adolf: Collected Works, edited by Eunice E. Winters, Vol. 2, pp. 63, 78 and 100, Baltimore, Johns Hopkins Press, 1951.

[470] ——: Misconceptions at the bottom of hopelessness of all psychology, Psychol. Bull., Vol. 4, 1907.

is in the mind. Our interest, Meyer insisted, lies not in the intricate psychic fact but in what brought it into *being* and what can be done about it. In the early formulations of his therapy, Meyer spoke of the mind as an "organized living being in action," and hence psychotherapy was the regulation of action; as a corollary, "habit training is the backbone of psychotherapy." [471] Later it came to be known as distributive analysis and synthesis. The general principle is that every analysis leads to synthesis, the analysis being

> distributed by the physician along lines indicated by the patient's complaints and symptoms, by the problems which the physician himself can recognize, by the patient's imaginings concerning the present and the past as well as by actual situations, attitude to the future and outstanding features of his personality.[472]

A slow revolution was occurring in attitudes toward hospital patients, signalized by the entrance of "plain sense" in treatment. To the doctor, Meyer pointed to the need to shed the protective halo of Latin names and consider the patient a living being in action. This brought him to the simple things of the patient's background, how he lived with his family, how he suffered or reacted to the pressures of daily work. The orientation was away from diagnostic categories to "reaction types." [473] "Why," Meyer asked, "must we be blinded by the notion of disease?" Let us look into the dynamics of the patient's life in terms of events! Medicine had overinfluenced psychiatry, he suggested, by making the diagnosis the "fetish of medical men." A response to a demand made on the organism constituted a symptom—a faulty, insufficient, protective response of the individual in terms of his life events. Until then, with a diagnosis made, one chiefly applied specifics or speculated on probabilities of spontaneous improvement or further deterioration, but with a life-plan of the patient outlined, one was in position to re-educate and retrain for a better adjustment. The practical outgrowth of Meyer's conceptual framework changed the hospital attitude from a custodial to a therapeutic one. It also vitalized the mental-hygiene concept, bringing it into relation with medicine and reflexly back to psychiatry. To use an example from common knowledge,[474] "As long as consumption was a leading concept of a dreaded tuberculosis, recognition was too late to make therapy tell: if dementia is a leading concept, recognition is a declaration of [therapeutic] bankruptcy."

As early as 1904, while at the New York Pathological Institute, Meyer

[471] *Ibid.*

[472] Diethelm, Oskar: Treatment in Psychiatry, p. 111, New York, Macmillan, 1936.

[473] Meyer, Adolf: Objective psychology or psycho-biology with subordination of the medically useless contrast of mental and physical, J.A.M.A., Vol. 60, September, 1915.

[474] ——: "Fundamental Conception of Dementia Praecox," *in* Collected Works, p. 436.

sent his wife[475] to the patient's home to investigate his life, background and family, to bring the patient in relation to his own environment, so that the background of disorganized habits could be studied and the patient then re-educated. Here was a combination of a philosophy based on a minute study of all that was known of psychiatric disease and a practical *doing* something about it.

The lessons of psychobiology lend themselves more readily to discerning attitudes toward patients seen in every sanitarium and mental hospital today than to precise psychological description. In two directions, in the hospital and in society, Meyer taught his followers to see the meaning of mental illness as a reaction to life's stresses, leaving open a way to do something about it. The psychobiologic attitude got down to simple things like sleep, eating, elimination, recreation and occupation and went on to particular emotional problems in the patient. The psychiatrist does not "talk to" the patient or read him a lecture based on his own knowledge, rather he utilizes the material of the patient's life in his attempt at guidance. These talks with the psychiatrist, free of embarrassment or fear, give the patient an appreciation of the meaning of his emotional crises in the development of his breakdown. And, finally, the underlying idealism which directs the patient's life is attacked. He is helped to develop a philosophy of life which will serve him in *his own environment.* It was no new thing for Doctor Meyer to insist on the importance of the little things that go to make up the relationship (rapport) between physician and patient. The attitude he taught was implemented in the "unhurried" conversation, which nevertheless keeps to essentials in the patient's illness, gives the patient a feeling of support, a feeling that someone is interested in his condition. Nor is he subject to the constant irritation of living among those to whom he is emotionally sensitized. There is also the effect of the unburdening of the patient's troubles to a sympathetic listener.

In many ways the psychobiologic attitude, which took perhaps a quarter of a century to infiltrate psychiatric thinking, was a compilation of all that had been known and thought before. It did not exclude specific psychotherapy, suggestion or even psychoanalytic therapy; there was no relinquishing of all that had been laboriously acquired by medicine and psychiatry, there was merely a dedication to the idea of re-education in living. The new attitude was a perspective, a viewpoint, a humanitarianism not necessarily new but freshly integrated with sound knowledge of disorders of the nervous system and of mental reactions.

Gradually it became obvious that psychotherapy, as applied to the chronic types of mental illness, was assuming a perceptibly different tone.

[475] Meyer, Adolf: Presidential address: 35 years of psychiatry in the United States and our present outlook, Am. J. Psychiat. 85:1, 1928.

Specific technics for treatment continued to be broached, but the main stream of psychiatric thinking on which attempts at therapy were based bore the imprint of Darwinism. The path which psychotherapy pursued in these years was psychobiologic and genetic in direction, aside from faith-healing methods of the neoreligious groups and the continued but desultory interest in hypnosis ("Hopes conceived for hypnotism as treatment of obsessions are fading every day . . . suggestion has only a modest value," wrote Bianchi,[476] Italy's leading psychiatrist, in 1906). Mental and emotional troubles no longer were thought of as peculiar visitations or inexplicable outcroppings of defective heredity; they were considered symptomatic representations of poor personality adaptation to the pressure of realities in the patient's environment.

Neurology had utilized the evolutionary principle in the concept of levels of nervous activity enunciated by Hughlings Jackson in 1881. This most provocative and valuable theory indicated that the highest, most recently developed, functional unit, the brain, inhibited and controlled the lower spinal tract activity. Thus automatic (pathologic) movements and reflexes appeared as "release phenomena" when destruction of brain centers occurred through disease. Jackson's observations on epileptic seizures led him to state as a general principle that diseases of the nervous system could be considered as "dissolution, the reverse of evolution." [477]

In psychology, Stanley Hall, the vivid head of Clark University, presaged the concept of the ego as an adaptive organ by his genetic psychology. The statement that "there are just as many rudiments and vestiges in our psychic activity . . . as in our bodies . . . a product of slow evolutionary tendencies" summed up Hall's decades of study of the child and the adolescent mind.[478] Psychoanalysis also rested on the genetic view of the emotions and the instincts where archaic structures in personal and phylogenetic terms were found active in unconscious mentation.

The dynamic view of the human personality as an organ of adaptation which may fail for reasons of physical, emotional, instinctual inadequacy or malfunctioning made psychotherapy an intelligible process to a generation trained in scientific methodology. Simultaneously, the basic attitude toward inadequate adaptation allowed one to contemplate modification of the ego to permit a better adjustment to social realities. If the mind and the emotions were essentially dynamic quantities, they were movable and treatable. If they were products of degeneration, of deterioration of nerve-

[476] Bianchi, Leonardo: A Text-book of Psychiatry, translated by J. H. MacDonald, p. 644, New York, Wood, 1906.

[477] Jackson, J. H.: Selected Writings, edited by James Taylor, p. 29, London, Hodder & Stoughton, 1932.

[478] Hall, S. G.: Adolescence, Its Psychology and Its Relation to Physiology, Anthropology, Sociology, Sex, Crime, Religion and Education, New York, Appleton, 1904.

stuff, they were less easily dealt with. The higher mental elements forming the ego, though formidable in their complexity, were part of an evolutionary chain and hence modifiable. The genetic viewpoint provided an intellectual atmosphere which permitted therapeutic optimism. The revotionary principle in psychiatry was distasteful to some, for it swept aside revered philosophic postulates. Complaints from orthodox philosophic quarters against psychic materialism, and especially against psychoanalytic determinism, arose: "Psychoanalytic materialism makes the existence of an ego outside the mental content (i.e., soul) impossible." [479] Nevertheless, the evolutionary viewpoint answered a pressing need for a discouraged generation of psychotherapists—answered a need and provided a tool for a determined attack on insanity and mental illness. Neurology and biology had launched their younger sibling, psychiatry, in the ways of science.

[479] Allers, Rudolf: The New Psychologies, London, Sheed & Ward, 1932.

8

The Emergence of Dynamic Psychotherapy

Dynamic psychotherapy is that type of mental healing most closely identified with modern psychotherapy. For many it is the only rational type of healing through mental means worthy of the name. For dynamic therapy is essentially *causal* in viewpoint, and, it is hoped, final in its aim, since it attempts to understand and remove the effects of antecedent pathogenic emotional elements in the development of the illness. It differs, for example, from faith-healing because it bases its operations on causes beyond those assigned to adventitious, supernatural, cosmic influences. These "causes" are then brought before the patient through a "sequence of *dialogues*" [480] and emotional reactions in the treatment situation. Properly speaking, dynamic psychotherapy was not discovered; it emerged from the ancient concern with the reasons for man's distress and ways to alter it. Plato's "beautiful logic" and Christian ethics, with its searching of the conscience and its concern for life of the soul, were dynamic methods of influencing men's minds. The originally decisive step in medical thought, Riese indicates, was taken by the Greeks "to turn to the sick himself as the sole source of knowledge," which would be used for subsequent treatment.

It is obvious that dynamic psychotherapy did not burst upon medical consciousness as a new idea, a "sport" among mental achievements; it evolved in the same tortuous way characteristic of other mental-healing forces discussed to this point. But it did have correlations with the historical progress of human thought. The notion of a dynamic psychotherapy inherent in the Greek philosopher's notion of *catharsis,* which attended the passage from ignorance to knowledge, had to wait for its revival for the Renaissance when the individual attained significance. Medicine then could shift its viewpoint from disease as a matter of humoral changes, impersonally conferred upon a patient, to disease *in* a person. This Renaissance

480 Riese, Walter: An Outline of a History of Ideas in Psychotherapy, Bull. Hist. Med. 25:442, 1951.

attitude in regard to mental illness appears in Paracelsus, who, writing in the vernacular German rather than Latin, prefaced in *The Diseases That Deprive Man of His Reason* (1567) [481] by saying:

> We must not forget to explain the origin of the diseases which deprive man of his reason, as we know from experience that they develop out of man's disposition. The present-day clergy of Europe attribute such diseases to ghostly beings and threefold spirits: we are not inclined to believe them.

In his introduction to this translation of Paracelsus, Zilboorg points out that the Renaissance author "intuitively perceived and conceived the concept of personality . . . and the fact that mental disease was a highly individual phenomenon . . . for which . . . a high degree of individualization of one's point of view was needed."

The view that the "complexions" of patients, i.e., their personality, and not the humours per se, were the cause of mental diseases, was mixed in Paracelsus' writings with complex medications derived from minerals and a vigorous espousal of chemistry (alchemy) as the essential equipment of the physician. His reliance on astronomy, which taught Paracelsus that minerals derived their power of cure from the heavenly bodies, further obscured his dynamic viewpoint. For "astronomy, which heretofore has never been taken up by physicians, teaches me to recognize such diseases [as] . . . the crazy dance which the common man calls St. Vitus' dance." [482] Astrology, human disease and human destinies were brought into relation with each other by the iconoclastic Theophrastus. Medieval astrology, served in this wise, allowed astrologists and mystics of later days to "worship him as their master into whose works they could read whatever pleased them." [483]

By a curious twist of medical fate, from this mixture of Paracelsian common sense, rudimentary chemistry and mystical astrology, dynamic psychotherapy took its roots. Two centuries after Paracelsus, Mesmer revived his theories in discovering the fact of animal magnetism, namely, that the celestial bodies influenced the human body through a magnetic fluid's passing from planets to man. Half a century later, magnetism became mesmerism, and soon mesmerism gave way to hypnosis. Another half century saw hypnosis yield to analytic psychology. Schematized and foreshortened, this progression spells out the genealogy of dynamic psy-

[481] Paracelsus (Theophrastus von Hohenheim): The Diseases That Deprive Man of His Reason, Such as St. Vitus' Dance, Falling Sickness, Melancholy, and Insanity and Their Correct Treatment, translated by Gregory Zilboorg, p. 142; Four Treatises, translated from the original German, edited by H. E. Sigerist, Baltimore, Johns Hopkins Press, 1941.

[482] Paracelsus: "Seven Defensiones, the Reply to Certain Calumniations of His Enemies," *in* Four Treatises, p. 16.

[483] Paracelsus: Four Treatises, Preface, p. ix.

chotherapy, the heritage of Paracelsus and Mesmer. The present chapter will relate the devious story of this evolution.

THE BIRTH OF ANIMAL MAGNETISM

In his student days Mesmer had displayed great interest in occult theory. His thesis, presented at the time of his graduation from the Medical Faculty of Vienna in 1765, bore the title "De Planetarum Influxu in Corpus Humanum" (The Influence of the Planets on the Human Body). In it he tried to show that the celestial bodies acted upon human beings through a kind of subtle magnetic fluid which he called "animal magnetism." The opportunity to test this theory clinically came to Mesmer eight years later when he learned of Father Maximillian Hell's cures through the use of the magnet.

Mesmer's first case [484] was so dramatic that it determined the course of his life. It concerned one Fräulein Oesterline, aged 29 years, whose convulsive illness, characterized by a rush of blood to the head, attacks of vomiting, neuralgia in ears and teeth, agitation and syncope, was of several years' standing. The periodicity of the patient's symptoms suggested the opportunity for proving the "flux and reflux" action of animal magnetism, which Mesmer had deduced theoretically. Mesmer applied a magnet over the stomach and to both of Fräulein Oesterline's feet. In a short time she experienced "extraordinary sensations" and spasmodic pains moving through her body, due to a "subtle fluid" coursing in different directions, which finally passed out her lower extremities. For six hours thereafter the patient was free of symptoms. Mesmer repeated the experiment the following day with the same success. "My observations," wrote Mesmer, "opened up a new horizon. . . . They taught me that another principle acted on the magnet, itself incapable of this action on the nerves." He concluded that the magnetic fluid, passing from the magnets, had revitalized the nervous tissues. Mesmer conceived the nature and the action of animal magnetism to be analogous to those of the magnet and electricity; further, that the body was susceptible of receiving this magnetic principle, that the (magnetic) fluid could penetrate everywhere and, like electricity, "could operate at a distance." [485]

Convinced of his findings, Mesmer hastened to invite Doctor Stoerck, president of the Viennese Faculty of Medicine, to witness his experiments. Baron von Stoerck declined. Presently Mesmer was able to induce Ingenhousze, a renowned botanist and inoculator of Vienna, to watch a demonstration on Fräulein Oesterline at Mesmer's home. The doubting Ingen-

[484] Mesmer, F. A.: Mémoire sur la découverte du magnétisme animal, p. 12, Geneva and Paris, Didot, 1779.

[485] *Ibid.*, p. 23.

housze was asked to touch the patient. No movement resulted. Then Mesmer "magnetized" the botanist by touching his hands and bade him repeat the action. A convulsion resulted. They repeated the experiment many times and each time, "to his great astonishment," Ingenhousze, when magnetized, obtained the same convulsive response. Subsequently he magnetized a porcelain cup with a like result. As a final demonstration to Ingenhousze, Mesmer showed how magnetism could be conveyed over a distance:

> I directed my finger toward the patient at a distance of eight steps; an instant after her body went into convulsion, to the point of rising from the bed. . . . I continued, in the same position, to direct my finger towards the patient, placing M. Ingenhousze between her and me; she experienced the same sensations. These experiments having been repeated to the satisfaction of M. Ingenhousze I asked him if he were satisfied, and if he were convinced of the marvelous properties which I had announced to him.

The botantist appeared convinced but asked Mesmer not to communicate to the public what he had discovered to avoid the possible ridicule that would follow. A short time later the Faculty of Medicine in Vienna appointed a committee of which Ingenhousze was a member to investigate Mesmer's claims. After painstaking tests, it concluded that his cures were based on imagination and expelled him from the medical fraternity. Unwilling to drop his new-found science of magnetism, Mesmer set out for France, the land of enlightenment.

The discoverer of the universal fluid reached Paris. Louis XVI, hearing of the new discovery, welcomed him; the liberal atmosphere of Paris encouraged Mesmer's desire to aid humanity through his science. In the interim he had discarded the magnet (1776), relying on the action of an "incomparably subtle" fluid not unlike the "universal spirit" of the seventeenth-century theoreticians. This hypothesis has a history. Earlier, Paracelsus had expounded the theory that the human body was a magnetic microcosm endowed with polarity, and Van Helmont and Maxwell further developed [486] this notion by assuming that this polarity, if joined to a universal spirit, could be harnessed to influence the human body in disease. By linking astrologic concepts with seventeenth-century vitalism, Mesmer masked the basic fact of an interpersonal emotional reaction exerted by one person on another. He thought that the passage of magnetic fluid was responsible for effect of doctor on patient; hence, everything was magnetized—water, bread, silk, wood, clothes—and each magnetized object achieved healing power. Although Mesmer began to believe that a *rapport* had to be established between patient and physician for the *fluidum* to be

[486] Van Helmont: *Quoted in* Bertrand, Alexandre: Du magnétisme animal en France, p. 8, Paris, Baillière, 1826.

effective, the nature of this interpersonal relationship was unknown to him, although archly surmised by his critics.

In Paris, meanwhile, the work of magnetizing went on. One of his spectacular pieces of equipment was the *baquet,* a large wooden tub filled with bottles round which magnetized water flowed. Patients sat round the *baquet* while Mesmer gravely touched each with his previously magnetized iron wand. Soon signs of restlessness appeared, the patients would twitch and tremble violently while jerky movements of the hands and body muscles increased in tempo until, palpitating and convulsed, they achieved the *grand crisis.* With the patient's nervous system brought to a state of crisis, the cure was ensured, as was Mesmer's practice. Parisians craved entertainment, and the "copious leisure of the rich fools of pre-Revolution Paris" [487] was filled with talk of Mesmer and his *baquet.*

Popularity brought changes in Mesmer's technic; his salon acquired rich appointments, he himself wore a lilac robe and his assistants were chosen for their "comeliness." Thomas Carlyle [488] painted the scene:

> Long-stoled he walks, glancing upward in rapt commerce . . . soft music flits. . . . Round their Magnetic Mystery . . . sit breathless, the circles of Beauty and Fashion, each a living circular Passion-Flower. . . . O Women . . . great is your infidel faith.

Eyewitnesses were equally impressed. Deleuze,[489] the librarian, recounts the picture:

> The patients then drew near to each other, touching hands, arms, knees or feet. The handsomest, youngest and most robust magnetizers held also an iron rod with which they touched dilatory or stubborn patients. . . .
>
> The women, being the most easily affected, were almost at once seized with fits of yawning and stretching: their eyes closed, their legs gave way and they seemed to suffocate. . . . Sardonic laughter, piteous moans and torrents of tears burst forth on all sides. Bodies were thrown back in spasmodic jerks.
>
> Another room was padded and presented a different spectacle. There women beat their heads against padded walls or rolled on the cushion-covered floor. In the midst of this panting, quivering throng, Mesmer, dressed in a lilac coat, moved about, extending a magic wand . . . gazing steadily into their eyes, while he held both their hands in his, bringing the middle fingers in immediate contact, to establish the *communication.*

Medical men who observed Mesmer's treatment were generally coldly disapproving. Chemist Berthollet [490] stated:

487 Simpson, Helen: The Waiting City, p. 68, Philadelphia, Lippincott, 1933.

488 Carlyle, Thomas: The French Revolution, A History, p. 46, New York, The Colonial Press, rev. ed. 1899.

489 DeCourmelles, Foveau: Hypnotism, translated by Laura Enser, p. 8, London, Routledge, 1891.

490 Bertrand, Alexandre: Du magnétisme animal en France, p. 62, Paris, Baillière, 1826.

I did not see anything in the convulsions, spasms, crises which are said to be produced by magnetic processes, that cannot be attributed to imagination or to the mechanical effect of friction on very nervous parts . . . or to the law of imitation.

ACADEMICIANS INVESTIGATE MAGNETISM

Mesmer's social and financial success did not satisfy him. He wished to receive the approbation of the French Academy; again and again he sought to interest the Academicians, but without success. Doggedly he submitted a paper composed of twenty-seven propositions which theoretically explained his "animal magnetism." Against their inclination the Academicians examined the writings. Mesmer started with the premise that (Proposition 1) [491] "a reciprocal influence exists between the heavenly bodies, the earth, and animated bodies." Proposition 2 stated, "A fluid universally diffused, so continuous as not to admit of a vacuum, incomparably subtle, and of its nature susceptible of receiving, propagating, and communicating all motor disturbances, is the means of this influence." He went on to elaborate vaguely the mechanism of this influence in Proposition 4, "Alternative effects result from this action, which may be considered to be a flux and a reflux," and concluded by, "The art of healing [through this method] reaches thus its final perfection."

The doctors were outraged at this effrontery. Thouret, regent physician of the Faculty of Paris, wrote a book criticizing "animal magnetism," in which he accused Mesmer of fraud. The fact that certain diseases were not susceptible to magnetic action was a "resource contrived in order to account for failures . . . in certain cases." Thouret continued, "To pretend to the discovery of a means . . . a universal medicine, is an illusion which cannot be excused in an enlightened age."

Nevertheless, a commission from the Academy tested the effect of Mesmer's treatment on themselves. They reported that during the séances nothing was felt but a "slight nervous irritability and a pain in the hollow of the stomach" where the magnetizer had touched them. Their report admitted the peculiar effects observed in the crises, but concluded that they were due to imagination in the subject. "Magnetism minus imagination is nothing." Since the patient's imagination was involved, there was nothing more to be said.

Alone of the prominent physicians in Paris, Charles d'Eslon, professor in the Faculty of Medicine, gave credence to Mesmer. What if imagination had the greatest share in the effects of "animal magnetism"? If it helps, then it is a valuable "invention" for patients. This new agent, explained M. d'Eslon, "might be none other than imagination itself, whose

[491] Mesmer: *Op. cit.*, p. 74.

power is as extensive as it is little known." The Academicians were unmoved; they condemned Mesmer and his magnetism, and came close to expelling d'Eslon also. Disillusioned, Mesmer left Paris.

Meanwhile, d'Eslon continued to experiment, and a group of enthusiastic followers organized the Society of Harmony for the Spread of Magnetic Ideas. The nobility took up Mesmer's struggle and pressed Louis XVI for an appeal to the Academy to consider magnetism once more. In 1779, Mesmer returned to Paris to deliver a series of lectures on his system.

In 1784, after several years of wrangling, the Academy of Science and Faculty of Medicine appointed several illustrious men to investigate the situation.[492] The commissioners included Benjamin Franklin, the American ambassador; Lavoisier, who discovered oxygen; Doctor Guillotin, inventor of the instrument of death; Bailly; and others. D'Eslon took an active part in the tests and proposed to show how the fluid worked. Before the commissioners, d'Eslon magnetized a tree in an orchard. Then he led a boy with bandaged eyes among the trees. As he approached the magnetic tree, and while still some feet away, the subject went into a crisis, with limbs rigid and arms extended. The examiners were sure that the boy was party to a preconceived plan. They experimented with many other tests also, but concluded with a "unanimous voice that the presence of animal magnetism was not proven." The commission decided against the usefulness of magnetism. They put the crisis down to three causes, "imitation, imagination and contact." Mere imagination had no place in science. The commission countered d'Eslon's arguments:

> If, then, M. d'Eslon . . . says . . . these effects are to be ascribed to the agency of a fluid which is communicated from one individual to another by touch . . . he cannot avoid conceding . . . that only one cause is requisite to one effect and . . . since the imagination is a sufficient cause, the supposition of the magnetic fluid is useless.

The Academicians had focused their attention on the "fluid," the means by which the crises were established, and not on the essential fact that a changed state of mind had arisen. Their report conceded the main issue, "that which has been proved through our examination of magnetism is that *man can affect man* . . . almost at will by stimulating his imagination," but did not understand its import. One member of the commission, de Jussieu, dissented, and in a minority report indicated that there might be the germ of a psychological idea in Mesmer's work.

At the same time, a secret report was rendered King Louis showing the moral dangers of magnetism. "It is apparent," wrote the commissioners,

[492] Rapport des commissaires chargés par le roi, de l'examen du magnétisme animal, Paris, L'imprimerie royale, 1784.

"that the crisis occurs more frequently in women than in men. . . . Women have, as a rule, more mobile nerves; their imagination is more lively and more easily excited." The Academicians, aroused by the seductive nature of the crises, were compelled to denounce it in the interest of public morality. The women who went for magnetization were, the commission observed, "not really ill; many came out of idleness or for amusement." They retained "their senses unimpaired and the sensitiveness of youth . . . their charms are such as to affect the physician." The secret report closed with the warning:

> There is nothing to prevent the convulsions in this case also from becoming habitual, from producing an epidemic, and from being transmitted to future generations; such practises and assemblies may also have an injurious effect upon morality.
>
> *Signed:* Franklin, de Bory, Lavoisier,
> Bailly, Majault, Sallin,
> d'Arcet, Guillotin, Le Roy.
> (Paris, August 11, 1784)

Mesmer, disheartened, protested that d'Eslon had wrongfully presented animal magnetism to the commissioners and had, in fact, committed an offense "as odious as it was reprehensible" by claiming discovery of animal magnetism for himself.[493] Retirement was Mesmer's only recourse. "Let him walk by the shore of Bodensee, by the ancient town of Constance," wrote Carlyle, "meditating on much."

MAGNETIZATION ON TRIAL

The demise of the embittered and empty-handed Mesmer occurred in the year of Napoleon's downfall—1815. Clinging to his astral explanation of a "universal fluid" that influenced the body, with which he had brought the art of healing to its "final perfection," Mesmer rejected the expansion of his hardy and esoteric offspring. In the hands of others, animal magnetism was evolving into a branch of a new department of natural philosophy-physiology. New facts which called for explanations of more naturalistic type of the magnetic force were accumulating. Marquis de Puysegur obtained somnambulism without crises in his subjects, and Abbé Faria was able to put his patients in a state of somnambulism by making them comfortable, suggesting drowsiness and then saying with authority, "Sleep!"[494] Nor was the circus spirit of public exhibitions found to be necessary to achieve results. Physicians at the Salpêtrière in Paris, experimenting with magnetism, achieved sleepiness in their patients without con-

[493] Mesmer, F. A.: Lettre à messieurs les auteurs du Journal de Paris, 1784.
[494] Bernheim, Hippolyte: Hypnotisme, suggestion, psychotherapie, ed. 2, p. 87, Paris, Octave Douin, 1903.

vulsions. Both Abbé Faria (1814), the Portuguese priest, and later Bertrand (1825) concluded that suggestion was the motive force behind magnetism. The latter clearly stated in his thorough review [495] of the subject that although he believed in the phenomenon of somnambulism, "magnetism is a mere chimera."

The problem of the nature and the action of magnetism was temporarily solved by assuming that the magnetic fluid, responsible for the *rapport* which Mesmer insisted passed between magnetizer and subject, was secreted in the brain, passing along the nerves to the peripheral organs in response to the operator's will.[496] This hypothesis obviated Mesmer's universal-fluid theory, and competent medical men—Husson, at Hôtel-Dieu, and Georget, at Salpêtrière—spoke less of magnetic "fluid" and more of the magnetizer's will in their reports. Nevertheless, Deleuze [497] ironically counseled his magnetizing students to

> forget for a while all your knowledge of Physics and Metaphysics. Dismiss from your minds all objections that may occur. Have an active desire to do good, a firm belief in the power of Magnetism, and an entire confidence in employing it. . . . Be very credulous, be very persevering, reject all past experience and do not listen to reason.

At all events, a more naturalistic theory was being evolved when the Academy of Science's committee, in response to pressure from lay and medical groups, commenced its deliberations in February, 1826, on the "Magnetical Experiments." [498] This commission, authorized to restudy the subject, was composed of eminent physicians, including men like Itard, the father of the movement for training the feeble-minded; Magendie, a pioneer in anatomy of the nervous system; Laënnec; and others. In 1831, Husson, the secretary, presented the commission's report, which affirmed the existence of "animal magnetism" in a few cases, but declared that in many others "weariness, monotony or the imagination" produced the phenomena observed. The commission affirmed that magnetism was a "therapeutic expedient" and as such had a place in medical science. They recommended that it be practiced by physicans only, and concluded, "The Committee has collected facts . . . to allow it to believe . . . the Academy should encourage . . . researches on magnetism, as being a very curious branch of psychology and natural history."

The commission also had gone far enough in experimentation to indicate that the phenomenon of somnambulism and certain new faculties as

[495] Bertrand, Alexandre: *Op. cit.,* p. 303.
[496] *Ibid.,* p. 237.
[497] Deleuze, M.: Histoire critique du magnétisme animal, Paris, Belin-Leprieur, 1813.
[498] Husson: Report of the Magnetical Experiments Made by the Commission of the Royal Academy of Medicine, Paris, June 21 and 28, 1831, translated by Charles Poyen, St. Sauveur, Boston, Hitchcock, 1836.

clairvoyance and *intuition* were, in their opinion, due to definite physiologic changes: [499] "A certain number of phenomena . . . [were] produced by magnetism alone and could not be produced without it." This report was read at a meeting of the Academy on the 21st of June, 1831, but it was not accepted.

The question of clairvoyance, reading through closed eyes in the somnambulistic state, was particularly vexing; it ran counter to Gallic logic. Certain committee members were dissatisfied, pointing out the opportunity for fraud in subjects whose eyelids were pressed down by examiner's fingers. One member, Burdin,[500] offered a prize of three thousand francs if it could be scientifically proved that one could read through closed eyes. In 1837, another commission of scientists undertook to restudy the question more critically. Husson, chairman of the earlier commission, felt himself personally attacked; feeling in scientific circles ran high. Apparently no conclusive report of this investigation was filed.

Although medical officialdom in France decreed, through the commission, that magnetization "ranked within the framework of medical knowledge," the subject did not retain interest in France. A group of magnetizers, nonmedical in background, carried their art to other countries at public gatherings, on the lecture platform and in *conversazioni,* where the demonstrations were watched with awe. Often these peripatetic magnetizers healed patients, read diagnoses through their subjects made clairvoyant by magnetization, and gained followers for their art among laymen. One such was M. Poyen, whose demonstration in New England stimulated Quimby to embark on a career of mental healing; another was Richard Chenevix, who exhibited in London. At many of these *conversazioni* curious physicians were present, prepared to disprove the induced somnambulism that they witnessed and to prick the bubble of scientific romanticism which had infiltrated social thinking in that day. In 1829, Dr. John Elliotson, brilliant professor of practice of medicine at University Hospital, London, became so impressed at Chenevix' séance that he commenced magnetizing at the hospital in spite of the cries of "Humbug!" from his associates. A man of vigor and vision, Elliotson had already been marked a radical in medicine by discarding the knee breeches and the silk stockings, the orthodox dress of physicians of that era.[501] In the same spirit he espoused the use of the stethoscope recently invented by Laënnec in Paris, insisted that the University College be affiliated with a hospital, and generally improved standards of teaching to the point at which his confrères' classes were relatively deserted by students. It was his outright

[499] *Ibid.,* p. 165.
[500] DeCourmelles, Foveau: *Op. cit.,* p. 17.
[501] Newbold, George: Famous names in hypnotism. John Elliotson (1791-1868) Brit. J. M. Hypnotism 1:2, 1950.

support of medical mesmerism, however, that won for Elliotson the strongest abuse by colleagues, culminating in a request for his resignation from his professorship. The year before (1837) the Council of the College had ordained that "animal magnetism" or mesmerism be barred from the hospital. With this blow, Elliotson practically withdrew from organized medicine, bending his efforts and practice in the direction of mesmerism. Since the columns of the *Lancet* were closed to him, Elliotson organized and edited the *Zoist,* a journal of mesmerism which contained all the work in that field in England for a span of 13 years (1843-1855). With the slander of his colleagues ringing in his ears,[502] Elliotson attempted once more to plead for scientific appraisal of mesmerism at the 1846 Harveian Lecture, but to no avail. The inevitable "Humbug!" greeted his pleadings.

THE EMBATTLED MESMERISTS

A thorny issue lay in the value of mesmerism in its anesthetic properties during surgical operations. Reports of major surgery done under mesmeric stupor had been already published sporadically in France, but Elliotson's espousal allowed Dr. James Esdaile to report in full his remarkable surgical results from a Calcutta hospital. Under induced trance Esdaile described a series of more than two hundred major operations.[503] Many recommended it in preference to ether and chloroform, then coming into common hospital use. The case reports were dramatic enough to compel attention from English surgeons. Though Esdaile could prove the authenticity of mesmeric anesthesia, his papers were not accepted for publication in England, save in the *Zoist*. His Indian experience with 261 major operations under mesmeric influence only served to make him, in his own words, "the best abused man in the world." [504] Such dramatic operations as the removal of a tumor of the eye "involving half the cheek" without the patient's knowledge or perception of pain under mesmerism, even "when nitric acid was used to clean the socket" postoperatively, were disbelieved. Esdaile's work in the Mesmeric Hospital in Calcutta, for a time under government auspices, was greeted by the ready cry of "Fraud!"

At a meeting of the Royal Medical and Chirurgical Society in 1842, an amputation was demonstrated in which mesmeric anesthesia only was used.[505] Doctor Copland led the attack by denying that "agony during the operation" was absent in the patient, and, if it were true, that "pain is a

[502] The Zoist 7:4, No. 25, London, Baillière, April, 1849.
[503] Esdaile, James: The Zoist, No. 26, p. 125.
[504] ——: Natural and Mesmeric Clairvoyance with the Practical Application of Mesmerism in Surgery and Medicine, London, Baillière, 1852.
[505] Bramwell, J. Milne: Hypnotism, Its History, Practice and Theory, London, Grant Richards, 1903.

wise provision of nature, and patients ought to suffer pain. . . . They are better for it and recover better." The vituperation of English physicians toward contributors to the *Zoist* was couched in words like "liar," "impostor," "satanic agency." In answer, the pages of the *Zoist* carried reports of mesmeric cures of rheumatism, eye inflammations, headaches, insanity and numbers of intractable conditions given up by regular practitioners of medicine as irremediable. Testimonials appeared in every issue. Doctor Elliotson stood his ground to the end, but the barbs of his enemies struck deep; his practice faded to a trickle. His devotion to a new idea, his closer understanding of functional nervous disorders, his use of "spiritual" forces in therapy of neuroses (not yet dignified by that name), constituted his professional tombstone. Though his colleagues called him madman, admirers were steadfast; Doctor Ashburner [506] wrote a year before the iconoclast's death, "John Elliotson . . . [became] an object of mortal envy to a host of pismires."

The contumely heaped on Elliotson and his confrères by medical men was pointed; a London surgeon, one Mr. Wakely, said quite seriously: [507] "Mesmerism is too gross a humbug to admit of further serious notice. We ought to regard its abettors as quacks and imposters. They ought to be hooted out of professional society [1842]." In part this was due to the fantastic theories promulgated of mesmerism and the phenomenon of clairvoyance during this period. Indeed, the explanation of the efficacy of mesmeric passes over the body of patients as due to a "quasi-electric chain," or to a "transference" of thought from doctor to patient, or to a "mesmeric fluid . . . emanating from the active brain," was not far from the "universal fluidum" of Mesmer himself. In the pages of the *Zoist* [508] were descriptions of the vital principle which appeared like a "halo . . . its color blue, like the electric spark, from lightest to deep violet," varying with the sensitivity of the mesmeric subject. The theory of odylic force, the luminosity emanating from "sensitives" under mesmerism and that behind the magnetoscope of Rutter [509] which measured each individual's specific magnetic force were persistent remnants of a primitive astrology which attempted to describe astonishing psychological findings in physical terms. Parenthetically it may be remarked that overtones of the influence of metal on the body lingered in Charcot's acceptance of Burq's metalo therapy (1878) [510] as the scientific basis for hypnosis (transfer of anesthetic effects from copper to the skin). Even later, in 1886, another French

506 Ashburner, John: Notes and Studies of Animal Magnetism and Spiritualism, London, Baillière, 1867.
507 The Zoist, No. 25, p. 4.
508 The Zoist, No. 27, p. 231.
509 Ashburner: *Op. cit.,* Chap. 5.
510 DeCourmelles, Foveau: *Op. cit.,* p. 29.

expert in hypnosis, Luys, placed hermetically sealed tubes containing iron and other metals under the head of the patient to obtain hypnotic effects. Nevertheless, crusty realists of Esdaile's day could only splutter, "The parties concerned in the infamous publication [the *Zoist*] . . . bite and rail: the leper [sic] must be taken with his spots." [511]

Nevertheless, the undeniable confluence of thought of mesmerist on patient, which in the presuggestion days was called "transference of thought," became the object of some remarkable hypotheses. It was explained that the ideas in the operator's mind were transferred to the patient's mind via a "double consciousness" evoked by the functional effect of mesmerism. It was this notion of an accessory consciousness which led in a tortuous way over a half century to the concepts of "subliminal consciousness," "unconscious cerebration," "subconscious mind," and "the unconscious." Early in the course of mesmerism the transference was considered a movement of thought of a sort which could then be retransferred from somnambulist to another person for therapeutic purposes. This was the explanation advanced for clairvoyant diagnoses. A remarkable passage in the *Zoist* by the Rev. Mr. Sandby,[512] who wished to explain clairvoyance, postulates that "transference of thought" may be based on the perception of facts in the brain of the mesmerist by the "ecstatic," a synonym for patient, which the former had forgotten. "We may suppose," Sandby wrote, "that these thoughts (memories and images) are latent in the cerebral region" and can be transferred to the sensitive brain of the somnambule without the mesmerist being "conscious of their re-existence."

This speculation was adduced to explain the production by the somnambule of material of which he could have had no conscious knowledge (i.e., an ancient tongue, unheard conversations, scientific material, etc.). But the persistence of other memory changes, posthypnotic amnesia or hypermnesia, i.e., increased memory, during the hypnotic state, forced a closer study of that which was "latent" in the mind of the patient and recoverable only in a subsequent hypnosis. In the mid-century, however, these problems were unevenly understood and speculatively explained. The position of scientific medicine regarding mesmeric phenomena can be assumed to be that of Radcliffe Hall [513] who, in 1845, published a sober, critical series of articles in the *Lancet*. Hall concluded his unbiased examination of mesmerism by summarizing the evidence:

Proved—Induction of sleep.
Probable but needs confirmation—Rigidities, convulsions, changed sensations, double consciousness.

511 Editorial: Lancet, July 31, 1847.
512 The Zoist. Comments by Rev. George Sandby, Review of book by A. Cahagnet, No. 28, p. 415.
513 Hall, R. C. H.: On the rise, progress and mysteries of mesmerism, Lancet 1:112, 1845.

Possible, not probable—Insensibility to severe pain.
Impossible—Clairvoyance, intuition, etc.
No shadow of evidence for a new agency as magnetism.

Among physicians, wedded to a mechanistic view of physiology of the nervous system, the vitalist concept that magnetism exerted a molecular force on the nervous system in the production of somnambulance, trance-states and so on remained in disrepute. It was not until Braid's work that the effect of mesmerism was brought to a level of physiologic respectability. Visiting a séance by M. Lafontaine in 1841, James Braid, a medical practitioner of Manchester, was impressed that the subject was unable to lift his eyelids during the mesmeric state. This he felt was a physiologic effect neither imaginary, magnetic nor magical. It represented a weakened function of certain muscles, perhaps due to excessive fatigue. Doctor Braid proceeded to test out his theory on a young friend, a Mr. Walker, and upon Mrs. Braid. To his amazement, when Walker looked fixedly at a bright object—Braid used his metallic lancet case—he almost immediately fell into a trancelike state. Braid had proved that "animal magnetism" was not essential in acquiring the mesmeric state of stupor. The subject had merely to fix his gaze on a bright object for a short time, induce pathologic fatigue of the eye muscles, and forthwith he passed into a stupor.

At the end of a six-month period Braid had already written a paper, entitled "Practical Essay on the Curative Agency of Neuro-Hypnotism," which he proposed to offer before the British Medical Association at its annual congress in 1842.[514] He was anxious to demonstrate the scientific validity of the condition he called *hypnotism* as a curative power. By this time he had amassed a large series of cases in which striking improvements had been accomplished through hypnotism in rheumatism, paralysis, pharyngitis, spasmodic torticollis (wry neck), migraine, spinal irritation, epilepsy, valvular heart disease, frontal-bone abscess, deafness, nearsightedness and strabismus. The program committee of the British Medical Association was not impressed. Caustically they replied to his offer that they were "pleased to decline entertaining the subject."

BRAID DISCOVERS HYPNOTISM

Braid continued his therapeutic experiments. Using his lancet case, he had his patients look fixedly at it until they fell asleep. Awaking from the hypnotic state they had no memory of what had happened. The effects of the hypnosis itself were sufficient to cause improvement in the patient's symptoms. Doctor Braid stressed relaxation, "absolute repose of body, fixed

[514] Bramwell: *Op. cit.*, p. 22.

attention and suppressed respiration." Braid freely professed that he did not understand the reason for the overpowering reaction that occurred in his patients; nor was he willing to ascribe hypnosis to any personal power in himself.

For a time Braid's results met with the usual objections and censure. The rebuff of the British Medical Association irritated him not a little, especially since he desired to subject his method to the most careful scientific scrutiny. Because he denied the fact of magnetism or mesmerism in any of its esoteric settings or odylic modalities, among magnetizers Braid's innovations were regarded as those of an upstart and a detractor. In a letter, Doctor Elliotson complained that "a man, a most vain and swaggering mechanic of a surgeon, named Braid, at Manchester," declared he could produce all the phenomena of mesmerism merely by having a person keep his eyes fixed on a light suspended above the level of his eyes.

The phenomenon of "nervous sleep" or "neuro-hypnotism" accomplished without mesmeric passes was sharply differentiated in Braid's mind from the "ordinary mesmerizing process." In his book, *Neurypnology, or, The Rationale of Nervous Sleep,*[515] he established the subjective nature of hypnotism. Like Abbé Faria and Bertrand several decades before, Braid called for a study of the patient rather than of the magnetizing fluid, remarking that patients became susceptible "according to their expectation or belief," by which was meant suggestibility.[516] In this paper he wrote, "I adopted the term 'hypnotism' to prevent my being confounded with those who have extreme notions . . . of exoteric influence being the cause of sleep." It is apparent that Braid was an excellent observer, and, within limits of the psychology of the times, perceptive to the emotional influence of doctor on patient, as witness the statement:

> It is well known, however, that so long ago as December, 1841, I particularly pointed out the remarkable docility of patients during hypnotism, which made them most anxious to comply with every proper request or supposed wish of others.

The braidian theory that hypnosis followed upon concentration of attention on an idea, so-called monoideism, was an early concept which was modified later to encompass hypnosis as an "artificial condition created by suggestion." [517] The problem of memory alterations also concerned Braid. The "extraordinary revivification of memory," [518] of things long

[515] Braid, James: Neurypnology, or, The Rationale of Nervous Sleep Considered in Relation with Animal Magnetism, illustrated by numerous cases of its successful application in the relief and cure of disease, London, Churchill, 1843.
[516] ———: On hypnotism, Lancet 1:627, 1845.
[517] Bramwell: *Op. cit.*, p. 294.
[518] Braid, James: Observations on mesmeric and hypnotic phenomena, M. Times, London 10:31, 1844.

forgotten, under hypnosis brought him to the notion that a "double consciousness" existed, a circumstance that offered a naturalistic explanation for clairvoyance. "The mesmeric intuition [clairvoyance?] very probably is nothing more than extraordinary memory referred to."[519] Rather than being "old fashioned and a believer in phrenology,"[520] as Zilboorg concludes, Braid was a careful investigator, oriented physiologically and alert to artifacts or loose thinking.

Indeed, the "swaggering mechanic of a surgeon" had brought hypnosis back to physiology sufficiently so that Professor Velpeau could reopen the question at the French Academy of Medicine meeting in 1860. Azam's paper on surgery under hypnotic anesthesia[521] made Braid's name synonymous with hypnosis (braidism) on the Continent, and, as contemporaries remarked, "distinguished physicians were now anxious to study these phenomena, without fear of compromising themselves."[522]

The pivotal figure round which hypnosis underwent its scientific renascence was that of Jean Martin Charcot. The authority of Charcot, which was in the main that of French neurology, and the serious approach of his students to the effects of hypnosis conferred an enduring sanction upon hypnosis as a legitimate medical technic. An associate, Dr. Charles Richet, in 1875 took the problem to Charcot, who by now had literally carved a clinical science of neurology from the motley group of syphilitics, chronic invalids and paralytics that thronged the halls of the Salpêtrière. Charcot set himself the task of unraveling the nosologic position of hypnosis among abnormalities of the nervous system. With the same unremitting observation and patience with which he had studied multiple sclerosis, muscular atrophies, tabes dorsalis and other poorly understood neurologic conditions, Charcot applied scientific method to the demonstration of the reality of a "special state of the nervous system." On the whole, interest at the Salpêtrière was concentrated more in method and experiment than in therapeutics.[523] Painstaking tests of sensibility under metallic contact of anesthesia, catalepsy, the effect of scalp stimulation by galvanic electricity, neuromuscular excitability under hypnosis, the occurrence of contractures, reflex changes under hypnosis, production of hysterical stigmata, etc., formed the basis of Charcot's classic nosologic description of the hypnotic state. This encompassed the states of lethargy, catalepsy and somnambulism representing levels of hypnotic effect in hysterical subjects. Charcot's

[519] *Ibid.*, p. 47.
[520] Zilboorg, Gregory, and Henry, G. W.: A History of Medical Psychology, p. 356, New York, Norton, 1941.
[521] Azam: Note sur le nerveux ou hypnotisme, Arch. gén. méd. 1:1, January, 1860.
[522] Binet, Alfred, and Fere, Charles: Animal Magnetism, p. 78, New York, Appleton, 1889.
[523] Charcot, J. M.: Oeuvres complètes, Vol. 9, Paris, Lecroshier & Babé, 1890.

summation [524] of the clinical limits of hypnosis established both himself and his subject within the Académie des sciences.

SCIENTIFIC HYPNOSIS UNDER CHARCOT

Out of this mass of experimental work arose another generalization which the Salpêtrière school upheld in the decades of debate that raged over the problem, namely, that hypnosis was a selective state of the nervous system closely related to, if not identical with, hysteria. Hysterical seizures could be induced by hypnosis and subsequently removed by it. In a word, the two states were synonymous affections of the nervous organization. The paralysis and the anesthesias of the hysteric, the *arc de cercle,* a condition wherein the patient formed a rigid arc with his body, resting on head and heels, were induced and removed by Charcot on the wards of the Salpêtrière.

His precise delineations of neurologic conditions brought physicians from all over the world; his demonstrations of *les états hystériques* brought the *cognescenti* to his famed Tuesday morning clinics. Charcot's lectures on hypnosis were alike a milestone in medical history and a landmark in the life of Paris. The penetrating perception of hysterical neuromuscular patterns, Charcot's gifts as a lecturer, his feeling for the poetry of distorted movement in hysterics, for the meaningfulness of postural changes reflecting intense emotional states, soon led to charges of theatricality by others. Clinicians elsewhere could duplicate neither the three phases of hypnotic action (lethargy, catalepsy, somnambulism) nor the grotesque contractures of Salpêtrière patients. That apperception of tonic distortions which Charcot identified both in the demoniacs of medievalism and in hysterical seizures and contractures, in a study of medieval art,[525] was considered as evidence of mass suggestion peculiar possibly to the Gallic psyche. Bernheim [526] remarked that only once did he see the three stages of hypnosis reproduced in his Nancy clinic, and that in "a girl who had spent three years at the Salpêtrière." Dubois noted that Charcot's patients acted like "marionettes or like circus horses." [527] German clinicians treated these dramatic demonstrations with disdain, pointing to the decadence of the Latin race.

Workers at the Salpêtrière rallied to Charcot's defense. Against the

[524] Charcot, J. M.: Essai d'une distinction nosographique des divers états compris sous le nom d'hypnotisme, Compt. rend. Acad. sc., Vol. 44, 1882.

[525] Charcot, J. M., and Richer, Paul: Les difformes et les malades dans l'art, Paris, Lecroshier & Babé, 1889.

[526] Bernheim, H.: Suggestive Therapeutics, A Treatise on the Nature and Uses of Hypnotism, translated by C. A. Herter, p. 90, New York, Putnam, 1889.

[527] Dubois, Paul: The Psychic Treatment of Nervous Disorders, translated and edited by S. E. Jelliffe and W. A. White, p. 16, New York, Funk, 1909.

charges that the patients had been rehearsed by the Master for clinical presentation, Pitres asked, "What if they were? The findings in extreme cases did not negate general principles: where else could one see these extraordinary seizures except in *la grande hystérie?"* [528] Binet and Fere journeyed to Nancy to review Bernheim's cases, and, on the inability of Bernheim to produce contractures by electrically stimulating nerves during hypnosis, asked, "What can be thought of subjects so devoid of material signs? Can one evade physiology?" [529] And in relation to Braid, who also perceived the suggestive aspect of hypnosis, these investigators commented on the obviousness of Braid's being "a believer rather than an observer." [530] No, medicine for the imagination was distinct from hypnotic therapeutics.

Demonstration of the reversibility of hysteria and hypnotic phenomena presumably placed these findings on a physiologic basis. Though warmly contested by Bernheim and others, the basic observations started a chain of thinking that led eventually to a soundly established psychopathology. Activity, experimental and therapeutic, surrounding hypnosis involved neurologists and psychotherapists whose names are meaningful in the history of modern medicine. Charcot, Janet, Forel, Babinski, Krafft-Ebing, Bernheim, Freud, Déjerine, Hack Tuke, Binet, Vogt, Schilder, are but a handful of the neurologists and the psychiatrists whose work has filled the pages of medical journals from 1870 to our day. Journals devoted solely to hypnotism, *Revue de l'hypnotisme et de la psychologie physiologique* (1887-1902), *Zeitschrift für Hypnotismus, Psychotherapie sowie andere psychophysiologische und psychopathologische Forschungen* (1892-1902), and recently the *British Journal of Medical Hypnotism* (1950-   ), attest to the widespread and persistent interest in hypnotism.

The literature on the subject is vast and confusing, its content varying from speculative assumptions to painstaking investigations, dominated first by physiologic theories and later by psychological concepts, marked early by chauvinism and conflict and more recently by efforts at co-operative correlation of neurophysiologic and psychic data. The seemingly magical relationship between two individuals, wherein one exerts a directive influence on the other's feelings, behavior and mental functioning, has been, and is, a challenge to both experimentalist and clinician. Though the therapeutic value of hypnosis has been agreed upon, its limits of application tested, its depth of penetration increased, no definitive explanation of the hypnotic state has yet been reached. In a sense, the history of hypnotic investigation mirrors the alternate phases of mysticism, idealism, materialism and relativistic realism through which natural

[528] Pitres, A.: Leçons cliniques sur l'hystérie et l'hypnotisme, Paris, Douin, 1891.
[529] Binet and Fere: *Op. cit.,* p. 174.
[530] *Ibid.,* p. 72.

phenomena pass in their scientific life histories. From the astrologic theories of Mesmer to the psychoanalytic concept of the instinctive-emotional basis of human relatedness, hypnosis recapitulates, to a degree, the process of relentless clarification of assumption, inference, hypothesis and theory which underlies the scientific method.

SUGGESTION VERSUS HYPNOSIS

The literature on hypnosis during the 1880's centered in whether the phenomenon was of a physiologic or a psychological nature. Chief criticism of the theory of "selective" responsiveness of certain persons to hypnotism which the Salpêtrière school argued was evidence of disordered physiology, i.e., hysterical disposition, came from Hippolyte Bernheim, of Nancy. Convinced by Liébault, a fellow-townsman of Nancy, whose quiet work over a decade proved that the trance-state was possible because of a "side-tracking" of attention, Bernheim became the spokesman for the Suggestion School. As early as 1864, Liébault, an unassuming country doctor, was magnetizing his patients with marked success through the simple suggestion that they sleep. His book,[531] contending that magnetism and somnambulism represented no more than the obedience of one person to the suggestion of another, received scant attention until Bernheim, as a young physician recently graduated from the Salpêtrière, joined him. Bernheim was impressed by Liébault's theory of hypnosis: "The concentration of attention causes the isolation of the senses, the cessation of muscular movement and the rapport between the somnambulist and the hypnotizer."

Liébault's technic was on a nontheatrical but personal level. He placed the patient in a recumbent position, requested him to fix his eyes on a glittering object, then suggested in a soothing voice: "You are sleeping; your breathing is slow and deep; you are becoming calm and relaxed; your body is warm; you are getting sleepy; now go to sleep!" With this technic, Liébault had asserted that one fifth of his patients could be placed in a state of somnambulism; Bernheim insisted that 90 per cent of all persons could be hypnotized. The contentions of the Salpêtrière group were exposed as inadequate by the new theory. To Bernheim, hypnotism was an intensification of normal suggestion. Due to restriction of attention, the patient became an automaton, in a state of "helpless obedience." The demonstration of anesthesia induced by copper plates placed on the skin of hysterics, nominated *Aestheogenism* by Charcot, was clearly unnecessary: "There is no hypnotism; it is all suggestion." Bernheim considered it

[531] Liébault, A. A.: Du Somneil et des états analogues considérés surtout au point de vue de l'action du moral sur le physique, Paris, Masson, 1866.

gratuitous to define the hypnotic state as a hysterical neurosis; sleep and somnambulism were identical conditions. How could sleep be considered pathologic, asked Bernheim; how could hypnosis be a disease?

The technic of the Nancy school was simple and powerfully therapeutic. Delivered in a tone which implied certainty and quiet authority, the psychotherapist at first used general suggestions of well-being. Then specific suggestions for the disease followed. "You will get well," said Bernheim. "Your state will improve. You will become calm at first, less frightened, then stronger. Your aches will grow less: the pains will grow less. Gradually the muscles will loosen up, your joints will be less stiff, your limbs will become stronger and stronger." These suggestions were repeated for several days in the same manner.

The majority of workers, in believing that suggestion represented the motive power in therapeutic hypnosis, deviated from the Salpêtrière school. Babinski, a pupil of Charcot, recognizing that persuasion could cure hysterical symptoms coined the term *pithiatisme* [532] to describe the essential characteristic of hysteria. The positive findings of Salpêtrière were explained on the basis of "expectant attention in the patient," the action of an "idea" (of anesthesia or *arc de cercle,* for example), bringing about an ideomotor reflex through increased ideosensorial excitability. This later explanation advanced by Bernheim was accompanied by the caution that this was "only a formula." [533]

The notion of "idea" conceived in broad terms, implanted by the therapist and resulting in bodily action in the patient, became the essential contribution of the psychological school of hypnosis.[534] By 1890, the theory of specificity of hysterical disposition for successful hypnosis yielded to the generalized theory that inhibition of psychic activities in most persons could be pushed to a state of inattention approximating sleep without abolishing receptivity of ideas and reflex expression thereof in motor terms. This reorientation in theory initiated a change in therapeutic aim; direct suggestion of symptom disappearance became the accepted goal of treatment.

General adoption of Bernheim's ideas led to a widening of the area of hypnotic usage. Treatment was extended to alcoholic, neurasthenic, medical problems of every description, and hypnosis was regarded as an adjuvant to a rationalistic medical therapy. Moreover, the simplification of hypnosis lent itself to pedagogy and treatment even of "vicious and degen-

[532] Babinski, J.: Hypnotisme et hystérie, Gaz. hebdomadaire méd. et chir., July, 1891. The dismemberment of traditional hysteria (pithiatism), St. Paul M. J., October, 1909.

[533] Bernheim: Suggestive Therapeutics, p. 138.

[534] Janet, Pierre: The Major Symptoms of Hysteria, p. 324, New York, Macmillan, 1907.

erate children."[535] Suggestion is a force, said Bernheim, which is close to daily life.[536] It is used in everyday affairs. Suggestion is used by the mother on her child, by the teacher on his pupil, by the state on its citizens. Indeed, suggestion is an essential part of education and provides the encouragement which causes people to control the old and try the new.

The area of suggestive therapy extended to schools and prisons; a single hypnotic séance in the public schools of Nancy was reported to have converted lazy children into children of industrious habits. The press[537] carried accounts of idiotic children's being taught reading and writing in two months' time under the efforts of hypnotists:

> Stupid children are made gifted by this discovery of hypnotism with mere verbal suggestion and instruction. By this process children become mere machines, and their studies may be directed the way their parents incline. . . . The confirmed bad habits of years' standing are now also cured by hypnotism. It is claimed that in fifty years more such a thing as a chronic drunkard will be unknown.

Accent on the suggestive relation between patient and therapist brought to the fore the moral implications of influencing the will, since the hysterical trance-state was now acknowledged to be almost entirely a property of the subject's psychic structure. Many observers agreed with Bernheim's tentative hypothesis that the transfer of idea from therapist to patient could achieve its effect by a process of autosuggestion within the patient. Wetterstrand, a Swedish psychotherapist, in expressing the growing conviction that it was very difficult to influence hysterics with suggestive technics, pointed out that "in one sense" hysterics were helped by a "firmly rooted auto-suggestion."[538] Aside from the practical use of autosuggestion, the subjective aspect of the patient's receptivity raised questions of responsibility for criminal suggestion whose medicolegal implications were discussed at length in the literature. Fifty years of hypnotizing had convinced medical men that posthypnotic actions could not be expected to occur when contrary to the subject's customary ethical standards. Nevertheless, laymen continued to express anxiety by "praying that scientific investigators stop where they are lest we learn too much of the secrets of the nervous system"[539] and expose the mind to Pandora's box of human evils. In a hopeful vein the editor of the *New York Ledger*[540] asked how

[535] Berillon, editor: Rev. hypnotisme et psychol. physiol. 14:255, February, 1900.
[536] Bernheim: Suggestive Therapeutics, p. 159.
[537] Hypnotism, New York Sun, June, 1890.
[538] Wetterstrand, O. G.: Hypnotism and Its Application to Practical Medicine, translated from the German edition by H. G. Petersen, p. 52, New York, Putnam, 1897.
[539] Beard, G. M.: Current delusions relating to hypnotism, Alienist & Neurologist 3:57, 1882.
[540] Bell, Clark: *Quoted in* Hypnotism, Proc. Med.-legal Soc. New York, J.A.M.A. 14:247, February 15, 1890.

far "hypnotism could be used as a moral remedy to correct evil habits, bad practices or evil inclinations."

PERSUASION AND AUTOSUGGESTION

Psychotherapy which strengthened the will through suggestion moved naturally along the lines of intellectualism, of rationally explaining away disturbing bodily ailments and distressing mental states. Babinski had already indicated that persuasion was a potent therapeutic weapon; and Dubois, the urbane and affable Swiss, raised persuasion to the level of a method of "moral" treatment of neurasthenia and neurosis. Dubois called his method "moral orthopedics," a synonym for a forthright type of mental hygiene. Although Pierre Janet, dean of French psychiatry, complained that the moral method bordered on the mystical, a retrogression to faith-healing, Dubois spoke of "education of the will and reason" and recommended his patients to "pass a sponge over [their] past and wipe out [their] phobias." [541] Persuasion was successful in suppressing neurotic symptoms, disarming in its directness and pragmatic appeal. In a similar vein, William James, in America, spoke of unlocking our mental energies, of striving, working against our weaknesses; and Dubois, in Berne, recommended his patients to take a "rosy view of life." He spoke in direct, intimate terms of their life problems. Contrary to the "circuitous path of insinuation" by which suggestion worked on patients, the ebullient Swiss persuaded the ill to relinquish their troubles in such words as:

> Your intestinal troubles will surely improve. . . . You are going to gradually get stronger. You are intelligent and have a taste for work: your whole state of helplessness is due to a conviction of helplessness. . . . Go back to an active life after your treatment is over.

The rational therapeutics of the persuasionists is recognizable as a lineal descendant of Pinel's moral treatment of the insane and the kindly intellectualism with which Leuret treated psychotics. In addition to its "paternal spirit," it had the value of spending much time on the patient's life-history. "I am not at all anxious," Dubois wrote, "to juggle with the patient's symptoms. . . . I wish, on the contrary to study him . . . to discover by what circuitous route he arrived at the pains in the head." The kinship of this method of therapy was closer to Weir Mitchell's rest cure than to hypnotic treatment. It comprised rest and food and the regulation of every-day life, the *how* of living combined with a vigorous optimism of good hygiene. Said Dubois to a tuberculous patient:

> "You cannot put on weight unless you take your food properly. . . . A consumptive who is losing weight is on the downward path: but it is a happy

[541] Dubois, Paul: *Op. cit.*, p. 330.

augury when such a patient puts on flesh." The patient answers: "I'll try to eat, doctor." "Try! What's the use of that? The word 'try' conveys a doubt of the result, and the doubt will not fail to reduce your impetus. What you must say to yourself is, 'I am going to eat!' "

The psychotherapeutic philosophy of persuasion, of which Janet complained that it contained "too much exaltation," was shadowed in a more modest manner by the apothecary of Nancy, Emile Coué. Starting with suggestive therapy, Coué stimulated autosuggestion within his patients. Coué's quiet personality, his kindliness, forceful yet dignified manner, contributed to the success of his method. He did not indulge in theoretical explanations to his patients; scientific theory was quite secondary with him. Only occasionally did he present the result of his work to a psychological congress. Light, humorous, "sometimes firm, sometimes gently bantering," varying his tone to suit the temperament of his patient, he taught his autosuggestive therapy [542] to his patients. The first exercise was a demonstration of the power of implanted ideas over the will by a simple experiment. The patient, his hands clasped together, was instructed to think, "I cannot open them;" contrary to an order to open them, the patient could not do so. The subject was then ordered to think, "I *can* open them;" and immediately the cramped hands were loosed. So with the various diseased and nervous states presented to him. With kindly persistence and vigorous suggestion, Coué insisted that these patients "will" to move a stiff joint or exercise palsied legs. His patients were to carry away with them the idea that day by day they were able to overcome this notion of disease by the notion of willing their bodies to be healthy and straight. "Go home and will that *tous les jours, à tous points de vue, je vais de mieux en mieux*" (Day by day, in every way, I am getting better and better), he suggested. Coué insisted that his formula be said in an effortless, sing-song way accompanied by a feeling of complete faith. Coué never mentioned any specific disorder or diseased condition, but merely the contrary state of health.

The exhortative and inspirational type of psychotherapy claimed to pass beyond hypnosis and suggestion. Although attitudes of inspiration and persuasion are common currency of all physicians in their practice at one time or another, scientific psychotherapists regarded this spirit to be blatantly antipsychological. Forel, the Swiss authority, wrote, "Professor Dubois slangs hypnotism and suggestion, while in reality, he practises suggestion from alpha to omega." [543]

[542] Coué, Emile: How to Practice Suggestion and Autosuggestion, New York, Am. Lib. Service, 1923.

[543] Forel, Auguste: Hypnotism, or, Suggestion and Psychotherapy, A Study of the Psychological, Psychophysiological and Therapeutic Aspects of Hypnotism, translated by H. W. Armit, New York, Rebman, 1907.

A century of experience with hypnotism had established its usefulness among the healing arts; a century of experimentation had yielded the final explanation of its secret in the notion of suggestibility. Suggestion was a satisfactory theory from an operational point of view, but it neither answered questions concerning the psychological mechanisms involved nor quieted the vague anxiety physicians felt that they were utilizing, in hypnotism, a quasi-magical power. The one true supposition of Mesmer, that a special *rapport* existed between mesmeriser and patient, defied understanding. Vitalistic theories of a "nervous electro-magnetic fluid" were rejected completely; Braid's final hypothesis [544] that rapport was an artificial condition, created by suggestion, was tentatively but generally accepted. But the notion of a "double consciousness," a subterranean area of mental functioning, remained as an intriguing possibility in the background. The facts of posthypnotic suggestion and increased memory, or, more accurately, recall of forgotten memories under hypnosis, seemed to point toward a second consciousness, the Doppel-ich (double ego) of Max Dessoir, or the "unconscious cerebration" of Carpenter.

UNCONSCIOUS FACTORS IN HYPNOSIS

The concept of a second consciousness related to our state of awareness, but not readily accessible, had been foreshadowed in prepsychological days by metaphysicians. Kant spoke of "unconscious ideation," and, in the infancy of psychological science, Herbart discussed degrees of consciousness.[545] Kant's oft-quoted statement—"Innumerable are the sensations and perceptions whereof we are not conscious. . . . The clear ideas indeed are but an infinitely small fraction of the same exposed to consciousness." [546]—was a recognition of perceptual possibilities. As refined by Herbart, these degrees of consciousness were represented in focal, marginal and inhibited (repressed?) ideas. The theory of associationism, the ranking psychology of the nineteenth century, provided the background for an additional possibility that marginal or inhibited ideas were in reality unassociated, or "unconscious." W. B. Carpenter,[547a] an English neurologist, noted that a large part of our intellectual activity was automatic, due to "reflex action of the Cerebrum, i.e. unconscious cerebration." The com-

[544] Bramwell: *Op. cit.*, p. 294.

[545] Flügel, J. C.: A Hundred Years of Psychology, ed. 2, p. 18, London, Duckworth, 1951.

[546] Kant, I.: Anthropology, 1798. *Quoted by* von Hartmann: Philosophy of the Unconscious, translated by W. C. Coupland, ed. 9, New York, Macmillan, 1884.

[547a] Carpenter, W. B.: Principles of Mental Physiology with Their Applications to the Training and Discipline of the Mind and Study of Its Morbid Conditions, New York, Appleton, 1874.

mon experience of sudden reappearance of forgotten ideas, described by Holmes,[547b] was identified as unconscious cerebration:

> We wish to remember something. . . . No effort of the will can reach it. . . . Presently, some minutes later the idea we are in search of comes all at once into the mind, delivered like a prepaid bundle, laid at the door of consciousness, like a foundling in a basket.

Carpenter was aware also that not intellectual ideas alone but "emotional states, or, rather, states which constitute emotions when we become conscious of them," underwent the same process. It can be safely said that the notion of an unconscious was part of German metaphysics from the time of Leibnitz, as witness, among other writings, three heavy volumes about physiologic and mental phenomena written by Eduard von Hartmann (1868) in which inductive reasoning established the validity of an unconscious.[548] The oft-repeated "iceberg theory" of the subconscious, that consciousness is "as a sheet of water of some depth . . . the whole process of our thought seldom lies on the surface," [549] is Schopenhauer's concept.

Experiences under hypnosis of recalling long-forgotten memories made clear the fact of another type of consciousness. Especially conclusive were studies in multiple personalities, elicited by hypnosis, or automatic writing and some types of spontaneous somnambulism where a few ideas, at first forced into the unconscious, were "incubated and after synthesizing became egocentric systems on their own." [550] Cases of double or multiple personalities, the Beauchamp (Prince), the Hanna case (Sidis),[551] and others, proved that emotional shock, actual trauma or even "voluntary repression" could produce a dissociation of the personality entirely analogous to that evoked through hypnosis. The work of the early students of spiritualism,[552] Myers and Gurney, pointing toward a "full exploration of subconscious mind," resulted in the concept of "subliminal consciousness" wherein "automatic, nervous, vasomotor and circulatory system" functions operated below the threshold of consciousness and hence could be dissociated by hypnosis.

Further studies on psychic mediums seemed to indicate that the split in

[547b] Holmes, Oliver Wendell: Mechanism in Thought and Morals, p. 38, Boston, James R. Osgood & Co., 1871.

[548] von Hartmann, Eduard: Philosophy of the Unconscious, translated by W. C. Coupland, ed. 9, New York, Macmillan, 1884.

[549] Margetts, Edward: The concept of the unconscious in the history of medical psychology, Psychiat. Quart. 27:126, 1953.

[550] Prince, Morton: Clinical and Experimental Studies in Personality, p. 130, Cambridge, Mass., Sc.-Art. Pub., 1929.

[551] Sidis, Boris, and Goodhart, S. P.: Multiple Personality, An Experimental Investigation into the Nature of Human Individuality, p. 83, New York, Appleton, 1905.

[552] J. (and Proc.) Soc. for Psychical Res. (1882-), London, July-October, 1952.

the personality of the spiritualistic medium, the "obsession" of the medium by another character sometimes long deceased, represented a dissociation not unlike that of double personality.[553] More recently, this intuitive telepathic function of the unconscious has been investigated by psychoanalysts as evidence of an active subliminal quality [554] and function of the mind observable in the analysis of patients.[555] The perception by the patient's unconscious of thoughts and occurrences relating to the analyst (or other patients), of which the former could have no knowledge, has obtruded itself in dreams, reminding one of the "thought transference" that concerned early mesmerists. Observations by analysts [556] seem to show that telepathic communications function, when analyzed, according to laws of the unconscious mental life.

A practical consequence of such hypothecating was to prepare the way for the reception of a dynamic psychiatry in which an unconscious, with its emotional and volitional forces, was conceded to exert a hitherto undreamed-of influence on human behavior and thinking. With Janet, Prince, Sidis and others, hypnosis, particularly of hysterical patients, demonstrated a structural dissociation in the ego accounting for manifold neurotic symptoms as trance-states, somnambulism, paralysis and phobias. With Freud, under hypnosis and later psychoanalysis, this dissociation was predicated on a dynamic quality of the mental apparatus through which ideas and complexes of ideas unacceptable to the ego were split off, reappearing in disguised form as symptoms. The development of a psychopathology flowing from these experimental and therapeutic findings altered psychotherapy during the subsequent half century to a degree that literally transformed the treatment of nervous states and mental illnesses. In a word, "moral" treatment became scientific and objective, humanitarianism was tempered with insight, and understanding replaced exhortation and inspiration. Theories of personality disposition, in this period of emerging dynamic psychotherapy, played a more important role than practical methods of mental healing. Although this evolution belongs more to a history of psychiatry than of psychotherapy, theory and practice are in this case inseparable historical phenomena.

[553] Prince, W. F., and Hyslop, J. H.: The Doris case of multiple personality, Proc. Am. Soc. for Psychical Res., Vols. 9, 10 and 11, York, Pa., York Printing Co., 1915-1917.

[554] Freud, Sigmund: New Introductory Lectures on Psycho-analysis, translated by W. J. H. Sprott, p. 46, New York, Norton, 1933.

[555] Eisenbud, Jule: Telepathy and the problems of psychoanalysis, Psychoanal. Quart. 15:32, 1946.

[556] *Ibid.*, p. 36.

THEORY OF DISSOCIATION

In view of rapid accretions of knowledge of the pathology of the nervous system, it was natural that theories of mental malfunction should be couched in psychophysiologic terms. The proposition that hysteria and other functional nervous diseases were based on an inherited neuropathic diathesis or predisposition, an offshoot of the degeneracy theory of Morel (1857) and Magnan (1876), was upheld for several decades chiefly on the authority of French neurology. From this viewpoint Janet developed the notion that dissociation in hysterics and neurasthenics rested on a basic *enfeeblement* of consciousness, manifested in an inability to synthesize ideas due to a contraction of consciousness and psychic exhaustion. The theoretical formula started with the view that hysteria was due to a "depression, exhaustion of the higher functions" [557] of the brain: the lowering of nervous strength resulting in a retraction of consciousness. The resulting enfeeblement yielded to emotional shocks, which caused dissociation. The difficulty then lay in the disordered physiology of the nervous system which permitted dissociation under stress. As early as 1889, Janet spoke of emotional trauma's causing a dissociation in hysterical subjects in which certain fixed ideas pushed into subconsciousness caused a "psychological disaggregation" resulting in symptoms.[558] The split-off idea was "emancipated," pursuing its own development into an autonomous system of symptoms, e.g., convulsions, paralysis, etc. Later, this mechanism was extended to account for obsessions, impulsions and phobias where a fixed idea [559] (sexual or emotional trauma, dread of loneliness, need to be loved, etc.) forced the dissociation of consciousness through a weakened nervous system. Similarly, suggestion by a hypnotist introduced ideas to the patient's subconscious which then developed automatically "outside the will and personal perception" of the latter. Janet's psychophysiologic explanation of neurotic symptom-formation plus suggestion betokened an advance in the direction of a planned psychotherapy.

Other explanations of the effectiveness of suggestion were couched in terms of the neuron theory and the more precise cytologic descriptions of the nervous system enunciated by Golgi, Cajal and Gerlach. For example, Forel [560] followed Oscar Vogt's explanation of neurodynamic inhibition in sleep and hypnosis because of cortical exhaustion. Here the energy of cor-

[557] Janet, Pierre: *Op. cit.*, p. 333.

[558] ——: Psychological Healing, A Historical and Clinical Study, translated by E. and C. Paul, p. 596, New York, Macmillan, 1925.

[559] ——: The Mental State of Hystericals (Etat mental des hystériques), translated by C. R. Corson, p. 278, New York, Putnam, 1901.

[560] Forel: *Op cit.*, p. 165.

tical stimulation underlying thinking, feeling or any mental state was expressed in the term *neurokyme*—the molecular wave corresponding to, and accompanying, any nerve element activity. Every psychological phenomenon was therefore assumed to be accompanied by the expression of cerebral energy called neurokyme activity. In dissociation, as occurred in hysteria under hypnosis, Breuer,[561] working with Freud, used the theory of "intra-cerebral tonic excitation" to mean the potential energy in nerve fibers which became kinetic when used for psychic activity. When the potential energy was high, the dynamic equilibrium became disturbed, followed by increased excitation through emotion or motor discharge. If resistance existed to this discharge, anomalous reactions occurred, i.e., hysterical reactions. This explained how energy in nervous individuals flooded from the idea to the "nervous apparatuses of circulation and digestion" in hysterical symptoms. At the start, Freud's explanations of defense and repression were in terms of physicalistic neurophysiology.[562] Vogt's explanation of hypnosis and suggestion hypothecated that neurokyme activity was deflected from consciousness and guided to other cerebral areas as vasomotor or extrapyramidal centers, then to cause hysterical paralyses, rigidities, intestinal disturbances, or headache from which neurotic patients suffered. More recently, new neuropathologic and neurophysiologic findings and theories have been invoked to explain hypnotic effects by assuming that stimulation of a sleep center near the third ventricle alters the hypnotizability of a given brain, i.e., increases inhibitions of cortical centers.[563]

Mechanistic theories of the action of hysteria and suggestion have not settled obscure problems concerning reciprocal influence of mind and body; nor have they contributed to the essential technic of hypnosis. The vast literature on physiologic implications of hypnosis can be summed up in the general statement that it induces an "altered state . . . in the subject . . . which is followed by transcendence of normal limits of voluntary control." [564] In this state, deep emotional strivings and constellations, to some degree malleable by the therapist, are mobilized. This generalized statement of the hypnotic state, modified from Brenman and Gill, contains an indication of the emotional aspects of the hypnotic relationship. It also sums up the result of a half century of continued interest in hypnosis, much of it spurred on during the last two decades by the needs of a brief

561 Breuer, Joseph, and Freud, Sigmund: Studies in Hysteria, translated by A. A. Brill, New York, Nerv. & Ment. Dis. Monographs, 1936.

562 Bernfeld, S.: Freud's earliest theories and the school of Helmholtz, Psychoanal. Quart. 13:341-362, 1944.

563 Schilder, Paul, and Kauders, Otto: Hypnosis, translated by S. Rothenberg, New York, Nerv. & Ment. Dis. Monographs, 1927.

564 Brenman, Margaret, and Gill, M. M.: Hypnotherapy, A Survey of the Literature, New York, Internat. Univ. Press, 1947.

psychotherapeutic method. At the time of Freud's crucial contributions in the field of neurosis, hypnosis was widely used, but as widely disclaimed, as a decisive method of treatment. Freud's exploration of the intricacies of the interpersonal relation between patient and hypnotist, however, provided a new stimulus for a renascence of interest in hypnosis in the twentieth century. Study of *rapport,* that elusive relation at which Mesmer had hinted in his spectacular treatments with the *baquet,* was virtually begun by Breuer and Freud in their studies on hysteria. At this point we will postpone the outline of the further development of hypnosis to trace the new departure in psychopathology initiated by two Viennese physicians, a departure which was to precipitate an entirely new concept of the dynamics of the therapeutic relationship.

ABREACTION IN PSYCHOTHERAPY

Freudian psychoanalysis started from the base-line of French psychopathology. Among the foreign students who in 1885 attended Charcot's clinics at the Salpêtrière was Sigmund Freud, lecturer in neuropathology at the University of Vienna. On his return home, impressed by Charcot's treatment of hysterics, Freud, who had produced several noteworthy contributions to neurology at the neurophysiologic laboratory of the famous Brücke in Vienna, devoted more time to hypnosis. In company with Dr. Josef Breuer, a well-established Viennese practitioner, they studied many cases through hypnosis, publishing a paper in 1893 [565] which affirmed the presence of mental trauma associated with mental pain, shame or fright in the patient's history as the causative mechanism for the hysterical attack. By evoking the memory of the trauma through light hypnosis, allowing pent-up emotions to be discharged in words, the patient was freed of symptoms for the time being. Commenting on the paper, Janet remarked,[566] "We are glad to find . . . MM. Breuer and Freud have recently verified our interpretation, already somewhat old, of subconscious fixed ideas with hystericals."

For more complex cases, Breuer found it necessary under hypnosis to carry each symptom back to its original traumatic event in order to revive the patient's memory of forgotten events and thus achieve relief. The process of "abreaction" is described in the historic case of Anna O.,[567] a young woman afflicted with a multitude of symptoms, convergent strabismus, hearing difficulties, paralysis and contractures of three extremities

[565] Freud, Sigmund, and Breuer, Josef: On the psychical mechanism of hysterical phenomena, Neurolog. Zentralbl., 1893. Translated by J. Rickman *in* Collected Papers, Vol. 1, p. 24, New York and London, Internat. Psychoanal. Press, 1924.

[566] Janet, Pierre: The Mental State of Hystericals, p. 290.

[567] Breuer and Freud: Studies in Hysteria.

and neck muscles, as well as a series of bizarre psychic symptoms, delirious episodes with hallucinations of snakes and rodents, aphonia, periods of speech in English supplanting an inability to speak her native tongue and so on. These varying transient difficulties followed in part the trauma of her father's lingering illness and subsequent death. Each day, after observing the patient's depression and fright, Doctor Breuer hypnotized her, listened to representations of horrifying scenes and "took away the whole supply of fantasms" which had collected during the intervening period. The patient herself referred to this process as "chimney sweeping" or the "talking" cure. Laboriously the doctor probed the hypnotic state until each symptom was related to a specific image or story of a traumatic event. The effect of hypnotic suggestion to recall forgotten memories was to bring affect-related events out of another state of consciousness, a *condition seconde,* into the clear light of memory. Treatment by abreaction or mental catharsis allowed the motor discharge of emotional charges associated with unpleasant or terrifying experiences, and hence cured the symptom. In Freud's hands, the Breuer technic developed into an *analysis,* originally under hypnosis and later through a "pressure procedure," in which the patient in the waking state was urged to recall forgotten events, occasionally aided by the doctor's firm hand placed on the patient's forehead.[568]

The striking impression that Freud obtained while he patiently and tenaciously tracked down the emotionally tinged occurrences behind each symptom was that his patient's troubles fitted into a mosaic of his life story; they did not stand alone as an isolated pathologic process. Painful ideas found at the base of hysterical symptoms had been turned away from consciousness by a psychic force for the purpose of defense against mental pain (Unlust). The idea being incompatible with the ego was "converted" into a symptom; the "dynamic lesion" which Charcot had surmised lay at the base of hysteria proved to be a psychological one. As the mechanism of defense against unacceptable (predominantly sexual) ideas became clearer in his cases, Freud settled on a therapeutic technic that dispensed with hypnosis and, to some extent, with the "talking" abreaction as the primary tool of treatment. The psychic force which had to be overcome in uncovering amnesias for significant affective events in the life of the patient—resistance—proved to be the same force which initially *repressed* the affect and hence caused its representation in physical (functional) changes. Recognition of repression as an intrapsychic activity brought the inescapable conclusion that the contents of amnesias were in reality ideas held in the unconscious until liberated by associative connections, after resistance within the patient was reduced.

The notion that psychic splitting, or dissociation, occurred because of a

[568] *Ibid.,* p. 109.

psychic act called "repression," and not as the result of a physiologic change in levels of consciousness (Breuer's hypnoid states), provided the dynamic accent that started psychoanalysis as an independent therapeutic system. In a letter unearthed by Oberndorf,[569] Breuer expressed himself as aware, as far back as 1880, that in the study of hysteria "a glimpse was being offered into deeper layers of psycho-pathological processes." As Freud developed the basically sexual nature motivating this repressing force, Breuer apparently deemed it wise not to pursue investigations further. A gradual deviation occurred between the two men as Freud demonstrated to his satisfaction that sexual elements lay behind the rapport (transference) of patient and physician, and announced the sexual etiology of the neurosis in later papers. The disbanding of the joint investigation was spurred, Freud notes, by Breuer's dislike of the sexual connotation. Simmel put it more positively in saying that Breuer was "a slave to conventional beliefs." [570] At any rate, Breuer "stopped his investigations right there." [571] Breuer had fixed psychotherapy on a dynamic level, and Freud carried it to its clinical and metapsychological conclusion. As Freudian psychology deepened, in the words of Bernard Hart, "it left the phenomenal plane and ascended to the conceptual." [572]

Probing behind the unexpected resistance in patients toward expressing fantasies, unpleasant and painful life experiences, brought insight to Freud into the contents and the laws of the unconscious. He studied dreams,[573] the sexual life of the child, the role of sexuality in formation of neuroses,[574] the defensive nucleus of neurosis, the manifestations in normal persons of unconscious mentation in wit, slips of the tongue, etc., the substitutive meaning of obsessions and phobias as a defense against intolerable ideas. For a decade following the publication of the now famous *Studien über Hysterie* Freud worked alone, constructing both a theory of neurosis and a therapeutic weapon. Although these deepening investigations were re-

[569] Breuer, Josef: Autobiography, edited and translated by C. P. Oberndorf, Internat. J. Psycho-analysis 39:64, 1953.

[570] Simmel, Ernst: Sigmund Freud, the man and his work, Psychoanal. Quart. 9:170, 1940.

[571] Freud, Sigmund: "A History of the Psychoanalytic Movement," *in* The Basic Writings of Sigmund Freud, translated by A. A. Brill, p. 936, New York, Modern Lib., 1938.

[572] Münsterberg, H., et al.: Subconscious Phenomena, A Symposium, p. 131, Boston, Badger, 1910.

[573] Freud, Sigmund: "The Interpretation of Dreams; Three Contributions to the Theory of Sex, Wit and Its Relation to the Unconscious; Psychopathology of Everyday Life," *in* The Basic Writings of Sigmund Freud.

[574] ——: "The Defense Neuro-psychoses" (p. 59); "The Justification for Detaching from Neurasthenia a Particular Syndrome: The Anxiety-Neurosis" (p. 76); "My Views on the Part Played by Sexuality in the Etiology of the Neuroses" (p. 272)—*in* Collected Papers, translated by Joan Rivière, Vol. 1, London, Internat. Psychoanal. Press, 1924.

ferred to by colleagues as "Freud's method of analysis," it was as often derided and spurned as the work of a zealot who read sexual connotations into his patient's life stories. Until about 1902, Freud worked alone in his office at 19 Berggasse, in Vienna, developing his dream theory, his theories on obsessions and phobias, his delineation of the sexual life of the child and the vital concept of repression and regression, sublimation and the levels of genital psychosexuality, etc. Abandoning a growing practice in nervous diseases, he became intensely absorbed in his work. From many descriptions and innumerable reports of personal contact with Freud, the picture emerges of a man of immense power of concentration, of scientific honesty, penetrating vision and meticulous concern with clinical minutiae that illuminated, rather than obscured, the broad fundamental hypothesis he was developing. As his small circle of pupils increased, he lectured, expounded his views before a privately organized Vienna Psycho-Analytic Society. To the few who went to his lectures the predominant characteristics of an enveloping humanity and a penetrating perception of the thread that unites human emotions were perceived as "a genius-given gift." [575] It was a matter of ten years before Freud's ideas on the significance of the unconscious were appreciated. Meanwhile he lived through the bitterness and the beauty of the "heroic era," [576] fortified against the "slings of outrageous fortune" by an inner sense of confidence in the overwhelming significance of the psychological world he was unearthing.

The most vociferous opposition arose from Freud's hypothesis as to the causation of neurosis, namely, that sexual malfunction lay at the base of anxiety, either as dammed-up and ungratified libido in the *actual-neurosis* or repressed infantile (fantasied) sexual components in the *psycho-neurosis*. As his penetrating work expanded, Freud was treated with increasingly sharp criticism.

Yet psychoanalysis gradually replaced suggestion and hypnosis in treatment of neuroses and personality dissociations which presented themselves to psychotherapists. While, in medical journals and at congresses, scientific ideas, arguments and counterarguments swirled, the technic of analysis of emotional trauma behind neurotic symptoms became an accepted part of psychiatry. Critics in Europe were shocked at Freud's intrepid entrance into the inner lives of his patients and his methods: [577] "It [psychoanalysis] is a criminal investigation which aims at the discovery of a culprit in the unearthing of a past happening. . . . It is more the work of a detective than a psychiatrist." American psychiatrists, stung by the irrationality of

[575] Deutsch, Helene: Freud and his pupils, a footnote to the history of the psychoanalytic movement, Psychoanal. Quart. 9:184, 1940.

[576] Freud: "A History of the Psychoanalytic Movement," *in* The Basic Writings of Sigmund Freud.

[577] Janet, Pierre: Psychological Healing, p. 610.

Freud's unconscious psychology, opined that "it would not hold my attention except for its astonishing standpoint and novelty. The whole book reminds one much of the thinking of primitive minds, of persons with unscientific, uncritical systemization of ideas."[578] To attacks of licentiousness, scientific frivolity, or worse, Freud had an answer, "I do not see what we shall gain by being ashamed of sexuality."

On the whole, Freud's theories of the etiology of neuroses excited more attention than did his therapy. As though to prove his findings about repression of painful ideas with their consequent vigorous defense, medical men generally repudiated him. Freud's attributing incomplete sexual gratification with its accumulated somatic excitation as the cause of anxiety neurosis was branded as "a curiosity of the absurd lengths to which medical men will go when seeking medical notoriety."[579] The period from 1900 to 1910 became roughly an incubation period during which Freudian ideas of the unconscious, the analysis of obsessive and phobic cases, the libido theory, Oedipus complex, the pleasure principle and the mechanisms observed in the dream were digested, pondered over, reported and re-reported. The small circle of followers around Freud in Vienna helped to build a theoretical structure of the instinct life to explain not only neuroses and psychoses as states reactive to movements of unconscious ideas and drives, but also social institutions as religion and man-made arts. Practitioners of psychiatry from areas outside Vienna were attracted to Freud's discussions and lectures.

By 1907 the "latency period" of psychoanalysis, as Freud has expressed it, had begun to move on to a stormy adolescence. A dynamic psychotherapy had emerged.

[578] Solomon, Meyer: Psychopathology of everyday life, a critical review of Dr. Sigmund Freud's theories, J. Abnormal Psychol., Chicago, pp. 23 et seq., April, 1916.
[579] Editorial: Sigmund Freud's foolish conclusion, Alienist & Neurologist 20:113, 1899.

9

Psychoanalysis and Its Derivatives

When Freud, pursuing his premedical career, entered Brücke's Institute of Physiology in Vienna, painstaking studies in comparative nervous system anatomy were beginning to fit into evolutionary concepts. Freud's histologic studies of nerve tracts and nuclei in the medulla oblongata (1885) clearly showed his genetic bent.[580] Comparative anatomy without reference to the "essences, entelechies . . . or ultimate purposes" of idealistic philosophy [581] furnished the ideologic background upon which Freud's intensive investigation of the mental life eventuated in psychoanalysis. From his original research [582] on the spinal cord cells of the Petromyzon (1877), to his valuable clinical report on cerebral diplegias in children (1893), Freud, the neuropathologist, shared the enthusiasm of his teacher, Brücke, for a "physicalistic" and evolutionary physiology.

It was perhaps for the reason of his evolutionary predilections that Prof. Stanley Hall, the genetic psychologist, invited Sigmund Freud, accompanied by Carl Jung, Ferenczi, and Jones, of Toronto, to lecture at Clark University in Worcester, Massachusetts, in 1909. Freud, respectfully received in America, was delighted with the reception accorded psychoanalysis; "it was a realization," he said, "of an incredible day-dream to lecture in Worcester." A reporter of a Boston newspaper [583] described one of Freud's appearances: "A man of refinement, of intellect, and of many-sided interests . . . his high forehead with the large bump of observation and his beautiful energetic hands are very striking. He speaks clearly, weighing his words carefully, but unfortunately never of himself." Nevertheless, Freud held a curiously deprecating attitude toward this country. Years after his American trip, Hanns Sachs [584] reported Freud's remark,

580 Bernfeld, Siegfried: Sigmund Freud, M.D., 1882-1885, Internat. J. Psychoanalysis 32:204, 1951.
581 ——: Freud's scientific beginnings, Am. Imago 6:3, 1949.
582 Jelliffe, S. E.: Sigmund Freud as neurologist, J. Nerv. & Ment. Dis. 85:696-711, 1937.
583 Albrecht, A.: Boston Evening Transcript, 1909.
584 Sachs, Hanns: Freud, Master and Friend, London, Imago, 1946.

"America is the most grandiose experiment the world has seen, but I am afraid it is not going to be a success."

This was an attitude which persisted all his life. In 1937, he remarked to an American colleague during a brief visit that the Boston psychoanalytic group could with advantage "add to the American self-sufficiency a few drops of the European spirit,"[585] a spirit which presumably did not pragmatically accept psychoanalysis as a proven part of psychiatry. The apparent thoroughgoing materialism lying alongside a deep spirituality and practical distrust of metaphysical theory, characteristic of the American mind, may have been the reason for Freud's dismal attitude toward this country. Or it may have been a mistrust of America's readiness to "believe." This singular reading of American thought-trends did not prevent the New World from providing a haven for psychoanalytic doctrine far in advance of that given by Mediterranean, Asiatic or Communist-influenced countries. Nevertheless, Freud's trip in 1909 brought psychoanalysis into official contact with neuropsychiatry and psychology, lifting it from its relative isolation and concentrated cultivation by a small band of disciples in Europe to the attention of the world.

SPREAD OF INTEREST IN PSYCHOANALYSIS

To return to the early years, while a small circle of doctors were reducing the "void" which surrounded Freud, the persistent work of checking and rechecking his observations and theoretical formulations completely absorbed Freud's attention. Analyses of cases of phobia, obsessional neurosis, paranoia, were painstakingly reported, while the vicissitudes of instinct-disposition in the psychosexual organization of the personality were being thoroughly worked out through clinical analytic material.[586] Within these dozen or more years, large sections of analytic theory were chiseled out of the granite of clinical work involving the unconscious, narcissism, the pleasure principle, sadomasochism, the place of oral, anal, phallic, urethral erotism in the ego-structure, ambivalence, the Oedipus situation, and so on. By 1907, psychiatrists in some sectors were actively testing psychoanalytic hypotheses.

Jung and Bleuler in Zurich, Switzerland, became deeply interested in proving that mechanisms of symbolization, repression, dream censorship, projection described for the neuroses, were present also among psychotic patients. At Burghölzli, in Zurich, a group of eager workers "unraveled every symptom to show . . . relations between cause and effect and the

[585] Peck, Martin: A brief visit with Freud, Psychoanalyt. Quart. 9:205, 1940.

[586] Freud, Sigmund: Collected Papers, 4 Vols., translated by A. and J. Strachey, London, Hogarth, 1933.

part played by repressed complexes." [587] The presence of unconscious motives in symptoms and daily life was enthusiastically followed as the staff analyzed each other's dreams at the breakfast table.[588] The Zurich school plumbed the bizarre productions of paranoia and schizophrenia (Bleuler) through application of freudian mechanisms, integrating psychoanalytic thinking into psychiatry, developing thereby a new viewpoint which George Kirby, Meyer's successor at the New York Psychiatric Institute, called an "interpretative psychiatry." [589]

One of Freud's brilliant disciples, Carl G. Jung, experimented with the now famous association-word test, wherein the reaction to key words, chosen out of a random sample, indicated in association with the word an emotional, unconscious significance to the individual tested. The time of response to the word was noted, and a delay in association, an unusual emotional response, a failure to respond or a superficial reaction, indicated a blocking or a repression of the idea related to the word, i.e., a complex.[590] The association test became in some hands [591] a diagnostic indicator not unlike the present use of the Rohrshach Test, aiding in enucleating emotional complexes responsible for symptoms, which could then be pursued therapeutically. Although Freud later noted [592] that the association experiments offered no essential contribution to the technic of treatment, it brought psychology into relation with psychoanalysis and popularized the concept of "complex" in the literate world and the world of literature.

Diffusion of psychoanalytic tenets spread widely during the next two decades. In 1908, the first psychoanalytic congress met in Salzburg,[593] and, in 1909, a *Jahrbuch für psychoanalytische und psychopathologische Forschungen* appeared, to be followed by journals devoted to the applications of psychoanalysis to pedagogy and cognate fields. The *Psychoanalytic Review* (New York and Washington), under the editorship of White and Jelliffe, published its first issue in 1913, and, in 1920, the *International Journal of Psychoanalysis* was founded by Ernest Jones, in London. An American Psychoanalytic Society was formed about 1911.

Spread of interest in psychoanalysis stirred up resistances in the medical and, somewhat later, the social worlds. Resistances evoked reactions of

[587] Brill, A. A.: Freud's Contribution to Psychiatry, p. 93, New York, Norton, 1944.
[588] ——: Personal communication.
[589] Jung, C. G.: The Psychology of Dementia Praecox, translated by A. A. Brill, ed. 2, pp. viii and ix, New York, Nerv. & Ment. Dis. Monographs, 1937.
[590] ——: Studies in Word-Association. Experiments in the Diagnosis of Psychopathological Conditions Carried out at the Psychiatric Clinic of the University of Zurich, translated by M. D. Eder, New York, Moffat, 1919.
[591] Rosanoff, A. J.: Manual of Psychiatry and Mental Hygiene, ed. 7, p. 884, New York, Wiley, 1938.
[592] Freud: Autobiography, translated by James Strachey, New York, Norton, 1935.
[593] Oberndorf, C. P.: A History of Psychoanalysis in America, p. 266, New York, Grune, 1953.

anger, then further criticism and rejection. The reactions in Viennese society (*circa* 1900), where "it was considered bad taste to bring up Freud's name in the presence of ladies," [594] was repeated in America. Translations of Freud's writings were under lock and key in public libraries. A few neurologists became viciously outspoken opponents of Freud. On a more restrained religio-philosophic level, critics appealed to the "Divine right in the realm of conduct . . . [where] psychoanalysis dethrones the will and places instinct in the vacant place." [595] Although the churchman who penned the sentence above felt that psychoanalysis was "a new and revolutionary method of healing—faith-healing with a difference," he also noted that many points were in curious agreement with the Faith, "however different its drift . . . may prove to be."

The storm which psychoanalysis engendered during the first two decades of this century extended into internecine strife, for Freud was uncompromising in his disinclination to conciliate those who in his judgment had lapsed from intellectual honesty.[596] In a sense, the developmental history of psychoanalytic therapy and theory coincides with the conflicts surrounding Freud. It has been customary to describe variations in psychoanalytic technic and theoretical background as "separatist" movements from the body of freudian knowledge. From the standpoint of loyalty to Freud, these deviations may be considered evidence of disloyalty. However, from the broad plateau of psychotherapy, separatist movements are more properly described as developments in a human endeavor that still is obdurate to claims of complete therapeutic success.

Conflict, the crucial dynamic factor in the formation of neurosis, was mirrored among his disciples and dissidents in lines of tension within Freud's circle in Vienna. Freud felt that deviations from his position meant a fatal fall from the plane of psychological science, as in the case of Adler. Aside from personal factors, the situation which often caused conflict was the fact that protagonist and antagonist in psychoanalytic struggles were literally speaking different languages. For Freud and his closest supporters, the need for scientific completeness of hypothetic constructions far outweighed the motive for therapeutic success which impelled other workers. In short, research goals took precedence over therapeutic aim. The conflictual aspect of the development of psychoanalysis could easily be overstressed if one did not recall that Freud himself often wrote in terms of bitterness and struggle. At one point he wrote that America was less prejudiced against psychoanalysis than the "centres of ancient cultures . . .

[594] Graf, Max: Reminiscences of Professor Sigmund Freud, Psychoanalyt. Quart. 11:465, 1942.

[595] Comment, How far the church can indorse psychoanalysis, Current Opinion 71:624, November, 1921. Quoted from the London Guardian, 1921.

[596] Sachs, Hanns: *Op. cit.*, p. 121.

[which] must be the scene of the final decisive battle for psychoanalysis." [597]

The drive for an integrated theory of psychic function was essentially philosophic in intent, a view which Freud's critics often pointed out, and to which Freud readily agreed. For Freud, who had built "his mode of life . . . for the sole purpose of his research work" [598] was primarily interested in investigations of man's mental life, a task for which his extraordinary psychological insight fitted him. As a working scientist in mental fields, he constantly reorganized his hard-won material into terms of a comprehensible metapsychology, a psychology based on the vicissitudes of instincts and their reaction in the human ego. It is perhaps because he was a seeker for truth rather than essentially a healer that he deplored the future absorption of psychoanalysis into medicine in terms that betrayed little sympathy for historical perspective: [599]

> We do not want to see psychoanalysis swallowed up by medicine, and then to find its last resting place in textbooks on psychiatry—in the chapter headed "Therapy" next to procedures such as hypnotic suggestion, autosuggestion, and persuasion, which were created out of our ignorance, and owe their short-lived effectiveness to the laziness and cowardice of the mass of mankind.

When, in 1914, Freud reviewed the progress of his science in the *History of the Psychoanalytic Movement,* activity in the field was acute. The storms and the schisms swirling round his head were at their height, defections from the ranks formed into "schools" of analysis, bitter attacks and valiant retorts barely survived the limitations of scientific courtesy. The pungent phrases used in assailing Elliotson, when his espousal of mesmerism had aroused organized medicine in London almost a century before, were more than matched by attacks against Freud and his students. Abundant criticism was based as much on his sexual theory of neurosis as on his racial derivation. In spite of the opposition evoked, or because of it, the new contribution of "depth" psychology, with its illumination of mythology, folklore, "normal" psychopathology, artistic creativeness, anthropology, as well as psychiatry, attained universal recognition.

EARLY ANALYTIC THERAPY

What constituted psychoanalytic therapy during the first decade of this century? Predominantly it followed the theory of sexual etiology of the neurosis. This stated in brief that "no neurosis is possible with a normal *vita sexualis.*" [600] Freud early had found that anxiety rested on dammed-up

[597] Freud: Autobiography.
[598] Sachs, Hanns: *Op. cit.*
[599] Freud: The Question of Lay Analysis, translated by Nancy Procter-Gregg, p. 121, New York, Norton, 1950.
[600] ——: "My Views on the Part Played by Sexuality in the Aetiology of the Neuroses," *in* Collected Papers, Vol. 1, p. 272, London, Internat. Psycho-analytic Press, 1924.

sexual outlets (so-called "free floating libido"), with consequent inadequate sexual gratification, dependent upon coitus interruptus, abstinence, frustrated sexual activity, etc. To cases of anxiety-neurosis due to dammed-up libido, Freud applied the term *actual-neurosis* in contradistinction to neurasthenia and to the *psycho-neuroses* wherein emotionally involved ideas, split off from consciousness, caused the symptoms. Further study showed that these unconscious ideas were also related to sexual disturbances, often fantasied and deriving from an infantile period. Analysis provided "incontestable" proof that psychoneurotic symptoms represented repressed and defended-against perverse sexual components which assumed a tortuous path into consciousness. The aim of treatment, then, was the release of unconscious sexual elements, infantile and perverse in nature, through free association and interpretation, and brought to the patient's consciousness against his resistances. Thus repression of traumatic events (or fantasied ones) was undone, the unconscious made conscious and the morbid condition removed.[601]

Considered schematically, early analytic treatment[602] commenced with a recital of the patient's life story with careful notations of amnesias presented. The association-word test of Jung was often used to find clues for further analytic work. In addition, slips, symbolic movements, dreams and free associations were, and still are, utilized to plumb unconscious elements. The central aim of treatment can be summarized in Jones's words as the "assimilation into the personality,"[603] against resistance, of unconscious wishes. The overcoming of resistances, the chief therapeutic endeavor in addition to uncovering complexes, led to technical problems which the patient posed for the analyst. These centered in the transference-resistance, a phenomenon in which the patient obstructs free associations which may lead to painful, repressed memories by *transferring* to the doctor unconscious love and hate feelings deriving from his relations to childhood figures of his environment.[604] Early attitudes toward parent figures, both positive and negative, lived out in the analysis, contributed major problems for the analysis, since transference manifestation ramified into every relation with the analyst, from stubborn silences, loquacity, promptness or tardiness in coming to treatment, paying the bill, etc. The transference-relationship became the fulcrum round which the patient accepted the analyst's interpretation of unconscious findings; it allowed

[601] Freud: "Freud's Psycho-analytic Method," *in* Collected Papers, Vol. 1, p. 264.

[602] Jones, Ernest: "The Psycho-analytic Method of Treatment," *in* Papers on Psychoanalysis, p. 193, New York, Wood, 1913.

[603] ———: "The Therapeutic Action of Psycho-analysis (1912)," *in* Papers on Psychoanalysis, p. 298.

[604] Freud: "The Dynamics of the Transference," *in* Collected Papers, Vol. 2, p. 312, Internat. Psycho-analytic Press, 1924.

assimilation into the personality of uncovered wishes and drives through the authority and the influence of the therapist.

The unexpected depth of relationship between neurotic patient and analyst, the complex expression of resistances within the patient, forced the necessity of an analysis of the analyst in order that the therapist might become acquainted with his own blind spots. Investigators of the unconscious "subjected themselves . . . to the same sort of searching character-analysis to which their patients were being subjected at their hands."[605] This preparation, now a regular feature of the psychoanalyst's training,[606] was further stimulated by the uncovering of counter-transference, a reciprocal re-experiencing of the analyst's unconscious wishes and attitudes in and through the patient. The eternal vigilance of analysts to their own unconscious trends represents the first occasion on which the human instrument of psychotherapy—the therapist himself—was subjected to analysis.

As treatment passed beyond the limits of anxiety neurosis and hysteria for which the freudian method was originally devised, the complexities of attempting to cure deep-laid patterns of instinctual and emotional responses became evident. Some physicians, inadequately trained yet equipped with Freud's theoretical formulations, proceeded to inform their patients of the active complexes unearthed, whereupon the "analysis" was then considered completed. "Cures" reported by physicians who indulged in "wild" analysis were commonly reported. Ferenczi characterized such extravagant claims of treatment as due to the "blissful mood into which acquaintance with the unconscious transports one." He recognized (1919) the "honeymooning months" of analysis as the period when the patient flourished on the permissivity and the understanding of the therapist.[607] In America especially, "wild analysis" grew in association with the psychoanalytic invasion of literature.[608] In the decade 1912 to 1922, stimulated by James Joyce's appropriation of symbolism, unconscious motivation and subjectification in literature (*Ulysses,* 1922), writers and playwrights adopted freudianism as their guide. Although the psychological effulgences that touched off literary persons, especially in America, were "one of the fads that periodically rage through the antechambers and subbasements of literature,"[609] utilization of the unconscious experience is and has been appreciated in fictional literature.

[605] Putnam, J. J.: On Freud's Psycho-analytic Method and Its Evolution, Harvey Lectures, Philadelphia, Lippincott, 1912.
[606] Knight, R. P.: The present status of organized psychoanalysis in the United States, Am. J. Psychoanalyt. 1:197, 1953.
[607] Ferenczi, Sandor: Further Contributions to the Theory and Technique of Psychoanalysis, translated by J. I. Suttie et al., p. 177, New York, Boni & Liveright, 1927.
[608] Oberndorf, C. P.: *Op. cit.,* p. 129.
[609] DeVoto, Bernard: Freud in American literature, Psychoanalyt. Quart. 9:236, 1940.

To return to the clinical problems of the period, analysis based on a "transference cure" was soon found to be insufficient for enucleation of deep patterns of resentment or other emotional fixations. Experience showed that emotions evoked by filling in amnesias of traumatic events in infantile life had to be "worked through" again and again in order to loosen their binding effect on the patient. Psychoanalysis did not seek to impart ethical teachings or superimpose the physician's attitude on the patient; it sought to "release the individual from the domination of regressive tendencies and infantile fixations" which appeared as neurotic symptoms. Treatment was an emotional experience, not an intellectual one, which required a "living through" of the infantile neurosis in the analysis, with all its frustrations, deprivations, rejections, denials, pleasure seeking and hostilities.[610]

Progression in treatment of neurosis, from an uncovering technic aimed at emotionally tinged memories exerting a pathogenic effect to an exposure of the "infantile neurosis" at the bottom of the adult neurosis, was the work of many hands. Spurred by Freud's unremitting testing and retesting of his theory of libido disturbance in neurosis, his steady stream of clinical and metapsychological papers and books, analysts slowly built a technic of treatment. Experiences among psychiatrists in World War I stimulated a fresh interest in emotional conflict as the etiologic factor in neurosis. Progressive military psychiatrists assumed an "interpretative attitude toward the soldier . . . [which] illustrates the fundamental principle of psychoanalysis."[611] The war brought home to physicians dealing with shell-shock cases the message Freud had been teaching; it also brought to analysts the realization of the narrowness of the sexual theory of neurosis. A re-evaluation of the problem resulted in enlarging the psychoanalytic view of the libido in relation to the ego; the self-preservative instincts within the ego were carefully restudied by Freud. The resulting reorientation of theory and treatment of neurotic conditions will be discussed presently.

Although the main body of freudian ideas was largely appreciated by psychotherapists who aspired to careful work following World War I, the detailed mechanism of the cure occasioned doubts. Earlier it had been felt that uncovering unconscious wishes, making conscious the unconscious, sufficed to remove the symptom which resulted from internal conflict. The "essential remodeling" was left to the patient, when the ego had been "weaned" from its infantile libidinal attachments. The ego, once more in control of instinctual impulses, could adapt itself to demands of reality in conformance with social rules and mores. The patient was free to work, love and relate himself to others unhampered by infantile, regressive tend-

[610] Ferenczi, S., and Rank, Otto: The Development of Psychoanalysis, translated by C. Newton, p. 19, Washington, Nerv. & Ment. Dis. Pub. Co., 1925.
[611] Brown, M. W., and Williams, F. E.: Editorial, M. Rec., p. 257, August, 1916.

encies. Analysis exposed the basic forces at work in the conflict, but what of *synthesis?* This was a question many asked. How could the mobilized infantile fixations be aided in their assimilation into the personality? Did the filling of gaps, restitution of distortions in the history of the patient's libido development, complete the therapeutic work? In general, analysts had depended on the *vis curatrix naturae,* that positive force of nature which, in preserving the integration of the ego, healed the neurosis. This was accomplished by repeated mastery of the original disturbing (unconscious) trauma by means of "working through." Some psychotherapists, however, aspiring to analytic technics, began to question whether the synthesizing element in analytic treatment was not a separate factor. Morton Prince,[612] for example, felt that "repersonalization," a process of integration occurring within the personality, as seen in the merging of multiple personalities within one ego after hypnosis, was the active force involved. And Jung departed from psychoanalysis in part on the issue of a need for active synthesis in a patient through the "therapist's ultimate conviction . . . and search of those religio-philosophic conceptions which correspond to the emotional state of the patient." [613]

JUNGIAN AND ADLERIAN DEVIATIONS

The theoretical differences which lay between Freud and Jung were great enough to divorce Jung's analytical psychology from psychoanalysis as a system of therapy. Disagreement occurred early regarding the concept of libido, the biologic instinctive force whose distortions during childhood were considered as the cause of neurosis. Jung viewed libido as a deeper force than implied by Freud; it was part of the creative energy, élan vital, common to the race of man. Hence Jung's analyses [614] searched for racial images and archetypes represented in the *racial* or *collective unconscious* shared by each individual. His therapy called upon the creative force, one aspect of which was the spiritual yearning encompassed in religion. Here we see a real difference of opinion. In its application, the difference would appear thus: For Jung, the explanation of night terrors in children lay in a revival of ancient racial fears; for Freud, it connoted the anxiety arising from the revival of the child's unconscious fear of its father, displaced and symbolized in some terrorizing dream figure such as an animal. The

[612] Prince, Morton: Suggestive repersonalization, Arch. Neurol. & Psychiat. 18:159, 1927.

[613] Jung, C. G.: "Psychotherapy and a Philosophy of Life," *in* Essays on Contemporary Events, translated by Elizabeth Welsh, Barbara Hannah and Mary Briner, p. 41, London, Routledge, 1947.

[614] ——: Modern Man in Search of a Soul, translated by Dell and Baynes, New York, Harcourt, 1933; Contributions to Analytical Psychology, translated by H. G. and C. F. Baynes, New York, The Bollingen Foundation, 1928.

archetype of the racial mother was of greater importance to Jung than was the father-image to Freud. The mother is immediate and deep in the consciousness of human beings. The first instincts of the child and the last thoughts of man are toward the mother. Freudian psychoanalysis, said the jungians, is a masculine movement.

The collective racial unconscious, Jung stated, passed beyond the mother and father imagos, reaching Lilith, mother of the world, the Sun God, or Wotan of the Norsemen. These eternal racial figures formed the final repository of unconscious life. "In the Jungian analysis, using the life experiences of the patient in terms of these concepts, the analyst shows how anxieties, phobias, obsessions and other bad habits of thought are but the effects of misdirected unconscious energy."

Treatment of the jungian school aims to analyze the patient into the archetypes which we have described, then direct the patient's life along the path of his type. The patient is taught to live out his life along the line of his innate tendencies. As the analysis proceeds, the patient is able to see how the attitudes which were responsible for his symptoms developed. The patient sees that he or she is fixating on impossible or undesirable objects, reaching back to racial and primitive levels for satisfaction. As this interpretation of dreams goes on, the patient is shown that his tendencies are those of universal mankind, and gradually the patient develops a feeling of "oneness" with all humanity. It is obvious that freudian analysis and jungian psychology are as mutually exclusive as their philosophic bases are extremes of mental polarity.

The basic ideologic differences between Freud and Jung has been the subject of a generation-long struggle. An English psychotherapist, a self-professed "eclectic," has attempted to evaluate objectively these two schools of analytic psychology. The "freudian therapeutic philosophy," writes Crichton-Miller, "is based on emancipation from infantile patterns, whilst jungian therapy looks toward spiritual freedom as the 'greatest human attribute.'" And again, "Freud leaves the impression of a closed circle: Jung's scheme is entirely reconcilable with the conception of creative evolution." [615]

But those who are jealous of the scientific, verifiable accuracy of the postulate of the unconscious in its effect on symptom formation reject the alleged impartiality of the eclectic medical psychologist wherein he sees some therapeutic value in jungianism. In a recent study, Glover,[616] an English analyst, has settled the incompatibility of the two psychologies (especially on theoretical grounds) by concluding that Jung has effectively

615 Crichton-Miller, Hugh: Psycho-analysis and Its Derivatives, pp. 84, 181, London, Oxford, 1933.

616 Glover, Edward: Freud or Jung, New York, Norton, London, Allen & Unwin, 1950.

scuttled the presence of the unconscious and has thus excommunicated himself from scientific psychoanalysis. To Glover

> the key to the riddle of Jung's psychology is that Jung is a conscious psychologist; . . . indeed his whole system is based on conscious and descriptive criteria. . . . His psychology . . . has little or no relation to Freudian psychology. The mostly implicit but often explicit tendency of his theories is to prove that Freud's discovery of the unconscious and of the laws that regulate its functions is either inaccurate, totally false, or totally unnecessary. Whether he knows it or not, this is Jung's consuming passion.[617]

The jungian use of dreams as a key to the future, the moral implication of analysis used as an educative measure, the mixture of Oriental, mystic symbolism prominent in this type of analysis, combined to convince Glover of the "petrifying influence of Jungian postulates."

Although Jung's accuser deals more with theory than with practice, Glover does point out that Jung's therapy is directly related to the latter's personal attitude and philosophy, a "variety of pre-destination." For jungians often complain of the lack of interest in the "creative" aspect of human life among freudians. Their own therapy of neuroses, according to Jung, is still essentially a form of pedagogic guidance admixed with a transcendentalism deriving from the collective racial unconsciousness. The view that the world is a "super-personal fact to which an essential personalistic psychology can never do justice"[618] brings psychotherapy into an exalted frame of reference and stresses use of a personal creative force, "individuation," in the patient's therapy. Glover's barrage includes an attack on the "reactionary" eclectic who obstructs the progress of clinical psychology by seeing some value in Jung's ideas as well as in others. Perhaps a clearer view of jungian psychology in its comparative and practical aspect is given in Crichton-Miller's paradigm: That Freud's psychology is most intricate, evading subjective (spiritual) difficulties in its objective approach, and hence most appealing to intellectuals and Jews; that Jung's psychology is most profound, congenial to limited groups, as mystics and introverts; that Adler's psychology is most practical, superficial and sociologic.[619]

The name of Alfred Adler brings forth another dissident who sought to supply what he considered a deficiency in the early libido theory, namely, the problem of the "character" of the neurotic individual. Just as Jung was intent on supplying a *Weltanschauung* for the patient to aid in synthesizing the ego after analysis, and as Horney later sought to remedy the lack of sociologic orientation of psychoanalytic theory, so Adler, starting with compensations for organic inferiorities, developed a therapy based on

[617] *Ibid.*, p. 86.
[618] Jung, C. G.: Essays on Contemporary Events.
[619] Crichton-Miller: *Op. cit.*, p. 241.

the total directiveness of the personality—the *life-plan.*[620] "Treatment by Individual Psychology, accordingly, is not so deep as in orthodox psychoanalysis. It aims in a practical way to satisfy the more or less universal desire that neurotics and non-neurotics have of achieving satisfaction from life. The patient's life is searched for evidences of the struggle between superiority and inferiority that run from childhood onward."

The infantile neurosis with its fixations and defenses against instinctual drives lost its importance for Adler. The moving factor in the emotional life of people, neurotic or otherwise, was the will to dominate.[621] The philosophy behind Adler's school of Individual Psychology was readily understandable, and for this reason Adler's theories were accepted, without much resistance, in Europe and in this country. The aim of the adlerians was to bring the message of Individual Psychology to the people, and the writings of his disciples deal as much with the problems of the unhappy, unfulfilled, but not actually ill, group of persons as with definite cases of neurosis. These developments, in addition to the denial of the sexual doctrines of Freud, gave the adlerian psychology a popular appeal that was lacking in the orthodox psychoanalytic school. Adler's emphasis had been on therapy primarily. He taught the patient the uselessness and the inefficiency of continuing on the road which he was following in life. He traced back through the life story of the patient those tendencies which he felt brought about the neurosis. The most important thing in life is the goal toward which each individual strives. It is unformed and undifferentiated in childhood, but more specific and recognizable in adult life. It is, indeed, a *life-plan.*

From the standpoint of the abstraction—psychotherapy, which is a name for a complex psychic operational relationship between doctor and patient, Adler had introduced a teleologic concept; [622] man had a purpose, a goal idea, to dominate those in the environment. Neurosis was a faulty method of implementing the drive for superiority. The emphasis of purposiveness which Adler contributed has returned in Schilder's [623] view of psychoanalytic therapy. But in the early 1900's the difference in this shift of accent from Freud's biologic-instinctual orientation was sufficient to sever Adler's psychology from psychoanalysis. Deserting the unconscious as an operational tool in psychotherapy, Adler, as did Jung, moved to another level of communication with the patient.

620 Adler, Alfred: The Practice and Theory of Individual Psychology, p. 4, New York, Harcourt, 1924.
621 ——: Understanding Human Nature, translated by W. B. Wolfe, New York, Greenberg, 1927.
622 ——: The Neurotic Constitution, translated by B. Glueck and John Lind, New York, Dodd, 1917.
623 Schilder, Paul: Psychoanalysis, Man and Society, pp. 5 et seq., New York, Norton, 1951.

Since psychotherapy depends much on intuition, empathy and the artful application of intangible judgment values, while psychoanalysis added a science of the ego, the temptation has been great to alter technics more in accordance with patient needs than with scientific laws. Inclusion of a philosophic-religious note into these analytic modifications altered the freudian viewpoint. Freud, in exposing the primary process (the direct discharge of psychic instinctual energy) as originating in that part of the unconscious ego which he called the "id," eschewed any religious connotation to our biopsychic natures. Although freudians are aware that "we sometimes vaguely feel that our primary function (process) links us with the cosmos," [624] Freud refused to embody any religio-philosophic construct beyond that of an "oceanic feeling" in his description of the basic reservoir of psychic energy within the ego. From the same frame of reference he conceded the psychoanalyst to be neither redeemer nor savior of his conflictful patients, but only a medical psychologist.

MODIFICATIONS IN PSYCHOANALYSIS

A small work published by Freud in 1922 [625] initiated decisive modifications in psychoanalytic theory and practice. Careful rethinking and reformulation of the relation of libido to the ego, beyond its relation to objects in the external world, formed the basis for a new conception of ego psychology. Clarification of unconscious ego forces—id and superego—and their interrelations with the conscious ego furnished illumination in clinical work for the therapist. Attention was focused rather on ego defenses against instinctual drives than on "id" drives themselves; in addition, study of the motives and operations of conscience (superego) in neurotic symptoms enlarged the scope of psychoanalytic theory.[626] A further consequence of the new ego psychology was the rethinking and the reformulation by Freud of the problem of anxiety. He regarded anxiety as a danger signal to the ego of unconscious threats, of loss of love, of injury or helplessness, which the ego warded off by the development of symptoms.[627] These traumatic influences were considered as deriving from instinctual dangers to the ego. When analyzed and brought to awareness in the treatment process, the ego was enabled to handle them objectively, as one deals with actual dangers. The theory of psychoanalytic treatment

[624] Wittels, Fritz: Freud and His Time, translated by Louise Brink, p. 422, New York, Liveright, 1931.

[625] Freud: The Ego and the Id, translated by J. Rivière, London, Hogarth, 1927.

[626] Alexander, Franz: The Psychoanalysis of the Total Personality; The Application of Freud's Theory of the Ego to Neuroses, translated by B. Glueck and B. D. Lewin, New York, Nerv. & Ment. Dis. Pub. Co., 1930.

[627] Freud: Inhibitions, Symptoms and Anxiety, translated by Alix Strachey, London, Hogarth, 1936.

established itself in consequence of the development of ego psychology. The scope of therapy broadened to include borderline states, as depression, schizoid characters and, later, psychoses, in addition to hysteria, anxiety neurosis, obsessions and phobias. Treatment manifestly required more time, two years or more of intensive work for patient and therapist. The goals of treatment were more clearly delineated, the "phases" of the analysis defined within limits and crucial technical problems of the transference worked out to the point at which they could be taught to students and practitioners of psychoanalysis.[628] This important relationship between patient and doctor, in which the patient uses the analyst upon which to project his early (unconscious) emotional drives and feelings, had been recognized earlier by Freud as an artificial situation, the "transference neurosis." It now formed a vital aspect of the treatment process. Through it the gamut of the neurotic's infantile affective life was relived, worked through in detail, until the ego unburdened itself of symptom-forming unconscious drives and the unconscious defenses thereto. Dependence on the analyst, inherent in the transference relation, was dissolved prior to the termination of the treatment.

Knowledge of the uniqueness of the transference situation placed the analysis of neurotic patients on a more certain basis. The task of therapy [629] could now be stated:

> Generally stated, [it] is to *mobilize* the energies of the id, to make the superego more tolerant, and to help the ego regain its synthetic and sublimating faculties as well as its own function of undisturbed perception and purposeful action. Through this change in the id, ego and super-ego, the neurotic will lose his anxiety caused by the danger which seems to accompany his instinct-demands, and will learn to react to them adequately and without fear. The task of therapy is therefore very complicated.

With organization of analytic technic and a fairly satisfactory metapsychological theory tracing the unconscious influences operating on superego, id and ego in functional nervous disease, psychoanalysis had advanced in the 1930's to the position of a vast body of illuminating clinical knowledge, an intricate and time-consuming therapeutic procedure. The main stream of psychoanalysts still consider psychoanalysis as (1) a body of knowledge of the ego and its unconscious elements, (2) a method of research into abnormalities and normalities of personality function, (3) a theoretical system covering behavior, feeling and thinking of human beings of genetic and dynamic type, and (4) a technic of treatment of

[628] Glover, Edward: The Technique of Psychoanalysis, London, Baillière, Tindall & Cox, 1928.

[629] Nunberg, Herman: "The Theoretical Basis of Psycho-analytic Therapy," *in* Psycho-analysis Today; Its Scope and Function, edited by A. S. Lorand, p. 56, New York, Covici Friede, 1933.

mental and emotional disturbances.[630] Psychoanalysis does not pretend to replace other types of psychotherapy with its technics, but it does aim to understand them. Whether this in fact will be the eventuality, as in the case of hypnotic phenomena, is a question for the future to decide. A corollary question arises as to the ultimate etiology of neurosis, for one may well ask if Fenichel's statement—"There are many ways to treat neuroses but there is only one way to understand them " [631]—will stand the test of future research.

Repeatedly in his writings Freud has pointed to the eventual merging of physiologic and psychological points of view, and, except in the case of his work on the dream, felt that theoretical improvements were both necessary and inevitable.[632] To its practitioners also psychoanalysis as a technic for modifying personality could not remain static. Forced by the baffling therapeutic problems which the many-sided aspects of neurosis posed, gradual changes in viewpoint and procedure developed. Resistances of the patient, chiefly deriving from the comfort experienced in the transference situation, slowing progress in uncovering unconscious roots of symptoms, occasioned one modification in technic, called "activity." This modified the accepted attitude of the analyst, a blend of passive attention to and tolerant acceptance of the patient. The bland emotional backdrop upon which patients projected their emotional life allowed them also to cling to the infantile dependency patterns which the therapist's attitude evoked; thus the work of unearthing unconscious motives virtually became stagnant. To interrupt this stagnation, Ferenczi [633] proposed, in accordance with Freud's basic view, expressed earlier, that since neurosis originated in frustration its treatment should be continued in an atmosphere of abstinence. The patient was therefore prohibited from activities which might interfere with exposure of unconscious libido during the analysis. Thus phobic patients were ordered to face their phobias, sexual activities which drained off unconscious gratification were prohibited, and symptomatic acts were curtailed. The meaning of these prohibitions was to have the patient face his inner fears without recourse to his symptomatic defenses. In addition, a time limit was set for the termination of the analysis.[634] Activity on the part of the analyst, recommended by Ferenczi and Rank in the service of shortening the duration of analytic treatment, was soon

[630] Knight, R. P.: *Op. cit.*

[631] Fenichel, Otto: The Psychoanalytic Theory of Neurosis, p. 554, New York, Norton, 1945.

[632] Alexander, Franz: Psychoanalysis revised, Psychoanalyt. Quart. 9:1, 1940.

[633] Ferenczi, Sandor: "The Further Development of an Active Therapy in Psycho-analysis (1920)," *in* Further Contributions to the Theory and Technique of Psycho-analysis, p. 198.

[634] Freud: "Analysis Terminable and Interminable," *in* Collected Papers, Vol. 5, edited by J. Strachey, p. 317, London, Hogarth, 1950.

curtailed when embarrassing theoretical considerations showed themselves. These derived from Rank's theory of birth trauma,[635] a theory which became the starting point for another departure from classical psychoanalytic theory.

THE RANKIAN DEPARTURE

The extension of Rank's methods which led to a new metapsychology arose from his consideration of anxiety as the prototype of the psychic experience of being born into the world. Although common to all mankind, the process of birth, for the neurotic-to-be, involves a basic anxiety situation, which reappears in the treatment process as a disinclination to leave the protective atmosphere of the analyst. Rank proposed to move directly to this anxiety-producing situation in the treatment, well marked in fantasies of all patients, work it through and liberate the patient from his "basic" anxiety. For this reason he proposed a time limit for the treatment (the rebirth itself, so to speak). While other analysts considered birth fantasies only one aspect of the neurotic problem, Rank elaborated a type of therapy from this base line called "will therapy," based on the concept that the transference is in reality a "duel of wills"[636] between patient and analyst. To Rank the idea of resistance was the idea of clash of wills in a situation guided by the personality of the analyst. To guide the patient to understand his will, not to accept the superimposed one of the analyst through the injunction to "associate freely," which Rank claimed was an educative process, not a true psychological one, became the way to successful therapy. The basis for freudian analysis was repudiated by Rank. He sought in the "dynamic" of the person, i.e., the organized forces within the individual, material to use in therapy of neurosis. Here was to be found the "creative energy" of the individual, which, once freed from its basic anxiety occasioned by the birth trauma, became usable for adaptation to life and reality.

Will therapy stressed the therapeutic situation as apart from the specific fixations of the patient, and hence was utilized by a school of psychiatric counseling[637] as well as by rankian analysts. As a method that shortened analysis by setting a time limit for its termination, Rank's views were given a hearing for a time among analysts. Freud agreed that the arguments of his lieutenant were "bold and ingenious," but felt that the clinical results of this group were not available for study. Furthermore, the emphasis on birth-trauma fantasies as the key to anxiety delimited therapy

635 Rank, Otto: The Trauma of Birth, New York, Harcourt, 1929.
636 ——: Will Therapy, and, Truth and Reality, translated by Jessie Taft, New York, Knopf, 1945.
637 Robinson, V. P.: A Changing Psychology in Social Case Work, Chapel Hill, N. C., Univ. North Carolina Press, 1930.

too severely. Critics noted that the rankian theories produced a school of psychiatrists who "ostracized the vagina;"[638] furthermore, its reflections in theory laid it open to medical criticism when, for example, it is reported a recommendation was made of cesarean section for all births to obviate psychic birth trauma for the infant! This and other improvisations which aimed to shorten treatment were rejected by freudians. Stekel, one of Freud's early associates, proposed, for example, that dream analysis be shortened by attending mainly to the manifest content, the "microcosm" of the patient's conflict.[639] Rank's and Stekel's innovations were alike greeted by the comment by Freud that the "best way to shorten analysis is to carry it out correctly." Treating the transference as a struggle of wills was, to Freud, the wish to "accelerate the tempo of analytic therapy to suit the rush of American life." By 1937 the final verdict on Rank was handed down,[640] "The theory of and practice of Rank's experiment are now things of the past—no less than American 'prosperity' itself."

If the birth trauma left little impression on analytic practice, the modification of "activity" with its implications has been incorporated in present-day practice. The passive attitude (never entirely so) on the part of the analyst has been shorn of its rigidity. The early attitude that every contact between patient and analyst was weighted with unconscious significance, that physical contacts, civilities and common amenities be eschewed as interfering with the transference, has been softened by the connotations of activity. Coincident with increased attention to the counter-transference attitudes of the analyst has come a more "friendly" expression, replacing the complete neutrality and personal anonymity inherent in the "passive" attitude.

RE-EVALUATION OF BASIC QUESTIONS

In quite another way, Rank's interpretation of the genesis of anxiety stimulated developments in viewpoint and technic. Although the original suggestion of the birth-trauma theory had come from Freud, he was not satisfied to allow this cataclysmic event in human life to be considered the sole influence on a fetal "mind" that manifestly did not exist at birth. To Freud, the problem of anxiety was far wider than its involvement with birth trauma. Rethinking the entire crucial question of anxiety, Freud revised his earlier notions in 1926.[641] He now conceived anxiety rather as a function of the ego than as the result of dammed-up libido. Anxiety was

[638] Kardiner, Abram: Lecture, A Critical Review of the Development of Psychoanalysis, New York, Psychoanalytic Institute, 1938-1939.

[639] Stekel, Wilhelm: The Interpretation of Dreams, translated by Eden and Cedar Paul, Vol. 1, New York, Liveright, 1943.

[640] Freud: "Analysis Terminable and Interminable," *in* Collected Papers, Vol. 5, edited by J. Strachey, p. 317, London, Hogarth, 1950.

[641] ——: Inhibitions, Symptoms and Anxiety.

a signal to the ego of an unknown fear: objective anxiety represented fear of a known danger; while neurotic anxiety signified fear of an unknown force, i.e., instinctual demands, that could not be met by the ego for reason of guilt or reality. The formulation that anxiety was an inner perception and response by the ego to pressure from unconscious id and superego forces was assimilated into the instinct theory,[642] molding the aims of psychoanalytic technic. Anxiety was the prototype of an original reaction to the helplessness of infantile life and was experienced repetitively by the ego when new danger arose. Repeated acquaintance with and control over these forces enabled the ego to master this fear. Treatment then could help to master anxiety by a process of re-education of the ego after revivification of unconscious memories and affective trauma responsible for anxiety.

One of Freud's major accomplishments, through his struggles to comprehend the etiology of anxiety and bring it into line with a psychological theory, was to lift this pervasive symptom from a nondescript position as a medical complaint into the forefront of a psychotherapeutic endeavor. The physical accompaniments of anxiety had been known and treated medically for centuries; the nervous heart, the nervous stomach, "cold sweats," the "shakes," were accepted conditions on the margin of medical practice. Undoubtedly the less obvious disquietude or sense of intolerable tension which accompanied anxiety has been part of human experience for untold time. But the recognition of the psychic component aspect of anxiety, so baffling to understand and so elusive to describe, had not been elevated to the status of a "neurotic symptom" which warranted attention by physicians.

After World War I and in the following decades, the infiltration of psychoanalytic thinking and psychiatric orientation toward somatic (functional) illnesses permitted the complaint of "jitteriness," the psychic component of anxiety, to be freely expressed. Until the struggle with the meaning of anxiety had been embarked upon, such descriptions of "queasiness," "worry" or "uneasiness" covered the most universal mental disturbance among men and women.

The problem of anxiety is a challenging one for psychiatry; to solve anxiety is to solve the therapy of the neurosis. In the last half century it has become the concern also of many thinking people, philosophers, theologians, psychologists, as well as psychoanalysts. Rollo May has demonstrated how, during the nineteenth century, through the efforts of Kierkegaard and, later, Freud, anxiety has "emerged as an unavoidable problem"[643] in the psychological life of the individual in consequence of the repression of emotion. Present-day existentialists, following Kierkegaard,

[642] Freud: New Introductory Lectures on Psycho-analysis, translated by W. J. H. Sprott, New York, Norton, 1933.

[643] May, Rollo: The Meaning of Anxiety, p. 29, New York, Ronald, 1950.

the Danish philosopher, have postulated anxiety as a natural state of man when he confronts the possibility of freedom of action in his world. Undoubtedly insecurity and anxiety are universal phenomena today among men not considered "neurotic" in the ordinary sense. It is this ubiquitous sense of inner insecurity which religionists have dealt with in invoking compliance with and submission to a larger Universal Will. Christian philosophers see anxiety as deriving from man's finiteness in nature in contrast with his potential freedom. A Catholic psychologist puts the paradox succinctly, "Anxiety, like guilt, springs from the attitude of revolt against man's limited nature" in contrast with God's.[644] That which has occupied theologians for centuries as a general problem of man has become an explicit one for psychiatrists, who seek to balance the emotional forces in their patients. Anxiety stands on the borderline between the status of man as a reasoning being, subject to tensions incident to life itself, and an illness defined as neurosis; anxiety is a precondition of neurosis as well as a disturbing illness itself.

It is outside the scope of this book to probe further into this fascinating problem, except to note its pervasive position in the history of psychotherapeutic development. Starting with the theory of birth-trauma anxiety, clinicians and experimentalists have made many careful studies to establish whether pathologic births or difficult deliveries actually demonstrated increased anxiety in infants in the nursery. Vital work by child psychiatrists (Gesell, Ribble, Fries and others) pointed to the possibility of an existence of preanxiety reaction occurring in fetal or neonatal [645] life which laid the foundation for later development of anxiety. On a physiologic basis the possibility existed that earlier speculations about anxiety's originating in the birth process, or soon after, were not without basis. These discoveries strengthened the need for prolonged analysis in cases of severe anxiety, although the fundamental problem of a "constitutional" factor in the genesis of this universal symptom is left unanswered.

HORNEY'S MODIFICATIONS

The issue of anxiety in neurotic patients and the theoretical basis thereof brought further divergences from the classical analytic method. Horney, whose early work was done in Berlin, Germany, pointed to the neurotic symptom as a device of the character itself to safeguard its feeling of security. She did not find that Freud's mechanistic-evolutionistic theory, which explained symptoms as defenses against unacceptable instincts, explained the functional meaning of anxiety as found in patients. Children,

[644] Allers, Rudolf: The New Psychologies, p. 76, London, Sheed & Ward, 1932.
[645] Greenacre, Phyllis: The predisposition to anxiety, Psychoanalyt. Quart. **10**:66, 1941.

Horney found, developed "basic anxiety" [646] as a condition of social life, out of a feeling of helplessness in a potentially hostile world. Basic anxiety could be considered rather a protective device for the individual, a "neurotic trend," than a symptom. Contrary to freudians, Horney, Fromm and others of this separatist group consider neurosis to be the outcome of conflict between human beings rather than between the environment and instincts. The answer to the pressing question of anxiety lay in the perception that "anything may provoke anxiety which is likely to jeopardize the individual's specific protective pursuits." How the patient protects his psychological needs arising from his character structure is of vastly greater importance than how individual symptoms are derived from instinct vicissitudes. On this basis Horney concluded that the drives which motivated a patient, not the infantile nature of neurotic symptoms, became the center of therapeutic work.

Horney's plan of therapy stressed the unconscious meaning of safety devices which have grown into the patient's character with subsequent demonstration to the patient of his use of neurotic trends to maintain emotional comfort in his social world. A consequence of this changed orientation was that the treatment [647] abandoned the passive approach and the analyst took a stronger hand in conducting the analysis. Reconstruction of the symptoms in terms of ego psychology lost significance in favor of a reconstruction of the consequences of the neurotic trend. This change in accent brought a closer appreciation of social pressures in the patient's life and also touched on the still unsolved problem of the will which Rank had raised. Horney's analysis tended to bring the current conflict more into view than the infantile life. Furthermore, it spoke in terms of "deliberately mobilizing the will power in constructive direction." [648]

Criticism directed against Horney's methods linked her work to Adler, who signalized neurotic strivings—for example, power, prestige, aggression—as basic trends in human nature. Horney aimed to understand the reason for these trends; against what basic anxieties did the patient demand power, etc. In this sense the cultural implications of a drive for prestige or any neurotic trend were honored as contributing to the neurotic's need to seek safety from deep feelings of helplessness. Competitiveness and the hostilities between individuals, the common bases for social intercourse in our modern world, were given value beyond those biologically based elements of freudian psychoanalysis.

With a reorientation in analytic theory there arose a concomitant, different attitude on the part of the therapist. As noted, the "imperturbable

[646] Horney, Karen: The Neurotic Personality of Our Time, p. 89, New York, Norton, 1937.

[647] ——: New Ways in Psychoanalysis, New York, Norton, 1939.

[648] *Ibid.*, p. 293.

tolerance" of the analyst, once regarded as indispensable, was now humanized. Value judgments, a derivative of every human being's personal philosophy, including the analyst's, must necessarily evidence themselves during the treatment relationship. To succeed in avoiding indication of the "moral" value of certain ways of adjusting to social pressures and relationships would be, in Horney's opinion, to attain an impossible ideal for the analyst. In similar vein ran Rank's objection to the therapist's unconcern with the *will* of the patient and the struggle in which it was enmeshed. The analyst's will must be brought to bear lest "the understanding psychoanalyst send the self-conscious neurotic back to the very self-knowledge from which he wanted to escape." [649]

CHARACTER ANALYSIS

Inherent in the Horney criticism of Freud's psychology is the question that recurs again and again, "What part does the analyst play in the synthesizing function of treatment?" And with it a corollary question arose as to the therapeutic strength of reconstructing the patient's infantile past from a knowledge of his unconscious reactions and attitudes. As a partial answer, Horney stressed the character structure of the patient as the therapeutic point of attack. Meanwhile, Wilhelm Reich, an outstanding Viennese psychoanalyst, had been meticulously restudying the neurosis from the standpoint of technic, i.e., the difficult task of dissolving resistances. Careful clinical work with patients forced the conclusion that one particular group of resistances, character resistances, deserved special consideration. As differentiated from symptom resistances, these arose from the "protecting armor" [650]—in short, the "character" formation which maintains the neurotic in a certain equilibrium. The function of character is to bind anxiety which wells up from within and to protect from external stimuli. Hence, analysis meets strong resistances in the character structure functioning as a narcissistic "protective apparatus" of the ego in patients who are rigid, aggressive, unnecessarily hostile and so on.

Reich's emphasis on the character enlarged the area of psychoanalytic treatment to include borderline psychotics, rigid characters, psychopaths whose "character" was their symptom, although neurotic difficulties, often in the sexual field, were also present in them. Direct approach to resistances, taking the form of a patient's "character" with which he has become familiar since it is his "person" greeting the world, aroused greater

[649] Rank, Otto: Psychology and the Soul, translated by W. D. Turner, Philadelphia, Univ. Penn. Press, 1950.

[650] Reich, Wilhelm: "On Character Analysis (1928)," translated by R. Fliess, *in* The Psychoanalytic Reader, Vol. 1, New York, Internat. Univ. Press, 1948.

hostility within the patient than when ego defenses to specific symptoms were attacked. The resulting "negative" transference made for more explosive outbursts and reactions on the part of the patient, but, by the same token, it allowed a deeper penetration into the real personality of the neurotic. The analysand developed an "objective attitude towards his character" as the attitudes with which he faced the world, as well as his symptoms, were worked through and their infantile basis demonstrated. Beneficial as this view of character resistances in handling borderline cases has been found to be, theoreticians have found difficulties with the concept. Writing in 1953, Sterba notes that "character resistance as formulated by Reich was an artifact of his suspicious personality, since he equates transference to it." [651] Notwithstanding, Reich's contribution in 1928 was a positive one.

This renewed emphasis on the character indicated the need for entertaining the effect of cultural forces on the personality or character, as apart from biologically based instinctual drives. Adaptation, or its failure, i.e., neurosis, was viewed as a continuous activity of the organism, its drives determined at birth but requiring constant revision as the result of numerous contacts with the environment.[652] In like manner, Reich wished to know "how social existence is transformed into psychic structure," [653] what our present economic system, our moral teachings, sex regulation, etc., do to people as eventually shown in their psychological character structure. What authority imposes on the child, particularly in sexual and anal habit patterns, bears a strong influence on character development for a given culture as well as for the individual. The theoretical views underlying treatment procedures, or more accurately the frame of reference of the therapist's thinking, came to assume a social-cultural aspect.

The realization that society through cultural patterns makes its imprint on the growing individual introduced several modifications of the freudian psychology of the ego (Fromm, Rado, Kardiner). This development had two ramifications: one was the great interest in contrasting the results of anthropologic study of primitive societies as their culture determined individual character development; the other was a trend toward considering social impingements on the neurotic patient in therapeutic systems (Horney, Rado, Kardiner). The theoretical realignments in psychoanalytic thinking due to infusion of cultural anthropology are of great interest but need not concern us here except to note, for example, Kardiner's statement that the concept "instinct" contains "too many processes all con-

[651] Sterba, R. F.: Clinical and therapeutic aspects of character resistance, Psychoanalyt. Quart. 22:1, 1953.
[652] Kardiner, Abram: The Individual and His Society; The Psychodynamics of Primitive Social Organization, New York, Columbia, 1939.
[653] Reich, Wilhelm: Character-Analysis, ed. 2, p. xviii, translated by T. P. Wolfe, New York, Orgone, 1945.

densed into one" to allow of unitary treatment.[654] For the history of psychotherapy, the view that the ego is an adaptive organism, an integrator of experience on unconscious and conscious levels, broadened the concept of neurotic reactions to mean "personal failures to adapt to conditions created by [social] institutions," [655] in addition to conflicts between unconscious forces in id, superego and the ego.

In accenting character structure, Reich fell back on Freud's initial idea that anxiety was a manifestation of dammed-up libido. In his delineation of the "neurotic" and "genital character," he traced anxiety to its source as excitation of the vasovegetative system (sympathetic nervous system), returning in this way to the area of medical experience. In a search for the active, possibly measurable, substance which underlies libido, he claimed to have found it in a unit of energy called the "orgone." Reich conceived "of orgone energy" as a cosmic energy, "a visible, measurable and applicable energy of a cosmic nature." [656] The energy which the human psyche uses—most observable in the sexual orgasm of man—was regarded as an aspect of the "biosystem," measured, apparently, as electrical energy. The orgone, discovered in 1931, filled the void left by the hypothesis of libido, for experiments at Reich's Orgone Institute (now located in New York) has succeeded in showing how organs of the body, genital organs, skin, etc., can be deficient in "orgonotic charge" and hence responsible for neurotic lack of orgastic gratification.[657]

The evolution of biophysics carried Reich to areas reminiscent of the latter-day magnetizers. The "bion," a basic unit of life energy (orgone), was measured by electrical devices, checked on the Reich Blood Test which determined the "shrinking capacity of blood corpuscles " [658] as seen in the microscope. Utilizing bionic energy in treatment, Reich developed an orgone energy accumulator which released bio-energy "bound in characterological armorings." Observations by followers agreed with Reich as to the ubiquity of orgone; Werner Grossmann, in Basel, Switzerland, wrote, "I became aware that the outside world appeared intensely blue at 7:00 A.M. a well-known orgonotic fact, the same that Reich produced in vacor tubes." [659] Although his laboratory experiments overstepped the limits of psychiatric preoccupation, Reich's sociopsychological ideas were in the direction of cultural anthropologic thinking. He clearly recognized that the

[654] Kardiner: The Individual and His Society; The Psychodynamics of Primitive Social Organization, p. 18.
[655] *Ibid.*, p. 484.
[656] Reich, Wilhelm: *Op. cit.*, p. 272.
[657] International Journal of Sex-Economy and Orgone-Research, New York.
[658] Reich, Wilhelm: Orgonomic Diagnosis of Cancer Biopathy 14:78, No. 2, Orgone Inst. Press, Orgonon, Maine, April, 1952.
[659] ——: Orgonomic Diagnosis of Cancer Biopathy 4:59, Basel, Switzerland, Werner Grossmann, January, 1952.

sexually suppressive influence of the patriarchal-authoritarian culture to which the civilized world had been subject for centuries brought about repression of the neurotic's ability to achieve orgastic potency. This he defined as the "capacity for surrender to the flow of biological energy." [660] An aspect of treatment was the disestablishment of sexual suppression.[661] In 1934, Reich, charged with being "in the service of Communist ideology," broke with organized psychoanalysis; his membership in the International Psychoanalytic Association "came to an end." Soon after, he moved to the United States, where his work in biophysics, vegetotherapy and orgonic research transcended those psychological problems which concerned his colleagues.

AMERICAN INFLUENCE IN PSYCHOANALYSIS

The upheaval in central Europe following the control of Germany by National Socialism and impending World War II started an exodus of psychoanalysts and psychiatrists to the United States and, to a lesser degree, to South America. This transplantation exerted a subtle effect on the development of psychoanalytic therapy through the further absorption of freudian theories into American practice. At the same time a reciprocal reaction on psychoanalysts themselves was exerted by the democratizing influence of American life. Much of the bitterness and "contempt" which Freud had withstood in Europe for his espousal of infantile sexuality, his views on the obsessional quality of religious ritual and his psychosexual investigations in neuroses, was softened in the New World in the 1930's. Though Freud has been continuously flayed by hostile critics as a "strong atheist, the bearded Viennese experimentalist was a pupil of the notorious professional hypnotist, Jean Martin Charcot," [662] and his science as a plague on the intellectual life of man—"Psychoanalysis has left behind a dry and sterile wasteland where the hot winds of analytic controversy raise blinding sand-storms, [and] there is no oasis and nothing grows" [663]—freudianism and its followers received a sympathetic audience and a secure refuge in this country. In spite of such vituperations, many critics in the medical profession and out assayed the usefulness of psychoanalysis with perspicacity and fairness: "Catholics ought to be respectful of this work. . . . Mutual respect and good relations having been established

[660] Reich, Wilhelm: The Function of the Orgasm, Vol. 1 of Discovery of the Orgone, translated by T. P. Wolfe, ed. 2, p. 68, New York, Orgone, 1948.
[661] ——: The Sexual Revolution; Toward a Self-governing Character Structure, translated by T. P. Wolfe, ed. 3, p. 19, New York, Orgone, 1945.
[662] O'Connor, John: Thought-Control, American Plan, The Sign, p. 23, Union City, N. J., November, 1949.
[663] Salter, Andrew: The Case Against Psychoanalysis, p. 13, New York, Holt, 1952.

with the analysts, Catholics can then hope to impart some of the wisdom which they feel is their own." [664]

Cultural attrition in turn forced recognition that the new culture, "in many ways so different from the European, allowed greater freedom from dogmatic beliefs." [665] Particularly the closeness of psychiatry with "social realities" in this country, the continued perception and formulation of the psychological *genre* of the people, woven so felicitously into mental hygiene concepts by Adolf Meyer and William James, encouraged those thinkers [666] who wished to correlate the findings of psychology and philosophy with a realistic psychoanalytic psychiatry. Imperceptibly psychiatric thinking moved in a cultural and anthropologic direction, and perceptibly psychotherapy moved into the position of observing social relationships, other than those relationships between child and parent, or parent figures in the infantile history of the patient. Psychological mechanisms, thought of in terms of interpersonal relationships and not solely derived from early patterns of relationship based on movements of libido, came to underlie psychological practice and therapy in some quarters. "Current conflict," "interpersonal relationship," "social ideology of the patient," were concepts that added social validity to those of "infantile neurosis" and "libidinous fixation."

Distortions of adaptation to life situation had always been the central problem of the neurosis, but in this period therapeutic eyes were lifted from troublesome conflicts within the ego structure to areas of conflict between ego and social milieu. Advances in character analysis stimulated by Reich, repudiation by some of the "death instinct" which Freud postulated as a polar antithesis to the life or libidinous instinct, a more active attitude by the psychoanalyst, an appreciation of neurotic social relationships, modification of transference use to include psychotic patients, all broadened psychoanalytic therapy. Many thought these measures increased its effectiveness, but others felt that the introduction of "brief" psychotherapy along psychoanalytic lines would spell a dissolution of the therapeutic structure which Freud and his followers had so arduously built.

Practical considerations arose also to alter the general course of analytic practice.[667] The five- or six-session week tended to become costly to patients and otherwise impractical. Psychiatrists, psychologists and others trained in the psychoanalytic tradition utilized analytic technics in their therapy, and the question of delimiting the name "psychoanalyst" to members of the International (and American) Psychoanalytic Societies was

[664] McNeill, Harry: Freudians and Catholics, The Commonweal, New York, p. 350, July 25, 1947.
[665] Horney, K.: New Ways in Psychoanalysis.
[666] Schilder, Paul: *Op. cit.*
[667] Oberndorf, C. P.: *Op. cit.*, p. 163.

discussed in 1947.[668] The question of "lay analysts," which Freud had endorsed, was again before professional groups, as was the general use of analytic procedures by psychiatric social workers and psychologists, either alone or under the supervision of professional psychotherapists.[669] Indeed, dynamic psychotherapy has come essentially to mean a method of modification of emotional and mental patterns into which have infiltrated some or all of the basic concepts of freudian psychology.

Since the 1930's the acceleration of psychiatric writings has been constant and the resulting volume mountainous. Henry Murray has remarked in this regard, "In these days of boundless, rootless zest for novelty experiment and revolution, twenty years is a century." [670] The "century" has been productive, however, not so much of primary conceptions of psychotherapy as of assessment and reality-testing of ideas in the context of an educated patient-society alert to its psychological and medical heritage. The new attitude which arose among patients gradually induced medicine, especially psychiatry, to relinquish some of its relative imperiousness. Individuals were entering into psychotherapy, not as inert "patients" waiting for the magic skill of the physician to wield its wonders, but as participants in a social relationship, an "expert-client" [671] relation, rather than a benevolent despot-subject situation. The "new" social viewpoint in psychiatry, far from new among sociologists interested in personality dissociations, had particular relevancy to psychotherapy which had transcended treatment of hysterias and phobias to deal with "social neurosis" or states of unhappiness or ineffectiveness.

SOCIAL ORIENTATION IN ANALYSIS

The tendency within analytic psychotherapy to move into current conflicts in the patient, whatever the earlier pattern determinants had been, in part signalized the "new" approach. But this statement does little justice to the rich implications and philosophic breadth of the psychotherapy of Schilder and Sullivan. The orientation receives a clear formulation in the background furnished by Schilder's views that "desires and instincts cannot be understood as mechanical agents . . . they have aims and purposes." [672] Neurotic symptoms, understood as resulting from the distorted

[668] Kubie, L. S.: Practical and Theoretical Aspects of Psychoanalysis, p. 201, New York, Internat. Univ. Press, 1950.

[669] Group for Advancement of Psychiatry, Topeka, Kansas: Relation of clinical psychology to psychiatry, Rep. No. 10, 1:1-5, 1949.

[670] Murray, H. A.: Introduction, *in* Contemporary Psychopathology, edited by Silvan S. Tomkins, Cambridge, Mass., Harvard, 1946.

[671] White, M. J.: "Sullivan and Treatment," *in* The Contributions of Harry Stack Sullivan, edited by Patrick Mullahy, New York, Hermitage House, 1952.

[672] Schilder, Paul: "Psychoanalysis and Philosophy," *in* Psychoanalysis, Man and Society.

expression which instincts were forced to undergo in the patient's historical development, could not be conceived as existing in isolation within the ego. One has to understand how "experience is social" in its final expression, and that instinct derivatives (neurotic symptoms) are attached to real "ideologies" in the patient's life. By these Schilder meant the limited number of basic problems which each person must master—those relating to superiority and inferiority in the physical sense, to the body, aggression and submissiveness, the concepts of masculinity and femininity in social and interpersonal terms, sex and love, health.[673] Most of these attitudes require a deep analysis, for each individual's "ideology" about his body, his family, his aggressiveness, etc., is rooted in early experiences, unknown and unconscious to the patient. Nevertheless, accent on the "meaning and conceptual purpose existing in the inner life history . . . the meaning in the stream of experience [for] the personality"[674] is a quality which calls for attention in psychoanalysis beyond the casual relationship, for example, of repression and neurotic symptom. This philosophic background for analytic therapy recalls Adler's somewhat discredited idea of a life-plan which one must recognize in the analysis of a patient's problems. Adler had written, "Every psychic phenomena, if it is to give us any understanding of a person, can only be grasped and understood if regarded as a preparation for some goal."[675] Hence Adler advised that therapists look for the life-plan, the goal toward which the patient had unwittingly striven and for which the neurotic symptom, for example a feeling of inferiority, was an overcompensation.

In the sense that there is a purposiveness in life strivings, a view which McDougall advanced in his discussion of human instincts,[676] a somewhat different attitude was taken in relation to nervous symptoms, a turning away from the more mechanistic or causal theories of freudian ego-psychology. Thus Harry Stack Sullivan brought analysis to focus on the interpersonal relationship which had become dissociated in mental patients or was disturbed in neurotic patients. Paul Schilder carried his treatment of neurotics into areas where their ideas of social value of their body-image disturbed their social relationships, and Horney recommended "self-analysis"[677] for a fuller development of each individual potentiality. These three workers did not entertain analogous ideas or technical procedures, but the central notion of modification of instinctive processes, the making

[673] *Ibid.*, p. 61.
[674] Schilder, Paul: Goals and Desires of Man, New York, Columbia, 1942.
[675] Adler, Alfred: The Practice and Theory of Individual Psychology, p. 4, New York, Harcourt, 1924.
[676] McDougall, William: The Energies of Men, New York, Scribner, 1933.
[677] Horney, Karen: Self-analysis, New York, Norton, 1942.

conscious of the unconscious, lost its primary importance in their therapeutic methodology. Sullivan achieved a closer, realistic view of the early relationship with "significant people" in the patient's background by becoming a "participant observer" in the treatment process. He entered into the private world of the patient through an interpersonal setup in which the therapist could observe and point out inhibitions which made free relationships difficult for the patient. Schilder, by noting the meaning of symptoms in social life, was able to analyze their relevancy or irrelevancy for the neurotic patient. This, in a broad way, is the significance of some of the later developments of analytic therapy.

Purposiveness and the social implications of the therapeutic situation comprised the main elements of later developments of analytic therapy. Tersely put, therapy broadened to include more than a "group of two." Moreno's [678] studies on interrelations between individuals in a group-therapy situation and Schilder's theorizing on the social meaning of neurosis gave further validity to group therapy, a field rapidly receiving attention in the 1930's. Group therapy will be discussed in a later chapter, but it needs to be pointed out here that therapists were gradually, yet not too slowly, succumbing to the emphasis of sociology in analytic thinking and practice. Not only was this exemplified by group therapy, but it came to acute realization in Sullivan's views of the therapeutic process as part of a complex social situation "expressing the interactions of numerous individuals and of a cultural matrix beyond." [679] The distinction between this frame of reference and the older psychoanalytic one is seen in Murphy and Cattell's summarizing statement: [680]

> We might . . . [say] that when clinical psychiatry appeared as an entity, in the hands of Emil Kraepelin, the disease was inside the patient . . . ; that with Freud the phenomena of transference began to make embarrassingly clear that two persons were involved in every symptom and in every step toward cure, the analyst serving as temporary surrogate for the persons who were . . . that with Sullivan the conception of a disease inside the person, carried around by him intact from one situation to another, was frankly abandoned, with a clear recognition that all we really see and deal with is a career line of interactions between individuals; and that if this be so . . . the relationships, not the individuals . . . become our concern.

This newer viewpoint involving the social implications of neurosis is in effect a sufficient departure from psychoanalysis as no longer to merit the

[678] Moreno, J. L.: Who Shall Survive?, Washington, D. C., Nerv. & Ment. Dis. Pub. Co., 1934. (Revised 1953, New York, Beacon House.)

[679] Murphy, Gardiner and Cattell: "Sullivan and Field Theory," *in* The Contributions of Harry Stack Sullivan, ed. by Patrick Mullahy. Copyright, William Alanson White, Institute of Psychiatry, Psychoanalysis and Psychology. Published by Hermitage, New York, 1952.

[680] *Ibid.*, p. 162.

name. For psychoanalysis revolves round the concepts of ego psychology and considers the handling of the transference and resistance as its inescapable function. In the 1930's it was not difficult to identify psychoanalysis as the science of the unconscious, deriving directly from the work of Freud, Abraham, Ferenczi, Reich, Jones, Fenichel, Alexander and a host of investigative analysts. But after that period the "deviations" increased in number and vocality, and the inevitable splits brought with them the need for the "orthodox" group to defend themselves against attacks of illiberality.[681] Personal loyalties to Freud and fealty to his metapsychology conflicted with a growing appreciation of the presence of hiatuses in the analytic psychological system as therapeutic successes with cases other than the "transference-neurosis" type did not appear to be guaranteed through the use of orthodox technic of psychoanalysis. In 1933 it was clear that

> use of a purely psychological approach in therapeutics . . . is necessarily based upon the assumption that certain disorders . . . are of psychogenic causation and have primarily a mental or emotional origin: . . . but, it follows as an obvious corollary that the greater the degree to which a given psychotherapeutic method embodies this assumption, the more rational and thorough-going and genuinely "causal" it will be.[682]

Later, this certainty diminished. To those who wished to relate the total configuration of the ego to environmental influences, present as well as past (Horney), it did not seem so certain that a genetic, causal chain of life events, worked out in a given patient, would relieve symptoms. Agreement of metapsychological theory with the view that social realities in the current situation of the patient react on the individual ego, provided the greatest theoretical difficulties. Although Freud has been rightly represented as never being entirely satisfied with his theoretical formulations, and ever willing to modify his ideas, a synthesis of the findings of sociology, anthropology and psychoanalysis has not yet been adequately made. It can be stated at this point, however, that the limits of psychoanalysis appeared to be broadening during the decades we are discussing, even while retaining its primary psychogenic perspective and reliance on knowledge of the unconscious in treatment technics.

Nevertheless, the "social" view of psychotherapy comes of good theoretical parentage. In the range of its multiple progenitors are Schilder's synthesizing of analytic concepts of the ego and instincts with his study of the psychological meaning of organic changes in muscle tone, body image or sensory perception; the experimental integration of motivation

[681] Knight, R. P.: *Op. cit.*

[682] Bunker, H. A.: "Psycho-therapy and Psycho-analysis," *in* Psycho-analysis Today; Its Scope and Function, edited by A. S. Lorand, p. 280, New York, Covici Friede, 1933.

and perception among Gestalt psychologists;[683] Moreno's "sociatry,"[684] a science which studies human beings as "social atoms" living under certain cohesive group forces of spontaneous origin; the dynamic psychology of Kurt Lewin, wherein the individual's psychology is intimately related to the "social field" in which he lives; the growing area of "culture-and-personality rapprochement;" the biosocial interpretation of mental function[685] deriving from the process of role-taking in infancy—in effect, a behavioral psychology without benefit of psyche.

This diffuse parentage has brought into being an offspring which, under the name of "social psychiatry," represents a cross-fertilization of ideas and experiences in the area of normal and abnormal behavior. It is this confluence of viewpoints, originating from various clinical and experimental disciplines which has provided a background for a perception of neurotic illness characteristic of our present period. In general, social psychiatry "stands upon the shoulders of Freud"[686] and his discovery of the involuntary (unconscious) psychic processes. Undoubtedly, also, social psychiatry developed from the pressures of an international atmosphere of conflict, arising from the struggles of opposing political-social ideologies during the past two decades, plus a conscious global effort to learn to live together. At all events, the therapeutic reflections of social psychiatry attain a more naturalistic direction from the standpoint of twentieth-century living. They embody, likewise, operational concepts more congenial to psychotherapy's fellow travelers—sociologists and anthropologists.

SULLIVAN'S INTERPERSONAL RELATION TECHNIC

Arising from, and simultaneously forming, the matrix of a social psychiatry, Sullivan's conception of interpersonal relationship offered a different slant to analytic psychotherapists. He took his departure from the conviction that the psychiatrist deals with living, and that the therapeutic situation is specifically a "relationship," not a working of one person on another. Without discarding Freud's discoveries of the influence of the unconscious on human motivations and symptoms, he took the stand that the patient's problems could best be approached by demonstrating how the

[683] Brosin, H. W.: "A Review of the Influence of Psychoanalysis on Current Thought," *in* Dynamic Psychiatry, edited by Franz Alexander and Helen Ross, Univ. Chicago Press, 1952.

[684] Moreno, J. L.: Sociometry, Experimental Method and the Science of Society, New York, Beacon House, 1951.

[685] Cameron, Norman: The Psychology of Behavior Disorders; A Biosocial Interpretation, Boston, Houghton, 1947.

[686] Thompson, Clara: *In* The Contributions of Harry Stack Sullivan.

patient had maintained his security and self-esteem through life.[687] This meant a somewhat different way of handling the patient. It meant also a new scientific language, which Sullivan notes "might well be refined from common speech through which the therapist and his patient have acquired some skill in communicating." [688] From this new language arose a viewpoint embodying "a rich store of intuitive wisdom " [689] which Sullivan developed first from treatment of schizophrenics and later from obsessional neurotics. Using practical "operational" methods, he and his associates [690] listened to the patient as the "marginal thoughts" brought up the points at which anxiety was experienced in the therapeutic situation. The doctor himself becomes a participant observer, also entering into the situation through communication by words and gestures and the emotional fact of his presence. Free association was given up in favor of the importance of fleeting marginal thoughts. Therapy of the neurotic or the psychotic patient became less a microscopic scrutiny of the movements of the ego and instinctive forces within the ego than a living together, a "togetherness" through which the patient again could dare face reality.[691] In this connection the psychosexual derivations of symptoms, the distortion of libido disposition, were considered much less important than the interpersonal relationship of the patient with his early figures usually centering in vital modalities, as security, relief of loneliness and self-esteem. Thus, also, hostility, so common a force in the neurotic and in everyone else, was viewed as a measure to protect severe insecurity. Therapy from this standpoint relied less upon the natural forces of restitution in the ego for healing and more upon the therapist's obligation to assist by "pressure direction and education" to aid the transition from neurotic infantilism to social satisfaction in living. "In this sense Sullivan was more Meyerian than Freudian." [692]

It is to be expected that this attitude of "rectifying impractical evaluation systems . . . by reducing personal distance," which is the essence of Sullivan's therapy, involves an almost entirely new set of concepts and, therefore, an initially confusing terminology. The crucial point of therapy, the relief of anxiety,[693] handled by the therapist as a participant observer since "anxiety arises from relationships with particular significant people," obviated the necessity of searching for instinct defenses within the patient.

[687] Sullivan, H. S.: Conceptions of Modern Psychiatry, p. 102, New York, Norton, 1953.
[688] *Ibid.*, p. vi.
[689] Stanton, A. H.: *In* The Contributions of Harry Stack Sullivan.
[690] Sullivan, H. S.: The theory of anxiety and the nature of psychotherapy, Psychiatry 12:3, 1949.
[691] White, M. J.: *Op. cit.*, p. 141.
[692] Wagner, P.: *In* The Contributions of Harry Stack Sullivan.
[693] Sullivan, H. S.: The theory of anxiety and the nature of psychotherapy.

Nevertheless, Sullivan's concepts lie close enough to those of Freud to allow an attempt at an approximation of equivalence. For purposes of orientation, free association can be equated to "marginal thoughts;" "the significant others," to "parental imagos;" the transference situation is seen as "parataxic phenomena"; the ego becomes a "self-system," and "object libido," empathy, "a term referring to peculiar emotional linkage that subtends the relationship of infant with other significant people." [694]

The primary difficulties of understanding the sullivanian language ought not to obscure advances which these concepts encompass for therapy. They represent more a view of neurosis formation as a correlate of social living in a psychobiologic atmosphere than a specific technic of therapy. From this view arises a series of usable operational concepts. For example, problems of countertransference within the analyst constitute a vital factor, because the therapist is a participating person in the therapeutic relationship. Minute interference with analyst-patient communication,[695] in tone of speech and its expressive quality, in facial expression of therapist, etc., is necessarily a subject for awareness on the part of the therapist. The personality of the therapist and the "new private worlds [occurring] between therapist and patient" [696] render the therapy an active relationship of real social meaning. Of course, it has always been recognized that the "group of two" which comprised the analytic situation was an area of social interaction. Flowing from this consideration, the question of countertransference generally has been more actively discussed in recent years than before, but concentration on the therapist as participant observer forces even more sedulous attention to this problem. In a recent book outlining intensive psychotherapy,[697] the designation which Sullivan preferred for his "school," five chapters are devoted to discussion of the therapist's own personality problems as they may be unmasked in the patient-doctor relationship. These and other advances in the total therapeutic situation were not apparently so regarded universally, for Fromm-Reichmann's exposition was placed by a psychoanalytic reviewer,[698] "In this twilight of electicism based on three-fourths rejection and infinitesimal acceptance of Freudian concepts . . ."

It is perhaps this very intensity of therapist-reactions, stemming from group and personal identifications, biases and role-taking, that has brought forth the acidulous criticism with which each newly proposed therapeutic system has been greeted. For the critical comments so liberally reported throughout these pages pointedly show the vital part that therapist-feelings

[694] Sullivan, H. S.: Conceptions of Modern Psychiatry, p. 8.
[695] Cohen, M. B.: Countertransference and Anxiety, Psychiatry **15**:231, August, 1952.
[696] Sullivan, H. S.: The theory of anxiety and the nature of psychotherapy.
[697] Fromm-Reichmann, Frieda: Principles of Intensive Psychotherapy, Univ. Chicago Press, 1950.
[698] Review of Fromm-Reichmann, Frieda: *In* Psychoanalyt. Quart. **24**:834, 1950.

have played in this history. Were the patient's critical comments as easily obtainable by the recorder of psychiatric history, a more revealing, and possibly more humanistic, story could have been written. For one can easily be persuaded that the therapist is a vital factor in the therapeutic process, both as a personality and a technician.[699] But analysts are men and women aspiring to a difficult task, each equipped with slightly varying perceptive gifts, unconscious predilections and individual adaptations. That attention is shifting somewhat to the intangible aspects of the therapist's make-up and its influence on what happens within the patient, is evidence of a scientific objectivization of human relations that cannot help but have a beneficial, if sobering, effect on psychotherapy.

MODIFICATIONS IN FREUDIAN ANALYSIS

Analysts adhering more closely to freudianism were, of course, not unmindful of the need for refining their instrument. Treatment of deeper states of ego disorganization, schizophrenic psychoses, earlier considered to lie outside the scope of psychoanalysis, called for modification of technic. Brill, who had started his life-long espousal of psychoanalysis working with hospital material at Burghölzli, recognized early that even the so-called chronic dementia praecox cases benefited from psychotherapy. Beginning about 1912,[700] Brill treated analytically every case that was approachable, in the hope that "an unknown something might change him to a normal being." Such simple, yet for the time profound, measures as telling the patient the truth helped many schizophrenics who were immersed in their private worlds of delusion and hallucination. The high inner tension of the patient, the terrible sense of isolation which Sullivan had perceived and described so penetratingly, were found to be the stimulus to the flight into autism and a dereistic (Bleuler) world. This perception that the schizophrenic's odd behavior meant something real in terms of ego defense encouraged a therapeutic attitude which emphasized the renewing of a relationship experience with another person, the therapist. The aloof, perhaps dilapidated, patient extended his pseudopods of feeling toward the therapist, who shed the classical passive position of psychoanalytic tradition. In this development of therapy, Sullivan's perceptions deserve recognition as being crucial. Other analysts, however, soon saw the possibility of developing a transference in the schizophrenic patient by modification of their attitude.

Among these latter was Federn,[701] who painstakingly enlarged the

[699] Oberndorf, C. P.: Constant elements in psychotherapy, Psychoanalyt. Quart. **15**: 435, 1946.
[700] Brill, A. A.: Schizophrenia and psychotherapy, Am. J. Psychiat. 9:519, 1929.
[701] Federn, Paul: Psychoanalysis of psychoses, Psychiatric Quart. **17**:3, 246, 470, 1943.

technic, originally suggested by Ferenczi, by "nourishing the transference through sincerity and kindness," avoiding free association and watching the reality relationship which lay behind the unconscious material. He made other innovations, as supplying another figure in the environment, a woman assistant, to build up the plausibility of a usable ego for transference development. Empathic sensitivity of the therapist and freedom to express his or her personality in a warm, "motherly" way toward the patient mitigated some of the desolate loneliness of the schizophrenic. Gertrude Schwing, a Viennese worker, carried this instinctive "motherliness" to her patients to the point of offering them fruit or candy, combing their hair or indulging infantile longings for attention and love.[702] It was essential to establish the long road back to an emotional situation which would then lead to the possibility of analytic treatment, the "pre-analytic" phase, before the autistic world of the patient could be invaded. It was this sensitivity to the unconscious feelings in patients which analysts like Fromm-Reichmann utilized as they set the stage for an interpretative treatment process.

More recently Rosen has carried this attitude almost directly to the doors of the unconscious, so to speak. Rosen "talks directly to the unconscious" in his patients.[703] Without fear or hostility toward schizophrenics, even deteriorated ones, this therapist directly attacks the traumatic infantile events in the patients' life in words laden with emotion. While he gives a "continuous drip . . . of affection and protection" to his patients,[704] he interprets their oral, sexual needs in Anglo-Saxon words to which are attached living realities of old. Based on the countertransference feeling that the "therapist cannot let the child be unhappy and cannot rest until the child is at peace," Rosen allows the infant within the schizophrenic to grow in a new, secure environment wherein he can see the meaning of his autistic symptoms. As all workers in this new field point out, the essential nature of the therapist attitude is changed, his warmth of personality becomes a therapeutic tool, and countertransference attitudes are recognized as natural concomitants of a changing "object-relation." Adaptations of this type have been made, for example by Stern,[705] in borderline neurotic cases with schizoid features by increased activity, a more natural attitude and seating the patient in a chair. Indeed, work with psychotic individuals has shown analysts the

[702] Brody, E. B.: "Treatment of Schizophrenia," *in* Psychotherapy with Schizophrenics, edited by E. B. Brody and F. C. Redlich, p. 46, New York, Internat. Univ. Press, 1952.

[703] Rosen, J. N.: The treatment of schizophrenic psychosis by direct analytic therapy, Psychiatric Quart. 21:3, 1947.

[704] *Ibid.*

[705] Stern, Adolph: Transference in borderline neurosis, Psychoanalyt. Quart. 17:527, 1948.

importance of changing their theoretical constructs from the original "biological or physiological bias," on which Freud erected his theories of instinctive expression in the unfolding of the human psyche, to a greater concern with object-relations attendant upon the physiologic instinct drives. The practical meaning of this reorientation has been stated by Balint to be seen in the transference, still the basic situation in which the neurosis is exposed and treated. The transference is now considered a two-way situation in which tensions of both analyst and patient require consideration,[706] the object (person) to which the basic instinct directs its drives gaining in importance in the handling of transference.

These gradual changes in analytic technic were spurred on by the somewhat disappointing and often unpredictable results of psychoanalytic therapy. Oberndorf, in a series of papers,[707] courageously brought attention to the lack of any investigation which "correlated permanency and quality of result with length and/or depth of treatment." He further speculated whether "too great or too deep preoccupation with the unconscious . . . retards synthesis between conscience and primitive drives." Analysts in the decade of the 1940's were aware that technical innovations were necessary to shorten treatment because of the prohibitive expense of treatment to some patients and the exorbitant time demands, as well as the interminability of some analyses. The staff of the Chicago Institute of Psychoanalysis utilized the original ideas of Ferenczi and Rank wherein they sought to minimize the long-standing dependence of some patients which served the cause of resistance to getting well. Alexander, French and their associates replaced intellectual understanding of the cause of neurosis by the "emotional experience" of the treatment in certain cases.[708]

Several other technical principles were developed arising from treatment of neurotic and psychosomatic cases which modified classical analysis to form a more economical "brief psychotherapy" suited to the patient's need for relief from anxiety and emotional tension. These included variations in the rule of daily sessions, interruption of treatment when emotional dependence on the analyst became too pointed, manipulation of the transference through choice of interpretations to the end that a complete transference neurosis becomes obviated, change in position of the patient "once bound to the convention of the couch" [709] and so on. The principles of flexibility were applied with a full appreciation of the psychodynamics of the case in hand and with a wish to discourage long-drawn-out, frequently nega-

[706] Balint, Michael: Changing therapeutical aims and techniques in psycho-analysis, Internat. J. Psycho-analysis 31:117, 1950.

[707] Oberndorf: Factors in psychoanalytic therapy, Am. J. Psychiat. 98:750, 1942; Considerations of results with psychoanalytic therapy, Am. J. Psychiat. 99:374, 1942.

[708] Alexander, Franz, et al.: Psychoanalytic Therapy; Principles and Application, New York, Ronald, 1946.

[709] *Ibid.*, p. 53.

tive (hostile) transference reactions and to bring the patient directly to his conflict. The gains from Alexander's "flexibility" procedures, apart from economy in time, resided in the translation into actual life situations of emotional experiences occurring within the analytic framework; it planned to co-ordinate the patient's actual and analytic lives. The significance of principles underlying "brief" therapy lies in the "corrective emotional experience" [710] consequent on re-enactment of early emotional patterns through a nonaggressive, nonretaliatory understanding analyst. The patient's ego is assisted by a real, rather than a surrogate, therapist-figure to handle emerging unconscious material.

In a similar direction lies Deutsch's "sector psychotherapy," in which the focus during the treatment is limited to psychological conflicts centering in specific symptoms. The present reality is kept in constant view to the end that the analysis is efficiently held to the problems of which the patient complains. Thus the therapist limits the goal to which the associations are pointing, and interpretations of unconscious material are considered less vital than confrontation of past material in direct relation to present psychological reality. Felix Deutsch [711] has found this modification especially helpful for psychosomatic conditions—for example, skin conditions—where the analyst wishes to protect the patient from overflow of anxiety in many directions, dealing with it in relation to the somatic symptom. In this work the analyst is active rather than passive, guiding rather than permissive. As with other brief methods of analysis, in sector analysis the implications of the transference and its lengthy working-through tend to be obviated.

The essential contribution of brief psychotherapists can be subsumed under their clarification of the processes of analytic cure expressed in a surer hold on the therapeutic situation. "Flexibility . . . in preference to routine," the recognition that the ego is reconditioned during analysis [712] to tolerate and assimilate repressed material uncovered and the goal of inducing the patient's ego "to accept self-government" represent significant changes in therapeutic aims. Accent on therapy as a learning process, implied in the awareness of reconditioning of the ego, brought the therapeutic process closer to the conceptions of experimental psychologists.[713] The learning which the neurotic ego undergoes during treatment is chiefly an emotional one, although intellectual insight aids integration into the

[710] Alexander, Franz: Analysis of the therapeutic factors in psychoanalytic treatment, Psychoanalyt. Quart. 19:482-500, 1950.

[711] Deutsch, Felix: Applied Psychoanalysis; Selected Objectives of Psychotherapy, New York, Grune, 1949.

[712] Alexander, Franz: "Developments of Fundamental Concepts of Psychoanalysis," *in* Dynamic Psychiatry, edited by Franz Alexander and Helen Ross, p. 31, Univ. Chicago Press, 1952.

[713] Dollard, John, and Miller, N. E.: Personality and Psychotherapy, An Analysis of Learning, Thinking and Culture, New York, McGraw-Hill, 1950.

ego of hitherto repressed emotional and behavioral patterns. Whether psychoanalytic therapy is shortened or intensified, activated or brought closer to reality of the patient's current life, the modifications outlined above have adapted psychoanalysis to present-day patient needs.

The original findings of Freud and his followers, assiduously adapted over a half a century to clinical material, were further elaborated, directed by the exigencies of emergency clinical situations. During World War II a large number of war neuroses occurring before, during and after combat were treated by psychiatrists of analytic training. Indeed, the infiltration of psychiatry by dynamic thinking altered the face of military medicine. Brief psychotherapy, narcosynthesis and narcoanalysis were developed by some psychiatrists into effective therapeutic weapons in combat areas and behind the battle lines. Pioneer work [714] utilizing sedatives (narcosynthesis) to help the neurotically ill soldier abreact the immense emotional trauma of war has proved the enormous usefulness of analytic concepts of the ego when worked out for the traumatic neurosis. Their experience [715] indicated that "every war neurosis is a psychoneurosis since old unsolved conflicts of the past are stimulated by stress to assist in the production of a neurotic reaction," and that "it is not possible to remove the effects of combat without encountering the soldier's conscious and unconscious complex character structure and neurotic patterns."

Cataclysmic events of modern war, in their devastating neurotic results to many individuals under combat conditions, were explicable as the consequence of a contraction of the important ego function of mastery of the external world. Kardiner, who studied the war neurosis following World War I, helped to develop an appreciation of the impact of traumatic experience on the ego.[716] With others, he found that overwhelming catastrophes, such as bombing, threw the ego's adaptation mechanisms into confusion, as witnessed in the characteristic nightmares all such patients experience, in which the original accident with its sudden, terrible power is re-enacted over and over again. Repetition of the occurrence represents the ego's attempts to master the tremendous excitation introduced by the original accident or injury. Symptoms of the traumatic neurosis proclaim this attempt while they simultaneously state the ego's helplessness in nervous tremors and the familiar train of physical concomitants of anxiety. These changes in the patient's mental state, characteristic of industrial injuries, automobile accidents and casualties of wartime, were rendered approachable therapeutically by the enlarged concept of the executive function of the ego in its adaptation to the external world. As Fenichel has summarized this concept,[717] "The Ego may be regarded as

[714] Grinker, R. R., and Spiegel, J. P.: War Neuroses, Philadelphia, Blakiston, 1945.

[715] ———: Men Under Stress, p. 354, Philadelphia, Blakiston, 1945.

[716] Kardiner, Abram: The Bio-analysis of the Epileptic Reaction, p. 104, Albany, New York, Psychoanalyt. Quart. Press, 1932.

[717] Fenichel, Otto: *Op. cit.*, p. 117.

having been developed for the purpose of avoiding traumatic states" by its ability to "bind" excitation from external stimuli. When influx of excitation is high, it is discharged through ego activity of "flight or fight;" if the stimuli overtax the individual's capacity, a neurosis results.[718] The way to therapy of these conditions then lies in abreaction of the original traumatic stimuli and in strengthening the ego, with the psychoanalytic handling of the secondarily disturbed involvement of other aspects of the personality.

Infiltration of psychoanalytic theory and practice into hypnosis, i.e., hypnoanalysis, has proceeded actively in recent years. In brief treatment, technics devised to circumvent resistances, initiated earlier by Simmel and Hatfield,[719] dreams have been explored under hypnosis, resistances brought to the surface and dissolved, and associations directed. More recently, Wolberg [720] has utilized automatic writing and artificially induced dreams, either during hypnosis or in the posthypnotic state, thus reaching and analyzing material which may have been buried by the lethargy, "traditionally accepted as an inevitable concomitant of the hypnotic trance state." Variations in technic have been developed in ingenious directions by Milton Erickson,[721] who pioneered in inducing dreams under hypnosis by causing the patient to relive, under hypnosis, specific emotionally significant events in his life. Erickson has even "implanted" complexes in a subject's mind under hypnosis. Other workers have utilized automatic writing (Rosen), [722] crystal gazing (Wolberg), direct attack on repression through insistence on recall of forgotten memories (Brenman; Gill and Menninger).[723] In this area, Lindner [724] used a similar technic in a psychopathic individual, forcing revival of memories reputed to belong to the sixth month of the patient's life. Harold Rosen forces the actual living out during the hypnotic trance of anxiety-laden events, unrecognized in the patient's conscious state, thus intensifying "the emotion of the moment" to the point at which the patient may become actually terror-stricken during the hypnotic state. Such technics dissolve resistances dramatically, and, although they constitute "calculated risks," they do result in rapid revivi-

718 Kardiner, Abram: The Traumatic Neuroses of War, sponsored by National Research Council, New York, Harper, 1941.

719 Brenman, Margaret, and Gill, M. M.: Hypnotherapy; A Survey of the Literature, New York, Internat. Univ. Press, 1947.

720 Wolberg, L. R.: Hypnoanalysis, New York, Grune, 1945.

721 Erickson, M. H.: Experimental demonstrations of the psychopathology of everyday life, Psychoanalyt. Quart. 8:338, 1939.

722 Rosen, Harold: The hypnotic and hypnotherapeutic unmasking, intensification and recognition of an emotion, Am. J. Psychiat. 109:120, 1952.

723 Brenman and Gill: Some recent observations on the use of hypnosis in psychotherapy, Bull. Menninger Clinic 10:104-109, 1946.
Gill, Merton, and Menninger, Karl: Techniques of hypnoanalysis illustrated in a case report, Bull. Menninger Clin. 10:110-126, 1946.

724 Lindner, R. M.: Rebel Without a Cause; The Hypnoanalysis of a Criminal Psychopath, New York, Grune, 1944.

fication of pathogenic experiences which are then subject to working through in the waking state.

The essential point of these variations is the use of hypnosis as an aid in manipulating the mobile aspects of the personality in order to resolve the effect of pathogenic disturbances. As Rosen put it, "Patients with emotional disease can be treated . . . not *by* but *under* hypnosis." It is characteristic of modern hypnotherapy that the various measures employed depend more on knowledge of patient-therapist relationship than upon the authoritarian frame of reference which characterized hypnosis in the days of direct suggestion. Present-day hypnosis stresses the need for the patient to participate actively in a reorganization of his psychic life. Hypnosis, in becoming patient-centered rather than doctor-centered, has lost some of its mystical connotations and is better suited for the purpose of reintegrating the personality with material obtained during the hypnotic trance. Jacob Conn,[725] for example, feels that relaxation without attendant sleep, suffices to bring about a patient situation wherein material and attitudes which otherwise cannot be faced are brought forth. His use of hypnosynthesis is in the service of "unifying inter-personal experience" in the patient, under the guidance of a therapist, but without the employment of an authoritarian attitude or direct suggestion.

Widespread appropriation of analytic principles has distinguished modern dynamic psychotherapy from its antecedents in an unmistakable way. In the modifications and alterations of psychotherapy, outlined in this chapter and a later one, the vitalization of its spirit, the broadening of its scope, can readily be seen as the result of psychoanalytic influence. At the same time it cannot be said that psychoanalysis has been impoverished by being subjected to the pragmatic, empirical test of treatment experience. Essentially, the value of psychoanalysis to the philosophy of medicine lies in its description, in psychological terms, of the assets and the limitations of man's nature. Man, as Freud saw him, was conditioned "by his biological heritage (id), [and] by his long cultural history (super-ego)." [726] Trilling appraises Freud as a true rationalist, "Like any tragic poet, like any true moralist, Freud took it as one of his tasks to define the borders of necessity in order to establish the realm of freedom."

The labors of three generations of workers epitomize the growth of Freud's science. They have built on the foundations laid down by one man, erecting thereby a fitting monument to house Freud's gift to mankind.

[725] Conn, Jacob: Hypno-synthesis; hypnosis as a unifying interpersonal experience, J. Nerv. & Ment. Dis. 109:9, 1949.

[726] Freud, Sigmund: An Outline of Psychoanalysis, reviewed by Lionel Trilling in the *New York Times* Book Review, February 27, 1949, Vol. 54, part 1, page 1.

10

Mental Hygiene, Psychotherapy's Catalyst

Entrance of the social viewpoint into psychotherapy was indefinably stimulated by the impetus of the mental-hygiene movement. As catalyst and energizer, mental hygiene, essentially American in spirit as in factual origin, wove its influence through the tissue of social psychiatry. Because this movement involves public participation in intimate matters as mental health, representing a need to improve social and personal relations, it is practical in its therapeutic meaning. Accepting our common human frailties and wishing to confer the inalienable right of adjustment, mental hygiene is a concept which could originate and flourish in a democratic atmosphere. Again, because it uses salesmanship and public-relations technics, depicting graphically and insistently what it wishes to demonstrate, yet containing a social ideal of vast significance, the movement reflected American practical idealism. It arose from the mind of one man, Clifford Whittingham Beers, yet it caught the imagination of the world. Mental hygiene does not deal in psychotherapy predominantly, but it was, and is, social psychotherapy in a larger sense.

A distinctive characteristic of our modern era has been the infiltration of applied science into social consciousness. Nowhere can the malleability of the human psyche with its responsiveness to ideas and attitudes be more clearly observed than in that exerted by the mental-hygiene movement. Concepts of mental hygiene are synonymous with modern social thinking, woven into our social "body image" as a built-in concern over the functioning of our emotional equipment. The nineteenth century prepared us for an absorption of technologic and scientific attitudes toward the world in which we live, but the twentieth century contributed an introspective slant and a mental set toward emotional problems much as earlier centuries infused religion and morality into the social mind of the day. As Commager[727] has put it:

> The Decade of the nineties is the watershed of American history. . . . On the one side lies an America predominantly agricultural; concerned with domestic problems; conforming . . . to the . . . moral principles inherited from the seventeenth and eighteenth centuries. . . . On the other side lies the modern America . . . inextricably involved in world economy and politics.

To borrow the historian's figure, the watershed of psychotherapy was likewise the advent of the twentieth century; on one side lay a body of knowledge and concept of practice involving a personal relationship between doctor and patient, healer and supplicant, while on the other was a consciousness of the interdigitating influence of mental life in health and disease on society as well as the individuals involved. In America first, and later in the rest of the world, society assumed a compelling interest in mental disturbances and their alleviation. Discovery of the presence of the fact of a mental life, with its corollary tendency to do something about it, i.e., psychotherapy, occurred under a general "shift in emphasis of philosophy from the salvation of the individual to the reconstruction of society."[728] In this general movement toward self-realization within social limits, it is difficult to overestimate the influence of psychiatry and psychology. It is a "forward motion," the century's sociopsychological revolution. The mental-hygiene movement has played the alternate roles of standard-bearer, combatant, supporting public and propagandists in this world change.

PREMENTAL HYGIENE DAYS

In 1900, the man in the street knew little about psychiatry or its technics save as a personal misfortune brought his attention to the gray-walled asylums or to the electrical machines and tonics of neurologists or the spas for the "nervously debilitated" in Europe. The term "alienist" was better known than "psychiatrist," and, although psychology assumed a respectable place in the university curriculum, it was generally recognized in the mind of the average man as a revered but somewhat impractical subject. Concerning insanity and its treatment, his interest was occasionally stirred by a current murder trial involving the issue of insanity, but in the main he was content to stand by the dictum accepted by everyone, "Once insane, always insane." His scientific reading, as purveyed in magazines[729] and the press, touched on discoveries of radium, the neuron theory of brain function, chemistry, the newly discovered "subconscious" region of the

[727] Commager, H. S.: The American Mind, p. 41, New Haven, Yale, 1950.
[728] *Ibid.*, p. 100.
[729] Harper's Magazine, Vols. 99-105 (1900-1905), New York, Harper.

mind, psychic experiments and spiritualism, and hypnosis. He was interested in descriptive anthropology of the "backward races" inhabiting Africa and the South Pacific,[730] discoveries in metallurgy and biology, but of mental hygiene as a way of emancipation from emotional tensions he was uninformed. The dark history of psychiatry, illuminated by the gentleness of Pinel, the persistence of Dorothea Dix, the industry of Charcot and the penetration of Freud, was an unopened, even unwritten, book to the vast majority. True social uplift was in the air in 1900; political, social, eugenic, economic, public-health, enfranchisement, improvement doctrines, were being advanced in many corners of the world. Society was stirring to its responsibilities for the welfare of man, but the concept of freeing the insane or the neurotic from the chains of neglect and indifference remained a Utopian dream in the minds of a few. Psychotherapy as a discipline, an application to living, was external to the concerns of men bent on practical achievements.

The attitude of medical men was not dissimilar to that outlined above for the man on the street. Preventive medicine at the turn of the century was already accepted as a legitimate outgrowth of advances in bacteriology and chemistry. Sanitary engineering reduced the incidence of typhoid fever; inoculation of immune substances was eradicating diphtheria; syphilis and tuberculosis were being controlled. Even social participation in hygienic projects [731] proceeded rapidly: the National Association for the Study and Prevention of Tuberculosis was established in 1904; the American Association for the Study and Prevention of Infant Mortality was organized in 1909, thus revitalizing older movements for ameliorating conditions among the ill and the indigent (American Public Health Association—1872, Charity Organization Society—1877, etc.). Physical hygiene, compounded of physiology and moral preachments, admitted as a study of prevention of illness in the schools, exposed the evils of alcohol, tobacco, excessive eating, tight clothing, poor ventilation, inadequate rest and lack of exercise to the oncoming generation. Physical hygiene and the companion social activities of calisthenics, sports, open windows and outdoor life grew as a conscious movement, but its mental-hygiene aspect remained moralistic. Later texts repeated older warnings; [732] to illustrate, the schoolboy of 1884 was advised, "Many boys are throwing away their manly strength and dwarfing their minds, by the use of tobacco," [733] and

[730] Macmillan Magazine, Vols. 82-93 (1900-1905), London, Macmillan.

[731] Deutsch, Albert: The Mentally Ill in America, ed. 2, revised, p. 301, New York, Columbia, 1949.

[732] Beecher, C. E.: Physiology and Calisthenics for Schools and Families, Chap. 18, New York, Harper, 1856.

[733] Smith, W. Thayer: The Human Body and Its Health, A Text book for Schools, Having Special Reference to the Effects of Stimulants and Narcotics on the Human System, p. 154, New York, Am. Bk. Co., 1884.

the student of 1909 learned, "Bad habits . . . sooner or later wear out the nervous machinery." [734]

Still, a hygiene of the mind, based upon broad psychological principles borrowed from medical practice, had been adumbrated through the nineteenth century by an occasional anxious physician writing to seemingly unhearing readers. Albert Deutsch states that the first use of the phrase "mental hygiene" is to be found in Sweetster's book, *Mental Hygiene, an Examination of the Intellect and Passions, Designed to Illustrate Their Influence on Health and Duration of Life* (New York, 1843).[735] Isaac Ray, dean of American psychiatrists, published a book in 1863 entitled *Mental Hygiene,*[736] and Kirkman, an English asylum superintendent, advocated mental hygiene [737] to attain a "balanced performance" of the nervous system. From the 1870's on, the term "mental hygiene" passed into general use,[738] concentrated initially in movements concerning the welfare of the insane, their civil rights and mistreatment by restraint. As recounted in stirring detail by Deutsch,[739] the running controversy between neurologists in practice and physicians in the asylums resulted in the formation of a National Association for the Protection of the Insane and the Prevention of Insanity, organized in 1880. The association succumbed within a few years because of professional jealousy and a too narrow base of public support. The term and concept "mental hygiene" was therefore not unfamiliar to alienists and welfare workers when Clifford Beers, the Connecticut Yankee, burst upon the world with his book, *A Mind That Found Itself.*[740] Beers's book proved to be "the shot heard round the world," the catalyst that set off mental hygiene chain reactions which have increased to the present point of national and international concern.

THE FOUNDING OF THE MOVEMENT

A graduate of Yale, Beers had experienced several breakdowns as a young man; he was treated in private sanitaria and state hospitals with the prevailing methods of restraint and isolation. The vigor of the treatment accorded him so injured his sense of human dignity that he vowed

[734] Hoag, E. B.: Health Studies, Applied Physiology and Hygiene, p. 52, Boston, Heath, 1909.
[735] Deutsch, Albert: *Op. cit.,* p. 310.
[736] Ray, Isaac: Mental Hygiene, Boston, Ticknor & Fields, 1863.
[737] Kirkman: Mental hygiene, annual report of county asylums, Asylum J. Ment. Sc. **2**:277, 1856.
[738] Deutsch, Albert: "The History of Mental Hygiene," *in* One Hundred Years of American Psychiatry, p. 332, New York, Columbia, 1944.
[739] *Ibid.,* p. 340.
[740] Beers, C. W.: A Mind That Found Itself; An Autobiography, ed. 2, New York, Longmans, 1910; 25th anniversary ed., New York, Doubleday, 1935; American Foundation for Mental Hygiene.

to expose these conditions to an indifferent public. His plan was not unlike that of many others in similar situations. But, unlike others, Beers added to memories of indignities a wish to inaugurate a "permanent campaign for improvement in the care and treatment of mental sufferers, and the prevention of mental illness itself." [741] When Beers regained his health in 1905, that itself somewhat of a miracle in that period, the book and the campaign were undimmed in his mind. The book was penned in white heat, but, since his chief interest lay in ameliorating the condition of the insane in institutions, he sought consultation with William James and later with Adolf Meyer. Professor James was enthusiastic. Writing to Beers, he said, "[Your book] reads like fiction but it is not fiction." Meyer, who had anticipated the direction of psychiatric development by attempting to develop an after-care program for his mental cases in the New York State Hospital System, sensed the confluence of psychiatry with social consciousness of the problems encountered in treating the insane in Beers's book. Alert to the book's significance, he urged both publication of the manuscript and formation of a mental-hygiene association. To Meyer, Beers was an ally for the "cause" of sorely needed public education regarding the insane. "Active psychiatry and public sentiment seemed to be meeting on the same errand," he wrote.[742]

The Mind That Found Itself was published in 1908. It was widely read and acclaimed throughout the literate world. But, for Beers, publication of his book was merely the opening salvo of a campaign that was to endure throughout his lifetime. The local group which Meyer and Beers had succeeded in interesting decided to organize a local committee first; the Connecticut Society for Mental Hygiene was born in 1908. Soon after, a National Committee for Mental Hygiene was formed in New York. Later, other states followed, and the organization began to function on a National level. "It looks," wrote Meyer to his fellow psychiatrists, "as if we had at last what we need—a man for the cause." [743] The early aim of these groups was to draw public attention to abuses, brutalities and neglect to which the mentally sick had traditionally been subject; [744] to focus public attention on the need for reform and, in general, to raise the standards of care for the mentally ill and to promote measures for the prevention of mental ills. Beyond this, the effort to remove the stigma from mental illness, to build up a prophylactic attitude toward mental defect and mental disease, to turn the medical profession toward mental illness as its legitimate concern, was the material goal of the movement. Dissolution of the age-old dictum, "Once insane, always insane," became

[741] *Ibid.*, p. 255.
[742] Lief, Alfred: The birth and development of the mental hygiene movement, Ment. Hyg. 19:29, 1935.
[743] ——: Connecticut Society for Mental Hygiene, National Committee, 1909.
[744] Beers, C. W.: *Op. cit.*, p. 324.

the unceasing objective of Beers and a growing army of professional and lay mental hygienists.

One of the early implementations of the movement was a survey made by Thomas W. Salmon, appointed by the Public Health Service in 1912 as medical director of the National Committee for Mental Hygiene. It concerned facilities for care of mental defectives and the insane in many states of the Union. Another was the work of psychiatrists in World War I. With the outbreak of war, creation of a division of psychiatry in the Army's Surgeon General's office allowed Salmon, who was chief psychiatrist for the American Expeditionary Forces, to plan for prompt treatment of shell-shock cases as near the front lines as possible.[745] The new attitude toward what are now known as war neuroses represented a revolutionary step, cutting across military distrust of specialism[746] and the accusation of "softness" in psychiatric handling of men made neurotically ill by brutal trench warfare. It required a man of Salmon's magnitude—in the words of Strecker,[747] "psychiatrist, humanitarian . . . and gallant leader"—to forge a military psychiatry consonant with mental-hygiene principles and to alter traditional military attitudes to the extent implied in the following letter, written from France:

> I have seen guards armed with a rifle and a fixed bayonet in an observation ward but since . . . the clinical supervision of all mental cases has been placed in our hands . . . such a thing is as impossible as it would be in a pneumonia ward.[748]

Home again, Dr. Salmon, the medical director of the National Committee, with his associates pushed on with their mental-hygiene objectives. Psychiatry had meanwhile expanded, and the number of men available for special work increased. Social workers were enlisted in the campaign as a new profession of psychiatric social work arose. State mental-hygiene societies arose in many areas. Through statistical analyses, hospital surveys, assistance to community clinics and educational institutions, consultation services, legislative pressure and encouragement, and, above all, publicity, the work of mental hygiene moved forward. The decade of the 1920's witnessed mental-hygiene ideas flowing into many areas. Prominent among these was the illumination of the psychological bases of criminology. Healy's work at the Juvenile Psychopathic Institute in Chicago had opened up the terrain of genetic dynamic causes of delinquency.[749]

[745] *Ibid.*, p. 390.
[746] Strecker, E. A.: "Military Psychiatry, World War I," *in* One Hundred Years of American Psychiatry, p. 389, New York, Columbia, 1944.
[747] *Ibid.*, p. 416.
[748] Bond, E. D.: Thomas W. Salmon, Psychiatrist, p. 104, New York, Norton, 1950.
[749] Healy, William: The Individual Delinquent, Boston, Little, 1915; and Mental Conflicts and Misconduct, Boston, Little, 1917.

His findings that emotional conflict was the cause of social misdeeds stimulated other pioneer work among adult prisoners.[750] Widening concepts of criminality as behavioral expression of emotional conflicts were slowly accepted in prison clinics, detention homes, criminal courts and other institutions and agencies. Children's courts spectacularly demonstrated the place of psychiatry in delinquency. The plea of Clarence Darrow, defense attorney for two generations of wrongdoers, expressed the "current" view which the mental-hygiene movement had actively promulgated for a decade, "When public opinion accepts the belief that punishment is only cruelty, that conduct is the result of causes . . . investigation and sorting and placing of the unfortunate [offender] can be done fairly well." [751] The endeavor to provide psychotherapy for criminal offenders had slowly developed on its own out of much sporadic work which tried to read psychological meaning into antisocial behavior.[752-754] The stimulus of mental hygienists, however, was the force that gave the required social impetus to the task of applying psychotherapy to the eternal problem of crime and delinquency.[755]

The efforts of the National Committee were more closely related to the rapid evolution of the child-guidance movement, from which interest in delinquency arose. This stemmed in part from the infiltration of psychoanalytic thinking, with its stress on the infantile emotional life, into American psychiatry, and in part from the logical wish to prevent the development of emotional problems at their point of origin—childhood. When the child-guidance movement was in full motion in the 1920's, the Commonwealth Fund had established a series of fellowships in child guidance at various centers throughout the country, school departments were staffed with psychiatrists, juvenile courts assumed the burden of investigating and decreasing the emotional conflicts that underlay delinquency. Mental-hygiene instruction of teachers was being arranged, parent-teacher organizations sprang up in many communities, parents were bombarded with books devoted to psychological child care. The state mental-hygiene committees and the National Committee printed and distributed hundreds of pamphlets, taking to the home explanations and advice about daily problems among children which had hitherto been neglected or lightly

750 Glueck, Bernard: First Annual Report of Psychiatric Clinic, Sing Sing Prison, National Committee for Mental Hygiene, New York, 1917.
751 Darrow, Clarence: Crime; Its Causes and Treatment, p. 128, New York, Crowell, 1922.
752 Bromberg, Walter: Crime and the Mind, Philadelphia, Lippincott, 1948.
753 Friedlander, Kate: The Psycho-analytical Approach to Juvenile Delinquency; Theory, Case-Studies, Treatment, New York, Internat. Univ. Press, 1947.
754 Karpman, Ben: Case Studies in the Psychopathology of Crime, New York, Mental Science Publishing Co., 1939.
755 Salmon, T. W.: Some new problems for psychiatric research in delinquency, Ment. Hyg. 4:29, 1920.

regarded as concomitants of physical immaturity. Leaflets used everyday words describing everyday troubles: Habit Training in Children, The Job of the Parent, How to Treat Jealous Children, The Problem of Bedwetting, The Nervous Breakdown, How to Teach Children to be Honest, etc. Child psychology and child guidance nurtured an influence which all but revolutionized our seemingly eternal cultural attitudes toward children.

CENTURY OF THE CHILD

Paced by the feminist movement, equally active in Europe and America, a reorientation in family alignment was preparing the way for the "Century of the Child" [756] just as laws for the abolition of child labor had altered the economic-social position of children in society. Ellen Key, a Swedish feminist, calling for a new morality which would escape the man-centered ethos imposed on Western society for centuries, pleaded that the child had a right to live in a world where its personality might "receive a free self-development." In the subsequent emancipation of the child, mental hygiene played a major role.

Child Study Associations intensively studied phases of the child's development, implementing the lessons learned by parents from magazines, lectures and books.[757] Education reversed itself as parent education seemed to take precedence over education of the child.[758] The brief popularity of Watson's behaviorism added weight to the warning that parents had better watch themselves more than their offspring in matters of child rearing. Stressing the finding that responses (and, later, behavior) in the infant were, chiefly, learned behavioral responses to the parent figures in the environment, Watson advised the "modern" parent to "learn not to talk to children in endearing and coddling terms" lest dreadful neurotic conditions be initiated. "Mother love is a dangerous instrument," he wrote, "an instrument which may inflict a never-healing wound." [759] It was a time for objectivity, for careful screening out of parental emotion, for the primacy of the child.

Many social and economic factors in postwar America contributed to the ascendancy of the child and the dethronement of parents in the 1920's. The entire movement of progressive education, the accent on emotional training in schools, project methods of teaching, permissiveness and other emancipating moves in the new child life lie within the scope of a cul-

[756] Key, Ellen: The Century of the Child, translated by M. Franzos, New York, Putnam, 1909.
[757] Fisher, D. C., and Gruenberg, S. M.: Our Children, New York, Viking, 1932.
[758] Blatz, W. E., and Bott, Helen: Parents and the Pre-school Child, New York, Morrow, 1929.
[759] Watson, J. B., and Watson, R. R.: Psychological Care of Infant and Child, p. 87, New York, Norton, 1928.

tural history of the twentieth century. For our purposes, however, it may be noted that the mental-hygiene movement was a major factor in what one psychologist called the "infantilization of adults:" "America, a land where adults are preoccupied with children and themselves becoming more and more like children."[760] Not only was elementary education and child raising revamped, but physicians applied mental-hygiene concepts to their practice, as pediatricians became the first medical converts to the "cause." From child guidance the psychiatric view spread to secondary schools and colleges, represented in curricula as courses in mental hygiene and in clinical applications. At the college and university level, where a serious problem of mental illness had always existed, psychiatrists were laboring to catch incipient mental disturbances among some students and to guide others over emotional hurdles.[761] As late as 1936, one author pointed to the "broad possibilities still untapped, even unrealized" of mental hygiene among college students.[762]

But perhaps one of the most fruitful developments of the mental-hygiene movement was that of psychiatric social work. This group, interpreting the message of mental hygiene to parents of disturbed children, came in time to bridge the gap between psychiatric plans for prophylaxis of mental conditions and the actual conditions in the "field," i.e., the home, where these plans were to operate.

SOCIAL WORK IN MENTAL HYGIENE

The informal origin of psychiatric social work is traced to the stimulus of Adolf Meyer, who, while director of the Psychopathic Institute in New York, desired to learn more concerning the home life and the history of emotional antecedents of mental patterns in his hospital patients. He suggested to Mrs. Meyer that she do an unprecedented thing—visit the homes of these patients to inquire into their emotional histories and gather data as to their personality structure and illness. Later, this social investigation prepared the way for the patient's return to a more informed environment. From this move grew the after-care planning program. At the time (*circa* 1905), however, this rudimentary social work was in the service of psychiatrists in the hospital.

A sharp increase in this development was occasioned by the war emergency in 1918. At that time a course of psychiatric lectures was given to social workers at Smith College, Northampton, Massachusetts, to acquaint

760 Roback, A. A.: The Psychology of Common Sense, A Diagnosis of Modern Philistinism, Cambridge, Mass., Sci.-Art. Pub., 1939.
761 Blanton, Smiley: A mental-hygiene program for colleges, Ment. Hyg. 9:478, 1925.
762 Raphael, Theophile: The place and possibilities of the mental hygiene approach on the college level, Am. J. Psychiat. 92:855, 1936.

them with state hospital practice and experience. In the hands of pioneers like Mary C. Jarrett, head of the Social Work School, and Dr. E. E. Southard, director of the Boston Psychopathic Hospital, the field spread as mental-hygiene and psychiatric concepts lifted social work to a new professional level. The application of psychoanalytic principles and the viewpoint of dynamic interpretation enlivened the older "direct aid" types of social work. One observer stated that the National Conference for Social Work in 1920 proved to be a "landslide for psychiatry."[763] Re-examining cases of social maladjustment, which were accepted until then as misfits, the subject of bad heredity or malevolent fate, demonstrated underlying emotional problems which could conceivably be modified or eradicated by mental-hygiene attitudes.[764] Social work, which was related to direct aid or relief prior to the mental-hygiene era, seemed a sterile thing in comparison.

The new orientation revitalized casework; child placement, for example, became a procedure calling for more than a survey of the economic or the living standards of a family to whom children might be sent, or the food allowance per child in institutions for abandoned or orphaned children. This new area of psychiatric casework became a field calling for rigorous discipline and inclusive training. The therapeutic accent led to the workers' evaluating themselves and, later, personal psychoanalytic treatment. It meant also an identification with the therapeutic aims of medicine as contrasted with ameliorative aims of practical sociology. The decades 1930-1950[765] witnessed a burgeoning of the field. Training centers increased, and the application of psychiatric casework methods to patients in state hospitals, clinics, military services, welfare agencies, etc., continued actively. In this endeavor mental hygiene, child psychiatry and clinical psychology each played a stimulating role.

Meanwhile the fountainhead of mental-hygiene inspiration continued to flow. In 1928, Beers suggested that a fund-raising organization be founded, the American Foundation of Mental Hygiene, to assist the National Committee in carrying out its projects. The preamble to the Foundation's constitution reflected the continued enthusiasm of its progenitor and his associates:

> Nature has her hidden remedies for the torture of a broken mind or body, and science is on the march in search of those remedies. . . . The knowledge so gained forms a sacred trust of civilization.[766]

[763] Taft, Jessie: The new impulse in mental hygiene, Pub. Health Nurse, October, 1919.

[764] Southard, E. E., and Jarrett, M. C.: The Kingdom of Evils, New York, Macmillan, 1922.

[765] Am. J. Orthopsychiat., Vols. 1-10, 1930-1940.

[766] Beers, C. W.: *Op. cit.*, p. 348.

The "golden age" of mental hygiene coincided with the mass euphoria of the predepression prosperity of 1928:

> But mental hygiene has a message also for those who consider themselves quite normal, for, by its aim, the man who is fifty per cent efficient can make himself seventy per cent efficient; and the man seventy per cent perhaps eighty per cent; and so on.

Areas of human activity wherein mental-hygiene principles could be applied seemed to increase without limit. Since our project is restricted to tracing the therapeutic effect of the mental-hygiene movement and its influence as a catalyzer for the modern tendency to modify tensions arising within social relationships, only a few significant trends of mental-hygiene application will be surveyed. Perhaps Coleman's phrase, "participant psychiatry," [767] wherein the psychiatrist assumes the position of functional integrator in organizations, e.g., school, military service, industry, etc., serves to illustrate the responsibility and the wide scope of service toward which mental hygienists are striving.

FURTHER AREAS OF GROWTH

An interesting area of mental-hygiene application was that of industry. Programs of health maintenance and prevention of accidents in industry, which had been proving practical to management and labor alike, provided a congenial soil for the growth of mental hygiene in the larger organizations, once the notion that psychiatry belonged only within "gray walls" was dispelled. Problems of labor turnover, collective bargaining between management and labor unions, self-government plans in industries, brought to light minor personality eccentricities, sensitivities, poor adjustment capacities which fell to the industrial psychiatrist and the consulting psychologist for solution. Personnel practices and supervisory principles, directed toward specific problems in the industry, utilized the general aim of mental hygiene to reduce interpersonal friction due to less tangible yet disturbing emotional problems in individual workers. That this field is enlarging is attested by the slowly growing number of psychiatrists in industry and their publications on the subject.[768] Even the amenities and regular rest periods, now standard practices in large (and small) offices, plants and working organizations, can be traced to the humanizing influences of the mental-hygiene idea. It is quite probable that the loosening of repressive authoritarianism in the family by the head of the household and the increased freedom of children were reflected in industry and commerce in the disappearance of the repressive "ogre" type of employer. And

[767] Coleman, J. V.: "Mental Hygiene," *in* Progress in Neurology and Psychiatry, 1948-49, edited by E. A. Spiegel, Vol. 3, p. 435, New York, Grune, 1949.
[768] Group for Advancement of Psychiatry, Topeka, Kansas: Rep. No. 20, July, 1951.

here one may also mention the social-psychological influence of the softened paternalistic spirit in government during the depression and post-depression years.

The decade 1940-1950 witnessed an even more spectacular spread of psychiatric thinking and of mental-hygiene attitudes. Competent publicists like Albert Deutsch, Albert Q. Maisel, Waldemar Kaempfert and others familiarized the public with the contributions of psychiatry and mental hygiene in popular journals, in the daily press and on the radio. Many avenues for dispensing public information were utilized to strike home the lessons of psychological investigations into human reactions in health and disease. Implementation of these preventive and therapeutic ideas in the form of laws proceeded under the stimulus of the National Committee for Mental Hygiene. In 1942, the Vocational Rehabilitation Act was passed by the Congress, providing for state planning for the rehabilitation of disabled individuals. Soon after, psychiatric services were added.[769] A broadening of the benefits of mental hygiene was furthered by the passage, in 1946, of the National Mental Health Act, which provided for wider use of psychiatric skills. This Act provided for the training of personnel, research opportunities and improvement of mental-health services in the various states under the guidance of the U. S. Public Health Service.[770] Grants-in-aid were advanced to workers in the various states, a National Mental Health Institute was established in the District of Columbia, and the enormous problem of mental disease and its prevention in this country was attacked systematically. Alertness to the needs of more hospital construction throughout the country resulted in the passage, in 1946, of the Hill-Burton Act, which stimulated hospital construction in areas insufficiently supplied with medical facilities. This move also supplied a stimulus for construction of more mental hospitals and the inclusion of psychiatric facilities in general hospitals throughout the country.[771]

Medicine, led by psychosomatic physicians, became interested in mental attitudes and emotional reflections in their patients. Dentists, surgeons, obstetricians and gynecologists perceived the mental-hygiene aspects of their work. From the period when Adolf Meyer pleaded against "the absolute distinction between mental disorders to be dealt with by the teacher and moralist, and the disorders which must be left to the physician," [772] to the present, is a short period of five decades, but a universe in changing social values.

[769] The Vocational Rehabilitation Act Amendment of 1943, J.A.M.A. **123**:572, 1943.
[770] Russell, W. L.: Comment; the National Mental Health Act, Am. J. Psychiat. **103**:417, 1946.
[771] Stevenson, G. S.: Personal communication, April, 1953.
[772] Meyer, Adolf: "Promoting a Practical Interest Among Practitioners," *in* Commonsense Psychiatry, edited by Alfred Lief, New York, McGraw-Hill, 1948.

World War II brought to a focus both psychiatric trends in medicine and the infiltration of mental-health concepts into the handling of large bodies of men and women. Activity in the military services, screening neurotic, psychotic individuals, including a myriad of personality problems, became a gigantic task for the psychiatrists and the psychologists of the combatant nations. Morale problems and therapeutic tasks exercised the ingenuity of psychiatrists and their adjunctive workers in social work, psychology and personnel.[773] The stimulus of air-borne catastrophe under war conditions in Britain and other European centers, the problems of displacement of homeless refugees and countless other social-psychological problems attendant on war destruction, called upon the resources and the methods of mental hygiene. It would be beyond the purpose of this work to outline the vast accomplishments of the mental-hygiene movement which underlay these developments. It will suffice to point out that in 1950 the several organizations in America were reorganized under the title National Association for Mental Health, a commentary on the changing connotation of "hygiene" in the positive statement of "mental health."

Until his death in 1943, Beers was the spearhead of new applications and wider spread of mental-health ideas. Envisaging a world-wide movement (the Canadian National Committee for Mental Hygiene had been established in 1918), Beers laid plans for an International Congress, which became a reality in Washington, D. C., in 1930. Further work was planned, only to be interrupted by World War II. Finally, under the title of World Federation for Mental Health, thirty-three countries co-operating with the World Health Organization (under United Nations), held their first meeting in London in 1948. Addressed to "administrators, workers in social sciences, in psychiatry, medicine and allied professions, and to thinking people everywhere,"[774] the International Preparatory Commission asked the profound question: "Can catastrophe of a third world war be averted? Can the people of the world learn to co-operate for the good of all? On what basis is there hope for enduring Peace?" Their provisional answer was, "Perhaps the most important contribution of the social sciences in their joint approach . . . is the recognition of the plasticity of human behavior."

The impetus to explore the findings of social sciences, to improve human relations, has become an insistent force in the World Health Organization and its subsidary committees. The knowledge psychiatrists gained and the cross-fertilization of related fields have made realistic the plea of Dr. Brock Chisholm, executive secretary of the Interim Commission, World Health Organization, that those concerned with international affairs have a personal

773 Schreiber, Julius: Psychological training and orientation of soldiers, Ment. Hyg. 28:537, 1944.

774 International Preparatory Commission, International Congress on Mental Health, London, H. K. Lewis, August, 1948, p. 5.

responsibility, along with mental hygienists, for a co-ordinated attack on world problems of interrelationship.[775]

As the membership of the World Health Organization—comprising men from the satellite nations, the U.S.S.R., the entire Western world and the Orient—found, these world problems are, in the last analysis, questions of understanding. The uniting of the peoples of the world in a great, benevolent community devoted to human progress, the plea of reformers and idealists for centuries, is being implemented as a practical reality through mental-hygiene concepts.

Incredible as this aspiration may appear on the surface, it has roots in a very real social situation. Just as the technology and the industrial revolution of the past two centuries changed the "social values" under which men lived, so a new revolution has been created which reassesses human value in relation to the spread of psychological findings. The mental-hygiene movement in all its ramifications has "been drawn into this power vacuum" which will guide the evolution of new social values attendant upon this century's "attention on the inner life." [776] The concept of preventing mental illness, an inspiration which burned in the mind of Beers as he emerged from his third hospital commitment, is being achieved. The concept of prevention was couched in terms of the individual, but, because of the democratic nature of the movement, it has fanned out to include all of society. For slowly and inexorably this psychological century is orienting its institutions and cultural patterns around the needs and the satisfactions of the whole social man. In this connection it is interesting to note that mental hygiene in the Soviet Union carries an overwhelmingly social connotation. Mental hygienists use slogans, as "Healthy Nerves," "United Front for the Establishment of New Healthy Society," and so on.[777] Here mental hygiene is viewed as a "continual adjustment in a rapidly changing" society, based on the ability to "co-ordinate . . . in the building of a new socialist society." [778]

Of necessity mental hygiene, the idea, is inspirational and idealistic even though the implementation is practical. Of necessity it is wide in its coverage, being a movement for improved care of the mentally ill, a social psychiatry, a science of behavior, a cult of living for some, a form of social action, a process of education and a system of ethics for healthy living.[779]

[775] Chisholm, Brock: Organization for world health, Ment. Hyg. 32:364, 1948.

[776] Seeley, J. R.: Social Values, The Mental Health Movement and Mental Health, Annals of American Academy of Political and Social Science, Philadelphia, March, 1953, p. 15.

[777] Zacharoff, Lucien: Mental hygiene in Soviet industry, Ment. Hyg. 15:522, 1931.

[778] Pinkevitch, A.: *Quoted in* Sigerist, H. E.: Socialized Medicine in the Soviet Union, p. 268, New York, Norton, 1937.

[779] Kramer, Ralph: Attitudes and action in mental hygiene, Bull. Ment. Health Soc. Northern California, 1953.

It is indeed a pragmatic test of the "validity of an idea." [780] Yet out of its substance the stimulus of mental hygiene will tend to merge into the processes of life and living. It shares with all scientific discoveries the quality of losing itself as an identifiable element in its result. The eloquent statement of Meyer's credo [781] implies the life history of the mental-hygiene idea, conceived as psychotherapy:

> We see ourselves as organisms that rise and bloom and pass and do their best under the ideal of ultimately making themselves in a way unnecessary through their own achievements. . . . So it is with medicine. The goal of medicine is peculiarly the goal of making itself unnecessary; of influencing life so that what is medicine to-day will become mere common sense to-morrow or at least with the next generation. The efforts of the worker of to-day become so assimilated in the common sense of to-morrow that it must be our pride to see that it has passed into the real objective nature of the world about us, no longer burdening our attention, but allowing us or those after us to do the same for ever new problems, with ever new achievements and satisfactions.

[780] Schreiber, Julius: Personal communication, 1951.
[781] Meyer, Adolf: The "complaint" as the center of genetic-dynamic and nosological teaching in psychiatry, New England J. Med. 199:360, 1928.

11

The Return of Physiology

While social psychiatry and the mental-hygiene movement were extending into fields neighboring on psychiatry, medicine itself was slowly taking up the torch with which to illuminate the dark shadow of mental disease. From the second decade of this century, the tempo of physiologic research in methods for treating the mentally and the nervously ill matched, to an increasing degree, the wide activities of psychological medicine. Psychiatry, the Cinderella of medicine, was taken into the medical household and refitted with the methodology of clinical experimentation. Empiricism and objectivity toward psychic events were added to psychiatry's more intuitive and subjective approach. At first contemporaneously, and quite recently synchronously, the two disciplines of physiology and psychology have bent some of their interests and energies to the same elusive problem of successful psychotherapy. The co-ordinated attack has been a scientific advance, for, although contemporaneity of methodologies has been characteristic of medicine throughout its history, the concept of converging, co-operative scientific interest has been the hallmark of recent predominance of technology in human affairs.

Earlier, contemporaneity in mental treatment was more apt to be the rule. When the value of depleting medicines and bloodletting was extolled in the early 1800's in one quarter, in another men were relying on the "bland arts of conciliation." When the neurologists of the 1880's were employing spine-stimulating medications such as strychnine and electric current over the skull and the spinal column, others considered suggestion to be the only force worth its salt in psychotherapy. In this century, while insulin and shock treatment were being pushed as the most promising method of treatment for mental illness yet devised, psychoanalysis and various types of dynamic psychotherapy were being refined and intensified in their technical application. Some therapists have used both physiologic and psychological methods, daring to run counter to the charge of eclecticism, one of medicine's taboos. However ineffective or even obstructive eclecticism has been in the production of scientific theory, the attempt to modify the tenacious symptoms of nervous and mental disorders justifies the use of any group of technics. For therapy is the *raison d'être* of medicine. While it is true that theoretical constructs have followed therapeutic expedient, it is conversely true that scientific theory has nourished further therapeutic efforts. We cannot deny that the reciprocal relation between therapeutic method and scientific understanding and control has enabled psychotherapy to grow; nevertheless, the object of all this activity is therapy. Nor can it be successfully contradicted that in the intensely subjective area of psychiatry a basic therapeutic empiricism, refined by testing, controlling and hypothecating, rests its case on the reactions of the recipients of treatment—the patients themselves.

It is a historical commonplace to say that many treatment methods for mental disturbances have proved successful, no matter how crass or crude they appeared to contemporary critics insisting on the need for scientific verification, or how amusing they may have appeared in retrospect to subsequent generations. More accurately stated, a succession of therapeutic methods has reduced the discomfort of patients and the anxiety of relatives (and physicians), which, when measured by scientific standards rather than by the variables and the imponderables comprising the patient's subjectivity, appeared to promise little predictable success. In the general area of psychological therapy from about 1910 onward, the freudian metapsychology has had a tendency to unify dynamic psychotherapeutic technics on the basic principles of transference and the enucleation of pathogenic unconscious experiences or memories. In the physical sphere, however, the chief guides were principles derived from medicine and neurology. For example, electricity, which had a wide vogue in the nineteenth century, followed much authenticated work in muscle, nerve physiology. Advances in chemistry and bacteriology were responsible for other new departures in treatment. Neurosurgical methods of treatment were built in part on neuro-anatomy, neurophysiology and physics. In the main, however, the common denominator for physical methods has been empiricism evoked by the patient's need for relief.

BRAIN FATIGUE AND BRAIN DAMAGE—BASIS FOR THERAPY

To return to our narrative, as discussed in Chapter 5, physiologic treatment in asylums during the nineteenth century was "supportive." This included narcotics, diet, soporifics, hydrotherapy, diversion (occupational therapy) and surgery for appropriate conditions. Accent on the theory of malnutrition or toxicity of nerve cells as the cause of "spinal neurosis" and neurasthenia tended to popularize treatment which met the needs of depleted nervous system cells.[782] The concept of stimulating or feeding de-

[782] Cowles, Edward: The advancement of psychiatry in America, Proc. Am. Psychol. A. 2:47, 1896.

pleted brain cells rested on the rationale that exhausted cells were more prone to abnormal mental performance, a true "psycho-asthenia." Hence phosphates, ergot, koumiss, caffeine, cocoa and milk were prescribed in the Rest Cure. To this group of stimulants or stimulations belong vitamins, concentrated foods and, more recently, glutamic acid,[783] a complex amino acid which is alleged to improve specifically the function of cortical cells.

The period of neuropathologic research brought in its train wide differences in theories of treatment based on cell pathology. In 1895, Cowles wrote, "Advances in histology are so marvelous and rapid that the student of five years ago must recast his conceptions of physiology and pathology of the nervous system." The rapid reorientation in neuropsychiatric thinking was foreseen by Beard,[784] who insisted on a "total attack" rather than a program aimed at reviving nerve cells in treatment. To "produce a change in the patient's constitution" in the effective cure of neurasthenia, more than tonics, electricity and rest were required.

The reflection of extensive neuropathologic study in therapy has retained its nutritional accent to the present time. With the rapid advance in our understanding of proteins, amino acids and vitamins and minerals in the processes of metabolism, there has remained a tacit assumption of the value of nourishment to the nervous system in treating mental or nervous cases. This area of physiologic treatment has passed into nursing, home economics and common domestic folklore, to witness the appreciation of the brain-feeding qualities of certain foods, e.g., "Fish is good for your brains," or, in time of bereavement, "Eat and you'll feel better." It was a simple extension of the concept of nervous exhaustion to state that "errors in diet or other departures from physiologic laws" were a true cause of functional nervous disease. Since neurotics wasted their energy in worry, and energy was intimately related to food, advice of a popular medical nature included dietary injunctions, "Don't worry—take a neural bath at bedtime, eat biologically, abjure tea and coffee, move the bowels three times a day and cheer UP." [785]

The concern of neuropsychiatrists, however, was more closely related to diseases in which the damaged cellular elements in the nervous system could be resuscitated or modified to improve function. With demonstrable neuropathology as a scientific foundation, attention turned to methods of treatment that lay closer to the psychophysical interaction theory of body-mind activity. Von Jauregg's method of treating general paralysis with malarial

[783] Zimmerman, F. T., Burgemeister, B. B., Putnam, T. J.: The ceiling effect of glutamic acid upon intelligence in children and in adolescents, Am. J. Psychiat. 104:593, 1948.

[784] Beard, G. M.: A Practical Treatise on Nervous Exhaustion (Neurasthenia), p. 178, New York, Wood, 1880.

[785] Kellogg, J. H.: Neurasthenia, or, Nervous Exhaustion, p. 21, Battle Creek, Mich., Good Health Pub. Co., 1915.

blood belonged in this general theoretical framework. The therapeutic difficulty presented by progressive brain diseases, as general paresis, for example, had been immeasurably reduced by the final demonstration, in 1913, by Noguchi and Moore that syphilitic organisms were responsible for the brain destruction. In 1912, salvarsan, which had been introduced as a specific for syphilis several years before, was injected directly into the spinal canal by Swift and Ellis.[786] Following early attempts to treat nervous-system involvement of syphilis with tuberculin (1890), von Jauregg[787] announced in 1917, from the University of Vienna Clinic, the beneficial results from fever reactions occasioned by the inoculation of a strain of tertian malaria via the blood.[788] Neymann[789] states that the method of inoculating mental patients with typhus and malarial blood was surreptitiously used by Rozenblum in Russia as early as 1876, and obscurely published in 1880. In any event, von Jauregg's work was a great advance in the treatment of the invariably fatal disease, paresis, and was so accepted throughout the medical world. In the Western hemisphere, it was first used in 1922 at Saint Elizabeths Hospital, Washington, D. C.[790]

Special studies were conducted at various institutes, particularly New York Psychiatric Institute, under the direction of George H. Kirby[791] and his associates.[792] The response of psychotic patients to malaria showed remission in about 25 per cent of the cases. Cessation of the action of the micro-organism in the brain tissue due to the fever was conceded to be the mode of curative action. Malarial treatment of luetic infections was followed by methods which developed fever in other ways, by relapsing fever inoculation, various types of vaccine (streptococcic and typhoid organisms), types of foreign protein (milk, horse serum), etc. With the exception of malarial inoculation, which could be controlled by quinine, hyperpyrexial measures were not standardizable. For this reason fever production in baths and electric cabinets[793] was substituted. The results in fever therapy of neuropsychiatric conditions other than paresis did not justify further experimentation. Nevertheless, therapeutic tests were continued in the hope of producing artificial inflammatory reactions within the nervous system following injection

[786] Swift and Ellis: The direct treatment of syphilitic diseases of the central nervous system, New York State J. Med. 96:53, 1912.

[787] Note: Treatment of paresis by malaria, Am. J. Psychiat. 79:721, 1923.

[788] Wagner-Jauregg, J.: Treatment of paresis by malaria (translated), J. Nerv. & Ment. Dis. 55:369, 1922.

[789] Neymann, C. A.: The effect of artificial fever on the clinical manifestations of syphilis and the *Treponema pallidum*, Am. J. Psychiat. 93:517, 1936.

[790] Overholser, Winfred: Personal communication.

[791] Kirby, G. H., and Bunker, H. A.: Types of therapeutic response observed in the malaria treatment of general paralysis, Am. J. Psychiat. 6:205, 1926.

[792] Hinsie, L. E., and Blalock, J. R.: Treatment of general paralysis; results in 197 cases treated from 1923-1926, Am. J. Psychiat. 11:541, 1931.

[793] Neymann, C. A.: Artificial Fever, Baltimore, Thomas, 1938.

of sterile horse serum into the spinal canal.[794] The aseptic meningitis so developed, in the original work of Carroll (1923),[795] was based on the theory, or rather the wish, that "an injured choroid interfered with normal chemotaxis and . . . perchance dementia praecox might prove a food-chemical deprivation, rather than a toxic destructive process."

In general, this group of stimulating treatment procedures embodied the concept of a reactive influence on the part of the cerebral tissues to a foreign irritant with resulting body defensive mechanism activity. The nature of this reaction was, of course, unknown, but work of this type stimulated careful study of body-mind interactionism in relation to "organic" mental disease. Ferenczi and Hollos,[796] Hungarian psychiatrists, found, for example, that personality deterioration in general paresis cases, even in the presence of destruction of brain cells, represented a reaction to changes in unconscious libido distribution within the ego. Further studies in this direction by Schilder [797] brought further elucidation of the body-mind problem. The waning intellectual function and inadequacy of perception and memory, common in the clinical picture of organic psychotics, arouse an unconscious ego reaction; hence depression or euphoria appeared. It was not a point-for-point deterioration, wherein so much destruction or toxic injury to brain cells developed so much dementia or mania in the clinical picture, but an unconscious reaction of the intact part of the ego against perception of impoverished function induced by brain destruction.

The introduction of a psychoanalytic orientation to the understanding of organic brain diseases obviated the necessity of supporting solely the impoverished cell in therapy of these conditions. Also, it made more intelligible therapeutic attempts to alter chemically or physically mental disorders considered until then to be irreversible. This re-evaluation of psyche-soma interaction contributed a conceptual background for work in the shock therapies to be discussed later. In this period, the 1920's, it brought the physiologic and the psychological approaches into operational acquaintance. But this acquaintanceship did not determine which way physiologic methods would move. The general effect was to confer greater dignity on the empirical physiologic approach to mental disease.

[794] Carroll, R. S., Barr, E. S., Barry, R. G., and Matzke, David: Aseptic meningitis in the treatment of dementia praecox, Am. J. Psychiat. 4:673, 1926.
Kubitschek, P. E., and Carmichael, F. A.: Experimental aseptic meningitis: therapeutic and clinical studies, Am. J. Psychiat. 8:97, 1928.

[795] Carroll, R. S.: Aseptic meningitis in combating the dementia praecox problem, New York M. J. 118:407, 1923.

[796] Ferenczi and Hollos: Zur Psychoanalyse der paralytischen Geistesstörung, Beihefte zur int. Ztschr. f. PsA. Nr. 5.

[797] Schilder, Paul: Introduction to a Psychoanalytic Psychiatry, translated by Bernard Glueck, New York, Nerv. & Ment. Dis. Pub. Co., 1928.

PHYSIOLOGIC ALTERATIONS—BASIS FOR THERAPY

A more direct influence upon the physical substrate of mental disease was implied in a number of therapeutic experiments with narcotic drugs which are utilized clinically at the present time. Here a strong sedative of the barbiturate or opium derivative group was used to place the patient in a state of unconsciousness for periods ranging from hours to days. The patient was awakened to carry on bodily functions, but otherwise lay in a coma for that period of time. It was early recognized, with the narcosis treatment, that the accompanying ventilation of psychological conflicts lying behind the psychosis was essential; direct influence of cortical function was a means to an end, a means to reduce excitement or remove stuporous reactions. The medications employed differed widely: in Germany, Kläsi (1922) [798] used Somnifene; in Switzerland, Oberholzer (1925), Luminal or other barbiturates. The aim was the induction of prolonged unconsciousness which approached normal profound sleep. The mechanism of recovery was clearly more psychological than biochemical. Narcosis therapy rapidly attained adherents in this country as it showed practical results. Negativistic and catatonic patients began to eat under the influence of the sleep state, and chronic patients were reported to be much improved; 80 per cent cures were reported in one series of cases. Modifications were introduced in the sedative drug employed (particularly Amytal),[799] with the general finding that such narcosis had a profound effect not only in reducing agitation of manics and catatonics but in decreasing self-absorption and increasing the possibility of friendly contact. In seriously disturbed patients, "a period of normal existence" followed administration of the drug. Moreover, autism was markedly decreased, and the basic psychodynamics responsible for the illness became accessible.[800]

The further development of narcotic treatment has been extended to the use of Pentothal in what is known as narcoanalysis or narcosuggestive therapy. This was discussed in its psychological aspects in a previous chapter. Early in World War II, under pressure of catastrophic events, as the London bombing raids and the evacuation of Dunkirk, British psychiatrists employed heavy sedation with paraldehyde or barbiturates for acute war hysterias.[801] The slow injection of the drug gave immediate relief for a limited time. Uncovering buried traumatic memories through suggestion was fol-

798 Kläsi, J., and Oberholzer, W.: *Quoted in* Palmer, H. D., and Paine, A. L.: Prolonged narcosis as therapy in the psychoses, Am. J. Psychiat. 12:143, 1932.

799 Bleckwenn, W. J.: Production of sleep and rest in psychotic cases, Arch. Neurol. & Psychiat. 24:365, 1930.

800 Palmer, H. D., and Braceland, F. J.: Six years experience with narcosis therapy in psychiatry, Am. J. Psychiat. 94:37, 1937.

801 Sargant, William: Physical treatment of acute war neuroses, Brit. M. J. 2:574, 1942.

lowed by re-education and explanation; in this way the experiences of the patient were synthesized into his life situation. The method of the Americans Bleckwenn and Lorenz (the "drug-analytic" method) in the hands of British psychiatrists broadened to become narcoanalysis.[802] Recent practice emphasizes the simultaneous use of several means of psychic exploration with sedative drug therapy.

A somewhat different theory underlay the "twilight state" (Dämmerzustand) which increased rapport and freed inhibitions.[803] For this, gases such as carbon dioxide, oxygen or nitrogen were used. In this instance it was hoped that anoxia, a decrease in oxygen available for brain-cell metabolism, would reverse and possibly modify brain function and, hence, mental activity. Experimentation with gases, originated by Loevenhart [804] and Langenstrass,[805] resulted in direct but temporary improvement among stuporous schizophrenics or other types of inaccessible patients. For this reason, psychotherapeutic suggestions were added, treating the patient as if he were in "a transient state of hypnosis." For induction, nitrogen in the form of nitrous oxide was substituted.[806] This treatment was soon extended to neurotic patients [807] in addition to stuporous cases, on the general theory that a "shock" affect would produce disinhibition of rigid and inaccessible individuals.[808] Treatment of the "hyper-ventilation syndrome," a frequent finding among hysterical and anxiety patients, utilizes the same principles as gas narcosis. Rebreathing into a paper sack decreases the symptoms of lightheadedness, anxiety and panic consequent upon alkalosis by increasing carbon dioxide [809] content of the blood and, ultimately, of the brain.

Modification of the chemical environment of the brain and the processes of oxidation of the brain tissue have been the subject of a thorough study by physiologists during the last two decades. This work,[810] the theoretical basis of experiments with gas narcosis, also underlay a varied series of attempts to alter chemical processes in the brain through chemical agents. Of

[802] Horsley, J. Stephen: Narco-analysis; A New Technique in Short-Cut Psychotherapy, London, Oxford, 1943.

[803] Broder, S. B.: Sleep induced by Sodium Amytal, an abridged method for use in mental illness, Am. J. Psychiat. 93:57, 1936.

[804] Loevenhart, A. S., Lorenz, W. F., and Waters, R. M.: Cerebral stimulation, J.A.M.A. 92:880, 1929.

[805] Langenstrass, K. H.: Treatment of stupor, Am. J. Psychiat. 11:447, 1931.

[806] Alexander, F. A. D., and Himwich, H. E.: Nitrogen inhalation therapy for schizophrenia, Am. J. Psychiat. 96:643, 1939.

[807] Meduna, von, L. J.: Pharmaco-dynamic treatment of psychoneuroses, Dis. Nerv. System 8:37, 1947.

[808] Lehmann, H., and Bos, C.: The advantages of nitrous oxide inhalation in psychiatric treatment, Am. J. Psychiat. 104:164, 1947.

[809] Carryer, H. M.: The hyperventilation syndrome, M. Clin. North America 31:845, 1947.

[810] Kalinowsky, L. B., and Hoch, P. H.: Shock Treatments, Psychosurgery, and Other Somatic Treatments in Psychiatry, ed. 2, Chap. 7, New York, Grune, 1952.

this group, Benzedrine, Dilantin, histamine, malononitrile, Tolserol, vitamins and other alternatives of cerebral physiology have been tried on various theoretical levels. Thus Benzedrine was introduced for its stimulating effect,[811] histamine because it produced vasodilation,[812] and malononitrile (the work of Swedish physiologists) for its increase in neucleoproteins within ganglion cells.

Medical measures used to influence symptoms of mental illnesses have been legion. Based on the supposition that emotional illnesses may be due to sympathetic nervous system dysfunction, several workers introduced medications in an effort to restore this balance. Thus, ergotamine tartrate was given a group of men suffering from battle reaction (war neurosis) to attempt to stem the troublesome parasympathetic symptoms.[813] On one extreme are attempts such as that of Petit, who injected intravenously radioactive substances (thorium) in cases of dementia praecox or melancholia,[814] while on the other is the use of salt-free diet in the treatment of insomnia.[815] Allied to these therapeutic assays into the unknown is the fascinating field of artificial psychoses produced by various drugs, on the supposition that the synthetic formation of mental states may lead to discovery of rational measures for their treatment. Psychopathologic changes induced by such drugs as mescaline, *Cannabis indica* (hashish, marihuana) in their action on the mid-brain, the cortex and the basal ganglia, resembling schizophrenic reactions, have been amply studied.[816] Perception changes of motility, Gestalt function, the body-image and alterations in personality reactions generally, with particular reference to impulsiveness and aggression, follow use of these drugs.[817] Fascinating changes in time perception, perceptual disintegration of visual, tactile, auditory and proprioceptive experiences in the drugged subject have been known by experimentalists since the days of Weir Mitchell and William

[811] Davidoff, Eugene, and Reifenstein, E. C., Jr.: The results of eighteen months of Benzedrine Sulfate therapy in psychiatry, Am. J. Psychiat. 95:945, 1939.

[812] Marshall, W., and Tarwater, J. S.: Use of histamine phosphate and peptone solution in the treatment of neuroses and psychoses, J. Nerv. & Ment. Dis. 88:36, 1938.
Sackler, A. M., Sackler, M. D., and Sackler, R. R.: Nonconvulsive biochemotherapy with histamine and electric convulsive therapy, J. Nerv. & Ment. Dis. **110**:185, 1949.

[813] Heath, R. G., and Powdermaker, Florence: The use of ergotamine tartrate as a remedy for "battle reaction," J.A.M.A. **125**:111, 1944.

[814] Petit, Gabriel: Curiethérapie des psychoses, Bull. Acad. de méd. **109**:225, 1933.

[815] Miller, M. M.: Cutting down salt in diet relieves sleeplessness, Science News Letter, May 27, 1944, p. 343.

[816] Lindemann, Erich, and Malamud, W.: Experimental analysis of the psychopathological effects of intoxicating drugs, Am. J. Psychiat. 13:853, 1934.

[817] Bromberg, Walter: Marihuana intoxication; a clinical study of *Cannabis sativa* intoxication, Am. J. Psychiat. 91:303, 1934.

James. More recent workers,[818, 819] repeating these observations of schizophreniclike and depersonalization symptoms in patients, have not, however, been able to find a place for these drugs in the therapy of mental conditions.

Undoubtedly these profound effects of perceptive disintegration occurring in varying degrees among users of alcohol, opium derivatives and marihuana have been unwittingly utilized in self-medication by neurotic and psychopathic individuals. Whether consumed for hedonistic purposes or for their mood-lifting effects, the specific body-image distortions of these drugs exert a powerful therapeutic effect on addicts or occasional users. That these unpredictable but powerful psychotherapeutic agents have a widespread nonprescribed vogue, either socially sanctioned or illegitimate, does not exclude them from our consideration, for self-medication through alcohol and the common forms of sedative drugs is probably the most frequent type of physiologic psychotherapy.

The question of sedation has occupied the major attention of physicians in the therapy of mental disorders from the days of Hippocrates. Sedation for mental patients has been limited only by the diligence of herb-gatherers in ancient days, by the versatility of apothecaries in more recent times and by today's gigantic pharmaceutical industry. Relatively few physicians encountered in the medical writings which we have surveyed have failed to mention drugs which quieted the disturbed or suppressed the unruly. From opium to hellebore and nepenthe, bromides and chloral, to the infinite array of barbiturate compounds of today, sedation has been the mainstay of physicians in dealing with nervous afflictions. The vast powers imputed to sedatives psychologically and their actual physical influence on mental distress, from the patient point of view, would far outweigh all other methods in frequency of use. Psychological and physiologic methods of treatment which have been described in this volume represent a mercator projection upon the total surface of psychiatric treatment when viewed quantitatively, for self-medication with sedatives and homespun "talking out" of emotional tensions constitute the overwhelmingly largest groups of applied psychotherapeutic methods. However, medicine's interest and devotion have been to treatment methods applicable for illnesses beyond the range of self-medication, which, moreover, are controllable and standardizable. It is a fact rarely commented upon that an almost unnoticed conflict is in continual progress between the layman's wish for a blanket drug temporarily to still his anxieties or tensions and psychiatry's aim permanently to alter these emotional disturbances. That is why psychiatrists have persisted in searching for a therapeutic principle which would decisively alter the mental disorder presented by the patient.

[818] Kluver, H.: Mescal, The Divine Plant, London, Psyche Miniatures, London, Kegan, Paul & Co., 1928.

[819] Beringer, K.: Der Mescalinrausch, Berlin, J. Springer, 1927.

GLANDULAR AND BIOCHEMICAL CHANGES—BASIS FOR THERAPY

Such a principle underlay the vogue attending the use of endocrine-gland extracts for mental patients in the early decades of this century. The relationship between mental illness and thyroid deficiency, known for an extended period, indicated the wisdom of thyroid medication [820] and, later, ovarian [821] and testicular hormones for depressions and involutional melancholias. The Aschner treatment, which resurrected some of the older methods of drastic purging, also utilized thyroid and corpus luteum glandular preparations in depressions among women.[822] During the period of enthusiasm for glandular treatment in medicine generally, the "misbehaving ductless glands" [823] were looked to for solution of many of the secrets of nervous disorders. Although no magical relationship was discovered between ovarian, testicular, pituitary, thyroid or adrenal-gland extracts and a wide variety of mental disturbances, these substances, refined and concentrated in recent years, continue to be used, particularly in depressive conditions. In the same sense of substitutive therapy, vitamin E has been experimented with in various neuropsychiatric conditions.[824]

Another accepted medical procedure, the removal of focal infections, became the basis for a surgical treatment method that aspired to underwrite a new theory of the cause of mental illness. In the 1920's the discovery that infections in the teeth, the nasal sinuses, the tonsils, the abdominal or the pelvic organs were the causes of many obscure, generalized illnesses was turned to account with mental patients by Henry Cotton at the State Hospital in Trenton, New Jersey.[825] He reported 80 per cent cures in patients in whom foci of infection were removed. The success of his work induced Cotton to re-evaluate the functional psychoses as disturbances "arising from circulating toxins originating in chronic foci of infection." Indeed, mental illness itself was considered merely as a symptom of a "toxemia which acts directly on the brain." Although removal of focal infections did improve

[820] Hoskins, R. G., and Sleeper, F. H.: The thyroid factor in dementia praecox, Am. J. Psychiat. **10**:411, 1930.

[821] Bowman, Karl, and Bender, Lauretta: The treatment of involution melancholia with ovarian hormone, Am. J. Psychiat. **11**:867, 1932.

[822] Appel, K. E., Farr, C. B., and Braceland, F. J.: The Aschner treatment of schizophrenia; a therapeutic note, Am. J. Psychiat. **92**:201, 1935.

[823] Spaulding, E. R.: The importance of endocrine therapy in combination with mental analysis in the treatment of certain cases of personality deviation, Am. J. Psychiat. **1**:373-384, 1922.

[824] Stone, Simon: Evaluation of vitamin E therapy in psychiatric disorders, Dis. Nerv. System **11**:355, 1950.

[825] Cotton, H. A.: The etiology and treatment of the so-called functional psychoses; summary of results based upon the experience of four years, Am. J. Psychiat. **2**:157, 1922.

the general health of some patients, a careful analysis at the New York Institute [826] disproved the causal relation of body infection to mental disease in a controlled group of patients and relegated the treatment to a medical routine adopted by every well-run mental institution.

The search for a treatment method which would favorably influence the physical substrate of functional mental disorders continued. Each new group of empirical therapeutic tests seemed to promise, by its reported high percentage of cures, that the eventual goal had been reached. But subsequent studies did not always support claims of high therapeutic efficiency. Apparently enthusiasm on the part of the medical worker and its transference to his patient are factors in the therapeutic equation of new treatment methods. These factors, difficult of assessment, have not been analyzed in estimating the success of a therapy, except to lump them under the head of "psychological effect," which relieved the investigator of social psychological concern, allowing him to turn to the all-absorbing task of finding a physiologic or a biochemical method which would radically alter disordered mental processes. It is a clinical axiom that enthusiasm of the physician often communicates itself to the patient when a new method of treatment is tried in a chronically resistive medical problem. Enthusiasm is undoubtedly a potent factor in the success of a new treatment procedure. The nature of enthusiasm, only a part of which embodies generalized faith in scientific endeavors, needs to be studied if the assessment of factors in psychotherapeutic success is sought.

The uncalibrated factor of optimism, assumed or inherent, in the proponent of every new treatment process operating on the psychic organization of the patient is not completely a "transference" phenomenon from patient to physician as is commonly stated. In part, theraputic optimism embodies participation in a scientific social-ego ideal that identifies any scientific work with progress; in part, it involves faith in change, any degree of change, consequent upon medical intervention in body-mind processes. But whatever the precise psychological factors in optimism, the intensity of this feeling is greatest in both physician and patient upon introduction of a new treatment. It was to be expected that the inauguration of insulin and electric-shock therapy would bring a new increment of enthusiasm and vigor to the psychological attack on psychotherapy. As summarized by Kalinowsky and Hoch in 1951,[827] "The pharmacologic and biochemical approach to the treatment of psychiatric disorders with or without psychotherapy, is the most promising one."

[826] Kopeloff, N., and Cheney, C. O.: Studies in focal infection: its presence and elimination in the functional psychoses, Am. J. Psychiat. 2:139, 1922.
[827] Kalinowsky, L. B., and Hoch, P. H.: *Op. cit.*, p. 274.

THE METHODS OF INSULIN AND ELECTRIC SHOCK

The outstanding contribution of the past two decades was the hypoglycemic treatment method, originated by Manfred Sakel, of Vienna. In treating morphine addicts for withdrawal symptoms, Sakel, as early as 1930, noted a profound beneficial effect on certain schizoid characters among the addicts due to the insulin effect. He reasoned that an increase in insulin dosage might result in major personality changes among schizophrenic patients.[828] Experiments were initiated in bringing these patients to a state of coma, induced by lowered blood sugar following large doses of insulin. Profound physical changes, sweating, convulsive movements, pallor, coma and epileptic seizures resulted. When patients regained consciousness following administration of sugar to overcome the insulin effect, they showed mental clarity and relief from many of their delusional experiences. Sakel's method was recognized immediately as a most significant development, since a change in the chemical environment of the brain cells evoked definite observable alterations in mentation and mood in patients brought back from the hypoglycemic state. The treatment results were so striking among patients hitherto inaccessible that Sakel's method was hailed as a great advance and put into practice in many clinics throughout the world. Original work done by Sakel at the University of Vienna Clinic was continued in this country in various psychiatric and state hospitals, particularly New York, in association with Joseph Wortis, at Bellevue Hospital. By 1937, at the Congress of the Swiss Psychiatric Association,[829] representatives of European countries reported their already extensive experiences with insulin and other shock-producing methods. Within three or four years there appeared an enormous number of papers reporting results in hypoglycemic treatment with insulin.

Early reports of therapy indicated a level of from 70 to 88 per cent cures in cases recently ill.[830] When schizophrenic patients whose illness had lasted more than a year were treated, the rate of remission of the illness after insulin therapy dropped to from 40 to 50 per cent. Early experiences pointed toward insulin shock treatment as a specific for schizophrenia, and the press gave prominence to the new treatment in their science reports. *Time* put it in layman's language, "The Sakel cure is complicated, difficult and dangerous because the patient must die of insulin

[828] Sakel, Manfred: Zur Methodik der Hypoglykämiebehandlung von Psychosen, Wien. klin. Wchnschr. 49:1278, 1936; A new treatment of schizophrenia, Am. J. Psychiat. 93:829, 1937.

[829] ———: The nature and origin of the hypoglycemic treatment of psychoses, Am. J. Psychiat. (Suppl.) 94:24, 1938 (Proc. 89th Meet. Swiss Psychiatric Association, 1937, translated by S. Katenelbogen).

[830] Müller, M.: The insulin therapy of schizophrenia, Am. J. Psychiat. (Suppl.) 94:5, 1938.

shock several times before he can collect and use his wits like a normal human being." [831] Follow-up studies indicated less satisfactory results over a period of years than originally reported, but the indications were clear that schizophrenic patients showed gratifying immediate responses to treatment and were more quickly released from the hospital following treatment.[832] Technical modifications in treatment, details of method, number of comas, depth of coma attained, quantity of insulin used, factors assisting successful therapy and reported results have been summarized fully from the large world literature by Kalinowsky and Hoch. It would be merely repetitive to recount their excellent compilation. Insulin therapy has found a place for itself in routine treatment of major psychoses, especially when combined with other forms of shock treatment.

A valuable modification has been the use of subshock insulin treatment, wherein a dose smaller than a coma-producing one achieves a moderate hypoglycemia relieving tension state, mild depressions and transitory psychoses. Small doses of insulin result in a better contact with the patient, allowing for further psychotherapy and physical improvement such as an increase in appetite and a sense of well-being.

Almost simultaneous with the launching of insulin treatment was the discovery and the development of Metrazol and electric-shock therapy. The stimulant drug Metrazol [833] was introduced in 1935 by the Hungarian psychiatrist von Meduna, and electric shock, in 1937-1938, by Bini and Cerletti.[834] Whereas Sakel's origination of insulin was a clinical empirical procedure, von Meduna introduced Cardiazol (Metrazol) therapy on the deductive basis of antagonism between epilepsy and schizophrenia. Electric shock developed following animal experimentation, demonstrating reversible changes in animals on the passage of an electric current through the brain. The drug Metrazol was injected into the blood stream, whereas the technic of electric shock depended on the designing of a compact machine which would deliver a variable but safely tolerated quantity of electric current through the patient's brain. Insulin treatment required a hospital setting, nursing service and at least five hours per treatment of close supervision; Metrazol and electroshock called for briefer care and less extensive preparation and supervision of the patient. After much clinical experimentation, the chemical method of shock production (Metrazol) originated by von Meduna was rejected in favor of electric-shock treatment for cogent reasons, namely, the initial anxiety which the patient experienced, the possibility of fractures following the convulsion, and the unpredictability of

[831] Insulin for insanity, Time 29:28, March 25, 1937.

[832] Kalinowsky, L. B., and Hoch, P. H.: *Op. cit.*

[833] Meduna, von, Ladislaus: General discussion of Cardiazol therapy, Am. J. Psychiat. (Suppl.) 94:40, 1938.

[834] Bini, L.: Experimental researches on epileptic attacks induced by the electric current, Am. J. Psychiat. (Suppl.) 94:172, 1938.

convulsion. Electric shock produced an amnesia for the brief period prior to the convulsion and thus wiped out the anxiety-producing effect of an oncoming seizure. The ease of application and the time-saving factor of the latter treatment also recommended it to psychiatrists.

The production of an artificial convulsion, so-called electric convulsive therapy, had a long history, starting with Leduc's experiments (1902) on "electric sleep," which occurred on passage of an electric current through the brains of animals. The Italian originators, Bini and Cerletti,[835] made a series of careful experiments with dogs before they extended the technic to human beings. Improvements in the electrical apparatus and the lack of anxiety produced in the patient made electric convulsive therapy most feasible and effective for many unmanageable or self-absorbed patients, particularly in the affective group—depression, melancholia, neurotic tension states. The moderate dangers of electric shock, namely, production of fractures after convulsion, have been mitigated by the use of curare,[836] the introduction of the glissando method of induction,[837] the brief stimuli technic and the electrostimulator.[838] A large volume of experimentation has been devoted to induction of the convulsive seizure, to reducing hazards and improving results. Considering modifications such as electronarcosis (Tietz), electrostimulation (Reiter) and other types of subconvulsive treatment, as well as the original technic of Cerletti, the present attitude toward electroconvulsive therapy is that it has proved to be the "greatest single advance in the treatment of psychoses." Social and economic gains in terms of shortening the period of illness among depressive patients have been impressive.

Competent authorities are agreed that insulin shock has yielded to electric shock and psychosurgery to a large degree. Although all these methods terminate a mental attack in the major psychoses rather than cure a disease, the recent tendency has been to resort to electric shock in the majority of psychotic situations.[839] This is chiefly the result of expediency and a general trend toward individual and group therapy for schizophrenics. Within the difficulties of generalizations, the consensus at this stage is that for schizophrenia "the difference between the final outcome in shock-treated

835 Cerletti, Ugo: Old and new information about electroshock, Am. J. Psychiat. 107:87, 1950.

836 Bennett, A. E., and Cash, P. H.: Curarization with quinine methochloride to prevent traumatic complications of Metrazol shock therapy, Psychiatric Quart. 15:351, 1941.

837 Tietz, E. B., Olsen, C. W., and Rosanoff, W. R.: The suppression of the motor phenomena of electroshock and electronarcosis by modification of the current level, J. Nerv. & Ment. Dis. 109:405, 1949.

838 Hirschfeld, G. R.: Observations with non-convulsive electric stimulation, Psychiatric Quart. (Suppl.) 24:297, 1950.

839 Jones, G. L.: Psychiatric Shock Therapy, Current Views and Practices, National Committee for Mental Hygiene, Red Bank, N. J., Manfred Sakel Foundation, 1949.

and untreated schizophrenics may not be very striking, but the number of years spent outside the hospital is certainly higher in shock-treated patients."[840]

The attempt to explain the undoubted benefits of shock treatment for depressive cases has resulted in a great amount of theorizing. Psychological reaction of the ego to electric shock and physiologic changes in the brain substance have been invoked in most explanations. Admittedly, electric shock is a drastic physical assault on the nervous system, and it was expected by psychological investigators that a complete dissolution of the ego would be one of the major effects.[841] It was theorized that reactions to a threat of death to the ego, consequent on the electric shock and the impending feelings of disintegration accompanying disturbances of body-image and ego boundaries, were the probable causes for relinquishment of depressive or autistic states in psychotic patients. It was assumed further that circuits of action were disrupted and rearranged; in common parlance, the brain was "shaken up." The helplessness which invades the ego of the patient in shock evokes a mobilization of defenses which control earlier aberrant impulses. In a word, the integrating power of the ego receives a strong stimulus.

On the other hand, explanations of more purely physiologic type presumed that altered brain metabolism through reduced cerebral oxidation was the cause of improvement after shock treatment. Another suggestion is that the vegetative centers in the diencephalon are stimulated, or somehow altered, by the passage of the electric current, hence reintegrating the body economy and establishing homeostasis between the soma and the psyche. No one theory covers the common denominator of shock treatment.[842] Kalinowsky and Hoch conclude their study by stating that shock treatment is an empirical method operating on illnesses whose etiology is unknown.

PSYCHOSURGERY AS PSYCHOTHERAPY

Since the physiologic basis of disordered mental function was the subject of therapeutic attack, it was inevitable that some intrepid investigator should seek to alter the actual fiber tracts and cell bodies of the brain itself through direct procedures of surgery. Clinical experience with agitated and obsessive patients seemed to point toward the "circular" nature of symptoms which could easily be conceived as due to fixed misarrange-

[840] Kalinowsky, L. B., and Hoch, P. H.: *Op. cit.*, p. 192.
[841] Frosch, John, and Impastato, David: The effects of shock treatment on the ego, Psychoanalyt. Quart. 17:226, 1948.
[842] Kalinowsky, L. B., and Hoch, P. H.: *Op. cit.*, p. 324.

ments of cellular connections in the brain.[843] Destruction of these "circuits" in chronic patients which were hypothesized to relate to fiber tracts passing to the thalamus from the cerebral lobes might interrupt symptom cycles, thus far unaffected by other therapeutic methods. So fantasied the creative genius, Edward Bellamy, in a novel published in 1880 in which the heroine sought to extirpate obsessive "pangs of conscience" by a surgical operation. The "mental physician," speaking through the author, remarks that in "20 years . . . merely a question of mechanical difficulties to be overcome . . . a nice problem in surgery . . . we will be able to extract a specific recollection from the memory as readily as a dentist pulls a tooth."[844] And so reasoned Dr. Egas Moniz, a neurologist of Lisbon, Portugal, a half century later.

With understandable trepidation, Moniz, in association with Almeida Lima, a Portuguese surgeon (1936), initiated the operation of leukotomy in a group of patients by cutting the fibers in the motor areas of the frontal lobes. Their chronic patients all demonstrated improvement in behavior but there was no real change in intellectual capacity. Other brain surgeons followed Moniz cautiously, although Furtado remarks that it was not until Freeman popularized the procedure that much attention was given leukotomy, even in Portugal.[845] Technics of surgical intervention were modified, cutting the corticothalamic fibers running in the anterior and the inferior aspects of white matter areas in the frontal lobes. The original operation was done through a trephine opening near the vertex of the skull, a special scalpel called a leukotome being used. Later, other approaches were devised, a recent one being a transorbital operation in which an instrument is inserted through the orbital bone plate, immediately above the eye. Neurosurgeons in Italy, Britain, Germany and Switzerland repeated Moniz' experiences; in the United States, Freeman and Watts performed the lion's share of pioneering in developing operative technics and diligently studying postlobotomy patients.[846]

The operation of lobotomy and its variants were developed during the same period of therapeutic activity in which the electric shock was being given a thorough clinical test. Although this type of brain surgery met with considerable opposition from psychiatrists dedicated predominantly to a psychogenic persuasion, it has gained adherents among conscientious neurosurgeons and observers who deal with chronic state-hospital material. It is not unnatural that a treatment method which involves entering

843 Freeman, Walter, and Watts, J. W.: Psychosurgery in the Treatment of Mental Disorders and Intractable Pain, ed. 2, p. xvi, Springfield, Ill., Thomas, 1950.

844 Bellamy, Edward: Dr. Heidenhoff's Process, p. 95, New York, Appleton, 1880.

845 Furtado, Diogo: Notes on Portuguese psychiatry, J. Clin. & Exper. Psychopath. 8:1, 1952.

846 Freeman, Walter, and Watts, J. W.: *Op. cit.*, pp. 487 et seq.

the sacred precincts of the cranial cavity as an elective operation should evoke a stronger reaction than treatment which throws the contents of the skull into a state of shock by the passage of electricity. Some French psychiatrists object to lobotomy on quasi-moral grounds because it involves destruction of normal cerebral structures in patients with functional mental disorders; psychosurgery has been banned in the Soviet Union (1951) because it contradicts Pavlovian theory.[847] Nevertheless, a large series of cases, 20,000 lobotomies, had been recorded in the United States by 1951, together with much careful neurologic and psychological work. Although complications and dangers from the operation exist, they do not exceed those incident to shock treatment. The original work done on schizophrenics has been extended to other types of psychiatric patients. In actuality, workers in this field feel that neurosurgery can attain a more precise result because they are able to destroy fibers in the brain whose position is well known to neuroanatomists, in contrast with the generalized attempt to "shock" the entire cerebral structure.

There are as many shades of opinion regarding the value of psychosurgery as there are observers. Significantly, the space devoted to psychosurgery in the compendium by Kalinowsky and Hoch on somatic methods of treatment of mental disorders has increased threefold from the first edition in 1946 to the second edition in 1951. Correspondingly, the amount of space given to insulin treatment has decreased in the later edition. This commentary on the changing interest of those engaged in research in the field of physiologic therapy may be considered a trend in the ever-oscillating pendulum of therapeutic accent. One psychiatrist of long experience commented on this situation by remarking that we are now in an age of "mutilation therapy." Nevertheless, the value and the meaning of the several drastic methods of physiologic treatment have been fairly well defined. To summarize, electroshock reduces the acuteness of depression and other affective states; insulin minimizes tension, softens delusions and improves emotional accessibility; neurosurgery has a specific effect in quantitatively reducing anxiety.

Apparently generalizations about postlobotomy patients are of little prognostic significance. Individual patients require study before and after treatment. One of the interesting findings has been the relief after lobotomy of "self-directed anxiety" which impairs the "sense of one's self-continuity." [848] The patient who has been subject to lobotomy loses a depth of emotional experience, rendering the basic mental illness less troublesome; the patient loses his self-consciousness and is a different kind of individual from what he was before the operation. For this reason, the

[847] Freeman, Walter, and Watts, J. W.: "Psychosurgery," *in* Progress in Neurology and Psychiatry, edited by E. A. Spiegel, Vol. 7, New York, Grune, 1952.
[848] Robinson: *Quoted in* Kalinowsky and Hoch: *Op. cit.*, p. 239.

rehabilitative aspect of postsurgical treatment has assumed great importance. The patient after psychosurgery is an individual who, in a sense, has to be rebuilt to resume his place in social life. It is vital that the re-education and the retraining of the patient be given careful attention; a great number of technics have been developed to fit the patient into the home environment from which he came. The oft-quoted classic statement of a relative of one of Strom-Olsen's patients that "for him the operation did miracles, if we only did not have to live with him" illustrates one type of therapeutic dilemma following psychosurgery in many treated psychotic individuals.[849] The early justification for psychosurgery has been its use on chronic, apparently hopeless, schizophrenic patients. All workers agree that definite changes in the nature of a toning down of the affective urgency of many life experiences in the patient occur after the operation. Psychotherapy after lobotomy does not appear promising, although retraining in some simple behavioral patterns is necessary. This is due to the profound emotional "emptiness" observed in lobotomy cases.

Measured against those therapeutic technics which aim to rehabilitate patients to function in a realistic environment, itself perpetually encumbered by stress and conflict, psychosurgery leaves much to be desired. Its use at present is chiefly to relieve disturbing and disturbed behavior intractable to other forms of treatment, and to interrupt irreversible chains of obsessive reactions. As Kolb has pointed out in a careful summary of the subject,[850] to call lobotomy a therapeutic agent in the ordinary sense is "uncritical." Still, psychosurgery has done much for clinical and theoretical neurology, helping to reassess the localization of such abstract functions as creativeness, esthetic sensibilities, social deportment, etc., as well as gross forms of motor activity. In the converging streams of research in brain physiology, both shock therapy and lobotomy have stimulated areas of hypotheses which may, in time, result in new approaches to nervous disturbances now found refractory to psychological influences. Kubie[851] has recently brought together thinking and experimentation in psychophysiology which sheds possible light on the "organic inaccessibility" of some types of neuroses.

A basic speculation of nervous physiology made by Kubie in 1930 seems to have been borne out by recent study of circular causal systems. This notion surmised that reverberating circuits existed within the brain which carried nervous impulses that could continuously re-excite and, hence, isolate themselves. In this way the normal and pathologic repetitiveness,

[849] Strom-Olsen: *Quoted in* Kalinowsky and Hoch: *Op. cit.*, p. 240.

[850] Kolb, L. C.: An evaluation of lobotomy and its potentialities for future research in psychiatry and the basic sciences, J. Nerv. & Ment. Dis. 110:112, 1949.

[851] Kubie, L. S.: Some implications for psychoanalysis of modern concepts of the organization of the brain, Psychoanalyt. Quart. 22:21, 1953.

evident in obsessive and compulsive symptoms, and sometimes in normal individuals who get into a mental "rut," was explainable as resting upon a self-continuing series of action currents within the nervous system. From this phenomenon Kubie deduced the reason for success in shock therapy and psychosurgery; treatment in these cases interrupts reverberating circuits, thus rendering the patient accessible to psychological influence. This hypothesis raises the question as to whether the nervous system can generate its own energy, as demonstrated in these circuits, as apart from utilizing energy derived from external stimulation, as in the phenomenon of visual perception. The "one-dimensional cause-and-effect chain" concept is being replaced by the notion of "circular causal process" as physiologists contemplate systems which achieve automatic equilibrium—for example, in the chemical balance of body tissues, cellular elements in the blood stream or even the so-called "balanced" personality.[852] The application of the feed-back principle in regulation of human physiology may well reorganize our knowledge of body function.

Significant also is the analogy between the human brain and the electronic computing machine in the matter of storing "circulating" memories and self-regulation through successive feedbacks. Norbert Wiener's description of "neurotic machines,"[853] which are corrected by being subjected to abnormally large electrical impulses, suggests the possibility that electric shock to the brain also resets abnormal cyclic processes. We cannot go further into this fascinating analogy between the mechanical and the human brain beyond noting that an English psychiatrist, Ashby,[854] has offered the thought that in time the concept of "energy dynamics" will be substituted for that of "libido and instinct." Further evolution of this promising field waits upon the pooled work of scientists of multidisciplinary interests. It is they who may merge the discoveries of physicists and physicians and forge instruments which will heal disorders affecting that most intricate mechanism designed for human thinking, feeling and willing.

[852] "Cybernetics, Circular Causal and Feedback Mechanisms" *in* Biological and Social Systems, edited by H. Von Foerster, Tr. 8th Conf., March, 1951, Josiah Macy, Jr., Foundation, New York, 1952, p. xiv.
[853] Wiener, Norbert: Cybernetics, p. 172, New York, Wiley, 1948.
[854] Ashby, R. W.: Review, Cybernetics, by Norbert Wiener, J. Ment. Sc. 95:716, 1949.

12

The Breadth of Psychotherapy

As our survey nears the "now" of time, the panorama of psychotherapy becomes more and more densely peopled with innovators, adapters and modifiers. The scene depicted spreads to broader areas of human function; the background involves wider social and historical currents. The panorama of mental healing seems now to encompass almost all those attitudes and values by which men live. The need for psychotherapy has replaced the need for consolation which religion and philosophy contributed, the first in a practical way, the second more abstractly. From the early Christian Era, when Jesus' teachings introduced the concept of the "primacy of the person,"[855] through the doctrine of personal salvation to the Industrial Revolution with its accent on the economic and social primacy of the individual, psychotherapy has utilized and assimilated the changing basic postulates by which men live. Therapeutic methods and viewpoints have fallen about these base lines of world order, like points in a distribution graph.

We may summarize the "usurpation" by psychotherapy of cosmic attitudes by noting that magic and faith, to which was added a religiously derived humanitarianism, sufficed as a base line for what amounted to psychotherapy in the first three millennia of history. In the next millennium, faith, humanitarianism and scientific medicine, latterly supported and implemented by a growing science of psychology, provided an axis round which psychotherapy grew. During the past century, the rapid growth of dynamic psychology, the beginning intimations of man's social relationships and their interpersonal significance, has carried therapy along into a social direction, involving both anthropology and sociology. For a decade or two an increasingly astute perception of the analogy between human thinking and the operations of mechanical circuits and feedback systems has provided another base which may or may not draw psychotherapy in a different direction. In all this, psychotherapy has been a

[855] Mumford, Lewis: The Condition of Man, New York, Harcourt, 1944.

relativistic science; its aims remain undisturbed, but its methodologies have varied.

This chapter will trace the multitudinous developments of psychotherapy which in recent years have expanded in response to psychoanalysis and social psychiatry. As the field has spread, its practitioners have come from domains beyond that of medicine and psychiatry, encompassing psychologists, counselors, psychiatric social workers, nurses and hospital technicians especially trained in psychiatric attitudes. The ancillary workers, occupational, music, recreational, biblio-therapists, have also become part of the therapeutic picture. Important though these groups are, their work will not be discussed at any length because of limitations of space. For the same reason, psychotherapy of children will not be dealt with separately, since our interest is more in the history of method than the field of application. The developments traced in Chapters 8, 9, and 11 and this chapter refer to practices among children as well as adults.

EXPRESSIVE VERSUS SUPPRESSIVE PSYCHOTHERAPY

At the turn of the century, psychotherapy, which meant chiefly suggestion, persuasion and a belief in the power of the "subconscious mind," was slowly changing. Even though neurologists relied more on suggestion through medicinal channels, and persuasion through the intellectual acuity of the patient, the investigation of emotional conflict was taking precedence in the specialist's technic. Deeper motivations, unconscious sources of guilt, symbolic meanings of symptoms, occupied the forefront of the therapist's interest. Psychoanalytic theory was profoundly modifying the office and the clinic treatment of neurotic patients by general psychotherapists; in spite of this infiltration, support, explanation and persuasion remained as therapeutic weapons.

To obtain a clearer picture of the varieties of method in the general field of psychotherapy, it would be well to use a classification which has wide approval. Individual psychotherapy has been classified as falling broadly into two groups: (1) Expressive or deep; and (2) suppressive or supportive therapy.[855a] The former seeks to study and demonstrate these emotional conflicts, usually unknown to the patient, which are the cause of symptoms. In the former, exploration, abreaction, interpretation and free association are depended on in the main. Suppressive therapy, using inspirational or ego-strengthening measures through the reassurances of an understanding, palpably optimistic therapist, is less interested in "analyzing" and more in direct psychological aid. Realistically considered, the supportive aspect of therapy is a factor in every expressive or "analytic" method, although in psychoanalytic technics this factor is kept at a mini-

[855a] Menninger, Karl A. The Human Mind. N. Y., A. A. Knopf, 1947—3rd Ed. Rev. P. 378.

mum in order better to uncover unconscious motives and resistances. Conversely, the suppressive therapy also seeks to elucidate basic conflicts and to achieve abreaction to emotional trauma. Overlapping occurs in both groups of methods. The use of either depends on the character structure of the patient, his malleability, the fixity of his symptoms, time available for therapy, the scientific aims of the therapist and his therapeutic predilection and training. This generalization will suffice for orientation purposes. Of the factors noted, those related to the therapeutic work-plan have been chiefly considered.

In addition to technical devices and the prospective patient's psychological structure and problems, the science of psychotherapy involves factors within the therapist himself. These aspects deal with the intuitive gifts of the therapist, his loyalty to a set of principles—the *lege artis,* his artistic sense of application of these principles, his personal philosophy and unconscious bias, his narcissistic needs for success or approval and so on. In this connection it is conceded that training furnished by a psychoanalytic preparation immeasurably aids a therapist in his handling of his own and the patient's needs and problems. It has always been recognized that the psychotherapist utilizing expressive technics almost of necessity should himself have been psychoanalyzed. A trained psychiatrist of broad vision and life experience, interested in people and possessed of intuitive understanding of emotional problems, could do competent therapy without an analysis. Nevertheless, an analytic training provides the experience and the knowledge of perceiving the character of deeper ego changes, of estimating the forces and the defenses of unconscious nature, which are constantly encountered during a psychotherapy of uncovering type. By the same token, a basic personality rigidity in an analyzed therapist might vitiate effective therapy by rendering such an individual too orthodox in his dealings with patients or too unresponsive to their emotional needs. Both the inner core of the therapist's personality and his or her training in "depth" psychology are influential factors in expressive therapeutic procedures. The "ideal goal" of "equanimity and serenity which are desirable features in the psychiatrist's professional dealings with his patients" [856] is best attained through the combination of adequate training and a flexible, warm personality in the therapist. From these general remarks let us turn to methods of expressive psychotherapy employed.

One of the early simplifications of an expressive psychotherapy was the "psychological explanation." This was a species of re-education, making use of material from an exploration of the patients' life, aiming to bring

[856] Fromm-Reichmann, Frieda: Principles of Intensive Psychotherapy, p. 41, Univ. Chicago Press, 1950.

"comprehension of the rights of the denied instincts" and releasing the "fettering hold of unfortunate child habits." [857] In a similar strain, but with less reliance on "subconscious" factors, was the re-education technic of Austen Riggs. Discarding the disharmonious current concepts of psychopathology (1908), in "desperation" Riggs studied the individual whose neurosis he considered a matter of "maladaptation of intrinsically normal individuals." [858] The objectives of this technic, to readjust the patient to full social usefulness, were carried on at the Riggs Foundation in Stockbridge, Massachusetts. Re-education stressed the teaching of normal adaptation methods, imparting information with full perception of its appropriateness to the particular social and educational status of the patient. Primarily the patient's intelligence was utilized,[859] since advocates of this method mistrusted direct suggestion, such as that made under hypnosis, as a method which "lulled the critical faculties to sleep." Most of this work was done in the sanitarium, away from the usual habitat of the patient. The life situation which had given the patient distorted values and faulty habits of life based on innate hypersensitivity was reviewed with the patient, and an attitude of "living in the present" was furthered.

This form of psychotherapy, originating in New England, seems to share the intellectualistic bent and common-sense spirit of this region. It accepted the presence of unconscious conflict in the formation of neurosis, but insisted on the need for a philosophy of life which would permit the patient to view his symptoms objectively and in proper perspective.[860] And it considered William James's maxims on habit training of real value in a reassessment of daily life patterns.[861] This chiefly conscious psychotherapy recognized unconscious aggression and guilt, distortions in the patient's emotional response and so on, but recognized also the therapist's cultural orientation as a model for a reintegration of the patient's life. More recently, psychotherapeutic methods at the Riggs Foundation have been altered to include psychoanalytic theory and knowledge. "Broadly conceived," the therapy employed in recent years [862] does not necessarily always aim to "lift unconscious conflicts into full scrutiny," but the insights given psychoanalytic therapists helps them guide patients to mental

[857] Jackson, J. A., and Salisbury, H. M.: Outwitting Our Nerves; A Primer of Psychotherapy, New York, Century, 1921.

[858] Riggs, A. F.: The psychoneuroses; their nature and treatment, Am. J. Psychiat. 3:91, 1923.

[859] Forcheimer, Frederick, and Billings, Frank: Therapeusis of Internal Diseases . . ., ed. 4 (George Blumer, ed.), New York, Appleton, 1924.

[860] Thom, D. A:. Psychotherapy in private practice, Am. J. Psychiat. 13:77, 1933.

[861] Coon, G. P., and Raymond, A. F.: A Review of the Psychoneuroses at Stockbridge, Stockbridge, Mass., Austen Riggs Foundation, 1940.

[862] Austen Riggs Center, Inc., An Informational Report, Stockbridge, Mass., 1953, p. 6.

health. Terhune, summarizing this "eclectic" psychotherapy,[863] to which group Riggs's work belonged, spoke of it as an "intensive method employing analytic technic without deep analysis."

The influence of Meyerian psychobiology is evident in the therapeutic viewpoint outlined above, in the sense that emotional distortions are to be viewed as deviations of the "life-line" of the patient. Work is done with the patient with a full view of his capacities, appropriate goals and emotional assets. Expressed somewhat similarly by Appel,[864] the desired reintegration involves a "dynamic growth process" in the patient in which each experience, including the experience of psychotherapy, requires ventilation in an atmosphere of security. Efforts to understand the patient and the acceptance of his hostility with forbearance by the therapist are important steps in offering neurotic sufferers the opportunity to grow emotionally.

Accent on the living environment of the patient, past and current, brought up the question of intervention in life activities or even alteration of the environment by the therapist. Usually eschewed in classical psychoanalytic technic, the subject of directiveness and controlled emotional growth has been studied carefully. From the "dynamic growth" viewpoint, the patient is encouraged to assume, and "at times he is actually charged with," responsibility for attaining a total adjustment. He may also be "instructed" as to the general pace of life most compatible with his emotional capacities. This relationship of therapist to patient obviates an analysis of the transference to aid the patient's adjustment. Billings [865] remarks in this connection, "In my experience, it is not necessary to work toward creating any special type of . . . transference situation." The combinations of active measures, or, more properly described, directive methods, with investigation of deep emotional components in the patient, are numerous. The precise name of each "school" is less important than the common technic, which seeks to evaluate and use situational factors equally with emotional personal ones. For example, Herzberg,[866] who worked with the usual "uncovering" analytic accent, directed his patient's environment, following analysis of emotional factors, by imposing tasks calculated to "re-shape impulses and remove obstacles." Others stress participation of the therapist in the treatment process,[867] even to the point of

863 Terhune, W. B.: Advances in Individual Therapy, Emphasizing Brief Psychotherapy, Delivered at World Congress on Mental Health, London, August, 1948.
864 Appel, K. E.: Psychotherapy, The 4th in the 14th Annual Series of Conference Talks at the Institute of Living, February 4, 1948.
865 Billings, E. G.: General principles of psychotherapy in general practice, J. Indiana M. A. 42:1243, 1949.
866 Herzberg, Alexander: Active Psychotherapy, New York, Grune, 1945.
867 Bonime, Walter: Some principles of brief psychotherapy, Psychiatric Quart. **27**:1, **1953.**

advice and occasional attempts to influence but not coerce the "client." [868] This problem concerned a group [869] which devoted itself to separating out just what factors are needed, which are superannuated, which are truly "therapeutic" in the treatment relationship.

DIRECTIVE VERSUS NONDIRECTIVE THERAPY

Other variants of therapeutic relationships minimized the implied authoritarian or directive aspect of the therapist's position. Unwilling to distill dependent attitudes in the patient through frequent therapeutic contacts, Karpman [870] reduced the sessions in number and kept the entire relationship on an objective level. Karpman's cases, chiefly from a hospital population, were handled through reduced personal contact with avoidance of suggestion. By having the patient write an autobiography and subsequently write his detailed answers to questions framed by the physician covering particulars of the case history, including dreams, intimate revelations and reactions, Karpman maintained the relationship on an objective level. These communications were then individually analyzed and presented to the patient as a "memorandum," which was studied, commented on and assimilated. The interviews were limited to five or ten minutes, but much time was spent by the patient on the "memorandum," which incorporated all the therapist's observations and interpretations.

The "objective psychotherapy" of Karpman is related, in at least one respect, to "counseling," an approach developed by Rogers [871] and his associates, which was initially tried with college students in need of adjustment services. Since this type of therapeutic relationship was conceived primarily by psychologists, its frame of reference is nonauthoritarian and impliedly nonmedical. The recipient of counseling is called a "client," and the method, "nondirective." Treatment is more accurately described as a nice variety of noncommittal guidance. It is focused on a concern with the client's own attitudes as he develops them under counseling, and not on the transference situation. Stress is placed on the immediate situation: "[Past history] for therapy to take place, . . . is not necessarily important. . . . When there is no probing for the 'facts' of the history, a better picture of the dynamic development of the individual often emerges." [872]

[868] Thorne, F. C.: Directive psychotherapy: XIV, Suggestion, persuasion and advice, University of Vermont, Burlington, Vt. (J. Clin. Psychol. 4:70-82, 1948).

[869] Kubie, L., Hendrick, I., Shakow, D., Brosin, H. W., Bergman, Paul, Bibring, E., and Kris, E.: The objective evaluation of psychotherapy, Am. J. Orthopsychiat. 19:463, 1949.

[870] Karpman, Ben: Objective psychotherapy; principles, methods and results, J. Clin. Psychol., Monograph No. 6, Suppl., July, 1948.

[871] Rogers, C. R.: Counseling and Psychotherapy; Newer Concepts in Practice, Boston, Houghton, 1942.

[872] *Ibid.*, p. 30.

In an important sense, Rogers' method, which has become accepted in many predominantly educational circles and extensively by psychologists, has a psychobiologic rationale. Maturation of the individual, with its accretion and assimilation of new experiences, becomes the theoretical axis of counseling theory. Briefly stated, the postulates of nondirective therapy are (1) that every individual has a drive toward growth, health and adjustment, (2) that emotional blocks to integration of knowledge require removal, (3) that the immediate rather than the past situation is stressed, (4) that counseling is change, not a preparation for change, "The therapeutic relationship itself is a growth experience." It will be recognized that psychological "growth," as a function of maturation, has pervaded all psychiatric thinking since the genetic approach has become reality. It is obviously a major tenet of psychoanalytic theory. The contribution of Rogers has been essentially to allow the client to explore his own situation and behavior, accept responsibility for the forward movement of his escape from an emotionally blocked situation. The counselor is entirely permissive, neither interpreting nor directing the client, serving as a growth catalyst rather than a "doctor" in the ordinary sense, allowing and aiding the client to mature under his own self-scrutiny. The fundamental direction of counseling is opposite that of "doctoring"; neither dependence nor resistance is encountered, for, being "client-centered," the therapeutic process occurs within the client, who is helped to face his own problems and to make independent choices of solution.[873]

Psychologists working with this technic have made many experimental observations purporting to show how the forces of growth were released in the individual as the counseling proceeded. In fact, it is Rogers's hope that scientific investigation of therapeutic technics, through use of an electrical wire recording of an entire series of sessions, as has been done by his students, will put an end to "cultism in psychotherapy," substituting controlled measurement of therapeutic results for unsubstantiated claims.[874] In spite of the supremely objective setting of counseling, critics [875] have pointed to the inevitability of interaction between therapist and patient and the essential existence of a "transference" situation, whether explored or ignored. Others have pointed to the possibility that the "catalytic" influence of the counselor may be in reality one of identification of therapist by client.[876]

873 Curran, C. A.: Personality Factors in Counseling, New York, Grune, 1945.
874 Rogers, C. R.: Recent research in nondirective therapy and its implications, Am. J. Orthopsychiat. **16**:581, 1946.
875 Lowrey, L. G.: Counseling and therapy, Am. J. Orthopsychiat. **16**:615, 1946.
876 Chassell, Joseph: Review of Counseling and Psychotherapy by Carl R. Rogers, Psychoanalyt. Quart. **13**:232, 1944.

THERAPY BY THE SOCIAL CASEWORKER

The connotations of this experimentally derived method have infiltrated into social casework where the client's resistance to facing his problems is reduced by removing the "directiveness" of the therapist. This trend in the growing casework fields received its chief reflection in the technic which came to be known generally as "client-centered" therapy. Handling personal problems developing out of disturbed familial situations brought the need of adapting therapeutic relationships to a reality setting wherein the client's problems could not be considered apart from his family tensions. This type of social-work activity has been called *functional,* in that it does not imitate psychological analysis or indulge in "traditional concrete service of the family agency," [877] but deals with the question of how people may be helped to solve stated or unstated social-psychological troubles. This type of social casework was developed at the University of Pennsylvania Social Work School and involved an application of some of Otto Rank's ideas dealing with the psychology of accepting help and the neglected problem of the "will" in the therapeutic process. The essential feature of this "functional" casework attitude resided in a focus on the client's freedom to become himself, with help from the caseworker. Rather than being a patient, the client was regarded as a person asking for a specific piece of social service. Counseling, rather than therapy in the ordinary sense, pointed toward a troubled individual in a social setting, characterized the work of Taft and her group. This movement coincided with increasing awareness of the therapeutic opportunities facing the social worker, recognized simultaneously by other workers under analytic and psychiatric influence.

The social worker, who traditionally dealt with welfare needs, jobs or direct relief of clients, soon found her relationship to be implicitly a therapeutic one. Since she was ordinarily not equipped to enact the role of psychotherapist, the resources in the clients were mobilized to the maximum to help them help themselves. Still, the social-work relationship proved on analysis to be more complicated than at first appeared. The client's first contact in the search for help was found to embrace psychological elements [878] which could be used later in the treatment process. When "treatment [was] addressed to a person with a problem, not to a problem itself" the full import of the skilled use of relationship was appreciated. As social workers moved more deeply into treatment areas, it became evident that

[877] Taft, Jessie: "Family Case Work and Counseling," *in* A Functional Approach to Family Case Work, edited by J. Taft, pp. 8, 301, Philadelphia, Univ. Penn. Press, 1944.

[878] Hamilton, Gordon: Psychoanalytically oriented case-work and its relation to psychotherapy, Am. J. Orthopsychiat. 19:209, 1949.

direct work with individuals presenting personality deviations was resorted to more and more.[879] The reality situation, which, in addition to the psychological problem, bedevils a social-agency client, introduced new factors into casework. For this reason, among others, the type of therapeutic approach employed required modification which amalgamated the non-directive and directive plans.[880]

During the decades since the profession of psychiatric social work received recognition at Smith College, Massachusetts, by virtue of the merger of psychiatry and social work, progress has been steady. The social worker has advanced from the position of an aide to the psychiatrist to that of an independent, though co-ordinated, worker in the clinical team.[881] Treatment of the patient by the social worker parallels that of the physician with treatment and consultation among relatives, employees, teachers and others who constitute the interpersonal objects for the patient.

One of the specifically social-therapeutic aspects of casework with the mentally ill is the placement of patients in suitable family care or restricted environments. This so-called family-care program has advanced markedly during the past decade. The program is the sole responsibility of the psychiatric social worker, who confers with the caretakers, themselves psychiatrically oriented by virtue of experience and expert counseling. As in Gheel, Belgium, where the foster-care program started eight centuries ago, extension of the mentally ill into the community under care of families trained to the task has broadened the therapeutic personnel. Adolf Meyer's wish to vitalize state hospital care by bridging the gap from hospital to home has come to realization with this broader aspect of psychiatric casework.

With growth of psychiatric social work, the problem of distributing responsibilities and outlining the scope of work became apparent. A summary of opinions in the field in 1948 [882] considered that psychiatric social workers engaged in both direct and and indirect types of therapy, and that essentially there was a difference between interrelationship technics implicit in psychotherapy and in casework. So rapid has been the development of this field, however, that the same group, which summarized opinions as to the caseworker's therapeutic area, two years later [883] pointed

[879] Garrett, Annette: The worker-client relationship, Am. J. Orthopsychiat. **19**:224, 1949.

[880] Lowrey, L. G.: Trends in orthopsychiatric therapy; general developments and trends, Am. J. Orthopsychiat. **18**:381, 1948.

[881] Regensburg, Jeanette: Charting directions in social work education in the United States, Social Casework 33:47, 1952.

[882] Committee on Psychiatric Social Work, Group for Advancement of Psychiatry, Report No. 2, January, 1948.

[883] Committee on Psychiatric Social Work, Group for Advancement of Psychiatry, Report No. 16, September, 1950.

out how the range of therapeutic application of the caseworker became wider than that of the psychotherapist. A corollary of this has been the recent development of the psychiatric caseworker in the role of therapist with an independent professional relationship to patients. Like the psychiatric nurse who is in a "strategic position" to relate to patients, whose "every action and gesture" [884] has meaning for the rapport, the social worker meets the patient on the level of social objectives and everyday life problems.

Historically, the psychiatric caseworker was more restricted to social planning and less often engaged in the practice of therapy. With the change from a nondirective to an expressive, or psychoanalytically oriented, type of therapy, the psychiatric social worker began to emancipate herself (or himself) from the traditional pattern of social work, which stressed "conformity" of the client. Social "weaning" of the state-hospital patient became a new therapeutic goal. Borrowing from new work in analysis of psychotic or psychopathic individuals, and other active treatment technics, the concept of the "half-step home," [885] in which patients ready for discharge from a state hospital are taken to live with a social worker or a psychiatric attendant, is one technic that is being developed. In this development, the accent is directive and educational, but applied with full knowledge of the psychopathology of the patient involved. For example, a young woman recovered from schizophrenia is advised, as she resides for a month or more in a "half-step home," how to look for a job, how to dress, to meet young men, to deport herself socially and so on.

Technical innovations such as the half-step home encompass both the social and the psychological frames of reference, i.e., the new social realities the patient is required to meet at the moment of each step in the adjustment, and the psychological assets available within the individual. In the process, areas of emotional discomfort are soothed and new patterns encouraged and demonstrated to the ex-patient in consonance with the psychiatrist's decision that he is ready for a trial at living. This independent use of a social worker's knowledge represents an application to living of psychological findings, a merging of psychiatric knowledge with an acute perception of social needs in individuals whose adjustment had been interrupted or deviated by emotional illness.[886] It represents a "mothering" process of wide implications for the management of psychotic, psychopathic or character deviations that defied a purely medical psychiatric relationship.

[884] McLaughlin, Dorothy: "Contribution of the Psychiatric Nurse to the Clinical Team," *in* Education for Psychiatric Social Work, p. 57, New York, Am. A. Psych. Workers, 1950.

[885] Bromberg, Esther B.: Personal communication, 1953.

[886] ——: The Role of Authority in the Treatment of Delinquency, to be published.

THE MEDICAL PRACTITIONER AS PSYCHOTHERAPIST

Aided by the impetus from World War II and the corollary stimulation of the mental-hygiene movement, the physician in general practice imperceptibly enlisted his viewpoint and talents in the field of psychotherapy. Perhaps it would be more accurate to say that psychiatry had generally persuaded medicine by the 1940's to adopt its viewpoint of the sick patient as a total organism whose mind and body were mutually involved. The medical man, long alerted to the meaning of neurotic attitudes in terms of physical illness, rapidly accepted the tenets of psychosomatic medicine as something very close to his daily experience. The surgeon, the gynecologist, the pediatrician and other specialists had long seen the relation of psychic states to disease entities. World War II brought the general practitioner's attention to the problem in unmistakable fashion. The rise of psychosomatic medicine[887] is a chapter of unequaled interest in medical history, but our preoccupation is with its reflection in the evolution of mental healing. Since the medical practitioner had neither time nor training for intensive psychotherapy, his efforts were shaped to improve his understanding of and effectiveness with nervous cases through the limits of his daily contacts.

Social workers had shown how the interview itself was an opening wedge for therapy, and physicians found that they were already in an advantageous position to utilize their consultations for psychotherapeutic purposes. The primary notion to assist "the patient to express feelings," which would otherwise be masked under the usually perfunctory relationship of a medical examination, was stressed.[888] Following Carl Rogers's indirect approach, the medical practitioner was encouraged to be a passive mirror of the patient's emotions toward his family and work situation. Interview therapy was the name dignifying an attitude which competent family physicians had employed for years, which did not invade the privacy of a patient's inner life but helped him to verbalize common feelings that ordinarily would not be searched for by the medical man. A "folksy" approach, adapted to physicians distant from psychiatric centers in large cities, has grown in recent years through teaching in university centers aimed at providing the practitioner with the "gist of what modern psychiatry has to say about human personality and the way it works." [889] The experiment with practitioners at the University of Minnesota has been repeated and extended at the University of Cincinnati and other institutions. Deepened and broadened, it has played an increasing part in educating medical students to include a psy-

[887] Dunbar, H. Flanders: Emotions and Bodily Changes, New York, Columbia, 1935.
[888] Law, S. G.: Therapy Through Interview, New York, McGraw-Hill, 1948.
[889] Smith, Geddes: Psychotherapy in General Medicine; Report of an Experimental Postgraduate Course, New York, Commonwealth Fund, 1946.

chiatric attitude toward therapy of neurotic persons, who constitute the major portion of the practitioner's practice.[890]

Participation in psychotherapy by the medical practitioner has been outlined by Maurice Levine [891] to include many areas of contact where possibilities for helping patients both directly and indirectly exist:

1. Physical Examination as Psychotherapy
2. Physical Treatment as Psychotherapy
3. Medicinal Treatment as Psychotherapy
4. Reassurance
5. Hydrotherapy as Psychotherapy
6. Occupational Therapy
7. Diversion and Entertainment
8. Establishment of a Daily Routine
9. Development of Hobbies
10. Authoritative Firmness
11. Suggestion Therapy
12. Hospitalization, including the "Rest Cure"
13. Giving of Information
14. Removal of External Strain
15. Changing the Attitudes in the Environment
16. Guidance and Advice
17. Fostering of Socialized Living
18. Provision of Acceptable Outlets for Aggressiveness
19. Provision of Acceptable Compensations for Fears and Inferiority Feelings
20. Non-Condemning Constructive Relationship
21. Ignoring of Certain Symptoms and Attitudes
22. Satisfaction of Frustrated Basic Needs
23. Satisfaction of Neurotic Needs
24. Opportunity for Healthy Identifications
25. Bibliotherapy

In addition, he suggests measures which do not probe too deeply but allow expression of those emotional conflicts which underlie many somatic illnesses. Here Levine includes:

1. Confession and Ventilation
2. Life-History Discussion
3. Desensitization
4. Persuasion and Re-education
5. Applications of Psychoanalysis

The induction of physicians into the area of psychiatric intricacies has its parallel in the recent modification of the medical-school curriculum to include the science of psychobiology. The vitality which psychiatry has at-

[890] Committee on Medical Education, Group for Advancement of Psychiatry, Report No. 3, Topeka, Kansas, March, 1948.
[891] Levine, Maurice: Psychotherapy in Medical Practice, pp. 17-18, New York, Macmillan, 1942.

tained in medical education can be seen by the fact that more than half of the medical schools in this country consider psychiatry and its background as a "basic science" [892] which requires almost as many teaching hours as are devoted to anatomy, biochemistry or physiology. Just as colleges and universities in stressing mental hygiene in their nonprofessional schools have included psychotherapy in spirit if not in fact as part of the teaching of their psychological departments, so has psychiatry's inclusion in medical education betokened a major advance. The avowed trend to bring medicine into direct relation with psychotherapy, with which it has openly or surreptitiously dallied over the centuries, has encouraged the view that physical methods of treatment of neuroses (apart from those dealt with in the chapter on physiologic measures) do indeed belong in the physician's armamentarium. This trend draws attention to the relaxation technic of Dr. Edmund Jacobson and the treatment methods of nervous tension based on the Pavlovian physiology of conditioned reflexes.

NEUROPHYSIOLOGIC FACETS IN PSYCHOTHERAPY

Starting with the happy idea of investigating the neurophysiologic meaning of rest—medicine's most common and effective prescription—Jacobson determined that rest and complete muscular relaxation were not the same phenomena.[893] Through careful observation combined with kymographic and galvanometric recordings, Jacobson found that a residual tension, observable as a kinesthetic sensation of muscle (or nerve) restlessness, accompanied by an ill-defined but perceptible sense of emotional disquiet, existed in most subjects not specifically taught how to relax. The physiologist instructed his patients first to perceive this subliminal experience of tenseness and then to relax beyond the point which they would ordinarily consider that of relaxation. Pointing to each muscle group individually, he taught the patient to "relax past the point of apparent perfect relaxation." The patient was advised to exert effort in a "negative direction." Paying little attention to the troublesome thought-content which might accompany nervousness, insomnia or anxiety states, Jacobson achieved relaxation of both voluntary and visceral (autonomic) muscles, which in its train brought a reduction or a cessation of emotional tension or anxiety. Realizing that "psychic events, both conscious and unconscious, have their physiological correlates," he concentrated on the basic neuromuscular tension which was related to emotional experience. In a sense, Jacobson's method is one of physical reconditioning, a re-education of the neuromuscular structure of the body. Since he

[892] Committee on Medical Education, Group for Advancement of Psychiatry, Report No. 3, App. A, Topeka, Kansas, March, 1948.
[893] Jacobson, Edmund: Progressive Relaxation, Univ. Chicago Press, 1929.

showed in the laboratory that cerebral activity apparently diminished in the presence of "progressive relaxation," without recourse to inhibitory technics of suggestion or hypnosis, Jacobson felt that his technic was of practical value in treating nervous states. These included neurasthenia, which he generally subsumed under the heading "neuromuscular hypertension" and such conditions involving involuntary muscles, as asthma, mucous colitis and thyroid disease.

The exhortation to "relax" is common in ordinary life communications and is obviously implied in most psychotherapeutic contacts. Yet analysis of its meaning, hence its predictable use, in therapy involves rather complex formulations of the physiology of the nervous system. The meaning of psychic inhibitions, habit formation, cerebral excitation and response requires exhaustive analysis if the exact meaning of relaxation is to be stated. In this inquiry the challenging Pavlovian theory was encountered. Progressive relaxation addressed itself to the tense muscles of the patient, so to speak, the proprioceptive end of the reflex arc, and not to the cortical and the subcortical portions of the arc, where psychic correlates—ideas, fears, etc.—presumably lie. In this way the relaxation method hoped to achieve indirectly a psychological quieting effect. Therapeutic methods deriving, on the other hand, from the Pavlovian theory of excitation and inhibition as the basic modalities of central nervous system function, addressed themselves to the cerebral portion of the reflex arcs in the brain.

Although the great Russian physiologist's work was primarily in the area of mechanism of cerebral action, his followers utilized his research findings to propose a direction for therapy. Based on his production of artificial neuroses in dogs, Pavlov had postulated that hysteria was the result of conflicting, overwhelmingly strong or weak repetitive stimuli impinging on the balanced mechanism of conditioning: "Irradiation of the excitatory process [causes] summation of reflexes to appear. . . . While a summated reflex is momentary and transitory, the conditioned reflex is gradually reinforced to become a chronic manifestation." [894] The resulting inhibition of cerebral cells allowed powerful excitation (emotional traumas) to cause symptoms to appear; hence, rest, prolonged sleep induced by soporifics (bromides, Amytal), is the treatment of choice for neurotic and psychotic conditions.[895] Earlier, Soviet psychiatrists, on the theory that suggestion was a typical, though simplified, conditioned reflex, employed repeated word-suggestion to break the abnormal state of unconditioned excitation in the neurotic's brain. "New, more beneficial cerebral connections" were brought to the patient

[894] Pavlov, I. P.: Conditioned Reflexes and Psychiatry, pp. 102-103, translated and edited by W. Horsley Gantt, New York, Internat. Pub., 1941.

[895] Wortis, Joseph: Some recent developments in Soviet psychiatry, Am. J. Psychiat. **109**:641, 1953.

through education, rest, electrical stimulation and possibly hypnosis.[896]

Pavlov's work on conditioned reflexes in experimental animals (dogs), producing thereby artificial neurosis and reconditioning them back to normality, is difficult of translation into terms of human psychopathology and psychotherapy. In spite of the fact that Pavlovians speak of psychic states, i.e., "the irradiation process leads to the elaboration of a temporary conditioned connexion, an association," the entire concept is couched in physiologic terms, employing objective criteria, "ideas." In the ordinary sense, Pavlov's theory of excitation and inhibition cannot be the subject of therapeutic endeavor. Nevertheless, although conceptual incongruities exist, the hints which Pavlov's researches offered have been extended into a system of mental treatment by an American psychologist.[897] On the theory that the simplest form of conditioned reflex in man is suggestion, Salter aims to replace conditioned inhibitory emotional reflexes by "deliberate excitatory emotional reactions" which become conditioned. In general terms, Salter's technic, which he expects will replace psychoanalytic methods, consists in getting the "individual to re-educate himself back to healthy spontaneity" through removing inhibitions built into symptoms. This is done by constant excitation in connection with specific suggestions; for example, a patient who needed to relax was conditioned thereto by the excitation of sounds associated with the suggestion to close the eyes.

In another direction, in the problem of chronic alcoholism, the conditioned reflex theory has been used in mental treatment. The technic follows Pavlov's conditioning of his laboratory animals wherein he associated an indifferent excitation (a ringing bell) with presentation of food to produce a differentiated attitude of "mind." In Voegtlin's technic,[898] the alcoholic patient is offered whiskey or wine at the same time that he is given an injection of drugs causing intense nausea and vomiting. Thereafter the smell, the taste or the sight of alcoholic beverages induces a "reflex activity of the centers of nausea and vomiting." Repetition of these associated occurrences induces an aversion to alcohol which lasts from weeks to months or years. Later reports indicate the essential psychological nature of the treatment process.[899] This type of somatic overexcitation in association with the presentation of alcohol is partly responsible for the action of the Antabuse treatment of alcoholism [900] recently introduced into this country from Denmark.

896 Platonov, K. I.: Psychotherapy, collected papers from the state neuro-psychiatric institute in Kharkov, book review by J. Notkin, Am. J. Psychiat. 11:1206, 1932.

897 Salter, Andrew: Condition Reflex Therapy, New York, Creative Age Press, 1949.

898 Lemere, F., and Voegtlin, W. L.: An evaluation of the aversion treatment of alcoholism, Quart. J. Stud. Alcohol 11:199-204, 1950.

899 *Ibid.* 11:199.

900 Jacobsen, Erik, and Martensen-Larsen, O.: Treatment of alcoholism with tetraethylthiuram disulfide (Antabuse), J.A.M.A. 139:918, 1949.

HABIT TRAINING AS CONDITIONING

Habit training on a less physiologic level has, of course, been a mainstay of sanitarium treatment of certain types of mental and nervous illnesses for years. Correction, associated with reward or even censure and punishment, has been a common method of handling asocial or objectionable behavior among children and chronic mental cases. Recently the principle of constant repetitious stimulation has been developed into what is now known as the "total-push" method for chronic mental cases. When Myerson,[901] concluding that deterioration was neither a natural nor an entirely necessary product of schizophrenia, employed his total-push method in a Massachusetts state hospital, he was building on a basic principle that activity, or activation, tends to dissolve patterns of autistic withdrawal in chronic cases. Almost twenty years before, Bryan,[902] at the Danvers State Hospital, in Massachusetts, had used this principle, claiming improvements but no cures. The method emphasized the use of every known general medical measure, plus diet, exercises, games and accent on personal attention to patients, no matter how emotionally flattened and deteriorated. Its aim encompassed no more than the wish to stave off the dreaded deterioration of "backward" patients. The phrase and the technic, formulated by Myerson, have come to represent the personalized activities of all good hospital technicians and ward psychiatrists, and are widely used in many state institutions. Recently group therapy, which provides intensive psychological stimulation, has been added to the measures mentioned. Not the least result has been a "tonic effect" on the spirit and the energy of technicians, nurses and physicians who handle this discouraging type of human material. Weir Mitchell's epigram that psychiatry is "an art with assistive sciences," [903] is virtually lived out in the concept of the teamwork approach to the rehabilitation of chronic patients. Each member of the team contributes a therapeutic atmosphere, in addition to his personal effort, with individual patients, in combating the "Rip Van Winkle" hebetude so characteristic of the "backward" patient.[904]

The total-push technic employs the teamwork concept even to the use of patients to help other patients.[905] The combining of staff management and environmental control of patients has been worked through by William

[901] Myerson, Abraham: Theory and principles of the "total push" method in the treatment of chronic schizophrenia, Am. J. Psychiat. 95:1197, 1939.
[902] Bryan, W. A.: Re-education of demented patients, Am. J. Insanity 77:99, 1920.
[903] Southard, E. E.: Cross-sections of mental hygiene, Am. J. Insanity 76:91, 1919.
[904] Galioni, E. F., Adams, F. H., and Tallman, F. F.: Intensive treatment of backward patients; a controlled pilot study, Am. J. Psychiat. 109:576, 1953.
[905] Storchheim, Frederic: On utilizing institutionalized mental patients to influence other patients psychotherapeutically, Am. J. Psychiat. 92:69, 1935.

Menninger [906] to meet unconscious emotional needs in the patient through diversified activities, recreation, dances, ward parties or a host of social situations arising out of life in an institution. An extension of this is the use of "patient government" in the hospital, wherein the actual organization of the hospital by the patients themselves provides "those opportunities for choice, expression and creativity that are so prized in a democratic society." [907] The major accomplishment of patient government, which lies between group therapy and morale building, is evidenced in improved spirit among the patients in addition to their learning "social skills of democratic living." A similar technic was used in England in the form of Social Clubs,[908] run on democratic lines, devoted to therapy rather than entertainment. The medical staff attend, as do the patients, but without professional function; discussions are general and free, the desideratum being to "remove the dividing line between the man who is or has been a patient and the man who is not."

The merging of environmental management and individual or group therapy has characterized the modern state hospital program. Implicit factors in the hospital environment and explicit factors inherent in various treatments have taken on positive values in an integrated plan. The total-push program is merely one aspect of therapy in a modern institution. A theoretical "Outline of Psychotherapy Program in a State Hospital" is indicated in the paradigm shown on page 290 [909] planned for both acute and chronic patients.

EARLY GROUP THERAPY

The tendency to deal with individual patients on a social scale in a hospital setting was contemporaneous with the development of group therapy. It coincided also with the spread of psychoanalytic "depth" concepts to psychotherapy in general and to the recognition of the significance of social interactionism following World War I. Whereas the total-push method dealt with patients as integers in a population all of whom needed stimulation, group therapy evolved in response to study of social interactions between members of a group. And the group technics also grew as an extension of the depth analysis of reactions of the group to its leader following Freud's work

[906] Menninger, W. C.: Psychiatric hospital therapy designed to meet unconscious needs, Am. J. Psychiat. 93:347, 1936.

[907] Hyde, R. W., and Solomon, H. C.: Patient government: a new form of group therapy, Digest Neurol. & Psychiat. 18:207, 1950.

[908] Strauss, E. B., Ström-Olsen, R., and Bierer, J.: A memorandum on therapeutic social clubs in psychiatry, Brit. M. J. 2:861, 1944.

[909] Bromberg, Walter: Outline of Psychotherapy Program in a State Hospital, Mendocino State Hospital, Talmage, California, 1951.

Factors IMPLICIT in Mental Hospital Residence
- Therapeutic Atmosphere
- Effect of Hospital Figures
- Dependence on Hospital Staff
- Directed Activity
- Psychological Effect of Physical Examination and Treatment

Factors EXPLICIT in Mental Hospital Treatment
- Interviews
  - Cathartic Effect
    - Assurance
    - Reassurance
    - Ventilation
  - Exploration
    - Superficial
    - Deep Historical
  - Emotional Support
- Individual Therapy (Multiple Interviews)
  - Relief of Anxiety
  - Dynamic Investigation
  - Nondirective
  - Confrontation and Interpretation
  - Transference Analysis
  - Hypnosis and Narcoanalysis
- Group Therapy (Including Psychodrama)
  - Support (Through Sibling and Staff Identification)
  - Relief from Isolation Feelings
  - Abreaction of Acting Out
  - Recognition of Misbehavior
  - Psychological Situations on Stage Perceived by Audience
  - Insight Development
  - Relief of Anxiety
- Manipulative Therapy
  - Job Placement
  - Ward Changes
- Training of Attendants
  - Seminars
  - Group Discussion with Attendants
- Social Casework
  - Preparation for Leave
  - Social Application of Therapeutic Result

on group psychology.[910] Freud's ideas on the emotional relation between leader and group members have been followed by many group therapists. From about 1930 onward, group therapy as a discipline, or a series of re-

[910] Freud, Sigmund: Group Psychology and the Analysis of the Ego (1921), translated by James Strachey, London, Hogarth, 1948.

lated efforts at forming a discipline, developed rapidly on the wings of a vertical (depth) analysis of individuals and a lateral (social) analysis of groups.

The beginnings of this enlarging area of psychotherapy have been traced to Dr. Joseph Pratt's handling of tuberculous patients in a "class" in 1905. Dr. Richard Cabot's introduction of medical social service at the Massachusetts General Hospital stimulated Doctor Pratt to gather "home-bound" consumptives into a class to instruct them in measures of physical hygiene and the newly discovered outdoor treatment of tuberculosis.[911] The Emmanuel Church of Boston, through its pastor, Doctor Worcester, made the class possible. It was perhaps because of the therapeutic spirit which the Emmanuel movement fostered that Pratt discovered the "mental uplift" which his tuberculous patients experienced during his lectures on the proper care for this devastating illness.[912] This line of endeavor, of distinctly medical social-service origin, was continued in classes for diabetics (Doctor Joslin) and other groups of chronic sufferers.

It was not, however, until psychoanalytic influence had pervaded psychiatry and influenced management of chronic mental cases that group therapy achieved more than casual notice. Working with psychotic material at St. Elizabeths Hospital, in Washington, D. C., Dr. Edward Lazell about 1919 started lecture classes for mental patients. His lectures dealt with the dynamic meaning of such symptoms as delusions, hallucinations, inferiority feelings and sexual perversion.[913] The accent was patently psychoanalytic, as Lazell adapted his lectures to his audience as individuals, to whom he hoped to bring understanding of their psychotic symptoms. Lazell's work, aimed at encouraging insight and lightening feelings of isolation or decreasing paranoid attitudes, was soon to be modified and extended by Wender in a hospital setting.

In this period another psychoanalytically oriented type of group activity was developed by Trigant Burrow, an American analyst, which sought to re-examine the neurosis as the product of social tensions arising within the individual under social conditions. Burrow's groups were small in number, devoted mainly to the theory of *phyloanalysis*, the study of conflict between the self-image of one person as it interacted with the self-image of another within the group. This was related to physiologic correlates [914] involved in the thinking process. In his group treatment Burrow made no interpretations, but tried to divert attention in patients from their "symbolic psycho-

911 Pratt, J. H.: The class method of treating consumption in the homes of the poor, J.A.M.A. **49**:755, 1907.

912 ——: The principles of class treatment and their application to various chronic diseases, Hosp. Soc. Service **6**:401, 1922.

913 Lazell, E. W.: The group treatment of dementia praecox, Psychoanalyt. Rev. **8**:168, 1921.

914 Burrow, Trigant: The group method of analysis, Psychoanalyt. Rev. **14**:268, 1927.

logical adaptation" to the organisms' true physiologic function.[915] Burrow's wish to reveal an absolute physiologic truth in human behavior rather than a symbolic one took him quite beyond the pale of useful psychological technics.[916] At any rate, the main stream of analytic group therapy has moved away from Burrow's early experiments.

Returning to the inspirational atmosphere of the earlier lecture-groups, Dr. Cody Marsh (1930), working in a New York state hospital with psychotic individuals, developed a type of group therapy of a warm, friendly, nonanalytic variety. Starting with lectures on mental-hygiene topics, Marsh found that he no longer needed to "talk down" to his patients, and that a "distinct group bond" became perceptible as they discussed problems, entertained each other, sang community songs and held "spell-downs" in their meetings.[917] Marsh felt, in developing mutual group feelings not unlike those of a religious revival meeting, that his activities were based on social bonds that were easily managed. In recommending that societies of ex-patients be established on a local and a national level to maintain associations formed in the hospital, Marsh recognized that therapy of mental conditions should be approached from a "social science" rather than a "medical science" point of view.

From a totally different quarter the advanced suggestions of Doctor Marsh were furthered in the evolution of the science of spontaneous interpersonal groupings by Jacob L. Moreno, a Viennese physician. The apex of Moreno's science of *sociometry* was a socially ordered world where the spontaneous creativity of individuals would fall into congenial groups. Before this social theory [918] of interaction was advanced (it has since been studied anew by Lewin and social psychological proponents of the "field theory"), Moreno had originated a really distinctive form of group therapy, under the name of *psychodrama,* as an outgrowth of his interest in the theater. Moreno discovered the therapeutic value of psychodrama while experimenting with the Theatre of Spontaneity,[919] in which, using random actors from an audience of the curious, he developed plays that spontaneously enacted scenes and dramatic content from the "private worlds" of the actors. The actor, Moreno found, tended spontaneously to create plays mirroring "his private world, his personal problem, his own conflicts, defeats and dreams." In the course of this work, actually part of the experimental theater movement initiated in Russia and Germany (1922-25) which sought

[915] Burrow, Trigant: The Neurosis of Man, New York, Harcourt, 1949.

[916] Bromberg, Walter: The biology of human conflict, critical comment, Am. J. Orthopsychiat. 8:553, 1938.

[917] Marsh, L. C.: Group treatment of the psychoses by the psychological equivalent of the revival, Ment. Hyg. 15:328, 1931.

[918] Moreno, J. L.: Who Shall Survive?, Washington, D. C., Nerv. & Ment. Dis. Pub. Co., 1934.

[919] ——: Das Stegreiftheater, 1923 [The Theatre of Spontaneity], translated by the author, New York, Beacon House, 1947.

to free the drama from its traditional formalism (Stanislavsky), Moreno gradually recognized the therapeutic value of his "Impromptu Theatre." * The emotional catharsis which the actor achieved through spontaneous dramatic action moved to the audience as the audience-member automatically placed himself in the role of the actor. When the director reversed roles on the stage, the actor saw himself portrayed by another actor, enabling the former to visualize aspects of his own personality not ordinarily accessible or perceptible.

ACTION TECHNICS IN GROUP THERAPY

The earliest motivation for the Theatre of Spontaneity arose from Moreno's philosophic interest in the creative aspects of man. His observation, that expansion of the self in a spontaneous drama was so clearly beyond the cramped expression which an actor ordinarily expressed when assuming the role of a character in the play, led Moreno to feel that a release of creativity was possible for anyone in spontaneous psychodrama. From the wish to release "the living creative process" in man, Moreno moved to study the interpersonal situation, a term which he claims to have originated under the German phrase "Begegnungs Lage." In this endeavor he encountered several interesting social-psychological phenomena; for example, resistances arising within the spontaneous actor from his movements, his emotions, the emotions of other actors and from the audience itself. From this development an elaborate series of social vectors which underlay subgroupings within a group were outlined and bent to use in psychotherapeutic sessions.

From a therapeutic point of view several important principles stand out from Moreno's experimentation with "action" technics. These include the fact that the therapist becomes in part a member of the group, hence a participant-observer; that the patient and each member of the audience become participant-observers; that by means of the auxiliary ego, mirror, double and role reversal technics the patient may see himself through the eyes of another and so objectivize his own inner drives, emotions and conflicts. When the therapeutic possibilities of this form of group activity became apparent, Moreno felt that he had stumbled upon a treatment method for the nontransference groups, namely, children and psychotics, "by systematically developing play as a therapeutic principle." [920] The basic notion in psychodrama is reliving in dramatic action and counteraction the "unrealistic patterns of neurotic and psychotic patients," [921] a concept which stands opposed to psychoanalytic or individual methods where acting-out is discouraged in

* The earlier material on Theatre of Spontaneity appeared anonymously.

[920] Moreno, J. L.: Psychodrama, Vol. 1, p. 6, New York, Beacon House, 1946.

[921] Hulse, W. C.: The social meaning of current methods in group psychotherapy, Group Psychotherapy 3: No. 1, 1950.

favor of verbalizations of fantasies and impulses. In psychodrama, the primary data are the acts and the feelings of the actors, whereas in psychoanalytic treatment the primary data are recollections adduced. In psychodrama the aim is to understand conflict in its current form, its *status nascendi,* whereas in analysis the goal is the reconstruction of "bygone or regressive" acts and feelings. Hence psychodramatists feel that a reconstructive analysis does not have the truth of action "of the moment," that rehearsed emotional relations are distorted, being removed in time from their *locus* of occurrence. It is difficult to reconcile Moreno's concepts and his singular terminology with traditional psychological views of personal relationships, but the warmth and the human empathy and the matter-of-fact realism of the protagonists displayed in a psychodramatic session bring to view an aspect of people not perceptible in other types of therapy.

In the psychodramatic session, after a period of "warming-up" in which intellectual interest passes into a kind of emotional arousal, action starts when a patient becomes the protagonist for his own drama. The therapist or a trained staff member then portrays persons vital to the patient's world—parent, wife or husband, friends, employer, etc., the auxiliary egos. The action is spontaneous, but automatically it moves to a central problem of the patient. By changes in the cast who enact what they believe the patient and his auxiliary egos really feel, by giving the patient a "double," a reflection of his self, or presenting a "mirror" picture of the patient on the stage or suddenly reversing roles of patient and staff members, a remarkably clear picture of the patient in a conflictful situation emerges.[922] The sudden placing of an individual in a role to which he is not accustomed, frequently a completely novel experience in life, itself a basic technic of Moreno, is often productive of a startlingly new view of one's self. As the spontaneous play develops, the therapist and the staff withdraw gradually, becoming less participators than observers, more catalysts than direct therapists. The actual characters in the patient's life can then be brought in and the "conflict" acted by patient and wife, or patient and mother; or it may remain in a projected form. Psychodrama is an intuitive and artistic form of interpersonal relationship, still not completely formulated in sociopsychological terms, but withal humanly valid and therapeutically effective. In fact, psychodrama has been held to embody all factors in group therapy. Other types of group therapists have felt that recognition of unconscious sources of conflict should find a place in this type of therapy, a view which Moreno concludes to be unnecessary and, in fact, doomed in the psychotherapy of the future.[923]

[922] Moreno, J. L.: Psychodramatic production techniques, Group Psychotherapy 4: 243, 1952.

[923] ——: The ascendancy of group psychotherapy and the declining influence of psychoanalysis, Group Psychotherapy 3:123, 1950.

ANALYTIC GROUP THERAPY

The practical difficulties of providing hospital patients with individualized psychotherapy led Louis Wender, of New York, to use the group method for informal discussion of mental mechanisms with his sanitarium patients. Gradually the group discussion touched on emotional relations occurring in the hospital—sibling rivalries, patient-to-patient transference reactions, jealousies, envy, etc. Wender's benign and understanding attitude welded the group into a family unit which made analysis of current emotional trends possible, a veritable "catharsis-in-the-family." [924] While the hospital life was organized round this dynamic structure, individual psychotherapy continued, depending on the needs of the patient. A mutual association of ex-patients was formed in the wake of Wender's relation to his patients which was openly recognized and interpreted as a frank father-figure transference.

Analytic group therapy attained prominence rather slowly; psychiatrists were wary of personal involvements with their patients. The same attitude of professional disinclination to get close to patients in an everyday manner also showed in the nonacceptance of psychodrama. The results which Wender obtained, and Paul Schilder's energetic espousal of group therapy in a clinic setting, did much to give this form of treatment a status of respectability in psychiatric circles before World War II. Schilder, at the Bellevue Psychiatric Hospital in New York, worked with patients who had previously been treated individually. With these he found that group work illuminated problems which did not arise in individual psychotherapy, particularly neurotic symptoms centering in attitudes toward the body, toward family ideals and social "ideologies." Using psychoanalysis "in a spirit of complete inner freedom," [925] Schilder uncovered before the group itself material from patients that touched on their unconscious derivative attitudes toward sexuality and other neurotic "ideologies."

The technic in Schilder's group therapy was psychoanalytic in nature; interpretations were made, material developed through free association, and general remarks or discussions carried out with and by the patients. Transference phenomena were interpreted and the therapist talked with relative freedom about his own position and interest toward his patients. Two interesting technical modifications were utilized by Schilder, namely, the writing of a complete, detailed "freely associated" autobiography by each patient which became the subject of the sessions, and a series of questionnaires, prepared for the therapist's use, to guide or stimulate discussion in the group. These questionnaires related to intimate subjects: they included reactions to the mother's or the father's body, "their caresses, angers, breast (mother),

[924] Wender, Louis: Group psychotherapy: a study of its application, Psychiatric Quart. 14:708, 1940.

[925] Schilder, Paul: Psychotherapy (rev. ed. by L. Bender), New York, Norton, 1951.

sex parts;" reactions to the "own" body, "will you age early, what do you think of your buttocks, your bosom, beauty, your mind;" reactions to masturbation, to urinary tendencies and habits, to birth, disease, food mentality, etc.[926] The idea behind these detailed questions, asked by the physician as a means of stimulating associations from the patients, was the uncovering of neurotic constellations which rarely appeared during individual psychoanalysis. Questions were often so startling as they confronted the patients with views of their inner feelings that neurotic corners "which the individual hides from himself," and hitherto hidden or obscured in therapy, came to light in the group.

It was significant that Schilder used psychoanalytic concepts freely in his group and individual therapy without the "codifications of the psychoanalytic school" which was prescribed in the period in which he worked. For example, he disbelieved the rigid rule that the psychotherapist should not examine his patients physically should he plan to treat them analytically. Another point which Schilder acted on was his faith in and perception of the learning process implied in every psychotherapeutic contact, and undeniably so in group therapy. "I believe in the power of the intellect," he wrote, meaning in this connection the validity of studying the "ideas" of patients with their emotional and historical attachments. Respect for the social-world realities of the patient that Schilder contributed induced many workers to relax some of their professional caution in their therapeutic relations with patients. Activity and freedom were the watchwords of his therapist role. The exigencies of psychiatric needs during World War II which led to widespread use of the group therapy method received, in some quarters at least, support and humanistic meaning from Schilder's efforts in this field.[927] "The relation between the physician and his patient thus becomes a mirror of possible social relations between two human beings, in which the physician is no less affected than the patient himself." [928]

A strong force in the burgeoning of group therapy arose from the natural tendency to handle disturbed children in groups. This activity was recognized in the field of child therapy,[929] but Slavson's consistent experimentation with behavioral problems at the Jewish Board of Guardians in New York exerted a strong influence on group therapy as a method. The early groups which Slavson conducted (1934) had diagnosis and treatment as their rationale. When he allowed children free activity in groups, Slavson noted the transition from an infantile to a group superego as the children altered their misbehavior, habit difficulties and neurotic traits within the

[926] *Ibid.*, p. 203.
[927] Shaskan, D. A.: Trends in orthopsychiatric therapy; evolution and trends in group psychotherapy, Am. J. Orthopsychiat. 18:447, 1948.
[928] Schilder, Paul: *Op. cit.*, p. 12.
[929] Bender, Lauretta: Group activities on a children's ward as methods of psychotherapy, Am. J. Psychiat. 93:1151, 1937.
Bromberg, Walter: The Mind of Man, p. 291, New York, Harper, 1937.

group.[930] Allowing the group complete permissivity, giving them "unconditional love," the children appeared to be transformed as they experienced release from guilt and censorship reactions through activity and group interaction. Slavson's interpretation of the changes wrought in the children was based on the transference reactions of children to the therapist-figure. Extended to adolescents and adults, Slavson's "activity group" became an "analytic group" wherein the unrestricted activity, permitted the children under a permissive, comfortable parent-figure, gave way to the encouragement of verbalization; group therapy became identical in technic with individual psychotherapy on a freudian basis.[931] However, the aim was admittedly not to eliminate the basic conflict behind the neurosis but to modify "its derivative personality difficulty and over-intense affect as manifested in behavior." The dynamic factors operative in group experiences, as summed up by Slavson, consist in the following factors: "Transference, dilution, target multiplicity (therapist-parent), displacement (sibling situation), escape and deflection (attention on other member as relief from own problem), identification, mutual support (lateral hostility and aggression), catalysis (patients activate each other), universalization (other people have same problem)." [932] While these dynamic interrelations occur also in individual psychotherapy, the introduction of a social world of reality (the group) makes more meaningful the dynamic changes occurring in the patient.[933]

All observers agree that group therapy is a more "real experience" for the patient than is individual therapy.[934] This sense of vivid experience is even more intense in psychodrama and activity groups. Here the value of spontaneous "play-acting" has been exploited among disturbed children and character deviations (psychopaths).[935] Play allows the toleration of anxiety-laden situations whilst it permits a channeling off of emotional tensions; play has been found to enhance catharsis and bring conflicts into relief in three-dimensions, so to speak. Yet, in spite of the vividness of affect which group therapy evokes, it is questionable whether it can eventually replace individual psychotherapy. Whether it can supplant the aim to uncover unconscious forces in the patient as in psychoanalysis, whether the "group of two" which Freud called the analyst-analysand relation requires enlargement to more than two, to provide social significance to the situa-

930 Slavson, S. R.: An Introduction to Group Therapy, New York, Commonwealth Fund, 1943.

931 ——: Analytic Group Psychotherapy; with Children, Adolescents and Adults, New York, Columbia, 1950.

932 *Ibid.*, p. 93.

933 Klapman, J. W.: Group Psychotherapy; Theory and Practice, pp. 119 and 120, New York, Grune, 1947.

934 Ackerman, N. W.: Group psychotherapy with veterans, Psychosom. Med. 8:118 and 119, 1946.

935 Bromberg, Walter, and Franklin, G. H.: The treatment of sexual deviates with group psychodrama, rep. from group psychotherapy, J. Sociopsychopathology & Sociatry, Vol. 4, No. 4, March, 1952.

tion is problematical. It is a further question whether passage of implied authority and the therapeutic goal of the therapist to the group itself constitutes indispensable criteria for effective psychotherapy in the future.

Some therapists feel that translation of group dynamics into terms of psychoanalytic ego psychology is "fraught with complications;"[936] others feel that the primary aim of establishing insight into psychoneurotic mechanisms is not the function of group therapy. Its function as conceived by Cotton[937] is an attempt to "reinforce and strengthen the individual's defenses against anxiety by identification with . . . and support from the group," to which formulation many workers add: "[The doctor] is the strongest single influence on the functioning of the group. He sets the aims and mores of the group and determines the . . . therapeutic effectiveness of the relationships formed among the members."[938]

The authors of this last axiom have made a careful, controlled study over a two-year period at the Veterans Administration facilities, using 124 patients and 25 physicians, themselves checked by trained observers.[939] They studied events in the group activity which had positive or negative therapeutic significance, scrutinizing such occurrences as the doctor's security feelings, exhibitionism, leadership; hostilities in the group; the "monopolist" who insists on keeping his own case in the forefront of discussion; silences among the patients; differences in early and late meetings of a group; rises and falls in tension and so on. Their objective study showed, in part, that patients tend to associate personal problems with common themes, and that the doctor must be "unremitting in attention . . . to guide members toward and around their areas of greatest anxiety." They imply also that it may well be that "crucial aspects of psychotherapy, group or individual, cannot be communicated in objectively verifiable terms." It must be acknowledged that precise understanding of all factors operating in group therapy of any description is not at hand, although, in Slavson's opinion, divergent views and practices may soon be reconciled.[940]

SOCIAL THERAPY

While complete theoretical understanding eludes workers in this field, its area of activity enlarges rapidly. Group therapy has spread in many

[936] Ackerman, N. W.: Psychoanalysis and group psychotherapy, Group Psychotherapy 3:204, 1950.

[937] Cotton, J. M.: "Group Psychotherapy; An Appraisal," *in* Failures in Psychiatric Treatment, edited by P. H. Hoch, p. 121, New York, Grune, 1948.

[938] Powdermaker, Florence, and Frank, J. D.: Group psychotherapy with neurotics, Am. J. Psychiat. **105**:449, 1948.

[939] ——: Group Psychotherapy: Studies in Methodology of Research and Therapy, Harvard, 1953.

[940] Slavson, S. R., Hallowitz, Emanuel, and Rosenthal, Leslie: "Group Psychotherapy," *in* Progress in Neurology and Psychiatry, edited by E. A. Spiegel, Vol. 7, New York, Grune, 1952.

directions, ranging from groups in a church setting under a pastoral psychiatrist in which the "democratic voluntary principle so deeply imbedded in Christianity" [941] is relied on, to group activity in an industrial plant or the self-confessing therapeutic activity and mutual participation of emotional experiences in Alcoholic Anonymous meetings.[942] Included in this new field is group therapy among nursing mothers,[943] psychotics, epileptics,[944] mental defectives,[945] senile mental patients [946] and sexual deviates.[947] The areas of use could be multiplied indefinitely. But overshadowing its widespread use in clinics, hospitals, schools and private offices is the social or, we may say, political meaning of group therapy. An essential factor of group therapy is its breaking down of authoritarian-subject values which played so great a role in psychotherapy throughout the centuries. A virtual revolution in the relation between doctor and patient has been brought into being by group therapy. The position of the therapist who was once removed from his patient by a chasm of impersonality, no matter how disguised by kindliness and paternal interest, has been replaced by the position of therapist as participant observer. An anthropologist and a social psychiatrist [948] have studied the problem, always implicit but not always stated, of communication between persons in a social relationship as it bears on the new therapeutic alignment. They indicate how therapy in actuality "rests upon communication between people having different values traceable to differences" in perception of life-events.[949]

This accent on the current emotional relationships between people has been found to rest on a wide base molded by culture and insensibly influencing the patient's and the therapist's attitude. When the psychiatrist becomes part of the group, he himself must be alert to forces acting on him as well as to those acting on the patient. The reconstruction of the personality to find the missing links covered by amnesias or the traumatic events repressed into the unconscious is supplemented by a living reformation in current participation in the group. Emotional reactions of the

[941] Leslie, R. C.: Pastoral group psychotherapy, Group Psychotherapy **3:** No. 1, 1950.

[942] Medicine Looks at Alcoholics Anonymous (reps. of papers presented to the Medical Society of the State of New York and the American Psychiatric Assoc.), New York, Alcoholic Foundation, 1944.

[943] Bartemeier, L. H.: Concerning the Cornelian Corner, Am. J. Orthopsychiat. **17:**594, 1947.

[944] Deutsch, A. L., and Zimmerman, Joseph: Group psychotherapy as adjunct treatment of epileptic patients, Am. J. Psychiat. **104:**783, 1948.

[945] Cotzin, Milton: Group psychotherapy with mentally defective problem boys, Am. J. Ment. Deficiency **53:**268, 1948.

[946] Silver, A.: Group psychotherapy with senile psychotic patients, Geriatrics **5:**147-150, 1950.

[947] Cruvant, B. A., Meltzer, M., and Tartaglino, F. J.: An institutional program for committed sex deviants, Am. J. Psychiat. **107:**190, 1950.

[948] Ruesch, Jurgen, and Bateson, Gregory: Communication; The Social Matrix of Psychiatry, New York, Norton, 1951.

[949] *Ibid.*

individual arising from his culture and his family constellation, the living matrix of neurotic and psychotic reactions, are therefore involved.

The use of social psychiatry in therapy has rapidly come to the point where it constitutes practically an outdistancing of individual psychotherapy. An English group, headed by Dr. Maxwell Jones,[950] have developed a "therapeutic community" in which treatment is in terms of living in an environment where doctors, nurses and patients interact as a unit community. A concrete notion of the work of this group can be obtained by noting that the traditional doctor-nurse relationship with its hierarchical levels is dissolved. The patients are not "treated" in the ordinary sense; they are integrated into the social structure. The nurses, Dr. Jones notes, "would be more aptly termed 'social workers.' " A process of "acculturation seems to be an essential part of our social therapy techniques," Jones comments, as models of social adjustment are introduced to the patients by "casual contacts incidental to the affairs of living" rather than in a formal therapeutic way. Prof. Goodwin Watson, who writes a foreword to the book of the English group, comments that the therapeutic community may be an even more far-reaching development than those that flowed from psychoanalysis. It may well be proved in the future that the acculturation process, which virtually is a process of emotional and cultural education, will be the effective psychotherapy for neurotic, maladapted individuals in our society.

In view of the rapid appearance of new methods of therapy in recent years, it is impossible to foretell how broad the panorama of psychotherapy will become. Almost no aspect of psychological theory, as Gestalt therapy,[951] or Count Korzybski's general semantics,[952] or philosophic outlook, as existentialism,[953] has been neglected in the search for methodologic bases for psychotherapeutic technics. As seen in the current chapter, the interpersonal-relationship problem has stimulated many workers to find means of enlarging the benefits obtained from more intensive treatment, which aims to enucleate and resolve binding infantile patterns. Methods of therapy which take their departure from recognition of the social influences on the individual seem to be more palatable and possibly more useful to psychotherapists dealing with a seemingly expanding number of emotional difficulties. It may be that methods which deal with the currency of everyday life seem more acceptable because therapists work in a world that demands amelioration more than radical cure.

[950] Jones, Maxwell: The Therapeutic Community, A New Treatment Method in Psychiatry, New York, Rinehart (Basic Books), 1953.
[951] Perls, Frederick, Hefferline, Ralph, and Goodman, Paul: Gestalt Therapy: Excitement and Growth in the Human Personality, New York, Julian Press, 1952.
[952] Campbell, D. G.: General semantics, Am. J. Psychiat. 93:789, 1937.
[953] Weigert, Edith: Existentialism and its relations to psychotherapy, Psychiatry 12:399, 1949.

13

Observations

The sprawling, chaotic, often anachronistic, yet intensely vigorous and human, story of the predecessors and the contemporaries of present-day psychotherapy comes to an end. It represents one phase of man's attempt to rise above humanity, and as such passes through much of human history. In its development, mental healing touched on many areas of human concern but also by-passed others equally vital in the history of civilization. The rise and the decline of cultures, expansion and contraction of empires, economic and literary evolution and technological enterprise have been detoured in our survey. It is possible that these movements had a remote effect on the evolution of psychotherapy; however, throughout this narrative we have commented on factors that have influenced *directly* the growth of mental healing. It has been pointed out that psychotherapy interdigitated with political philosophies and institutions, religions and neoreligions, mythologies and folklore, scientific methodologies, theories of ego psychology and currents deriving from economic and social realignment. Though psychotherapy today is an identifiable group of activities clustering round knowledge of man's psychic apparatus, it had no conscious beginning as such. Much of what we refer to as psychotherapy was part and parcel of the individual's attempt, through social institutions (e.g., religion, witchcraft, humanitarianism), to adjust to internal and external stresses that confronted him. The history of mental healing is the history of continuous adaptations to problems of living, occurring in eras differing radically from each other as concerns their central ideology and technologic equipment. Our survey shows that, save for the activities of organized medical and psychiatric science during the last century and a half, a chronology of mental healing is, in reality, only possible in the form of an interpretative reconstruction.

The history of psychotherapy differs from the history of psychiatry by virtue of two contrasting accents: first, the former was not marked by an intensive search, sometimes clinical and descriptive, sometimes philosophic, for an understanding of the disorders of the mind; second, it was marked by the constant presence of conflict. The lack of a conscious search for meaning in psychotherapy will be considered first.

Psychiatry, it is true, has been beset with the difficulty of defining its subject matter, of finding terms and ideas to describe real, yet impalpable, deviations from normal behavior. However, once psychiatry removed itself from the influence of ethical philosophy and adopted evolutionary concepts and behavioral criteria, it, with the aid of scientific medicine, found a path along which to travel. (Thomas Browne is quoted as writing in the early 1800's: "The moral affections . . . I consider rather physiologically or, better expressed, 'psychologically' than ethically, as parts of our mental constitution, not as involving the fulfillment or violation of duties.")[954] Psychotherapy, on the contrary, until recently was neither limited nor aided by these frames of reference. The main consideration impelling men to seek ways of helping others through mental means was the urgent need of distraught human beings. Hence men, whose aspirations and ideas became embodied in psychotherapeutic principles, and social movements, which aimed to relieve broad social pressures, became interlaced in the hybrid genesis of mental healing. At one extremity the technics of mental healing touched on magic, mysticism, religious devotion and submission to a Divine Will and philosophic idealism; while on the other, technics reached into biochemistry, neurology, psychology and the psychoanalytic theory of the unconscious. Attitudes lying behind the employment of these ideologies varied from a sublime sense of participation in Deity to a plain-spoken, causal materialism. The figures through whom mental healing evolved ran the gamut of monks and medicine men, saints and sinners, kings and quacks, physicians and specialists, including men of every degree of genius or mediocrity, of knowledge and skill. Their actions have been inspired by human nobility, by lust for advantage, by scientific curiosity and workaday patience; in common they had vision, tenacity of purpose and often inexhaustible wells of courage against defeats and disappointments.

The second differentiating element, the presence of conflict in psychotherapy, is evidenced both in the "warring sects" within the profession and in the intrapsychic struggle which underlies symptoms within the patient. Hostilities between groups of adherents of specific psychiatric systems of practice stretch from Galen and his contemporaries to the latest freudian separatist. The internecine medical struggles reported throughout this narrative, the contumely heaped upon innovators, the scorn and the derision which greeted new ideas, were not accidental. For psychotherapy itself was born of strong emotion and conflict, conflict between desires of man and limitations of his nature, between his conscience and his impulses, and

[954] Browne, Thomas: *Quoted in:* Mackintosh, Sir James: Progress of Ethical Philosophy, ed. 2, p. 242, Philadelphia, Carey, Lea & Blanchard, 1834.

man and society. Indeed, discovery of the presence of unconscious conflict was the fulcrum round which psychotherapy turned, moving from an empirical set of practices to a discipline of scientific aspirations. Further, discovery of the conflict resident in the therapeutic process, between patient and physician, was a concept of incalculable value in illuminating some dark corners in treatment mechanisms. It also rendered clear the meaning of neurotic symptoms, psychotic regressions and bizarre behavior. The struggles of patients to free themselves of forces opposing health, whether called demons, madness, "mortal error," "wrong thinking," id impulses or social aggressions, called for the best efforts of mental healers of every persuasion. For psychotherapy, in its concern with conflict, lies on the firing line of the mental sciences. It is here that necessity becomes the mother of invention, that clinical probabilities and intuitive insight become transmuted into science. This vibrant, "living" quality of psychotherapy makes the writing of a sequential "history" of this subject difficult and an analysis of its underlying, unifying principles even more so.

Nevertheless, we have attempted in the first chapter to outline the forces operative in bringing about ease, or healing, of mental and nervous states. Throughout the body of this book these forces have been both implicitly and explicitly described as they appeared in the various technics employed. The forces of magic, faith, intellect, and the adaptive potential of the ego represent the matrix of effective psychotherapy. What makes mental healing of the Dark Ages appear so unrelated to twentieth-century psychotherapy is the time-relations of employment of these forces. In examining the events which have been chronicled in these chapters we can readily observe how the primordial elements, magic and faith, although never absent, have been superseded by the handling of adaptive ego tendencies, in conjunction with use of the intellect. These changes in therapeutic accent resulted from experience and experiment; they were hewn out of the granite of clinical work by physicians and psychological workers, and supported by painstaking, critical observation. In the last analysis, therefore, the history of mental healing belongs to those who have grappled with the application of these psychic elements.

But, we may ask, what is the meaning to the patient of this struggle to extract rational healing principles from irrational operations on irrational subjects? To attempt to answer this seems to require turning to the basic question of the motive, the essential rationale, for engaging in the pursuit of psychotherapy.

It can be agreed by everyone with experience in the field, whether professional or lay, that the unifying thread in all psychotherapy over recorded time has been the wish to heal. This wish to cure is a conscious desire on the part of men and women of good will. It is unconsciously motivated also by a vague and socially acceptable anxiety, as well as a strong curiosity, to understand the complex human mind. No one who deals with distortions of the mind escapes "this never-ending reverence before the fact of mental disturbance as a problem of human existence."[955] Partly identifiable as scientific curiosity, partly recognized as a projection of specific personality trends in the healer (sublimation), and partly regarded as a spirit of altruism, the wish to heal is a function of the healer, not the patient.

But from the patient's point of view this preoccupation with the meaning of mental illness is relatively casual. Philosophic or scientific curiosity may follow his request for immediate relief, not precede it. If the patient has an unconscious wish to be ill (projection of unconscious impulses), it is veiled from his mind or embedded in his illness. If the patient has an altruistic impulse toward himself, it is similarly hidden. The client, supplicant or patient chiefly desires immediate relief and the assurance that his distressing condition or disabling pain will not reappear; he may also want approbation, direction or even relief through absolution from his therapist. There is a marked difference in frame of reference of the patient versus healer or physician. It is the difference between recipient and donor, between the taker and the giver. This contrasting attitude between patient and physician partly answers the question why, over the centuries, magical or faith elements in psychotherapy have been, and are now, effective in removing symptoms. It explains also why mental healing became the province of physicians only comparatively recently in the life of Western civilization. In the history we have traced there has been but a corresponding growth of rational interest within the patient of himself. The gap between patient and physician in its psychological essence remains wide, but not as wide as it was in the days before a conscious and a scientific psychotherapy appeared.

A commentary on the slow change in psychotherapy over the centuries, with its increasing accent on the individual as a sharer in a possible mental health, is seen in the variation of the patient's position in the social scale. For several thousands of years the seeker of health was a supplicant; then, as medicine developed, he became an unfortunate sufferer. For the past two centuries, as psychiatry evolved, he attained the level of a patient. Recently, as psychotherapy broadened to include social relationships, he advanced to the stage of a client. With group therapy he became a social atom, and, in the foreseeable future, where therapy becomes a matter of propaganda and social planning, he may evolve into a psychological integer. In all this the patient remained the recipient.

[955] Loewenberg, R. D.: Karl Jaspers on psychotherapy, Am. J. Psychotherapy 5:502-513, 1951.

To return to the meaning to the patient of psychiatry's struggle to develop a therapy based on a realistic understanding of the psychic life, we note that attainment of insight among neurotic patients was strongly stimulated by the psychoanalytic school and its derivatives. Freudian psychology made the accomplishment of insight an integral part of therapy. However, it should not be forgotten that concern with self-knowledge evolved also from larger social and historical forces. Increasing literacy and a corresponding psychological self-perception during the past two centuries have paved the way for the cultural reorientation toward the self, characteristic of modern man in the Western world. There were distant forces of a social and an economic nature in this realignment, such as the overthrow of feudalism, the Industrial Revolution, and the lessening disparity between the authoritative classes and the subject classes. These forces represented a democratization of education and relief from the authoritarian position, wherein man's soul and mind were not appropriate subjects for his own scrutiny. The modern era tends to accentuate self-understanding, even though the more elemental tendencies of submission, of seeking for authoritative direction or reliance on suprahuman forces, still exert powerful influences within us.

An outstanding result of the last century's attention to the dynamics of mental therapy has been the removal of elements of magic from the deliberate application of psychotherapy. And with it can be counted the corollary search for knowledge of the "cause" of mental symptoms expressed in terms of the patient's historical psychic life. The relating of unconscious forces and impulses and the defenses against them to consciously perceived symptoms has constituted an enduring chapter in psychiatry. Nonetheless, demonstration of the influence of infantile patterns of reaction in an individual suffering from neurotic troubles has not always met with cure in a given patient. Where cure is achieved, it is not always possible to state the exact mechanisms by which enucleation of unconscious determinants and their incorporation within the functioning ego bring about relief. Competent psychoanalysts do not all agree on the precise forces operative between therapist and patient which are effective in psychoanalytic [956] or other psychological therapy. There is the further question of satisfaction of the logical meaning of causality in the sequential relation of infantile trauma to symptom formation. For a sequence of events is not necessarily proof of "causation." [957]

Quite apart from the philosophical problem of the logical validity of "cause" in the development of a mental or a neurotic symptom is the psy-

956 Fenichel, Otto: Problems of Psychoanalytic Technique, translated by David Brunswick, Chap. 7, Albany, N. Y., Psychoanalyt. Quart. Inc., 1941.

957 Ducasse, C. J.: Causality, Creation and Ecstasy, The Philosophical Forum, Vol. 2, p. 11, 1953.

chological meaning to the therapist of the theory of causation upon which he bases his work. Such a theory is an operational conception, a working tool, which among other things contributes a feeling of solidity to the therapist in the application of whichever therapeutic method he employs. It is not the proof of "cause" of symptom formation, but the belief in the validity of that "cause," which is effective in psychotherapy. From this point of view to which our historical review seems to have brought us, another force inherent in the action of psychotherapy must be added to those which we have observed to underlie all methods of therapy described in our survey. For it is possible that the help which a patient derives from a therapeutic method rides upon some other factor than those of "causality" demonstrated by each proponent of a therapeutic method to his own satisfaction. For, if each therapy is even occasionally successful, and each rests upon widely differing theoretical bases, the factor making for success may be in the patient, not in the method. We will attempt to elaborate this surmise of a hitherto unstated, although frequently implied, force which has been apparently active in the therapeutic methods described in this work.

We may start this exposition by pointing out that all methods of psychotherapy may be encompassed under the heads of inspirational or suppressive, and expressive or uncovering, methods of therapy (see Chap. 12). An examination of the action of inspirational forms of treatment may shed some light on the reactivity of the patient to both groups of therapeutic methods. In the so-called suppressive methods of psychotherapy, the aim is to supply a feeling of faith in the eventuality of cure. This faith utilizes the vehicle of belief in a spirit of "goodness" which exists in the therapist, combined with an implied alliance with an external Power or Powers able to work the changes necessary for cure. This Power has authority, knowledge and a wish to help, i.e., a partisan position toward the patient. These functions are encompassed in the idea that the Power is "good," since symptoms or illness is, to the patient, considered to be "bad" or destructive, or (in fact) defeating and painful. Thus, in addition to faith as a vehicle, belief in the "goodness" of the assisting Power is necessary to achieve those changes necessary for a cure.

The inspirational technic of psychotherapy is analogous to use of prayer as a therapeutic maneuver. Prayer presupposes a wish for change in that one is to be different in respect to a symptom or a personality characteristic. The psychic work required is the acceptance of a Power (God) who will make such a change through inner rearrangement. This expectation is based on the fact that the Power (God) is the creator of all things, the cause of human phenomena both normal and abnormal and a wisher for good in all human beings. A supplicant for health to be achieved through prayer is convinced that God or a supernatural power (1) knows the cause of symptoms and (2) wants human beings to benefit from his love and perfection and is willing to donate this omnipotence and omniscience to those who, in so believing, accept through willing submission the power and the knowledge of the God or Spirit so invoked.

In the uncovering technics which include psychological analysis, removal of symptoms is predicated on a discovery of their cause, either in the historical development of the personality of the patient or in the current life situation. The therapist believes in the psychogenic and the pathogenic power of these antecedents. By demonstrating to the patient that such traumatic events are the cause of such symptoms, the patient comes to believe, on demonstration, in their pathogenic power. This belief process is accompanied by a growth of the ego to a knowledge of its capacities and rights of control (i.e., maturation) and increases the capacity of the ego to control instinctive forces within it. The emotional nurture passing from therapist to patient, in and through identification and transference, gives the patient strength and surety to believe, to which is added the effective (moving) experience of believing itself. To this is added the "natural" tendency of the ego to express the claims of instinctual energy directly to the outside world. This tendency can be explained no further than by noting that it is the ego's trend toward mastery in adaptation, or that it relates to "a wish for health." Indeed, the process of working through in analysis means confronting the ego, for its ultimate control, of warded off—hence, unconscious—impulses revived through analysis.

On the basis of this psychobiologic tendency toward ego control, the "natural tendency toward 'synthesis,' "[958] the therapist, using uncovering technics, offers his reconstruction of the patient's mental life *to* the patient, so that the latter, after resistances are resolved, may comprehend and incorporate the unconscious forces released. Although the patient can appreciate the effect of unconscious activity when it is demonstrated and "worked through," he does not "know" whether the reconstruction and the causal relationship between conscious or unconscious factors in his life and his symptoms are correct or not: he is held to accept the reconstruction on the basis of belief in the therapist's belief.

The therapist, who does not insist that the patient accept the formulations adduced, implies that if the patient will accept the former's interpretations "as if" they were true, he will be benefited. The therapist believes this on the basis of his own teaching, proofs in his own analysis and the pragmatic test of explanation of such causal relationships in other patients within his experience. In this process the therapist also has the wish that the patient get well, that "good be done him"—all this in the face of his scientific certainty of the cause of symptoms or in the near certainty that

[958] Fenichel, Otto: *Op. cit.*, p. 114.

his reconstruction is accurate in the face of facts as developed through a study of the patient's psychic economy.

The ceding of belief to the therapeutic efficiency of an uncovering, reconstructing and working through of the psychic vicissitudes of a symptom is analogous on a logical basis to the ceding of belief in the reconstructive power of a God or a nonhuman Power. In both cases the "as if" postulate operates: If the basic causative theory is correct, then belief in it is productive of practical result. For a patient cannot know the absolute truth of either postulate, even though they be proven to the satisfaction of the therapist or the religious healer. The patient can only believe that such causal relationship operative in his case (that emotional trauma causes symptoms or that God's omniscience can bring about removal of symptoms), if believed, can have resulting practical benefit. That many, even diametrically opposed, types of therapeutic endeavors have produced relief and cures in patients, points to the one universal factor in psychotherapies which have succeeded. Our historical survey seems to indicate, then, that the *one* prerequisite factor in effective psychotherapy is the dynamic, i.e., emotionally moving, one of believing in the power of removal of symptoms. For the patient any one of a number of technics may bring, and have brought, this belief into being, whether they encompass an omniscient Being or Beings, a natural agency, a demonstrable discord within the ego or a maldevelopment of the personality.

In spite of this assertion of the importance of dynamic belief in the patient, a factor often hidden from superficial view, the refining of methods of psychotherapy and the coincident education of the patient-world in the behavior of his psychic apparatus do and should go on. But a realistic appraisal of the therapeutic situation demonstrates that the patient's ideologies are therapeutic first and scientific (i.e., causally oriented) later.

For that reason various methods of mental healing have been used simultaneously or successively with satisfaction to the patient. This means that an *eclecticism* is acceptable to the patient and even expected by him, except by those who have been educated toward loyalty to scientific purism. This does not mean that the scientific spirit of verification of one method of treatment by keeping it isolated from others is not a good principle. It has nothing to do with the tenets of scientific methodology. It merely means that a reluctance toward eclecticism is a function of the therapist and his scientific interests and has no realistic relation to the needs of the patient as developed in the paragraphs above. Nor does eclecticism throttle the impetus of science toward developing new methods and new directions.

In a discussion of eclecticism one must ask what is the central rationale for treatment in mental disturbances. Is it cure, is it alleviation, is it functional restoration? It seems more realistic to consider that the aim is a functional restitution of the ego, which may bring with it disappearance of symptoms. The broad field of biology may offer us analogies of instructive value on this question. The observation can be easily made that, truly, nature does not heal, but merely restitutes. In medicine, when an organ of the body is diseased, the reparative forces surround the infection, quiet the disturbance, and allow other areas to take up the burden. For example, when collateral circulation develops round a thrombosis of vein or artery or when, in surgical cases, a scar forms after operative work, the scar has no function but allows other parts of the body to function. Nature does not bring an organism or an organ back to its prime state of efficiency and intactness. We are content if a wound "heals," whether in the body or on the surface, if whole or part function is maintained with as little cosmetic distortion as possible.

So, in the mental sphere, scars are left after a mental breakdown or neurosis, or even an emotional upset, while the total personality is enabled to function satisfactorily. The ego, freed from unconscious inhibitions and blocks, supported in its faltering strength, pulled back from its regressions, helped to relinquish neurotic (symptomatic) gratifications, is in a better position to form acceptable patterns of adaptation. Psychotherapy's essential task, after paving the way, is to provide the ego with tools for adaptation; to allow emotional, instinctual energies and intellectual tendencies to integrate within the ego and move in a direction consonant with personal realities. The wise physician, therefore, has come in modern times to speak of adjustment or help rather than cure in the majority of mental and nervous patients. The same process of democratization that induced patients to support the modern aims of psychotherapy has influenced psychotherapists. Their wish to cure, with its occasional overtones of unconscious omnipotence fantasy, has been modified to fit the patient into a social world where he can have the maximum of comfort, enjoyment and efficiency in regard to his own pursuits.

The fading of authoritarianism in the doctor-patient situation in our century has brought the aims of psychotherapy out of the formalistic realm of cure. The healer has now been brought face to face with the larger purposes of living, for, in his reorientation from the absolutist idea of "cure" to the relativistic one of "adjustment," he perforce encounters the question indicated in the phrase, "Adjusted to what?" These larger purposes of living whose delineation religion and philosophy have pursued, when articulated with the aims of psychotherapy spread the panorama into the indistinguishable horizon. In that horizon lie the seemingly eternal problems of existence, but short of that is the large temperate zone in which most of us live. Here satisfactions—physical, esthetic and moral—may be defined and experienced. It is here that psychotherapy is attempting to serve many men. With an awareness of the scientific principles of the healing relationship, the biologic basis of the physical and the mental life, and the human values involved, mental healers are striving to perfect their calling. Whether their work is illuminated by intuition or spurred by seasoned clinical judgment, whether lasting or ephemeral, their history tells a story that never grows stale. It is a story involving the exercise of man's greatest heritage—the imperishable spirit of man.

Recent Literature

Alexander, Franz: *Psychoanalysis and Psychotherapy: Developments in Theory, Technique and Training*. New York, W. W. Norton, 1956.

Bennett, A. E., Hargrove, and Engle: *Practice of Psychiatry in General Hospitals*. Berkeley, Univ. of California Press, 1956.

Chlorpromazine and Mental Health, Proceedings of Symposium under Auspices of Smith Kline and French Laboratories. Lea & Febiger, June, 1955.

Colby, Kenneth: *Energy and Structure in Psychoanalysis*. New York, Ronald Press, 1955.

Corsini, R. J.: *Methods of Group Psychotherapy*. New York, McGraw-Hill Book Co., Inc., 1957.

Deutsch, Felix, and Murphy, William F.: *The Clinical Interview,* 2 vols. New York, International Universities Press, 1954-55.

Ehrenwald, Jan: *From Medicine Man to Freud*. New York, Dell, 1956.

Glover, Edward: *The Technique of Psychoanalysis*. New York, International Universities Press, 1955,

Hall, Calvin, and Lindzey, Gardner: *Theories of Personality*. New York, John Wiley, 1957.

Hill, L. B.: *Psychotherapeutic Intervention in Schizophrenia* (Univ. of Chicago Com. on Publ. in Biol. and Med., Emmet B. Bay, et al.). Chicago, Univ. of Chicago Press, 1955.

Himwich, H. E.: "Prospects in Pharmacology," J. *Nervous & Mental Diseases,* Vol. 122, p. 413, November, 1955.

Jones, Ernest: *The Life and Work of Sigmund Freud,* 3 vols. New York, Basic Books, 1955-58.

Jung, C. J.: *The Practice of Psychotherapy*. New York, Bollingen-Pantheon Books, 1954.

Knight, Robert P., ed.: *Psychoanalytic Psychiatry and Psychology,* Clinical and Theoretical Papers, Austen Riggs Center, I. New York, International Universities Press, 1954.

May, Rollo, Angel, Ernest, and Ellenberger, Harry F., eds.: *Existence: a New Dimension in Psychiatry and Psychotherapy*. New York, Basic Books, 1958.

Meduna, L. J., ed.: *Carbon Dioxide Therapy,* 2nd ed. Springfield, Illinois, Charles C. Thomas, 1958.

Menninger, Karl: *Theory of Psychoanalytic Technique*. New York, Basic Books, 1958.

Menninger, W. C.: "Psychiatry and the Practice of Medicine," *Mississippi Valley Medical Journal,* p. 93, July, 1956.

Moreno, J., and Masserman, J.: *Progress in Psychotherapy,* 3 vols. New York, Grune and Stratton, 1956-58. In progress.

Munroe, Ruth L.: *Schools of Psychoanalytic Thought*. New York, Dryden, 1955.

Nelson, Benjamin, ed.: *Freud and the 20th Century*. New York, Meridian Books, 1957.

The Newsletter, National League for Nursing, Council on Psychiatric and Mental Health Nursing, 1956, et. seq.

Nunberg, H.: *Principles of Psychoanalysis*. New York, International Universities Press, 1955.

Shore, P. A., Silver, S. L., and Brodie, B. B.: "Interaction of Reserpine, Serotonin, and Lysergic Acid Diethylamide in Brain," *Science*, Vol. 122, p. 284, August 12, 1955.

Weitzenhoffer, A. M.: *General Techniques of Hypnotism*. New York, Grune & Stratton, 1957.

Wisdom, John: *Philosophy and Psychoanalysis*. Oxford, Basil Blackwell, 1953.

Wolberg, Louis: *The Technique of Psychotherapy*. New York, Grune & Stratton, 1954.

Index